World Literatures
Exploring the Cosmopolitan-Vernacular Exchange

Edited by Stefan Helgesson, Annika Mörte Alling, Yvonne Lindqvist, and Helena Wulff

Published by
Stockholm University Press
Stockholm University
SE-106 91 Stockholm, Sweden
www.stockholmuniversitypress.se

Text © The Author(s) 2018
License CC-BY

Supporting Agency (funding): Riksbankens Jubileumsfond (The Swedish Foundation for Humanities and Social Sciences)

First published 2018
Cover designed by Karl Edqvist

Stockholm English Studies (Online) ISSN: 2002–0163

ISBN (Paperback): 978-91-7635-079-9
ISBN (PDF): 978-91-7635-076-8
ISBN (EPUB): 978-91-7635-077-5
ISBN (Mobi): 978-91-7635-078-2

DOI: https://doi.org/10.16993/bat

This work is licensed under the Creative Commons Attribution 4.0 Unported License. To view a copy of this license, visit creativecommons.org/licenses/by/4.0/ or send a letter to Creative Commons, 444 Castro Street, Suite 900, Mountain View, California, 94041, USA. This license allows for copying any part of the work for personal and commercial use, providing author attribution is clearly stated.

Suggested citation:
Helgesson, Stefan, Annika Mörte Alling, Yvonne Lindqvist, and Helena Wulff eds. *World Literatures: Exploring the Cosmopolitan-Vernacular Exchange.* Stockholm: Stockholm University Press. 2018. DOI: https://doi.org/10.16993/bat. License: CC-BY.

 To read the free, open access version of this book online, visit https://doi.org/10.16993/bat or scan this QR code with your mobile device.

Stockholm English Studies

Stockholm English Studies (SES) (ISSN 2002–0163) is a peer-reviewed series of monographs and edited volumes published by Stockholm University Press. SES strives to provide a broad forum for research on English language and literature from all periods. In terms of subjects and methods, the scope is also broad covering: language structure, variation, and meaning, both spoken and written language in all genres, as well as literary scholarship in a broad sense.

It is the ambition of SES to place equally high demands on the academic quality of the manuscripts it accepts as those applied by refereed international journals and academic publishers of a similar orientation.

Editorial Board

Frida Beckman, Associate Professor at the Department of Culture and Aesthetics at Stockholm University (email)

Claudia Egerer, Associate Professor at the Department of English at Stockholm University

Stefan Helgesson, Professor at the Department of English at Stockholm University

Nils-Lennart Johannesson, Professor at the Department of English at Stockholm University

Maria Kuteeva, Professor at the Department of English at Stockholm University

Peter Sundkvist, Associate Professor at the Department of English at Stockholm University

Titles in the series

1. Begam, R. and Soderholm, J. 2015. *Platonic Occasions: Dialogues on Literature, Art and Culture*. Stockholm:

Stockholm University Press. DOI: https://doi.org/10.16993/sup.baa
2. Shaw, P., Erman, B., Melchers, G. and Sundkvist, P. (eds) 2015. *From Clerks to Corpora: essays on the English language yesterday and today.* Stockholm: Stockholm University Press. DOI: https://doi.org/10.16993/sup.bab
3. Stefan Helgesson, Annika Mörte Alling, Yvonne Lindqvist and Helena Wulff (eds.) 2018. *World Literatures: Exploring the Cosmopolitan-Vernacular Exchange.* Stockholm: Stockholm University Press. DOI: https://doi.org/10.16993/bat

Peer Review page

Guidelines for peer review

Stockholm University Press ensures that all book publications are peer-reviewed in two stages. Each book proposal submitted to the Press will be sent to a dedicated Editorial Board of experts in the subject area as well as two independent experts. The full manuscript will be peer reviewed by chapter or as a whole by two independent experts.

A full description of Stockholm University Press' peer-review policies can be found on the website: http://www.stockholmuniversitypress.se/site/peer-review-policies/

Recognition for reviewers

The Editorial Board of Stockholm English Studies applies single-blind review during proposal and manuscript assessment. We would like to thank all reviewers involved in this process.

Chris Holmes, PhD, Associate Professor, Department of English, Faculty, Telluride Foundation (TASP)", Co-Director New Voices Festival, Ithaca College (review of manuscript)

Johan Schimanski, Professor of Comparative Literature, Department of Literature, Area Studies and European Languages, Faculty of Humanities, University of Oslo (UiO), visiting Professor of Cultural Encounters, University of Eastern Finland (UEF). ORCID: https://orcid.org/0000-0002-1849-2600 (review of proposal and manuscript)

Mads Rosendahl Thomsen, Professor with Special Responsibilities at the School of Communication and Culture – Comparative Literature, Aarhus University. ORCID: https://orcid.org/0000-0002-4975-6752 (review of proposal, after which Thomsen initiated a research collaboration with Stefan Helgesson, hence he was not eligible to review the full manuscript)

Contents

1. General Introduction: The Cosmopolitan and the Vernacular in Interaction   1
   Stefan Helgesson

PART 1: BEYOND NATIONS: ENGAGING LITERARY HISTORIES

2. Introduction to Part 1   15
   Annika Mörte Alling

3. *Le Vernaculaire*: A Brief Lexical History in French   19
   Christina Kullberg

4. One Country, Several Literatures: Towards a Comparative Understanding of Contemporary Literature in Spain   31
   Christian Claesson

5. Beyond Chineseness: De-Nationalising and De-Sinicising Modern Chinese Literature   42
   Irmy Schweiger

6. "The Original Romance of America": Slave Narratives and Transnational Networks in Theodore Parker's American Literary History   59
   David Watson

7. Reformist Discourses: Classical Literary Language Versus Modern Written Vernacular in Lu Xun's Short Story "A Madman's Diary"   70
   Lena Rydholm

8. Reflections on Gender and Small Languages in World Literature Scholarship: Methods of Inclusions and Exclusions   89
   Katarina Leppänen

PART 2: NEITHER HERE NOR THERE? LOCATIONS AND ORIENTATIONS IN CONTEMPORARY LITERATURE

9. Introduction to Part 2   103
   Helena Wulff

10. Locating Chronic Violence: Billy Kahora's "How to Eat a Forest"   107
    Ashleigh Harris

11. Diasporic Divides: Location and Orientations of "Home" in Pooneh Rohi's *Araben*   119
    Helena Wulff

12. Zuhura the African Lioness: Performance Poetry, Digital Media and the Transnational Tangle in World Literature   129
    Paula Uimonen

13. Literary Ecologies and Post-9/11 Muslim Writing   140
    Adnan Mahmutović

14. Worldly Vernaculars in the Anglophone Caribbean   150
    Bo G. Ekelund

PART 3: WORLD ENOUGH, AND TIME: WORLD-MAKING AND LITERARY PRACTICE

15. Introduction to Part 3   165
    Stefan Helgesson

16. Literary World-Making under Apartheid: *Staffrider* and the Location of Print Culture   171
    Stefan Helgesson

17. Documentary Modernism: Worldly Sympathies, Ideal Collectivities and Dissenting Individualism   185
    Irina Rasmussen

18. In Conquest of the World and of Modernity: Movements from the Countryside to Paris in Novels by Stendhal, Balzac and Flaubert   199
    Annika Mörte Alling

19. The Contemporary Russian Cosmopolitans 211
    Anna Ljunggren

20. A World Apart and the World at Large:
    Expressing Siberian Exile 229
    Mattias Viktorin

21. Seclusion versus Accessibility: The Harems of Constantinople as
    Aesthetic Worlds in Stories by Elsa Lindberg-Dovlette 246
    Helena Bodin

22. The Travelling Story of Pettersson in the Pacific 261
    Anette Nyqvist

23. Indian Imaginaries in World Literature and
    Domestic Popular Culture 275
    Per Ståhlberg

PART 4: LOST AND FOUND: TRANSLATION AND CIRCULATION

24. Introduction to Part 4 289
    Yvonne Lindqvist

25. Translation Bibliomigrancy: The Case of Contemporary
    Caribbean Literature in Scandinavia 295
    Yvonne Lindqvist

26. Profiles of Italy: Localising Practices of Swedish Publishing
    Houses 310
    Cecilia Schwartz

27. Literary Migration as Transformation 324
    Paul Tenngart

28. A Cosmopolitan North in Nordic Noir: Turning Swedish Crime
    Fiction into World Literature 340
    Louise Nilsson

29. Swedes in French: Cultural Transfer from Periphery to Literary
    Metropolis 355
    Andreas Hedberg

30. Gender and the Circulation of African Lusophone Literature into the Portuguese Literary System   369
    Chatarina Edfeldt

31. World Literary Studies and East African Anglophone Literature   383
    Erik Falk

Notes on contributors   397
Index   405

1. General Introduction: The Cosmopolitan and the Vernacular in Interaction
Stefan Helgesson

The world seems to be up for grabs – conceptually speaking – in contemporary critical discourse. The anthropocene, globalisation, planetary thinking, world-system theory, worlding, worldedness: there is much evidence to support Eric Hayot's claim that "world" (and its variants) has become a word with "rhetorically unmatched prestige".[1] Literary scholarship, as will be discussed below, has its own version of world-speak, namely world literature, a concept and a field of study that has generated a significant amount of debate in recent years. The present volume, dear reader, that you either are holding in your hand or (which is more likely) reading on a screen, puts itself at an angle to that scholarly conversation, building on its insights but also presenting some alternative points of departure for thinking "world" and "literature" in conjunction.

If we agree with the fundamental phenomenological insight that the world is only possible to experience and think from within a given emplacement in time and language, it should be evident that the world is never just "out there" but always also "here". Transposed to the concerns of world literature, this calls for a conceptual framework that takes both the here and the there into consideration. Hence our overarching terms "cosmopolitan" and "vernacular",

---

[1] Eric Hayot, *On Literary Worlds* (Oxford: Oxford University Press, 2012), 30.

How to cite this book chapter:
Helgesson, Stefan. "General Introduction: The Cosmopolitan and the Vernacular in Interaction". In *World Literatures: Exploring the Cosmopolitan-Vernacular Exchange*, edited by Stefan Helgesson, Annika Mörte Alling, Yvonne Lindqvist, and Helena Wulff, 1–11. Stockholm: Stockholm University Press, 2018. DOI: https://doi.org/10.16993/bat.a. License: CC-BY.

which should not be thought of as opposites but as two modes – or vectors – of literary worldliness that may interact, merge or contest each other. As thoroughly relational terms, they are also implicated in the social construction of literary value and can have analytical force at a number of different levels, including style, language choice, emplotment, translation, book history and large-scale syntheses of literary history. How has the vernacular been defined historically? What is its place in world literature scholarship? How is it inflected by gender? How are the poles of the vernacular and the cosmopolitan distributed spatially or stylistically in literary narratives? How are cosmopolitan domains of literature incorporated in local literary communities? What are the effects of translation and language change on the encoding of vernacular and cosmopolitan values? These are some of the questions broached in the chapters that follow, all of which emerge out of a Swedish research programme called, appropriately, "Cosmopolitan and Vernacular Dynamics in World Literatures". (A more detailed presentation will follow.)

Before proceeding, however, it is probably wise to state what this volume does *not* claim to do. It is, first of all, not a world history of literature. The 26 chapters provide a considerable amount of historical knowledge and their temporal range stretches from the early modern period onwards. But the emphasis lies on contemporary literature and there is no attempt here to craft a coherent narrative of development and interaction. Nor is this anthology attempting "full coverage" in a geographical or cultural sense. There is nothing here on Arabic, Japanese or Persian literature, almost nothing relating to South America (excluding Brazil and the Caribbean), and only one piece on India. If we were to group contributions in terms of their geographical affiliations, one can note that that they gravitate around Scandinavia, western Europe, Turkey (Constantinople/Istanbul), Russia, China, Africa south of the Sahara, the Caribbean and North America.

This is geographically ambitious in its own right, but we are wary of reducing world literature to a matter of coverage. As Franco Moretti once famously stated, "[r]eading 'more' is always a good thing, but not the solution".[2] Even though digital

---

[2] Franco Moretti, "Conjectures on World Literature", *New Left Review* 1 (2000): 55.

technologies make the "wild idea" of grasping the sum total of the world's literatures slightly less unattainable in practice than Claudio Guillén claimed in the early 1990s, this is still not where the interest of this anthology lies.[3] Rather, our premise is that the wide-ranging debates on world literature over the past two decades have important implications for how we frame the object of literary studies. Consider for a moment the criticism that has been levelled at world literature, mainly from postcolonial and comparative literature scholars. Peter Hitchcock has complained that the "world" in world literature is "studiously neutral", whereas Gayatri Spivak has accused it of remaining beholden to "Europe as guide to disciplinary objectivity", an observation that resonates with Aamir Mufti's point that "the Latinate term literature, and the set of its cognates in the Western languages ... now provide the dominant, universalizing, but by no means absolute vocabulary for the comprehension of verbal-textual expression worldwide".[4] Choosing a different tack, yet in the same critical spirit, Emily Apter has attacked world literature for being "oblivious to the Untranslatable" and suggests instead that "translation and untranslatability are constitutive of world forms of literature".[5]

These interventions all express dissatisfaction with aspects of the scholarly conversation on world literature, but are, for all that, no less intent on devising ways to study literature in planet-wide and transnational contexts than the main targets of their critique. Without rehearsing once again the arguments of those who are routinely identified as the leading thinkers on world literature – David Damrosch, Franco Moretti and Pascale Casanova – it would seem that they and their critics broadly agree that world literature is a matter of method and theory first, and only then, as a consequence of this, also about *what* we read and study. This is

---

[3] Claudio Guillén, "*Weltliteratur*", in *World Literature: A Reader*, edited by Theo D'haen et al. (New York: Routledge, 2013), 143.
[4] Peter Hitchcock, *The Long Space: Transnationalism and Postcolonial Form* (Stanford: Stanford University Press, 2010), 6; Gayatri Spivak, *An Aesthetic Education in the Era of Globalization* (Cambridge: Harvard University Press, 2012), 455; Aamir Mufti, "Orientalism and the Institution of World Literatures", *Critical Inquiry* 36 (2010): 488.
[5] Emily Apter, *Against World Literature: On the Politics of Untranslatability* (London: Verso, 2013), 9, 16.

at least the view adopted in the present volume. In doing so, we are clearly resisting both an older conception of world literature as a "world canon" (with European masterpieces occupying centre stage) and the newer equation between world literature and the global anglophone market for literary publishing.[6] Such reductive conceptions of world literature are inadequate, at worst harmful, and fail above all to address what could be seen as the core challenge of world literature: to provide alternatives both to methodological nationalism and to methodological eurocentrism. That is to say, neither the nation-state, nor a notional (above all cultural) "Europe", should be taken for granted as the frameworks within which the study of literature unfolds. But by the same token, nor should European literatures be *excluded* in such a way that their centrality is reinstated negatively in relation to "the rest" – hence the inclusion of very diverse European cases found in this book.

Methodological nationalism and eurocentrism pose two distinct challenges that can be associated with two different disciplinary formations. Comparative literature, in its various iterations, has at least had the potential to sidestep or complement the national framework, and postcolonial studies have by definition challenged the knowledge regime of eurocentrism. Combining these two disciplinary traditions (or sets of traditions) in world literature studies is however easier said than done, as exchanges among Spivak, Damrosch, Apter, Mufti, Graham Huggan, Pheng Cheah, Mads Rosendahl Thomsen and others demonstrate.[7] But beyond

---

[6] For a more detailed discussion of different conceptions of "world literature", see Stefan Helgesson and Pieter Vermeulen, eds., *Institutions of World Literature: Writing, Translation, Markets* (New York: Routledge, 2015). Birgit Neumann and Gabriele Rippl also provide an excellent account of central issues in the current debate. Birgit Neumann and Gabriele Rippl, "Anglophone World Literatures: Introduction", *Anglia* 135, no. 1 (2017): 1–20.

[7] Apter, *Against*; Pheng Cheah, *What Is a World? On Postcolonial Literature as World Literature* (Durham: Duke University Press, 2016); David Damrosch and Gayatri Spivak, "Comparative Literature/World Literature: A Discussion with Gayatri Chakravorty Spivak and David Damrosch", *Comparative Literature Studies* 48, no. 4 (2011): 455–85; Graham Huggan, "The Trouble with World Literature", in *A Companion to Comparative Literature*, ed. Ali Behdad and Dominic Thomas (Oxford:

the specific disagreements, which often have an ideological slant, a bigger methodological question looms: Is there anything that remains to hold literary studies together? Is there anything internal to the phenomenon we choose to call "literature" in, say, West African, eastern European and Chinese settings that keeps it from splintering into so many discrete traditions and cultural fragments?

Two fairly recent interventions in the world literary field have provided strikingly different answers to that question. The first is *Combined and Uneven Development: Towards a New Theory of World-Literature* by the Warwick Research Collective (WReC). Here, a group of Marxist scholars present a restricted conception of "world-literature" (note the hyphen) as an effect of the capitalist world-system – to be precise, as "the literary registration of modernity under the sign of combined and uneven development".[8] This is a "strong" definition in the sense that it does posit a single, if complex, framework for reading, and leaves everything not connected to the modern and global capitalist era (such as classical Chinese poetry, or the Provençal troubadours) to one side. This approach provides a clear focus for a global and non-national mode of literary studies, while at the same time disallowing itself to engage with deep history.

In his book *An Ecology of World Literature*, Alexander Beecroft presents instead a typological model of what he calls "ecologies" that, hypothetically, could cover all modes of literary reception and circulation throughout human history. Working with *literatures* (and not just "literature" in general) as a unit of analysis, and with empirical cases from ancient China to the present day, Beecroft discusses six types of literary ecologies that arguably cover everything from minimal to maximal circulation: epichoric, panchoric, cosmopolitan, vernacular, national and global ecologies. If epichoric circulation is mainly oral and restricted to a

---

Blackwell, 2011), 490–506; Spivak, *An Aesthetic Education*, 455–65; Mads Rosendahl Thomsen, *Mapping World Literature: International Canonization and Transnational Literatures* (London: Continuum, 2008)

[8] Warwick Research Collective, *Combined and Uneven Development: Towards a New Theory of World-literature* (Liverpool: Liverpool University Press, 2015), 17.

tightly knit community, panchoric circulation draws together distinct polities within a common cultural identity – a case in point being the ancient Greek world and its sharing of a particular literary legacy. Cosmopolitan circulation emerges through religion or imperialism (or both), and is tied to a particular high-prestige language (Sanskrit, Latin, Chinese, Arabic). It is against such cosmopolitan cultural authority, Beecroft argues, that self-aware vernacular literatures then tend to emerge, not so much "from below", but through the formation of elites vying for cultural and political independence. It is only in the modern era, finally, that literature attaches to the newly invented nation-state, and even more recently that a global market and modes of reception start taking shape. Each of these modes produces a distinct community, as well as a distinct understanding of what counts as literature. The oral-based, ideal-typical epichoric ecology is a case of exceptionally reduced circulation, while the global ecology – which is obviously dependent on a number of technological, economic and linguistic preconditions – has the planet as its scope. These ecologies do not simply replace each other, however, in a teleological line of progression. Instead, different ecologies may co-exist, serving separate purposes at a given moment.

Both WReC's and Beecroft's categories will fray at the edges when looked at more closely. How does WReC's notion of "literary registration" – once one has braved the thickets of their theoretical argument – actually escape the risk of reproducing a strongly determinist view of literature? And is it even meaningful to posit "ecological" types, as Beecroft does, on the basis of such vastly different historical cases? This is not the moment to engage in an extensive discussion of these matters, but it is instructive to place WReC and Beecroft side by side. Both their books are impressive in their scholarship and rank as significant contributions to world literature studies, and yet the trajectories of their arguments move in almost diametrically opposed directions: one is restricted, historicising, focused on the modern era, geared towards close reading and overtly political; the other is expansive, pan-historical, erudite rather than political, and engaged in distant rather than close reading. This contrast not only alerts us to the current diversity of world literature studies (and the attendant lack of consensus in the field), but provides also a backdrop against which we can outline the contribution of this volume.

Rather than present a single, strong theoretical framework (such as world-system theory), and rather than adopting a typological approach (such as the ecologies model), the organising principle of this book is that of an open-ended dynamic, or what we call the cosmopolitan-vernacular exchange. Inspired by Erich Auerbach's famous coinage of the *Ansatzpunkt*, the concrete point of departure necessary for the study of literature on a world scale, our wager is that the cosmopolitan-vernacular exchange provides not only a uniquely adaptable comparative fulcrum for literary studies, but redresses what has repeatedly been identified as the inability of the world literature paradigm to accommodate literature which does *not* circulate, accumulate global prestige or make it on the Euro-American market.[9] It is also for this reason that we collectively engage with more than a dozen different languages, so as to diminish the risk of reinforcing the limitations of the English language as – currently – the hyper-central mediator of world literature.

The notion of the cosmopolitan-vernacular exchange does not, perhaps, satisfy Auerbach's requirement of a distinctly *concrete* set of phenomena, but it does operate at various and interacting levels, as the sections of this anthology demonstrate. For Auerbach, an *Ansatzpunkt* involves "the election of a firmly circumscribed, easily comprehensible set of phenomena whose interpretation is a radiation out from them and which orders and interprets a greater region than they themselves occupy".[10] What our four sections – on literary history, locations and orientations, world-making, and translation and circulation, respectively – demonstrate is precisely how the cosmopolitan-vernacular optic can be employed in macro-historical and sociological registers, as well as on the micro-level of close textual analysis.

---

[9] See in particular Apter, *Against*; Aamir Mufti, *Forget English! Orientalisms and World Literatures* (Cambridge: Harvard University Press, 2016); and Neumann and Rippl, "Introduction".

[10] Eric Auerbach, "Philology and *Weltliteratur*", trans. Edward and Maire Said, *The Centennial Review* 13, no.1 (1969): 14.

The question, of course, is what the terms "cosmopolitan" and "vernacular" mean – or at least what the contributors to this anthology *take* them to mean. They are used here primarily as heuristic and analytical concepts that help to organise our investigations, and not as organic or "emic" concepts that emerge from within the texts or cultural contexts themselves. Sheldon Pollock's well-known discussion provides a model here: in his macro-historical comparison of South Asia and Europe, he treats cosmopolitanism and vernacularism "as action rather than idea, as something people do rather than something they declare, as practice rather than proposition".[11] By analogy, the short studies presented here focus more on what texts, narratives, journals, translations or historical processes *do* than on what they profess. The cosmopolitan trajectory involves, in this instance, a larger world than the nation or local community and culture, whereas vernacular literary cultures (drawing once again on Pollock) "reshape the boundaries of [the] cultural universe by renouncing the larger world for the smaller place".[12] A key boundary marker, of course, is language, which is how the term "vernacular" once originated. Etymologically, it signifies the language of the house-born slave in imperial Rome, a felicitous designation in so far as it connotes class and sociolect as much as multilingualism in a stricter sense. Speaking of the "cosmopolitan" and the "vernacular" always involves a social dimension of some sort, and resists thereby the reduction of literary language to a neutral, transparent fact.

Accordingly, this problematic should not be thought of exclusively in terms of distinct languages, but also in terms of place, power, poetics, ethics and gender. It is relational all the way down. The most salient point in both Pollock's and Beecroft's discussions is that the vernacular in literary contexts is never reducible to an organic authenticity, untouched by the artifice of a cosmopolitan model. The latter figure of thought, inherited from romanticism, obscures precisely the relational, historically situated nature of the terms "cosmopolitan" and "vernacular" (and this relationality

---

[11] Sheldon Pollock, "Cosmopolitan and Vernacular in History", *Public Culture* 12, no. 3 (2000): 593.
[12] Pollock, "Cosmopolitan", 592.

is also what gives our conceptual pair greater traction than, for example, more abstract terms such as "universal" and "local"). When looking at the historical evidence, both Pollock and Beecroft claim that self-conscious articulations of vernacular literary value always emerge in relation to a literary culture and language with cosmopolitan authority – such as Sanskrit and Latin in earlier eras, or French and English in the modern period. But if we take this a step further, it becomes just as evident – and this is perhaps more characteristic of the modern and contemporary period – that the cosmopolitan and the vernacular are directly implicated in each other in myriad ways. Migrant writers may have access to several cosmopolitan and vernacular literary cultures at the same time, which all have a bearing on their poetics. Or, what is cosmopolitan in one setting – such as Farsi in West Asia – becomes vernacular in another – as an "immigrant language" in Sweden. Similarly, if English and its literary tradition on the one hand has been associated with the cosmopolitan legacy of imperial coercion in Africa, it has also provided a repertoire of forms as well as material networks which have fed into the cultivation of local literatures. If we look at the domain of literary translation, it is just as evidently involved in complex negotiations of cosmopolitan and vernacular trajectories: of the outward and inward movements, of foreignisation and domestication, of sociolects and dialects, of major and minor languages.

Short summaries of the individual chapters are provided in the introduction to each subsection. The design of the book as a whole needs however some explanation. What we present here should be seen as an interim report. As mentioned previously, the contributions all derive from a Swedish research programme with the heading "Cosmopolitan and Vernacular Dynamics in World Literatures".[13] Funded by a generous grant from the Swedish Foundation for the Humanities and Social Sciences (Riksbankens Jubileumsfond), and based at Stockholm University, it involves all the contributing authors. Having begun in 2016, and with 2021 as its cut-off date, the sub-projects are still in their initial phase as

---

[13] See our website for more information: http://worldlit.se.

this manuscript is being put together. For this reason, the chapters have an exploratory and introductory character. They are organised according to the current thematic division of the programme: 1) literary history, 2) locations and orientations, 3) world-making, and 2) translation and circulation. We see these as four dimensions of world literature studies, with quite distinct methodological inclinations. One could at the same time claim that the book has a circular composition: beginning with "distant" methods of historical investigation, it moves towards different modes of close reading in parts 2 and 3, and then again outwards, into the distant reading of the circuits of translation and circulation. Another way to phrase this is that there are shifts in scale, from the macro-historical, macro-social and paratextual, to investigations (both literary and anthropological) of individual texts and cases. In this way, the volume presents a broad introduction to diverse methods of doing world literature. Our explicit intention in each case, moreover, has been to produce short, updated, informative pieces, accessible also to advanced students. For the continued fruition of our efforts, watch this space.

Bibliography

Apter, Emily. *Against World Literature: On the Politics of Untranslatability*. London: Verso, 2013.

Auerbach, Erich. "Philology and *Weltliteratur*", trans. Edward and Maire Said. *The Centennial Review* 13, no.1 (1969): 1–17.

Beecroft, Alexander. *An Ecology of World Literature*. London: Verso, 2015.

Cheah, Pheng. *What Is a World? On Postcolonial Literature as World Literature*. Durham: Duke University Press, 2016.

Damrosch, David and Gayatri Spivak. "Comparative Literature/World Literature: A Discussion with Gayatri Chakravorty Spivak and David Damrosch". *Comparative Literature Studies* 48, no. 4 (2011): 455–85.

Guillén, Claudio. "*Weltliteratur*". In *World Literature: A Reader*, edited by Theo D'haen et al., 142–49. New York: Routledge, 2013.

Hayot, Eric. *On Literary Worlds*. Oxford: Oxford University Press, 2012.

Helgesson, Stefan and Pieter Vermeulen, eds. *Institutions of World Literature: Writing, Translation, Markets*. New York: Routledge, 2015.

Hitchcock, Peter. *The Long Space: Transnationalism and Postcolonial Form*. Stanford: Stanford University Press, 2010.

Huggan, Graham. "The Trouble with World Literature". In *A Companion to Comparative Literature*, edited by Ali Behdad and Dominic Thomas, 490–506. Oxford: Blackwell, 2011.

Moretti, Franco. "Conjectures on World Literature", *New Left Review* 1 (2000): 54–68.

Mufti, Aamir. "Orientalism and the Institution of World Literatures". *Critical Inquiry* 36 (2010): 458–93.

———. *Forget English! Orientalisms and World Literatures*. Cambridge: Harvard University Press, 2016.

Neumann, Birgit and Gabriele Rippl. "Anglophone World Literatures: Introduction". *Anglia* 135, no. 1 (2017): 1–20.

Pollock, Sheldon. "Cosmopolitan and Vernacular in History". *Public Culture* 12, no. 3 (2000): 591–625.

Spivak, Gayatri. *An Aesthetic Education in the Era of Globalization*. Cambridge: Harvard University Press, 2012.

Thomsen, Mads Rosendahl. *Mapping World Literature: International Canonization and Transnational Literatures*. London: Continuum, 2008.

Warwick Research Collective (WReC). *Combined and Uneven Development: Towards a New Theory of World-literature*. Liverpool: Liverpool University Press, 2015.

PART 1:
BEYOND NATIONS:
ENGAGING LITERARY HISTORIES

2. Introduction to Part 1
Annika Mörte Alling

What is the place of the vernacular in literary history? The contributions of the first section all illuminate this question and inevitably also how the vernacular is related to cosmopolitan, global contexts. Literature is understood here to evolve through a constant struggle between the universal and the particular. This essentially historical point of departure allows for a series of problems to be addressed: What is the role of literary fiction in the formation of nations and of a national, cultural identity? What parts do translation and circulation play in the constitution of a literary history? How are authors and works presented and valued differently depending on the agenda of the receiver? As the chapters will show, a literary history cannot be a simple juxtaposition of "national" literatures. Instead, a comprehensive transnational and multilingual approach is needed, one that acknowledges ruptures as well as intercultural connections and one that promotes localised and gendered knowledge. The complex question of canonicity, closely related to power and politics, is also discussed in this section: Who has the power to decide what constitutes a canon? What is the role of minor and peripheral texts to our understanding of canon formation and quality? The section combines systemic, distant-reading approaches with close readings of particular cases, in order to analyse the cosmopolitan and vernacular exchange on a textual level. This double-edged approach resonates with the core premise of the book, namely that world literature can only

How to cite this book chapter:
Alling, Annika Mörte. "Introduction to Part 1". In *World Literatures: Exploring the Cosmopolitan-Vernacular Exchange*, edited by Stefan Helgesson, Annika Mörte Alling, Yvonne Lindqvist, and Helena Wulff, 15–18. Stockholm: Stockholm University Press, 2018. DOI: https://doi.org/10.16993/bat.b. License: CC-BY.

be understood in terms of the dynamic tensions between cultural introversion and extroversion.

Looking at early modern French definitions of the term *vernaculaire*, **Christina Kullberg**'s essay argues that while the vernacular may hold a revolutionary potential, it does not necessarily build on a radical rupture with other languages. Examples are taken from Rabelais's *Le Quart livre* and from a selection of major dictionaries and encyclopedias from the seventeenth century up to the nineteenth century. The purpose is to explore the (French) historical understandings of the term and to see if they can allow for new theoretical possibilities to use the term today.

In "One Country, Several Literatures: Towards a Comparative Understanding of Contemporary Literature in Spain", **Christian Claesson** outlines a comparative approach to the literatures in Spain of today. How did Castilian literature come to represent Spanish literature as a whole? What scholarly attempts have been made to break this monolingual paradigm? How do the vernacular languages of the country relate to the cosmopolitan Spanish? By way of such questions, the chapter problematises the conception of Spain as one single and harmonious entity and of Spanish as its universal expression. As Claesson argues, in order to avoid unnecessary inclusions and historically charged hierarchies, a comparative project would need to avoid naming its object of study "Spanish", "Peninsular", "Hispanic" or "Iberian" literature, and instead study literature *in Spain*, applying a more spatial, and more neutral, characterisation based on the paradigm of the Spanish state.

In a similar vein, yet coming from a different direction and drawing conclusions that contrast with those of Claesson, **Irmy Schweiger** outlines the conceptual framework of modern Chinese literature as an ambivalent nationalistic and coercive vernacularisation project in twentieth-century China. Her essay, "Beyond Chineseness: De-Nationalising and De-Sinicising Modern Chinese Literature", illustrates how the institutionalisation of modern Chinese literature was reinforced by canonisation, language policy and sinocentric identity discourses, framed by Marxist and teleological historiography. In recent years the monolingual and sinocentric mantra has been challenged by a growing corpus produced by writers with transnational and multicultural backgrounds from Chinese communities worldwide. Drawing on concepts of francophone or anglophone literatures, Schweiger advocates sinophone studies as a counter-hegemonic and analytical tool to de-nationalise and de-sinicise modern Chinese literature.

In his discussion of slave narrative and American literary history, **David Watson** asks us to imagine the vernacular cultures of the antebellum period in relation to various cosmopolitan networks. Theodore Parker's privileging of the slave narrative in the American literary field depends on transnational engagements with European discourses and translation work invisible within Parker's "American Scholar" address itself. As Watson points out, a history of American literature in the antebellum period may very well have to take as its starting point that we cannot take for granted what was meant back then, or even today, by "American", "literature" or even "literary history".

Lena Rydholm's chapter on classical versus vernacular Chinese traces the influence of reformists and writers in the early twentieth century – Liang Qichao, Hu Shi and Chen Duxiu – to show how their calls for reform of language and literature were embodied in a single literary work, Lu Xun's short story "A Madman's Diary". Rydholm shows how their reformist discourse on language and literature confronts literary tradition within this text, through the conflict between the juxtaposed classical, literary language narrative and the modern, written vernacular narrative. Although fiction had low status among intellectuals, it is clearly seen as a potentially effective "vehicle" for reformist discourses; according to Liang, fiction has the power to change people at many different levels as well as their conceptions of the world.

In the final chapter of Part 1, **Katarina Leppänen** contributes with "Reflections on gender and small languages in world literature scholarship: methods of inclusions and exclusions". She argues that gendered perspectives informed by feminist literary studies are often totally absent or activated only as a political context rather than as an analytical literary category. What is more, smaller languages seem to evaporate in highly globalised scholarly practices. Leppänen investigates three themes in her research:

quality, representation, and transfer/translation. She argues that national recovery projects of lost or forgotten authors, including women writers, need to be stepped up to the world literature scale and that gender and feminist issues need to be reflected in anthologies and handbooks, which is not at all the case today.

3. *Le Vernaculaire*: A Brief Lexical History in French

Christina Kullberg
French, Uppsala University

This chapter proposes to trace French early modern understandings of the word *vernacular* in order to see what kinds of conceptual possibilities lie in the very history of the word. The investigation takes its cue from what could be identified as a quest for the moment of emergence of literatures within recent theories of world literature, a search in which the notion of the vernacular has come to play a crucial role. Alexander Beecroft argues that "a language is a dialect with a literature" and that the process of language emerging through and with the creation of literature is best described in terms of *vernacularisation*.[1] Following Sheldon Pollock, he suggests that vernacularisation translates into "the historical process of choosing to create a written literature, along with its compliment, a political discourse, in local languages according to models supplied by superordinate, usually cosmopolitan, literary culture".[2] Some 15 years earlier Pascale Casanova made a similar case. Taking the European (or more precisely the French) history as her point of departure, she claims that vernacularisation is mainly economically motivated since it occurred at

---

[1] Alexander Beecroft, *An Ecology of World Literature: From Antiquity to the Present Day* (New York: Verso, 2015), 6.
[2] Beecroft, *An Ecology of World Literature*, 147–48.

How to cite this book chapter:
Kullberg, Christina. "*Le Vernaculaire*: A Brief Lexical History in French". In *World Literatures: Exploring the Cosmopolitan-Vernacular Exchange*, edited by Stefan Helgesson, Annika Mörte Alling, Yvonne Lindqvist, and Helena Wulff, 19–30. Stockholm: Stockholm University Press, 2018. DOI: https://doi.org/10.16993/bat.c. License: CC-BY.

the same time as the invention of print culture.³ Writing in a local language may enable the author to reach a wider audience at a deeper level, thus gaining both financial and cultural capital. At the same time the act of writing "locally" quickly taps into political discourses and into the nationalism that took shape as French became a universal and a highly coded literary language throughout the seventeenth century.

In both Beecroft's and Casanova's model, the choice to write in a vernacular language or to create a literature in order to constitute a language, is conceptualised in terms of "revolutions". Casanova ties this process to the appearance of a particular work, Joachim Du Bellay's *La Deffence, et illustration de la langue françoyse* (1549), and Beecroft singles out "pivotal moments" in the history of languages and literatures,⁴ as if the shaping of (a) literature can be localised to an Event or a Moment and is created through decisions taken by identifiable subjects. Literary history is no doubt filled with power struggles. But we should not forget that languages do not only enter into contact with one another to compete over which language rules the world. By looking at the ways in which the vernacular was used when it first appeared in French in Rabelais' *Le Quart livre* (1542) and how it has evolved in early modern times, I would here like to problematise the systemic understanding of vernacularisation in terms of localisable moments and constant power struggles and explore other possible interpretations of what the vernacular may mean. French is used as a case in point and I will investigate the etymology and the various understandings of the notion by drawing from a corpus of major dictionaries and encyclopedias from the seventeenth up to the nineteenth centuries.

Etymologically, the word derives from learned Latin *vernaculus*, referring to slaves born in the house, in the country and, in extension, to the domestic, indigenous or national. The vernacular is:

---

³ Pascale Casanova, *La République mondiale des Lettres* (Paris: Éditions du Seuil, 1999), 90–91. See also Pascale Casanova, *La Langue mondiale* (Paris: Éditions du Seuil, 2015), which is briefly discussed in Erik Falk's chapter in this book.
⁴ Beecroft, *An Ecology of World Literature*, 153.

"Propre à un pays, à ses habitants. Syn. autochtone, domestique, indigène" (particular to a country, to its habitants. Syn. native, domestic, indigenous).[5] This is the very first lexical definition of the word given in a French dictionary and it comes from Victoire Boiste *Dictionnaire universel de la langue française: avec le latin et les étymologies* from 1823.[6] This late first appearance in the dictionaries informs us that the notion of the vernacular was hardly common at the time of the so-called "vernacular revolution", and even in the nineteenth century it is rare. It does not, for example, merit an entry in Émile Littré's *Dictionnaire de la langue française* (1872–77). The dictionaries that do give the vernacular an entry, like the already mentioned Boiste or Pierre Larousse's *Grand dictionnaire universel du XIXe siècle* (1866–77), all point toward the implicit power dimension in the etymology of the word. It is conceived as the opposite in regard to the ruling elite, suggesting that the elite also possesses another, supposedly cosmopolitan or vehicular language that is not limited to a country or a restricted group of speakers. This does not mean that the vernacular is automatically less valued, rather its value depends on the political and aesthetic context. In fact, the association with slaves and oppressed might explain why scholars like Beecroft and Casanova enhance its revolutionary potential: even when used by a local elite, the vernacular is the linguistic articulation of resistance to power. But history shows that as soon as a vernacular is affirmed, replacing the elite language it originally contested (this is what happened to *la langue françoyse* in the sixteenth and seventeenth centuries), other vernaculars surface and challenge the current linguistic order, in a perpetual dialectics of languages.

Even if the vernacular might etymologically possess a subversive power, the fact remains that it has no entry in ancient French dictionaries. Frédéric Godefroy's *Dictionnaire de l'ancienne langue française et de tous ses dialects*, covering the ninth to the fifteenth centuries, includes the masculine noun *vernicle*,

---

[5] All translations from French dictionaries and encyclopedias are mine.
[6] Pierre Claude Victoire Boiste, *Dictionnaire universel de la langue française: avec le latin et les étymologies* (Paris, 1823).

defined as "esclave né dans la maison" (slave born in the house).⁷ It seems like the only one using the notion *vernacular* in the era in which Casanova localises the "vernacular revolution" is – of course – François Rabelais. The term appears once in *Pantagruel* (1542), in the context of a conversation between Pantagruel and a student from Limoges in Paris. The student is the one using the word, giving it a comic rather than a radical connotation:

> Signor Missaye, mon genie n'est poinct apte nate à ce que dict ce flagitisse nébulon pour escorier la culticule de nostre vernacule Gallicque; mais viceversant je gnave opera, et par veles et vames je me en ite de le locupleter de la redundance latinicome.
> Par Dieu (dist Pantagruel) je vous apprendray à parler! [...]
>
> ("My worshipful lord, my genie is not apt nate to that which this flagitious nebulon saith, to excoriate the cut[ic]le of our vernacular Gallic, but viceversally I gnave opera, and by veles and rames enite to locupletate it with the Latinicome redundance."
> "By G–!," said Pantagruel, "I will teach you to speak." [...])⁸

In the student's jargon, vernacular means the language spoken by everyone, or the "langage usité", as Rabelais says, as opposed to written Latin.⁹ Coined in the context of corrupt Latin spoken by a student from Limoges who wants to sound like a Parisian,¹⁰ "vernacule Gallicque" exposes the emptiness of learned language: it appears as bad disguise, detached from the reference that it seeks

---

⁷ Frédéric Godefroy, *Dictionnaire de l'ancienne langue française et de tous ses dialects* (Paris: Émile Bouillon, 1895).
⁸ François Rabelais, *Pantagruel, roy des dipsodes, restitué à son naturel; plus Les merveilleuses navigations du disciple de Pantagruel, dict Panurge,* (Lyon: E. Dolet, 1542), 39. *The Whole Works of F. Rabelais*, trans. Sir Thomas Urquhart, Kᵗ & Bar of Cromarty and Peter Motteux (London and New York: G P Putman's Sons, 1905), 144.
⁹ Pierre Rigolot, *Les Langages de Rabelais* (Geneva: Droz, 1972), 33.
¹⁰ This can be compared to young Jean Racine travelling to Aix-en-Provence in 1661. In a letter to Madame de la Fontaine sent from Uzès, he writes that he is in as much need for an interpreter as a Muscovite in Paris would have been. Racine, a self-made man, exaggerates his linguistic alienation in order to pose himself as someone who belongs to the Parisian salons. Jean Racine, *Œuvres*, tome VII, (London, 1768), 23.

to designate; it has no connection to the world, which makes it ridiculous. Pantagruel's response is also part of the comic effect. Pantagruel, the common man, offers to teach his learned interlocutor how to speak properly, placing himself as the master and the "vernacule Gallicque" as the proper language and thereby reversing the hierarchy of power relations.

After this exceptional appearance in Rabelais "vernacular" seems to disappear from French, at least judging by the dictionaries, much like another strangely related term: *exotique*.[11] Curiously, the vernacular, like the exotic, resurfaces not in a linguistic dictionary but in Diderot's and d'Alembert's *Encyclopédie ou Dictionnaire raisonné des sciences, des arts et des métiers* in 1756:

> Vernaculaire: Maladies; est un mot qui s'applique à tout ce qui est particulier à quelque pays. Voyez local, &c. C'est pour cela que les maladies qui regnent beaucoup dans quelque pays, province ou canton, sont quelque fois appellées maladies vernaculaires, mais plus communément maladies endémiques.[12]
>
> (Vernacular: Maladies; is a word that can be applied to everything which is particular to a country. See local, &c. This is why the maladies that reign a lot in some country, province or canton, are sometimes called vernacular maladies, but more commonly endemic maladies.)

The vernacular has drifted from applying to spoken language used by everyone to referring to diseases, signifying endemic and local. As the word orbits, the spatial connotations, implied in the word endemic (i.e. native or restricted to a certain place), take over the more social connotations (i.e. slaves, domestics). Moreover, we are no longer in the domain of literature. Here, the vernacular

---

[11] Speaking of merchandise from a fictive island, Pantagruel describes the objects as "exotiques et peregrines". The word has no entrance in the dictionaries until the eighteenth century. See Vincenette Maigne, "Exotisme: Évolution en diachronie du mot et de son champ sémantique," in *Exotisme et création. Actes du Colloque International (Lyon 1983)*, ed. Roland Antonioli (Lyon: L'Hèrmes, 1985), 7–16.

[12] Denis Diderot and Jean Le Rond d'Alembert, *Encyclopédie ou Dictionnaire raisonné des sciences, des arts et des métiers* (Paris: Pellet, 1777). See http://encyclopedie.uchicago.edu/, accessed 26 January 2017.

is not a dialect in the language continuum seeking to form a literature; rather, it participates in the discursive configuration of knowledge.

A vernacular term translates into a local understanding of reality and appears as a piece in the project of putting together knowledge about the world. This has indeed been the function of vernacular language since the formalisation of the new sciences in the Academies in the seventeenth century, that is, during the same period as French asserts its role as the universal language. So even if the term vernacular is not used in the seventeenth century, the interest in local languages can easily be attested by the appearance of dictionaries in languages from faraway places, established by missionaries in Africa, the Orient and the Americas.[13] In travel literature and in scientific treatises written in French as well as in Latin, vernacular words are important elements. Terms used by locals, should it be in Breton, Occitan, Arabic or Taino, transmit a new form of knowledge that breaks with a bookish tradition by being connected to experience and empirical observation. The fact that the *Encyclopédie* identifies local knowledge as *vernacular* reflects two competing forms of knowledge. One is based on everyday life, whereas the other is systematised and universal, marking a return to Latin as no longer the scholarly language but the language of new science at the same time as the former vernaculars that have now become national and central languages are the languages through which thought is systematised and the world explained. The vernacular of the other (both the European other, i.e. peasants, and the foreign other) is linked to common practices as opposed to a more technical, scientific language, and the vernacular *name* and noun operate an alternative way to name the world and identify the uses of nature.[14] Even though such *savoir vernaculaire* is quickly trans-

---

[13] The openness to local languages is short. By the end of 1600 it is no longer acceptable to include foreign words within travel writing, at least not to a larger extent. See Marie-Christine Pioffet, *La Tentation de l'épopée dans les relations des jésuites* (Sillery: Septentrion, 1997), 497.

[14] See Centre national de ressources textuelles et lexicales, http://www.cnrtl.fr/definition/vernaculaire, accessed 26 January 2017.

lated into systems and ultimately loses its local connection as it enters into the domain of science, its importance within scientific discourse explains why the term "vernacular" is mainly linked to lexicography and onomastics when it finally appears in the dictionaries in the eighteenth and nineteenth centuries. But it also indicates that rather than referring to (a) language, vernacular is associated with *parts* of language, particular referential elements in language and not with a language system. Its meaning is clearly in constant transformation.

In the fifteenth to eighteenth centuries, the term commonly used for local languages is *vulgar (vulgaire)*, which has an entry in Jean Nicot's 1606 dictionary and shares features with the modern definition of "vernacular", but they are not complete synonyms. To Nicot "vulgar" means *common* and is directly linked to language: "Paroles vulgaires et communes" (Vulgar and common words).[15] *Dictionnaire de l'Académie française* from 1694 gives it a longer entry: "Qui est communément en usage. Il ne se dit guere que des choses morales. Ainsi on appelle *langue vulgaire, langage vulgaire*, Le langage qui est communément usité par toute une nation, par tout un peuple" (That which is commonly used. It is hardly said but about moral things. Thus one calls vulgar language, *vulgar tongue,* the language which is commonly used by an entire nation, by an entire people).[16] Furetière's dictionary defines "vulgar" as, "commun, trivial, ordinaire, du petit peuple" (common, trivial, ordinary, of the small people) and specifies that vulgar language "is sometimes opposed to ancient and savant".[17] Vulgar paradoxically seems to denote vernacular forms of Latin, but which have vehicular functions since they are spoken in everyday life and are used by many people. Interestingly, as French asserts its position

---

[15] Jean Nicot, *Trésor de la langue Françoiyse tant ancienne que moderne* (Paris: David Douceur, 1606), accessed 26 January 2017, http://portail.atilf.fr/dictionnaires/TLF-NICOT/index.htm.

[16] *Dictionnaire de l'Académie française t 2* (Paris: Chez la Veuve de Jean Baptiste Coignard, 1694), accessed 22 January 2017, http://dictionnaires.atilf.fr/dictionnaires/ACADEMIE/.

[17] Antoine Furetière, *Dictionnaire universel. Contenant tous les mots françois tant vieux que modernes, & les Termes de toutes les Sciences et des Arts* (A. et R. Leers: La Haye, 1690).

as political, intellectual and literary *lingua franca*, the notion of the vulgar is increasingly used to denote that which is low, vile and trivial. In the French Academy's dictionary from 1762, as well as in Jean-François Féraud's *Dictionnaire critique de la langue française* (1787–88), the moral meaning is placed first and vulgar language is understood only in opposition to learned language.[18] This definition remains through the nineteenth century and is preferred over "vernacular". Émile Littré, who does not give "vernacular" an entry, offers an interesting bridge between the two terms in claiming that vulgar languages are living languages.[19] He also underscores the medical and natural significations of "vulgar". Nevertheless, vulgar remains linked to the idea of the common not only as in ordinary or lower, but also as something shared: *ce qui est communément en usage*. A vulgar plant is something one comes across everywhere and vulgar medicine is used by everyone and the idea of opposition to the learned is always present. "Qui ne se dinstingue par rien" (that which lacks distinction) – from the latin *vulgus* meaning popular crowd, troupe or multitude. The key element is *common,* whereas the notion of vernacular is associated with the idea of particularity.

Thus, the comparison with the notion of the vulgar highlights that the vernacular is mainly understood in terms of difference, as an element that distinguishes itself from common language or a language distinct from vehicular language by virtue of it being restricted to a region and its culture. Interpreted as a foreign entity entering another language, marking difference, and in some cases suggesting a direct correspondence with foreign worlds, the vernacular here has another meaning than it has in contemporary theorisation of world literatures. In light of the historical (French) definitions, the vernacular can hence be used as a concept of difference that does not necessarily in itself constitute a literature, because it is not necessarily understood as a common language,

---

[18] Jean-François Féraud, *Dictionnaire critique de la langue française* (Marseille: Moissy, 1787-8), accessed 22 January 2017, http://artfl.atilf.fr/dictionnaires/FERAUD/.

[19] Émile Littré, *Dictionnaire de la langue française* (Paris: Hachette, 1863–72).

shared by everyone. The vernacular has no *common-place*, nor is it a commonplace, as the vulgar.[20]

This leads me to conclude that the two terms used to denote other languages hold two different revolutionary potentials. One – the vulgar – can counteract a linguistic and literary order by virtue of its commonality. The other – the vernacular – operates more discretely within the order. In Michail Bachtin's influential analysis of Rabelais, foreign words introduce a space of nonsense in the text, allowing for the carnavalesque disruption to have its effects.[21] This is precisely what happens when Rabelais inserts the word *vernacule* in a text written in *la langue françoyse* only a few years after Du Bellay's "vernacular revolution". Here the word "vernacular" itself appears at once as foreign and creative, carved as it is from a degenerated Latin. It begs for translation into the local idiom in which the narrative is written, thereby both exposing and undermining the hierarchy of languages. This way of conceptualising the vernacular as tied to the cosmopolitan vehicular language but denoting the local can allow for rethinking the notion today, not in terms of what Casanova identifies as the "Herder effect", i.e. a regional expression competing for a central position in the world literary market,[22] or in terms of the constitution of *a* literature as Beecroft seems to suggest. The study of the shifting meanings of the word shows that the idea of

---

[20] I draw on Édouard Glissant's idea of the common-place as a shared space and commonplace a kind of poetics of repetition. He writes in *The Poetics of Relation*: "This flood of convergences, publishing itself in the guise of the commonplace. No longer is the latter an accepted generality, suitable and dull – no longer is it deceptively obvious exploiting common sense – it is, rather, all that is relentlessly and endlessly reiterated by these encounters." Trans. Betsy Wing (Ann Arbor: University of Michigan Press, 1997), 45.

[21] Guy Demerson discusses this in "Le plurilinguisme chez Rabelais", in *Bulletin de l'Association d'étude sur l'humanisme, la réforme et la renaissance* 14 (1981): 4–5. See also Bachtin's essay "Le plurilinguisme dans le roman", in Mikhaïl Bakhtine, *Esthtétique et théorie du roman*, trans. Daria Olivier (Paris: Gallimard, 1987), and his work on Rabelais: *Rabelais and his World*, trans. Helene Iswolsky (Cambridge Mass: M.I.T. Press, 1968).

[22] See Casanova, *La République mondiale des Lettres*, 12–125.

a "vernacular revolution" rests on a contemporary interpretation that is highly dependent on a traditional narrative of literary history as being made up by important works and authors.[23]

It is here that the exploration of the historical understandings and uses of the notion of the vernacular has proven useful. While the vernacular may hold a revolutionary potential, it does not necessarily build on a radical rupture with other languages. Rather, vernacularisation can refer to that which emerges within a linguistic continuum but without necessarily taking over. For between the significant moments and publications that stand out in the history of literature, languages and literatures continuously take shape and interrelate with one another in less dramatic ways, and parts of the literary and linguistic condition are being formed beyond the control of speaking subjects or even beyond the control of institutions or centers. In other words, there is another molecular and non-systemic way of using the concept to identify literary and linguistic tensions. Seeing the vernacular as an ongoing production of linguistic and epistemic difference opens for another use of the notion as a potential tool for analysing how language can operate in terms of dynamic relationships to other languages and literatures across time and in an increasingly interconnected world.

Bibliography

Bakhtin, Mikhaïl. *Esthtétique et théorie du roman*. Translated by Daria Olivier. Paris: Gallimard, 1987.

———. *Rabelais and his World*. Translated by Helene Iswolsky. Cambridge: MIT Press, 1968.

Beecroft, Alexander. *An Ecology of World Literature: From Antiquity to the Present Day*. New York: Verso, 2015.

---

[23] The French tradition prefers vehicular over cosmopolitan when referring to language partly because cosmopolitan has different connotations in French, which there is no space to discuss here. The definition of vehicular is taken from *Le Centre national de ressources textuelles et lexicales*, accessed 23 January 2017, www.cnrtl.fr.

Casanova, Pascale. *La République mondiale des Lettres*. Paris: Éditions du Seuil, 1999.

Demerson, Guy. "Le plurilinguisme chez Rabelais". In *Bulletin de l'Association d'étude sur l'humanisme, la réforme et la renaissance* 14 (1981): 3–19.

Glissant, Édouard. *The Poetics of Relation*. Translated by Betsy Wing. Ann Arbor: The University of Michigan Press, 1997.

Maigne, Vincenette. "Exotisme: Évolution en diachronie du mot et de son champ sémantique". In *Exotisme et création. Actes du Colloque International (Lyon 1983)*. Edited by Roland Antonioli, 7–16. Lyon: L'Hèrmes, 1985.

Pioffet, Marie-Christine. *La Tentation de l'épopée dans les relations des jésuites*. Sillery: Septentrion, 1997.

Rabelais, François. *Pantagruel, roy des dipsodes, restitué à son naturel; plus Les merveilleuses navigations du disciple de Pantagruel, dict Panurge*. Lyon: E. Dolet, 1542.

———. *The Whole Works of F. Rabelais*. Translated by Sir Thomas Urquhart, K^t & Bar of Cromarty and Peter Motteux. London and New York: G P Putman's Sons, 1905.

Racine, Jean. *Œuvres*, tome VII. London, 1768.

Rigolot, Pierre. *Les Langages de Rabelais*. Geneva: Droz, 1972.

Dictionaries

Centre national de ressources textuelles et lexicales. Accessed 23 January 2017. http://www.cnrtl.fr.

Dictionnaire de l'Académie française, t 2. Paris: Chez la Veuve de Jean Baptiste Coignard, 1694. Accessed 22 January 2017. http://dictionnaires.atilf.fr/dictionnaires/ACADEMIE/.

Boiste, Pierre Claude Victoire. *Dictionnaire universel de la langue française: avec le latin et les étymologies*. Paris, 1823.

Diderot, Denis and Jean Le Rond d'Alembert. *Encyclopédie ou Dictionnaire raisonné des sciences, des arts et des métiers*. Paris:

Pellet, 1777. Accessed 26 January 2017. http://encyclopedie.uchicago.edu/.

Féraud, Jean-François. *Dictionnaire critique de la langue française.* Marseille: Moissy, 1787–88. Accessed 22 January 2017. http://artfl.atilf.fr/dictionnaires/FERAUD/.

Furetière, Antoine. *Dictionnaire universel. Contenant tous les mots françois tant vieux que modernes, & les Termes de toutes les Sciences et des Arts.* Haag: A. et R. Leers, 1690.

Godefroy, Frédéric. *Dictionnaire de l'ancienne langue française et de tous ses dialects.* Paris: Émile Bouillon, 1895.

Littré, Émile. *Dictionnaire de la langue française.* Paris: Hachette, 1863–72.

Nicot, Jean. *Trésor de la langue Françoiyse tant ancienne que modern.* Paris: David Douceur, 1606. Accessed 26 January 2017. http://portail.atilf.fr/dictionnaires/TLF-NICOT/index.htm.

4. One Country, Several Literatures: Towards a Comparative Understanding of Contemporary Literature in Spain
Christian Claesson
Spanish, Lund University

Since 2008, a severe and prolonged economic crisis has tormented Spain, forcing millions to leave their homes or even the country, fostering grassroots movements that have radically changed the political landscape, deepening the conflict between Catalonia and the central government and making large portions of the population question the Constitution and the Spanish democracy as a whole. This precarious and convulsive situation certainly raises questions to scholars interested in contemporary literature's role as a creative commentary to societal affairs. For example, how has literature in Spain generally represented and responded to this economic, social, historical and constitutional crisis? Which kind of social critique does it formulate? Well, nobody really has a complete picture, since very few people read the four official languages in which this literature is articulated, and no scholarly efforts have been made to make comparative, collaborative readings. This chapter is an attempt to map a comparative approach to the literatures in Spain.

The adjective *Spanish* (and its equivalent in Spanish) normally refers to something "Of or pertaining to Spain or its people", as the OED has it, but when it comes to language and literature, things become rather more complicated. Today, Spanish/Castilian

---

How to cite this book chapter:
Claesson, Christian. "One Country, Several Literatures: Towards a Comparative Understanding of Contemporary Literature in Spain". In *World Literatures: Exploring the Cosmopolitan-Vernacular Exchange*, edited by Stefan Helgesson, Annika Mörte Alling, Yvonne Lindqvist, and Helena Wulff, 31–41. Stockholm: Stockholm University Press, 2018. DOI: https://doi.org/10.16993/bat.d. License: CC-BY.

is the official language of Spain, while three languages are co-official and protected in the Constitution: Catalan, Galician and Basque, spoken altogether by some 26 per cent of the population. However, even though several languages have always coexisted within the borders of the country since its formation in the fifteenth century, Castilian – the vernacular spoken until then only in medieval Castile – soon became synonymous with Spanish, as the supposed lingua franca of the entire kingdom. Today, speakers in the monolingual parts of Spain tend to refer to the language as *español*, while most speakers in the bilingual parts of the country, and also in the majority of Spanish America, generally prefer *castellano*, as a way of avoiding connotations to Spain as a country. The use of one term or the other, as well as the view of Spanish as the common language, is complex and politically charged.

Equally complex is the question of Spanish literature. When scholars and laymen talk about Spanish literature, or *literatura española*, what they generally mean is literature in Spanish from Spain. Nonetheless, there are other vital and well-established literatures in Spain. Catalan and Galician have medieval literary roots that even antedate Castilian letters. Spain has been a unified country at least since the nineteenth century,[1] so even though its fiction is written in the four (or more) languages of the state, at the same time it concerns, represents and is produced in a shared national reality. How did Castilian literature come to represent Spanish literature as a whole? What scholarly attempts have been made to break this monolingual paradigm? Could literary studies encompass literature written in the four co-official languages of Spain? How do the vernacular languages of the country relate to the cosmopolitan Spanish?

---

[1] The popular belief – voiced even by the then Prime Minister Mariano Rajoy (see Patricia R. Blanco, "España no es la nación más antigua de Europa por mucho que Rajoy insista", *El país*, 15 March 2017) – is that the nation-state of Spain is born at the end of the fifteenth century. Most historians, however, rather situate the foundation of Spain in 1810; up until then, the different regions had separate laws, fiscal systems and currency. Henry Kamen, *Imagining Spain: Historical Myth and National Identity* (New Haven: Yale University Press, 2008), 1–37.

Literary-Historical Overview

Spanish history has been a constant struggle between the universal and the vernacular. After the marriage in 1469 of the Catholic Monarchs, Queen Isabella I of Castile and King Ferdinand II of Aragon, the country was further consolidated in the remarkable year of 1492, when Columbus first reached America, and Muslims and Jews were expelled from the Peninsula after having been present for 700 years. The first grammar in a vernacular language in Europe, Antonio de Nebrija's *Gramática sobre la lengua castellana*, was also published in 1492, at the same time marking the socio-political dominance of Castilian in a kingdom where several regionally rooted languages co-existed. Castilian thus became an imperial language, both in the Peninsula and in the overseas territories. By the time Sebastián de Covarrubias published the first dictionary of a vernacular language in Europe, *Tesoro de la lengua castellana o española* (1611), the interchangeability between the two denominations was signaled in the very title. Despite Spain's status as a unified nation in charge of a world-wide empire, with Spanish as its vehicle, Catalonia and the Basque Country nevertheless retained their vernacular languages and jurisdictions. Catalonia, the strongest and most populous of the non-Spanish-speaking regions, was definitely subdued as a consequence of the War of Spanish Succession in 1714, when Castilian replaced Catalan in all judicial aspects. Soon after, Spanish was established as the official language of the country, enforcing the monolingual paradigm, to draw on Yasemin Yildiz's phrase, at a time when languages were perceived as structuring principles for both national feeling and subjectivity, and multilingualism was seen as a threat to political and psychological cohesion.[2]

Spanish literature undoubtedly had one of its most glorious periods in the *Siglo de oro* (usually placed between 1492 and 1681), but not until the eighteenth century did there exist a historical consciousness of a Spanish literary past, and therefore also

---

[2] Yasemin Yildiz, *Beyond the Mother Tongue: The Postmonolingual Condition* (Fordham University Press, 2012), 6–14.

a concept of Spanish national literature as such.[3] According to Mainer, this occurred at a time when the concept of literature began to encompass a more general knowledge in written form, but also when Spanish intellectuals tended to compare a mediocre present with the glories of the past. In 1813, only a year after the end of the Napoleonic invasion and the first Spanish Constitution, a group of intellectuals proposed that literature should be an integral part of pre-university education – replacing the old rhetoric and poetics – while also establishing a link to the teaching of history. Reflecting the semantic shift from patriotism to nationalism, the education of both literature and history would be parts of the socialisation and national identification of the future citizen, and national literature would be understood as "the natural expression of a language, topics, attitudes and heroes that are the collective heritage".[4]

This institutionalisation of nationalism, based on the triad of national (i.e. Spanish/Castilian) language, literature and history, occurs in the 1860s, at the same time – or even because of[5] – the renaissance of vernacular cultures in the country. Industrialisation and modernisation brought renewal to vernacular cultures; both the Catalan *Renaixença* and the Galician *Rexurdimento* denote major cultural and linguistic upswings.[6] If Catalonia fostered a

---

[3] José-Carlos Mainer, "La invención de la literatura española," in *Literaturas regionales en España: Historia y crítica*, ed. José María Enguita and José-Carlos Mainer (Zaragoza: Inst. Ferdinando el Católico, 1994).

[4] "la literatura nacional, ahora entendida como expresión natural de una lengua, unos temas, unas actitudes y unos héroes que son patrimonio colectivo." Ibid., 32.

[5] Romero Tobar mentions a royal order of 1867 in which "the great number of dramatic works presented to the censorship in the different dialects threatened the generalisation of the national language" ("el gran número de obras dramáticas presentadas a la censura en los diferentes dialectos atentaba a la generalización de la lengua nacional"). Leonardo Romero Tobar, "Entre 1898 y 1998: La historiografía de la literatura española", *Rilce* 15, no. 1 (1999): 29. Note that the other languages are called "dialects" of "the national language".

[6] "Extraterritoriality and Multilingualism", in *Spain Beyond Spain*, ed. Brad Epps and Luis Fenández Cifuentes (Lewisburg: Bucknell University Press, 2005), 191.

cosmopolitan outlook and sought to be a part of the larger world, then the Basque Country, largely lacking the intellectual middle class that had been a driving force in Barcelona's cultural rebirth, responded to modernisation by turning inward and to traditional religiosity.[7] The Spanish-American war in 1898, when Spain lost its last overseas colonies (Cuba, Puerto Rico and the Philippines) and suffered a devastating military defeat against the US, was a major blow to the Spanish self-understanding.[8] The ensuing soul-search was channelled through the works of a brilliant group of writers, the *Generación del 98*, but it also fuelled "a monolithic conception of national identity constructed on a supposedly archetypal Castilian character".[9] The loss of the colonies hardened the attitude of Spanish nationalists towards non-State nationalists, and a royal decree declared Spanish as the only official language of the country in 1902.[10]

The latter part of the century also saw the birth of a philology in service of the nation state. Two towering figures of Spanish philology have greatly influenced how Spanish literature has been read as an expression of national character: Marcelino Menéndez Pelayo (1856–1912) and his disciple Ramón Menéndez Pidal (1869–1968). Menéndez Pelayo's philological project was to chart the Castilian dominance in the Iberian Peninsula, and his influence was to be long-lasting: "we can thus speak of the philological project of Menéndez Pelayo, with its deeply inscribed religiosity, frank justification of centralism, and socially conservative habitus, as having a time horizon of nearly a century

---

[7] Enric Ucelay da Cal, "The Nationalisms of the Periphery: Culture and Politics in the Construction of National Identity", in *Spanish Cultural Studies: an Introduction. The Struggle for Modernity*, ed. Helen Graham and Jo Labanyi (Oxford: Oxford University Press, 1995), 37.
[8] Sebastian Balfour, "The Loss of Empire, Regenerationism, and the Forging of a Myth of National Identity", in *Spanish Cultural Studies: An Introduction. The Struggle for Modernity*, ed. Helen Graham and Jo Labanyi (Oxford: Oxford University Press, 1995).
[9] Balfour, "The Loss of Empire", 30.
[10] Joan Ramón Resina, *Del hispanismo a los estudios ibéricos: Una propuesta federativa para el ámbito cultural* (Madrid Biblioteca Nueva, 2009), 169.

in length (1880–1980)".[11] But if the guiding principle in his search for Castile's soul was Catholicism, then for Menéndez Pidal it was language.[12] By the end of the nineteenth century, there no longer existed a need to justify the search for national character in terms of religion; literature and language were rather seen as the secular legitimations of the nation. In this sense, philology in the service of the State seems to reverse cause and effect: it perceived the present as eternal and mysterious in order to justify the search for national character by what Resina calls "'our' way of being".[13] What Menéndez Pidal saw as "Castile's original character" is at the same time a tool for charting a tradition and "the normative ethos of the national community".[14] As already stated, this view has been in force even until our days, which is also shown in Santana's review of Spanish literary history manuals.[15] Francisco Rico's monumental and widely acclaimed *Historia y crítica de la literatura española* (1980–present) clings unequivocally to the monolingual understanding of the Spanish nation, equating Spanish literature with artistic expression in Castilian, without further justification.

A Comparative Understanding

Although the field of Iberian Studies has provided a rich and refreshing perspective on Spanish letters and the place of literature in the Peninsula, above all in the study of large-scale, historical developments, the inclusion of Portuguese literature does not seem altogether justified in social and political readings of

---

[11] Thomas Harrington, "Belief, Institutional Practices, and Intra-Iberian Relations", in *Spain Beyond Spain*, ed. Brad Epps and Luis Fernández Cifuentes (Lewisburg: Bucknell University Press, 2005), 213.
[12] Resina, 73.
[13] "Post-Hispanism, or the Long Goodbye of National Philology", in *Writers In Between Languages: Minority Literatures in the Global Scene*, ed. Mari José Olaziregi (Reno: Center for Basque Studies, 2009), 205.
[14] "Post-Hispanism".
[15] Mario Santana, "Mapping National Literatures: Some Observations on Contemporary Hispanism", in *Spain Beyond Spain*, ed. Brad Epps and Luis Fernández Cifuentes (Lewisburg: Bucknell University Press, 2005).

literature, especially if we want to study contemporary literature.¹⁶ In fact, recent attempts to reconfigure the study of literary production in Spain often start from the paradigm of the country in terms that rather suggest a comparative approach to Spanish literature. Taking into account comparative literature's openness to the interconnectedness of literary systems, Antonio Monegal finds it "surprising that in a country which displays in such an obvious way its multicultural makeup, comparative literature has not found a more welcoming environment".¹⁷ The reasons behind this state of affairs are cultural, institutional and political, perhaps even to the extent that it is "only from a prudent distance, however, that a Hispanist can propose the inclusion of works written in Galician, Basque, or Catalan in Spain's literary histories" – such an approach would be unpopular not only among non-State nationalists, but among their State counterparts too.¹⁸ Delgado insists that Hispanists need to abandon the idea of a universal, harmonious normalcy, where Spain is one, single unproblematic entity and Spanish is its universal expression, and instead focus on "the ideological processes that differentiate between the particular and the general, the local and the universal".¹⁹ Mario Santana adds that we should "strongly object to the validity claims of presenting the study of literary production in

---

[16] For introductions to Iberian Studies, see for example *Reading Iberia* (2007; ed. Helena Buffery et al.); Joan Ramón Resina's *Del hispanismo a los estudios ibéricos: Una propuesta federativa para el ámbito cultural* (2009); the monumental *A Comparative History of Literatures in the Iberian Peninsula*, volume I (2010; ed. Fernando Cabo Aseguinolaza et al.) and II (2016; ed. Domínguez et al.); and *New Spain, New Literatures* (2010; ed. Luis Martín-Estudillo).
[17] Antonio Monegal, "A Landscape of Relations: Peninsular Multiculturalism and the Avatars of Comparative Literature", in *Spain Beyond Spain*, ed. Brad Epps and Luis Fernández Cifuentes (Lewisburg: Bucknell University Press, 2005), 245.
[18] Geraldine Cleary Nichols, "Blank Spaces: Literary History, Spain, and the Third Millennium", ibid., 258.
[19] Luisa Elena Delgado, "If We Build It, Will They Come? Iberian Studies as a Field of Dreams", in *Iberian Modalities: A Relational Approach to the Study of Culture in the Iberian Peninsula*, ed. Joan Ramón Resina (Liverpool: Liverpool University Press, 2013), 49.

only one language as a way of gaining knowledge of the totality of a culture" – here, the totality of a culture refers to "a reflection on Spain as a whole" – and that literatures of other languages are not studied lest the foundation on a monolingual conception of the nation be questioned.[20] Even an otherwise conservative critic as Menéndez Pelayo considered, in 1878, that taking Castilian literature for Spanish was a "fatal mistake" that has contributed to muddle and obscure literary studies to the utmost.[21]

There have certainly been attempts to include non-Spanish letters in overviews of the literature in Spain,[22] and more are underway,[23] as well as university courses that include elements of non-Spanish letters,[24] but no comparative project seems to have

---

[20] Santana, 117–18.

[21] "En sentir de ilustres críticos a quienes respeto, con el sentimiento de no poder seguirlos, la *Historia de la literatura española* no es más ni menos que la *historia de la literatura castellana*. Este error, a mi ver, funesto, y que no sólo a la literatura, sino a otras esferas trasciende, ha contribuído a embrollar y oscurecer hasta lo sumo, muy doctos juicios e investigaciones." Marcelino Menéndez Pelayo, *Estudios y discursos de crítica histórica y literaria*, vol. 6, Edición nacional de las obras completas de Menéndez Pelayo (Santander: Consejo Superior de Investigaciones Científicas, 1941), 3.

[22] Already in 1998, in an issue of *Foro Hispánico* characterised by an optimism not very common today, van Hooft Comajuncosas proposes a comparative Spanish literary history and conducts a survey among scholars in the field to come up with definitions and delimitations. His first calls the proposal "Peninsular literature", which he later changes, upon many scholars' disagreement, to "literature in Spain". Andreu van Hooft Comajuncosas, "Una historia de historias: encuesta sobre historiografía literaria", in *Foro hispánico. Literaturas de España 1975–1998: Convergencias y divergencias*, ed. Andreu Van Hooft Comajuncosas (Amsterdam: Rodopi, 1998).

[23] One example would be Delgado's forthcoming *A Cultural History of Spanish Literature*. See Luisa Elena Delgado, *La nación singular: Fantasías de la normalidad democrática española (1996–2011)* (Madrid: Siglo XX, 2014), 193, n. 79.

[24] The Spanish online university, Universidad Nacional de Educación a Distancia (UNED), offers a Master in "Hispanic literatures (Catalan, Galician and Basque) in the European Context". Denominations are difficult here, but more than a few representatives of non-Spanish letters would probably object to being a part of the "Hispanic".

been undertaken. As we have seen in this short overview, Spanish literature is a construction that needs to be problematised from the perspective of comparative literature, not only because regionalist movements are as strong as ever, but also because we cannot, as Santana says, pretend to say something about literature in Spain in general unless we find a way to include all languages. In order to avoid unnecessary inclusions and historically charged hierarchies, a comparative project would need to avoid naming its object of study "Spanish", "Peninsular", "Hispanic" or "Iberian" literature, and instead study literature *in Spain*, applying a more spatial, and more neutral, characterisation based on the paradigm of the Spanish state. There is no need to essentialise literature in Spain as the only frame of study – other limitations would certainly be justifiable in different historical periods – but rather to adapt the framework to the object of interest. In a study of contemporary literature, for example of fiction related to the ongoing economic and social crisis, the country as a construct has had and still has a strong influence on literary production and reception, regardless of the language of writing.[25] Likewise, the literatures would also need to be studied on a horizontal plane, without the Castilian-centric point of view that makes non-Spanish letters mere appendixes to the national literature. Here, the tools of comparative literature are required, since a study like this cannot be a simple juxtaposition of "national" literatures – such surveys already exist and do not contribute much to a larger understanding of the common ground between the literatures. Only then may we answer questions about how the literature of Spain has responded to nation-wide issues, such as the ongoing social and economic crisis, and evaluate the kind of critique formulated in contemporary fiction. A global understanding of contemporary letters in Spain demands a postmonolingual approach that may break with previous literary, cultural, institutional and political conventions.

---

[25] No limitation will be wholly satisfying here; arguably, literature in Spain could also include translations and writing in other, diasporic languages by authors in Spain. Translations would speak very little of the current situation, but diasporic literature would possibly constitute an important, albeit very minor, knowledge production to take into account.

Bibliography

Balfour, Sebastian. "The Loss of Empire, Regenerationism, and the Forging of a Myth of National Identity". In *Spanish Cultural Studies: An Introduction. The Struggle for Modernity*, edited by Helen Graham and Jo Labanyi, 25–31. Oxford: Oxford University Press, 1995.

Blanco, Patricia R. "España no es la nación más antigua de Europa por mucho que Rajoy insista". *El país*, 15 March 2017.

Cleary Nichols, Geraldine. "Blank Spaces: Literary History, Spain, and the Third Millenium". In *Spain Beyond Spain*, edited by Brad Epps and Luis Fernández Cifuentes, 253–69. Lewisburg: Bucknell University Press, 2005.

Delgado, Luisa Elena. "If We Build It, Will They Come? Iberian Studies as a Field of Dreams". In *Iberian Modalities: A Relational Approach to the Study of Culture in the Iberian Peninsula*, edited by Joan Ramón Resina, 37–53. Liverpool: Liverpool University Press, 2013.

———. *La nación singular: Fantasías de la normalidad democrática española (1996–2011)*. Madrid: Siglo XX, 2014.

Harrington, Thomas. "Belief, Institutional Practices, and Intra-Iberian Relations". In *Spain Beyond Spain*, edited by Brad Epps and Luis Fernández Cifuentes, 205–30. Lewisburg: Bucknell University Press, 2005.

Kamen, Henry. *Imagining Spain: Historical Myth and National Identity*. New Haven: Yale University Press, 2008.

Mainer, José-Carlos. "La invención de la literatura española". In *Literaturas regionales en España: Historia y crítica*, edited by José María Enguita and José-Carlos Mainer, 23–45. Zaragoza: Inst. Ferdinando el Católico, 1994.

Menéndez Pelayo, Marcelino. *Estudios y discursos de crítica histórica y literaria*. Edición nacional de las obras completas de Menéndez Pelayo, vol. 6. Santander: Consejo Superior de Investigaciones Científicas, 1941.

Monegal, Antonio. "A Landscape of Relations: Peninsular Multiculturalism and the Avatars of Comparative Literature". In *Spain Beyond Spain*, edited by Brad Epps and Luis Fernández Cifuentes, 231–52. Lewisburg: Bucknell University Press, 2005.

Resina, Joan Ramón. *Del hispanismo a los estudios ibéricos: Una propuesta federativa para el ámbito cultural*. Madrid Biblioteca Nueva, 2009.

———. "Post-Hispanism, or the Long Goodbye of National Philology". In *Writers In Between Languages: Minority Literatures in the Global Scene*, edited by Mari José Olaziregi, 199–212. Reno: Center for Basque Studies, 2009.

Romero Tobar, Leonardo. "Entre 1898 y 1998: La historiografía de la literatura española". *Rilce* 15, no. 1 (1999): 27–49.

———. "Extraterritoriality and Multilingualism". In *Spain Beyond Spain*, edited by Brad Epps and Luis Fenández Cifuentes, 189–204. Lewisburg: Bucknell University Press, 2005.

Santana, Mario. "Mapping National Literatures: Some Observations on Contemporary Hispanism". In *Spain Beyond Spain*, edited by Brad Epps and Luis Fernández Cifuentes, 109–26. Lewisburg: Bucknell University Press, 2005.

Ucelay da Cal, Enric. "The Nationalisms of the Periphery: Culture and Politics in the Construction of National Identity". In *Spanish Cultural Studies: an Introduction. The Struggle for Modernity*, edited by Helen Graham and Jo Labanyi, 32–39. Oxford: Oxford University Press, 1995.

van Hooft Comajuncosas, Andreu. "Una historia de historias: encuesta sobre historiografía literaria". In *Foro hispánico. Literaturas de España 1975–1998: Convergencias y divergencias*, edited by Andreu Van Hooft Comajuncosas, 61–80. Amsterdam: Rodopi, 1998.

Yildiz, Yasemin. *Beyond the Mother Tongue: The Postmonolingual Condition*. New York: Fordham University Press, 2012.

5. Beyond Chineseness: De-Nationalising and De-Sinicising Modern Chinese Literature

Irmy Schweiger
Chinese Language and Cultures, Stockholm University

Introduction

To what extent does Chinese American Ha Jin's work, written in English, with Chinese culture and politics as imaginary backdrop, qualify as Chinese literature? How about Chinese-born writer Gao Xingjian, French citizen and Nobel laureate writing in French? Are the writings of American Nobel prize laureate (1938) Pearl S. Buck, who spent most of her life in China and wrote exclusively about China, considered Chinese literature? Is Tibetan writer A-lai, who publishes fiction about Tibet in Chinese, writing Chinese literature? Is Husluma Vava, Taiwanese writer, writing in Chinese about Bunun culture, producing Chinese literature? And what of literature written in Chinese from Hong Kong, Taiwan, Malaysia and Singapore? There is no doubt: Writers of transnational and multicultural backgrounds are challenging conceptual frameworks of Chinese literature based on antagonistic binaries such as tradition and modernity, China and the west, national and local, Han Chinese and ethnic minority self, dialects and the standard language. However, the expanding corpus of literature produced by Chinese communities worldwide has only recently attracted scholarly attention to revisit histories of literary production and to challenge the concept of modern Chinese literature

---

How to cite this book chapter:
Schweiger, Irmy. "Beyond Chineseness: De-Nationalising and De-Sinicising Modern Chinese Literature". In *World Literatures: Exploring the Cosmopolitan-Vernacular Exchange*, edited by Stefan Helgesson, Annika Mörte Alling, Yvonne Lindqvist, and Helena Wulff, 42–58. Stockholm: Stockholm University Press, 2018. DOI: https://doi.org/10.16993/bat.e. License: CC-BY.

that is based on the notion of a monolithic Chineseness referring to mainland China exclusively.

The following chapter outlines the conceptual framework of modern Chinese literature as a highly ambivalent nationalistic and coercive vernacularisation project at the beginning of twentieth-century China. It claims that the emergence of modern Chinese literature mainly was due to an efficient politico-cultural institutionalisation that was reinforced by canonisation, language policy and sinocentric identity discourses, framed by Marxist and teleological historiography. In recent years, however, the monolingual and sinocentric mantra has been challenged by a growing corpus produced by writers with transnational and multicultural backgrounds from Chinese communities worldwide, prompting postcolonial counterhegemonic and analytical tools to de-nationalise and de-sinicise modern Chinese literature.

Modern Chinese Literature Between a Rock and a Hard Place

The predicament of modern China has affected the narrative of modern Chinese literature and culture ever since Chinese writers and intellectuals at the turn of the nineteenth century joined forces in a patriotic tour de force to "save China" and to "build a wealthy and powerful nation".[1] While being exposed to the brutalities of western and Japanese hegemonic imperialism on the one hand and internal social disintegration and the final collapse of the dynastical empire on the other, advocates of the New Cultural Movement sought refuge in a bold mixture of an iconoclastic anti-traditionalist worldview ("cannibalism" becoming the icon for Chinese traditional culture) and a romantic notion of western enlightenment and the modern nation-state (famously replacing "Mr Confucius" with "Mr Science" and "Mr Democracy").[2] It might

---

[1] On the interrelation of modernity and nationalism especially during the May Fourth period, see Zhao Suisheng, *A Nation-State by Construction: Dynamics of Modern Chinese Nationalism* (Stanford, CA: Stanford University Press, 2004).

[2] Cf. Lena Rydholm's chapter in this volume.

count as one of the ironies of transnational history that in late nineteenth-century China, western modernity became the object of desire when it was actually on the verge of collapsing; disillusionment and transcendental homelessness had already become the prevailing western zeitgeist and modernism an instrument of criticism instead one of affirmation.

In the China-related context, "modernisation" became equated with "westernisation" and the May Fourth period bred this primal cause that structured the cultural double bind, which would underlie any discourse on modern Chinese identity and literature through to the 1980s. The schizophrenic split can thus be traced back to different though overlapping forms of the event of modernity: a coercive one, forcing modernity on the colonial subject (through the opium war); and an aspirational one, thrilled by things modern and driven by a fascination for a unified nation-state (the New Culture Movement).³

Apart from external colonisation by imperialist powers, internal colonisation by authoritarian power has simultaneously been adding to the complex situatedness of literature and culture. The established presupposition of the mutual constitution of literature and nation is notably relevant in the case of China, yet has a decidedly political notion.⁴ Drawing excessively on parallels of Mao Zedong's infamous "Talks at the Yan'an" in 1942,⁵ current

---

³ These paradoxical historical experiences would later not only fertilise the principal nationalistic narrative of the "century of humiliation" but also fuel "patriotic nationalism" and political campaigns fighting westernisation like the "Anti-spiritual Pollution Campaign" (1984) or "Against Bourgeois Liberalisation Campaign" (1987). Alison Adcock Kaufman, "The 'Century of Humiliation', Then and Now: Chinese Perceptions of the International Order", *Pacific Focus* 25, no. 1 (2010): 1–33 and William A. Callahan, "National Insecurities: Humiliation, Salvation, and Chinese Nationalism", *Alternatives* 29 (2004): 199–218.
⁴ For a closer explication, see the chapter by Lena Rydholm in this volume.
⁵ Mao Zedong毛澤東, "Zai Yan'an wenyi zuotanhui shang de jianghua" [Talks at the Yan'an Forum on Literature and Art: 在延安文藝座談會上的講話], *Fenghuang wang*, 14 May 2009, http://book.ifeng.com/special/hongsejingdian/list/200905/0514_6459_1158238.shtml. See also *Mao Zedong's 'Talks at the Yan'an Conference on Literature and Art': A Translation of the 1943 Text with Commentary*, ed. and trans. Bonnie S.

president Xi Jinping reminded artists and writers as late as in October 2014 in his "Talks" to create works with "vivid national characteristics", and promote "socialist core values" to encourage Chinese people's "sense of national pride and honour".⁶ Since the Party never left much room for interpretation of the political role and social task of art and literature, the history of modern Chinese literature has consequently been read as an intersection of politics and literature moving forward in time, framed by Marxist and nation-obsessed teleological historiography.

Constituting the Chinese Modern: Enlightenment & National Salvation Narratives

Consequently, Chinese literary history is based on two plotlines: First, as a story of modernity, making the advent of western imperialism, the subsequent May Fourth Movement (1919) in its pursuit of modernity and its invention of "China as a nation", the cradle of modern Chinese literature;⁷ second, as a sequence of "realist comments" mirroring and negotiating political and social struggles of revolutionary China, since "realism came to carry the profoundest burden of hope for cultural transformation".⁸ In order to unfold its educative and incisive power of enlightenment, needed for the building of new China, new literature had to be penned in the standard written vernacular language (*baihua* 白話) that was to replace the "dead" and static classical language (*wenyan* 文言). More than half a century later massive globalisation,

---

McDougall, Michigan Papers in Chinese Studies 39 (Ann Arbor: Center for Chinese Studies, The University of Michigan, 1980).

⁶ Xi Jinping 習近平, "Zai wenyi gongzuo zuotanhui shang de jianghua" [Talks at the forum on literature and artwork 在文藝工作座談會上的講話], *Xinhua Net*, 14 October 2015, http://news.xinhuanet.com/politics/2015-10/14/c_1116825558.htm.

⁷ For a sharp summary of critical re-examinations of the discourse of Chinese modernity, see Charles A. Laughlin, "Introduction", in *Contested Modernities in Chinese Literature*, ed. C. Laughlin (New York, NY: Palgrave Macmillan, 2005), 1–15.

⁸ Marston Anderson, *The Limits of Realism: Chinese Fiction in the Revolutionary Period* (Berkeley: University of California Press, 1990), 3.

commodification and de-politicisation ran rampant, post-revolutionary China then coined the slogans to "march forward" (*wang qian zou* 往前走) and "take to the global stage" (*zou xiang shijie* 走向世界). In post-Tiananmen China (1990s), literature was turned into a cultural marker of Chinese postmodernism, mainly on the basis of the constant flow of imported western theories developing a "cultural fever" (*wenhua re* 文化熱).[9] These master narratives have shaped literary production and scholarship for decades and have been reinforced by orientalist complicity of the academic and general reading public: the conceptualisation of "belated Chinese modernity" conveniently allowed both, perpetuating supremacy of modern western culture and backwardness of traditional Chinese culture.[10] Furthermore, it created a defining space for a malleable binary perception of modern Chinese literature as cultural hybrid: originating as a "response to the West", while at the same time making use of indigenous traditional Chinese resources.

This constellation recalls Græcist Gregory Jusdanis' critique of modernisation theories as eurocentric and chronocentric projections. Belated modernisation, he argues, manifests itself in a sort of internalised structural deficiency, as local realities are necessarily incongruent with the assumedly western originals. In order to catch up, "delayed modernization necessitates centralised planning, since it entails the anxious attempt to acquire the characteristics of a model".[11] A decidedly programmatic approach to de-centralise the west by "provincialising Europe" is advocated by historian Dipesh Chakrabarty, whose approach has had a strong impact on sinological discourses. Advocating articulations

---

[9] Zhang Xudong, *Chinese Modernism in the Era of Reforms: Cultural Fever, Avant-Garde Fiction, and the New Chinese Cinema* (Durham and London: Duke University Press, 1997) and Wang Ning, "The Mapping of Chinese Postmodernity", in "Postmodernism in China", special issue, *boundary 2* 24, no. 3 (Autumn 1997): 19–40.

[10] It was only in the 1980s, when Edward Said's *Orientalism* (1978) started to be discussed in the field of China Studies that "Chinese modernity" was de- and re-constructed.

[11] Gregory Jusdanis, *Belated Modernity and Aesthetic Culture: Inventing National Literature* (Minneapolis: University of Minnesota Press, 1991), xiv.

of non-unitary experiences of political modernity, he inspired China scholars and postcolonial intellectuals. Wang Xiaoming, for example, argues for heterogeneity of the Chinese modern on the basis of a bidirectional globalisation process, passing off from outside and from inside, from the global appropriated by the local and vice versa.[12] Nevertheless, during the long twentieth century, the Chinese politico-cultural elite made sure to unify experiences of modernity, to homogenise the Chinese modern and to escape the "waiting room of history" by establishing a nationalistic and sino-centric political self as the agent of local history and as a global player.

Institutionalising a Modern Mode of Cultural Production: Language Policy

Understandably, a foundational myth conveniently leaves aside everything and everyone that complicates matters. One of the New Culture Movement's main pillars is the replacement of the classical language by the vernacular, thereby creating a new language allowing for a new literature. Language policy, for that matter, was an efficient means to institutionalise the modern in cultural production. The reportedly notorious quest for a modern Chinese script at the beginning of twentieth century was, however, neither a simple national decision nor a pure mainland phenomenon. Chinese communities in Taiwan, Hong Kong, Malaysia, Singapore or Indonesia, due to these countries' colonial histories and prevailing sense of belonging to their ancestral home, were at least sensitive to the May Fourth movement's call for a new culture.[13] Political activists' breathless search for a "national

---

[12] Wang Xiaoming, "The Trajectory of the 'Third World' in Early Modern Chinese Thought", *Inter-Asia Cultural Studies* 17 (2016): 84–90. Critics of eurocentrism argue that classical western social theory did not intend to establish modernity as a universal category but saw it as a condition characterising western societies.

[13] David Kenley, *New Culture in a New World: The May Fourth Movement and the Chinese Diaspora in Singapore, 1919–1932* (New York: Routledge Press, 2003).

language", taking to the "vernacular" as standard-bearer for a modern literature that was to strengthen and to create an image of the nation, was however much less successful among Chinese communities outside the mainland. Regional idiolects or "topolects" like Hakka, Fukienese or Teochew stubbornly persisted and remain up to this day a marker of ethnic, linguistic and cultural distinction.[14]

More importantly: the process of vernacularisation, "a rather militant and monolingual idea implemented and institutionalised by the May Fourth vernacular movement" was setting a dramatic end to an earlier diglossic linguistic landscape (populated with classical written Chinese and colloquial spoken dialects).[15] In 1912, after continuous script reforms during late Qing (1644–1911) and after negotiating between different regional dialects, the Ministry of Education of the newly established Republic of China decided in favour of Mandarin (*guanhua* 官話), an informal *lingua franca* that had long since been used for imperial administrative purposes, to be the new "vernacular" or "national language".[16]

The historical setting of this intricate transformation process was thus far from being monolingual or mono-cultural. On the contrary, leading late Qing and early Republican reformers had spend their formative years in study-abroad programs, mostly in Japan, Germany, France, Britain and America, which not only broadened their world view but also bred a peculiar nationalism. While this intellectual elite, driven by both megalomania and despair, aspired to build a strong and superior China by learning from foreign modern nations, they at the same time experienced displacement, linguistic estrangement and racist humiliation

---

[14] On the question of topolects, see Victor H. Mair, "What is a Chinese 'Dialect/ topolect'? Reflections on Some Key Sino-English Linguistic Terms", *Sino-Platonic Papers*, 29 (September 1991): 1–52.

[15] Gang Zhou, *Placing the Modern Chinese Vernacular in Transnational Literature* (New York: Palgrave Macmillan, 2011), 7. This is, to my knowledge, the most recent discussion of the vernacularisation process in China in a critical world literature perspective.

[16] For details, see Robert Ramsey, *The Language of China* (Princeton: Princeton University Press, 1987).

exactly in the environment that inspired awe and admiration.¹⁷ Even worse, not much later they became alienated in their own country too, when their work would disqualify as "dressed in European cloth and the academism of Oxford, Cambridge and Columbia [...] an exotic banquet made for the Europeanised gentry in order to give them some exciting varieties".¹⁸ The typical May Fourth writer was not simply "a hand writing the mouth"¹⁹ or a collector of "small talk" from the street corners and alleyways,²⁰ he actually was on a "mission impossible".²¹

In the decades to come Chinese language policies put a lot of effort into making the vernacular, Mandarin or *putonghua* (普通話 common language) the *lingua franca* in Mainland China and beyond, legitimising Chinese Communist Party's national aspirations and executing its soft power not least by way of the worldwide establishment of Confucian Institutes to "spread Chinese language and culture".²²

---

17 The writings of the decadent writer Yu Dafu (1896-1945), who spent nine years in Japan, are often read as *locus classicus* of a national inferiority complex, as his bold descriptions of the impotent sexual landscape of the Chinese male is read as encoding national weakness. See Yu Dafu, *Chenlun* (Sinking沈淪), 1921. http://millionbook.net/mj/y/yudafu/ydfz/002.htm.
18 See Gang Zhou, *Placing the Modern Chinese Vernacular*, 43, quoting Qu Qiubai (1899-1935), one of the most eminent literary figures and political activist who spent many years in Russia. Apart from Chinese, Qu spoke French, Russian and English.
19 This is a literal translation of the often-quoted catch phrase "*Wo shou xie wo kou* [我手寫我口]" of the late Qing scholar Huang Zunxian (1848-1905), which was often used to illustrate that the vernacular was nothing more than the spoken language written.
20 "Xiaoshuo [小說]", a term explicated in the *History of the Han Dynasty* which is credited to historian Ban Gu (32-92 AD), has become the term for fiction as a vernacular genre, which, if taken literally, means small talk.
21 For a critical reading of the role of May Fourth vernacular see Shu-mei Shih, *The Lure of the Modern: Writing Modernism in Semicolonial China, 1917-1937* (Berkeley: University of California Press, 2001), 71.
22 For a recent article on the issue see Rachelle Peterson, "American Universities Are Welcoming China's Trojan Horse", *Foreign Policy*, 9 May 2017, or the publications by the National Association of Scholars (NAS), https://www.nas.org/projects/confucius_institutes/the_report.

Canonisation of Modern Literature

Nationalism and sinocentrism were not only reflected in language policies but were just as well exhibited by the literary canon which by and large was set by a chauvinist communist ideological apparatus and found its first revisions only in the 1970s.[23] Those revisions meant a cautious extension of the canon by integrating "marginal" women writers together with "neglected" literary schools and individual literary figures. The national project of "rewriting literary history" (*chongxie wenxue shi* 重寫文學史) in the late 1980s was, however, more radical in questioning the "West-response" presupposition by pioneering explorations of late Qing fiction as the originating period of modern Chinese literature. The "re-discovery" of the Beijing and Shanghai Modernist schools of the 1920s and 1930s provided a feasible alternative to mainstream realism. Hence writers were no longer grouped according to their political or ideological affiliations but by gender, provenience, geographical area, literary style or topic, yet histories of literatures from Taiwan and Hong Kong were practically non-existent. One of the first western literary histories of Chinese literature was published in 1961 by the Chinese American literary scholar C. T. Hsia (1921–2013) and intended to "contradict rather than affirm the communist view of modern Chinese fiction".[24] In as early as 1986 at an international conference in Günzburg (Germany) with the prospective title *A Commonwealth of Chinese Literature*, more than sixty scholars, mainly from Europe and the United States, assembled to further adjust the perspective on modern Chinese literature by juxtaposing different literatures from Taiwan, Hong Kong and China, by investigating their translation and circulation and by making

---

[23] For a concise summary of literary historiography see, Zhang Yingjin, "Modern Chinese Literature as an Institution: Canon and Literary History", in *The Columbia Companion to Modern East Asian Literature*, ed. Joshua S. Mostow (New York: Columbia University Press, 2003), 324–332.

[24] C.T. Hsia, *A History of Modern Chinese Fiction* (1961; repr., New York: Columbia University Press, 1971), 498.

comparisons.[25] While western China Studies departments were still affected by Cold War sentiments and either bound to Taiwan or the PRC, this seems to be one of the first gatherings with a trans- and inter-local agenda for modern Chinese literature. In the early 1990s a paradigmatic shift took place in the field of Chinese literary studies, culminating in a "postcolonial turn" in the field, which at large followed the respective turns and trends in Anglo-American academia.[26]

Identity Politics: Modern Literature and "Chineseness"

Questions of identity went viral in post-socialist China. The rise of migration, a booming economy, an increasing need for self-assertion of cultural agents and their struggle for normative power provoked different notions of "Chineseness". Although each of those "(self)-definitions" either made place, cultural practice, language or history a marker of difference, every one of them explicitly or implicitly took China as the uncontested centre, as point of departure: "greater China", "cultural China", "Chinese diaspora", "overseas Chinese" etc. were basically denoting a detachment from physical space and everyday culture, separated by masses of water, apart from the authentic cultural home.[27]

Neo-Confucian thinker Tu Wei-ming[28] famously (re)defined "Chineseness" to be located in a Confucian Chinese modernity by

---

[25] Howard Goldblatt has edited results of this transatlantic cooperation in his book *Worlds Apart: Recent Chinese Writing and Its Audiences* (Armonk: Sharpe, 1990).

[26] To a large extent, contemporary postmodern and postcolonial criticism was the follow up of post-structuralism, New Historicism and New Criticism. For a detailed review of these trends, see Xiaoping Wang, "Three Trends in Recent Studies of Modern Chinese Literature and Culture", *China Perspectives* 4 (2009), http://chinaperspectives.revues.org/4934.

[27] The Tiananmen massacre in 1989 functioned as a sort of watershed for re-questioning "Chineseness", Chinese culture and Chinese script. This was largely due to the fact that many writers and intellectuals left China for good and settled either in Europe or in the United States.

[28] Tu Wei-ming was the former director of the Harvard Yen-ching Institute;

placing the "Chinese periphery" (Taiwan, Hong Kong, Singapore, Chinese overseas communities) – i.e. the Chinese mercantile culture with Confucianism as basis – at the centre of what he calls "cultural China" (*wenhua zhongguo* 文化中國). While the "roots of Chineseness", such is the implication, are clearly to be found in China, its strongest and most fructiferous "branches", however, have spread "over-the-seas". Although Tu's conceptualisation dismisses Chinese communism and western capitalism, his metaphor emphasises sinocentric oneness and hierarchy that perceives of Chinese diaspora as an extension of national interests and the culture of origin. The Singapore-based Chinese scholar from Indonesia Wang Gungwu suggests the concept of "local Chineseness" (*difangde zhongguoxing* 地方的中國性), implying a pragmatic engagement with the local on the basis of a Chinese legacy.[29] Leo Ou-fan Lee, eminent Chinese US scholar of modern Chinese literature prefers "Chineseness on the move" (*youzoude zhongguoxing* 遊走的中國性), implying a cosmopolitan being at home nowhere and everywhere but always committed to Chinese culture.[30]

Critical theory and postcolonial interventions have formulated alternative conceptualisations of China/Chinese, which generally aim at accommodating transnationalisation and translingualism on the one hand and "de-nationalising" and "de-sinicising" China/Chinese on the other. In short: de-constructing China as monolithic entity; re-conceptualising Chinese literature as an inclusive term; re-reading modern Chinese literatures as local appropriations of trans-local and global developments; countering both the "evolutionary" narrative, advocated by the New Culture Movement and continued by CCP literary historians, and the tedious dichotomy of "China and the West", which nonetheless still informs a large amount of scholarship.

---

for reference, see his edited book *The Living Tree: The Changing Meaning of Being Chinese Today* (Stanford: Stanford University Press, 1994).

[29] See, for example, his essay publication *The Chineseness of China: Selected Essays* (Oxford: Oxford University Press, 1992).

[30] For an in-depth insight see his *Musings: Reading Hong Kong, China and the World* (Hong Kong: East Slope Publishing Limited, 2011).

The Sinophone and Post-loyalist Writing

Inspired by highly contested and ideologically charged terms like anglophone, francophone, hispanophone and lusophone literatures, which broadly refer to the literatures in the ex-colonies using the ex-colonisers' languages, the term sinophone has become popular in China studies circles.[31] Most prominently the term has been defined by comparative literature scholar Shu-mei Shih as a critical response to what she calls Middle Kingdom hegemony. Shih coined the notion of sinophone to designate "Sinitic-language cultures and communities outside China as well as those ethnic communities in China where Sinitic languages are either forcefully imposed or willingly adopted".[32] Sinophone articulations, in her view, are voices against Han Chinese nationalism, originating from ethnic minority territories like Tibet, Xinjiang, Mongolia, Taiwan or Hong Kong. Shih is critical towards the notion of diaspora, which she considers being a unifying Han-centred Chinese identity category, denoting a hegemonic relationship between a nation and its nationals abroad. The sinophone is hardly a spatial concept only but above all an "analytical and cognitive category therefore both geographically and temporally specific […] a place-based, everyday practice and experience, and thus a historical formation that constantly undergoes transformation to reflect local needs and conditions. It can be a site of both a longing for and rejection of various constructions of Chineseness".[33] Shih's definition of sinophone is therefore not only counterhegemonic but also inherently comparative and transnational.

David der-wei Wang refutes Shih's postcolonial concept, stressing the heteroglossia and diversity of Chinese languages with their

---

[31] Sinophone can only partly be an equivalent; as for example the British colonised Hong Kong and Malaysia and Taiwan was colonised by the Japanese and not by "China proper". Besides the Chinese script has been used throughout Asia for centuries before countries like Japan or Korea, developed their own national scripts.

[32] Shu-mei Shih, "Against Diaspora: The Sinophone as Places of Cultural Production", in *Global Chinese Literature: Critical Essays*, edited by Jing Tsu and David Der-wei Wang (Leiden: Brill, 2010), 36.

[33] Ibid., 39.

multitude of Sinitic-Tibetan languages and dialects. Employing Bakhtin's term of "heteroglossia" he emphasises linguistic plurality inside China, despite mono-linguistic control, not only as a literary technique but also as a sign of "Chineseness". Adopting a historical perspective, he builds his argument on the fact that Chinese history is less a history of colonialism than a history of migration, with millions of Chinese being forced or having chosen to leave their homeland and to settle mainly in East and South East Asia (a statement, which does not contradict but rather strengthen Shu-mei Shih's concept of the sinophone). In his essay "Literary Traveling and World Imagination" from 2006, Wang uses the term Sinophone Literature as denoting all literatures in the Chinese language whether produced inside or outside China.[34] This additive definition is peppered by the concept of *Post-loyalist writing* (*houyimin xiezuo* 後遺民寫作), a term closely related to the notion of diaspora referring to migrants who keep alive their memories of an imaginary homeland. *Post-loyalism,* as Wang explains, does not refer to an ideology but serves as a critical interface through which to analyse political unconsciousness and cultural fixation.[35]

The least common denominator that these varied concepts of the Sinophone seem to share is to think beyond "Chineseness" and to de-nationalise and de-sinicise modern Chinese literature. So does the national imagery still play any role in writing and reading literature at all? What safeguards the coherence of modern Chinese literature?

---

[34] Sinophone literature integrates the different concepts of "literature in Chinese" (*huayu wenxue* 華語文學), "China Literature" (*zhongguo wenxue* 中國文學), "overseas Chinese literature" (*haiwai huawen wenxue* 海外華文文學), "world Chinese literature" (*shijie huawen wenxue* 世界華文文學) and "Taiwan, Hong Kong, Singapore, Malaysia sojourners' literature in Chinese" (*tai xiang xing ma lisan huawen wenxue* 台香星馬離散華文文學), see David Der-wei Wang, "Wenxue xinglü yu shijie xiangxiang" [Literary traveling and world imagination 文學行旅與世界想像], *Mingpao Monthly*, July 2006.

[35] For more details see his lecture at Cambridge University in 2014, "Sailing to the Sinophone World: On Modern Chinese Literary Cartography". https://www.youtube.com/watch?v=2F5ZdEyMgA8.

When the eminent literary scholar C. T. Hsia in 1961 published his seminal work, *A History of Modern Chinese Fiction, 1917–1957*, he explained the impossibility for Chinese literature to transcend China's borders and become world literature due to Chinese writers' "obsession with China". This clearly no longer holds true, however, "Chinese literature" still can be identified as a heavy burden on the shoulders of "Chinese writers". Yet American sinophone writer Ha Jin clearly votes against writing "national allegories"[36] and strongly objects to nationalistic, patriotic or any form of loyalist writing. He rejects the role of cultural ambassador mediating between China and the west or vice versa.[37] French sinophone writer Gao Xingjian in his Nobel Lecture leaves no doubt that he speaks "in the voice of an individual … not as a spokesperson of the people …"[38] These voices hardly harbour any desire for national or ethnic affiliation or post-loyalist ancestral belonging. That is why a conceptualisation of sinophone as analytical and cognitive category as well as a place-based, everyday practice actually may show a way out of essentialist notions of "Chineseness" and allow for critical positions debunking Chinese nationalism and Han-ethnocentrism.

Bibliography

Anderson, Marston. *The Limits of Realism: Chinese Fiction in the Revolutionary Period*. Berkeley: University of California Press, 1990.

Chakrabarty, Dipesh. *Provincializing Europe: Postcolonial Thought and Historical Difference*. New Jersey: Princeton University Press, 2000.

---

[36] See Fredric Jameson, "Third-World Literature in the Era of Multinational Capitalism," *Social Text* 15 (Autumn 1986): 65–88, where he argues that all third-world texts can be read as national allegories, as their forms developed out of western modes of representation.

[37] Instead Ha Jin builds his own writing experience on the model given by Conrad and Nabokov, who both found their destinies in their adopted language, see "Exiled to English," in *Sinophone Studies: A Critical Reader*, edited by Shu-mei Shih, Chien-hsin Tsai and Brian Bernhards (New York: Columbia University Press, 2013): 117–124.

[38] Gao Xingjian, "The Case for Literature", The Nobel Prize in Literature 2000, accessed 15 May 2017, http://www.nobelprize.org/nobel_prizes/literature/laureates/2000/gao-lecture-e.html.

Dirlik, Arif. "Literary Identity/Cultural Identity: Being Chinese in the Contemporary World". *Modern Chinese Literature and Culture Resource Center Publication*, September 2013. https://u.osu.edu/mclc/book-reviews/literary-identity/.

Callahan, William A. "National Insecurities: Humiliation, Salvation, and Chinese Nationalism". *Alternatives* 29 (2004): 199–218.

des Forges, Alexander. "The Rhetorics of Modernity and the Logics of the Fetish". In *Contested Modernities in Chinese Literature*, edited by Charles A. Laughlin, 17–31. New York: Palgrave Macmillan, 2005.

Gao, Xingjian. "The Case for Literature". The Nobel Prize in Literature 2000. Accessed 15 May 2017. http://www.nobelprize.org/nobel_prizes/literature/laureates/2000/gao-lecture-e.html.

Goldblatt, Howard. *Worlds Apart: Recent Chinese Writing and Its Audiences*. Armonk: Sharpe, 1990.

Ha Jin. "Exiled to English". In *Sinophone Studies: A Critical Reader*, edited by Shu-mei Shih, Chien-hsin Tsai and Brian Bernhards, 117–124. New York: Columbia University Press, 2013.

Hsia, C. T. *A History of Modern Chinese Fiction*. 1961. Reprint, New York: Columbia University Press, 1971.

Jameson, Fredric. "Third-World Literature in the Era of Multinational Capitalism". *Social Text* 15 (Autumn 1986): 65–88.

Jusdanis, Gregory. *Belated Modernity and Aesthetic Culture: Inventing National Literature*. Minneapolis: University of Minnesota Press, 1991.

Kaufman, Alison Adcock. "The 'Century of Humiliation,' Then and Now: Chinese Perceptions of the International Order". *Pacific Focus* 25, no. 1 (2010): 1–33.

Kenley, David. *New Culture in a New World: The May Fourth Movement and the Chinese Diaspora in Singapore, 1919–1932*. New York: Routledge Press, 2003.

Laughlin, Charles A. "Introduction". In *Contested Modernities in Chinese Literature*, edited by Charles A. Laughlin, 1–14. New York: Palgrave Macmillan, 2005.

Lee, Leo Ou-fan. *Musings: Reading Hong Kong, China and the World*. Hong Kong: East Slope Publishing Limited, 2011.

Mair, Victor H. "What is a Chinese 'Dialect/Topolect'? Reflections on Some Key Sino-English Linguistic Terms". *Sino-Platonic Papers* 29 (September 1991): 1–31.

Peterson, Rachelle. "American Universities Are Welcoming China's Trojan Horse". *Foreign Policy*. 5 September 2017.

Pollock, Sheldon. "The Cosmopolitan Vernacular". *The Journal of Asian Studies* 57, no. 1 (February 1998): 6–37.

Ramsey, Robert. *The Language of China*. Princeton: Princeton University Press, 1987.

Said, Edward. *Orientalism*. New York: Pantheon Books, 1978.

Shih, Shu-mei. *The Lure of the Modern: Writing Modernism in Semicolonial China, 1917–1937*. Berkeley: University of California Press, 2001.

———. "Against Diaspora: The Sinophone as Places of Cultural Production". In *Global Chinese Literature: Critical Essays*, edited by Jing Tsu and David Der-wei Wang, 29–48. Leiden: Brill, 2010.

Tu, Wei-ming. *The Living Tree: The Changing Meaning of Being Chinese Today*. Standford: Stanford University Press, 1994.

Wang, David Der-wei. "Wenxue xinglü yu shijie xiangxiang" [Literary traveling and world imagination 文學性旅与世界想象]. *Mingpao Monthly*. July 2006.

———. *Houyimin xiezuo* [Post-loyalist writing 後移民寫作]. Taibei: Maitian Publishing House, 2007.

———. "Sailing to the Sinophone World: On Modern Chinese Literary Cartography". Lecture at Cambridge in 2014. https://www.youtube.com/watch?v=2F5ZdEyMgA8.

Wang, Gongwu. *The Chineseness of China: Selected Essays*. Oxford: Oxford University Press, 1992.

Wang, Ning. "The Mapping of Chinese Postmodernity". In "Postmodernism in China". Special issue, *boundary 2* 24, no. 3 (Autumn 1997): 19–40.

Yu, Dafu. "Chenlun" [Sinking 沉沦, 1921] http://millionbook.net/mj/y/yudafu/ydfz/oo2.htm.

Zhang, Yingjin, "Modern Chinese Literature as an Institution: Canon and Literary History". In *The Columbia Companion to Modern East Asian Literature*, edited by Joshua S. Mostow, 324–332. New York: Columbia University Press, 2003.

Zhou, Gang. *Placing the Modern Chinese Vernacular in Transnational Literature*. New York: Palgrave Macmillan, 2011.

6. "The Original Romance of America": Slave Narratives and Transnational Networks in Theodore Parker's American Literary History

David Watson
English, Uppsala University

Theodore Parker's August 1849 address "The Position and Duties of the American Scholar" is perhaps best remembered today for the proclamation that "all of the original romance of America" is in its slave narratives, which he identifies with what appears to be "indigenous and original" in American literature.[1] This declaration is a pivotal statement within the antebellum period of 1820–60. With it, Parker declares that the emergent genre of the slave narrative, which usually focuses on a slave's flight to freedom, is endowed with literary and not just political value— the first such recognition to come from the literary culture of New England transcendentalism, which included such canonical figures as Ralph Waldo Emerson, Margaret Fuller, and Henry David Thoreau. He indicates implicitly as well that his abolitionist, anti-slavery work cannot be divorced from a consideration of the African American expressive vernacular culture growing

---

[1] Theodore Parker, "The Position and Duties of the American Scholar", in *The Collected Works of Theodore Parker*, vol. 7, ed. Frances Power Cobbe (London: Trübner & Co., 1864), 245, 244.

How to cite this book chapter:
Watson, David. ""The Original Romance of America": Slave Narratives and Transnational Networks in Theodore Parker's American Literary History". In *World Literatures: Exploring the Cosmopolitan-Vernacular Exchange*, edited by Stefan Helgesson, Annika Mörte Alling, Yvonne Lindqvist, and Helena Wulff, 59–69. Stockholm: Stockholm University Press, 2018. DOI: https://doi.org/10.16993/bat.f. License: CC-BY.

out of the institution of slavery. In effect, the statement links the transcendentalist literary culture to which Parker belonged to an emergent African American literature, even while proclaiming the importance of the latter for the future of American literature. But while the significance is indisputable of Parker's statement to a national literary history of the antebellum period, his address resists a reading of it as solely offering a national literary history. Instead, as I will show, it frames its remarks concerning the slave narrative within a world literary context, and asks of its audience to imagine the vernacular cultures of the antebellum period in relation to various cosmopolitan networks, even while asking of us to interrogate what we mean by the vernacular and cosmopolitan. In other words, Parker's address, as I will show, asks of us to engage with the historical specificity of his understanding of the vernacular and cosmopolitan, and how he mobilises this distinction in surprising ways.

Parker's claim concerning the slave narrative genre is, of course, informed by the debates within the United States during this period. His proclamation echoes that of Ephraim Peabody—the Boston Unitarian minister and abolitionist. A month earlier, Peabody began his review in *The Christian Examiner* of slave narratives by Fredrick Douglass, William W. Brown, and Josiah Henson by claiming that "America has the mournful honor of adding a new department to the literature of civilization—the autobiographies of escaped slaves", which, for him, resembled the Homeric epic more than any other literary genre.[2] While Parker by 1849 has resigned from his Unitarian parish in West Roxbury, Massachusetts and was preaching in an independent Boston pastorate, he, like Peabody, was firmly committed to the cause of abolitionism—he wrote the scathing "To Southern Slaveholders" in 1848, and helped finance in 1859 the abolitionist John Brown's Harper's Ferry raid. In "John Brown's Expedition", a public letter written after Brown's execution as a result of the raid, Parker argues in favour of violent resistance to slavery, and for the rights

---

[2] Ephraim Peabody, "Narratives of Fugitive Slaves", *The Christian Examiner* 47 (July 1849): 61.

of slaves to kill slaveholders. Parker's original address occurred at a volatile historical moment of increasing tension between anti-slavery and pro-slavery forces, which would soon result in the Fugitive Slave Act of 1850 and, ultimately, civil war. Like Peabody's review, it recognises in the slave narrative the emergence of a new African American expressive cultural form, and seeks to adjudicate this vernacular form's relation to American literary culture more broadly. Already over-determined from the outset by its entanglements with literary historical developments and the history of slavery, Parker's "American Scholar", as I will argue, raises questions as well concerning transnational comparison, translation histories, and 19th century conceptions of the long history of world literature. In other words, its engagement with the emergent genre of the slave narrative is embedded within an account of antebellum American literature that seeks to grasp this literature within a world literary framework.

By 1849, the terms whereby debates concerning American literature are to be conducted were well established. On the one hand, the so-called "Knickerbockers" such as James K. Paulding favoured a more cosmopolitan, or rather Anglophile, literary culture that would be reserved for a cultivated cultural elite. On the other hand, the "Young America" movement of Evert and George Duyckinck, and others favoured a more democratic and nationalist literary culture, with Herman Melville's exhortation that "men, not very much inferior to Shakespeare, are this day being born on the banks of the Ohio" perhaps best capturing the movement's vigorous celebration of American democratic values and their cultural promise.[3] Initially, in his address, Parker appears closest in spirit to the "Young America" movement even though he decries the materialist and imperialist inclinations of the period. Emphasising the democratic qualities of America's literary culture, which he sees as creating a definitive break with Europe, Parker assigns a particular kind of debt to the scholar. Arguing that the national community produces the scholar, he insists that

---

[3] Herman Melville, "Hawthorne and His Mosses", in *The Piazza Tales and Other Prose Pieces, 1839–1860*, ed. Harrison Hayford et.al (Evanston: Northwestern University Press, 1989), 248.

it is the duty of the American scholar to repay this investment, so to speak, by representing back to the nation "higher modes of human consciousness".[4] Comparatively historicising his country's literary output by comparing it to European literary production, Parker concludes however that American literature falls short of deserving entry to the world literary stage. Much of this literature appears to be imitations, he argues, of works by authors such as John Milton and Walter Scott. Adding nothing new, and nothing American to the literature of the world, this literature is cosmopolitan in a pejorative sense, taking both its form and content from abroad without giving anything of the "individuality of the nation" back to world literature—the hallmark of a successful national literature for Parker.[5] Arguing that all national literatures begin through a series of imitative gestures, Parker identifies a problem of coevalness within American culture: in comparison to European literatures, American literature is attempting belatedly to enter the world literary stage.

It is tempting to understand Parker's lament concerning American literature as a complaint concerning the preponderance of cosmopolitan literary influences in the United States, and a national failure to establish a properly vernacular culture. It may be though that such a reading would amount to an anachronistic mistranslation of his argument. Rather than subdividing American literature into cosmopolitan and vernacular strains, he offers instead two temporal categories whereby to classify his country's literary production:

> First comes the permanent literature, consisting of works not designed merely for a single and transient occasion, but elaborately wrought for a general purpose. This is literature proper. Next follows the transient literature, which is brought out for a particular occasion, and designed to serve a special purpose.[6]

Taking this division as a schematic whereby any literature can be mapped, Parker offers temporal categories—the transient and

---

[4] Parker, "American Scholar", 224.
[5] Parker, "American Scholar", 239.
[6] Parker, "American Scholar", 238.

ephemeral, the permanent and enduring—as a way of understanding the different parts of a literary culture. Coming perhaps closest to a vernacular conception of literature, the transient mode includes "speeches, orations, state papers, political and other occasional pamphlets, business reports, articles in the journals, and other productions designed to serve some present purpose."[7] Notably not including the slave narrative—a form understood to have an political purpose during this period—amongst his examples of the transient mode, Parker is expanding the sphere of what counts as literature by aggregating together forms of production that address historically-specific matters. Not quite, or rather exclusively, cosmopolitan in form, the permanent mode should on the contrary be at once universal as well as particular to the nation and author, the "private bottle", or bottles, into which should run the "public wine of mankind".[8] This literature gains its permanence via its synthesis of the general and particular, and it provides a model for other literary cultures as it circulates across the globe. Offering a synthesis of the arguments of the "Knickerbockers" and the Young America movement, Parker seems to be arguing that a universal literature is at its most worldly when national, and a national literature at its most national when it refers back to the universal.

The slave narrative occupies a privileged yet awkward space within this taxonomy of American literature. Superior to the "white man's novel", it is a mode of literary production that could only be written within the United States given its relation to the systems of slavery.[9] Yet it is ranked alongside, even while differentiated from, accounts of the "lives of the early martyrs and confessors… the legends of saints and other pious men… the Hebrew or heathen literature."[10] Parker writes as if all of these literatures belongs to a long, global literary tradition uniting Christian and non-Christian writing across epochs. This insistence on both the American particularity of the slave narrative and its position within

---

[7] Parker, "American Scholar", 245.
[8] Parker, "American Scholar", 241.
[9] Parker, "American Scholar", 245.
[10] Parker, "American Scholar", 244–5.

a long world literary history, in which secular and non-secular modes of writing are inter-linked, underwrites Parker's argument regarding its permanence. Yet, as Russ Castronovo has pointed out, this judgment does not lead to the full inclusion of the slave narrative in the body of American literature.[11] The fugitive slave is not sufficiently cultured, according to Parker, and the slave narrative does not make the necessary down payment on the debt produced by investment of the nation in its scholars. At once writing the exemplary form of American literature, yet not admitted fully to the ranks of the American scholar, the fugitive slave appears to be producing a literature that is American yet not. Is Parker, in the final instance, resisting the full association of American literature with the slave narrative, or is he acknowledging the difficulties in applying terms such as debt, which is overtly associated in the address with democratic opportunities for education, to the fugitive slave? He certainly appears to be doing both, at once resisting the miscegenation of the American literary field, and showing an awareness of the unevenness produced by the material realities of slavery. Despite this awkwardness, Parker's declaration concerning the slave narrative situates it within both a national and a transnational continuum, a world literary space stretching across deep time as well as a national sphere inflected by the on-going realities of slavery.

There are very few antecedents for Parker's mapping of the American literary field. It conforms to neither of the positions articulated in the debates between the "Knickerbockers" and the Young American movement, opting instead for a perhaps unstable synthesis of the terms they take to be antithetical to one another—the universal and the nation. Earlier national literary histories such as Samuel Lorenzo Knapp's *Lectures on American Literature, with Remarks on Some Passages on American History* from 1829, the first American literary history, focused on the progressive development of American literature and how it has been shaped by events such as the War of 1812 between the United

---

[11] Russ Castronovo, *Fathering the Nation: American Genealogies of Slavery and Freedom* (Berkeley: University of California Press, 1995), 158–60.

States and the United Kingdom, in which Knapp fought. In this history, American literature is identified overtly with the literature of New England to the detriment of writing from Southern states and what Parker would term "transient" modes of literary production. Parker's scope and his world literary reach makes for an obdurate comparison to such histories.

But we find a more persuasive antecedent for Parker's "American Scholar" in his own writing on religion. In fact, his mapping of the American literary field draws directly on this writing. It is in his then-controversial sermon of May 19, 1841, "A Discourse on the Transient and Permanent in Christianity", that Parker introduces the divisions that would assist him eight years later in organising the American literary field. He argues in the sermon that

> [i]n actual Christianity... there seems to have been, ever since the time of its earthly founder, two elements, the one transient, the other permanent. The one is thought, folly, the uncertain wisdom, the theological notion, the impiety of man; the other the eternal truth of God. These two bear the same relation to each other that the phenomena of outward nature, such as sunshine and cloud, growth, decay and reproduction, bear to the great law of nature, which underlies and supports them all.[12]

Noting that particular forms of worship and elements of Christianity change over time and even disappear, Parker argues for an historicising approach to religion that would distinguish between transient forms and beliefs, and enduring, or "permanent", religious truths. Advocating elsewhere a reading of the Christian Bible as a set of "conflicting Histories which no skill can reconcile with themselves or facts", Parker includes not only different forms of worship under the rubric of the transient, but the belief in miracles including the Christian resurrection.[13] What remains as permanent is "one Religion which is absolutely true"

---

[12] Theodore Parker, *A Discourse on the Transient and Permanent in Christianity* (Boston, 1841), 8.

[13] Theodore Parker, *A Discourse of Matter Pertaining to Religion* in *The Collected Works of Theodore Parker*, vol. 1, ed. Frances Power Cobbe (London: Trübner & Co., 1876), 217.

but which finds expression within "numerous systems of theology or philosophies of religion" whether Christian or not.[14] In other words, Parker, as in the "American Scholar", seeks to enlarge the category of the "permanent" to include both the general and the particular, articulating thereby a theological argument that particularise Christianity. As Barbara Packer has described, Parker's religious sermons and writings were controversial and contentious, leading ultimately to his break with the Unitarian church and the founding of his independent Boston pastorate.[15] I am less interested though in Parker's work on religion, or its consequences, than with his transposition of a classificatory system designed to distinguish between different modes of religious discourse onto the literary field of antebellum American literature. In this odd blurring of the secular and non-secular, religious discourse is transformed into a worldly phenomenon while literary production verges on becoming sacralised, especially once the slave narrative is linked across time to the "lives of the early martyrs and confessors… the legends of saints and other pious men." It may very well be that in Parker's discourse on religion and literature the alliance between secular modernity and the nation-state together with its literature is put under pressure until they disappear into a long history within which distinctions between the secular and sacred no longer appear to be functional.

The background to Parker's "American Scholar" becomes even more complex once we take into account that his religious discourse is sourced, in fact, in the German Biblical higher criticism of Wilhelm Martin Leberecht De Wette and Johann Eichhorn. This scholarship takes as its central premise the historicity of the Bible—it treats sacred scripture as a potentially secular script that often reflects its period rather than divine inspiration, which shows itself intermittently in both the Bible and other writing. Parker began producing in 1836 a paraphrastic translation of De Wette's *Beiträge zur Einleitung in das Alte Testament* as *A Critical and Historical*

---

[14] Parker, *Transient and Permanent*, 10.
[15] Barbara Packer, "The Transcendentalists", in *The Cambridge History of American Literature*, Vol. 2 ed. Sacvan Bercovitch (Cambridge: Cambridge University Press, 1995), 346–48, 414, 420.

Introduction to the Canonical Scriptures of the Old Testament, which would take him seven years to complete. De Wette writes in his preface to the volume that his aim is to reconnect biblical scripture to the history of its production—a claim that shaped Parker's own thinking. During the period in which he was translating De Wette, Parker would also write an extensive review of David Friedrich Strauss's *The Life of Jesus: Critically Examined* or *Das Leben Jesu, kritisch bearbeitet* in which the author sought to distinguish between the mythical and factual parts of the New Testament. Parker's own *A Discourse of Matter Pertaining to Religion* would testify to the impact of German philosophy and higher criticism on his thinking—the text is saturated with references to Kant, Hegel and Fichte, in addition to Eichhorn, Strauss and De Wette. There is little doubt about the importance of translation work and German philosophy within Parker's milieu.[16] Almost all of the New England Transcendentalists were translators and readers of German writing including Margaret Fuller, Frederic Henry Hedge, and James Freeman Clarke, who translated de Wette's *Theodore; or the Skeptic's Conversion*. Prominent New England intellectuals such as William Emerson, Ralph Waldo Emerson's brother, Edward Everett, George Ticknor and George Bancroft all went to Germany to study with Eichhorn and learn about Biblical higher criticism. Parker's translation work, his reading in German philosophy, and investment in the assumptions of Biblical higher criticism are all in strict continuity with the concerns and practices of the rest of the New England intellectual community. But Parker's translation of De Wette and his other engagements with German writing provide him with the coordinates whereby to map American literature. He turns to the historicising methodology of higher criticism to articulate a transnational history of American literature within which the slave narrative is central. To put this otherwise: Parker's elevation of the slave narrative to a privileged place within the American

---

[16] Cf. Kurt Mueller-Vollmer, "Translating Transcendentalism in New England: The Genesis of a Literary Discourse", in *Translating Literatures, Translating Cultures: New Vistas and Approaches in Literary Studies*, ed. Kurt Mueller-Vollmer and Michael Irmscher (Stanford: Stanford University Press, 1998), 81–106.

literary field depends on transnational engagements with European discourses and translation work invisible within the "American Scholar" address itself.

The complications abounding around Parker's "American Scholar" address are suggestive as to why it may very well be premature to associate antebellum America with the history of the emergence of American literary narrative, to paraphrase Jonathan Arac.[17] It is not only a matter of deciding what should be included and excluded in such a history—a question framing Parker's awkwardness concerning the slave narrative. An account of the antebellum period would have to take into account the diverse and often conflicting models of a national literary history and world literature informing such texts as Parker's address. It would also call for a reckoning with questions concerning the boundaries of the literary, whether to include what Parker terms "transient" literary expressions, and what to make of the porous relation between the secular and non-secular in his writing—a problem perhaps confronting all literary histories indebted to models of deep time. Moreover, it has to take into account the frequently invisible histories of translation, transnational comparison, and foreign influence shaping accounts of American literature. In other words, a history of American literature in the antebellum period may very well have to take as its starting point that we cannot take for granted what was meant back then, or even today, by "American", "literature" or even "literary history". More immediately, Parker's address shows that in mapping the cosmopolitan and vernacular tendencies of the period we need to attend carefully to their historical specificity and strange shapes.

Bibliography

Arac, Jonathan. *The Emergence of American Literary Narrative, 1820–1860*. Harvard: Harvard University Press, 2005.

Castronovo, Russ. *Fathering the Nation: American Genealogies of Slavery and Freedom*. Berkeley: University of California Press, 1995.

---

[17] Jonathan Arac, *The Emergence of American Literary Narrative, 1820–1860* (Harvard: Harvard University Press, 2005).

Melville, Herman. "Hawthorne and His Mosses". In *The Piazza Tales and Other Prose Pieces, 1839–1860*, edited by Harrison Hayford et.al, 239–53. Evanston, IL: Northwestern University Press, 1989.

Mueller-Vollmer, Kurt. "Translating Transcendentalism in New England: The Genesis of a Literary Discourse". In *Translating Literatures, Translating Cultures: New Vistas and Approaches in Literary Studies*, edited by Kurt Mueller-Vollmer and Michael Irmscher, 81–106. Stanford: Stanford University Press, 1998.

Packer, Barbara. "The Transcendentalists". In *The Cambridge History of American Literature*, vol. 2, edited by Sacvan Bercovitch, 329–604. Cambridge: Cambridge University Press, 1995.

Parker, Theodore. *A Discourse on the Transient and Permanent in Christianity*. Boston, 1841.

———. "Position and Duties of the American Scholar". In *The Collected Works of Theodore Parker*, vol. 7, edited by Frances Power Cobbe, 217–56. London: Trübner & Co., 1864.

———. *A Discourse of Matter Pertaining to Religion. The Collected Works of Theodore Parker*, vol. 1, edited by Frances Power Cobbe. London: Trübner & Co., 1876.

Peabody, Ephraim. "Narratives of Fugitive Slaves". *The Christian Examiner* 47 (July 1849): 61–97.

7. Reformist Discourses: Classical Literary Language Versus Modern Written Vernacular in Lu Xun's Short Story "A Madman's Diary"

Lena Rydholm
Chinese, Uppsala University

Introduction

In the wake of the Opium Wars in the nineteenth century, the semi-colonisation of China by western imperialist forces and China's defeat in the Sino-Japanese war (1894–95), many students, scholars and intellectuals called for economic and political reforms to strengthen China. Thousands of Chinese students went to study abroad, in Japan, Europe and United States. Some returned convinced that China needed profound reform, not only adopting western science and technology, but also breaking off ties with traditional culture and Confucian ethics. Anti-traditionalists advocated modernisation of education through "western learning", stressing science and democracy,[1] and reform of language and literature. David Wang states: "Language reform was the first stage of literary revolution, which in turn was key

[1] Tse-tsung Chow, *The May Fourth Movement: Intellectual Revolution in Modern China* (Stanford: Stanford University Press, [1960] 1967), 1.

How to cite this book chapter:
Rydholm, Lena. "Reformist Discourses: Classical Literary Language Versus Modern Written Vernacular in Lu Xun's Short Story "A Madman's Diary"". In *World Literatures: Exploring the Cosmopolitan-Vernacular Exchange*, edited by Stefan Helgesson, Annika Mörte Alling, Yvonne Lindqvist, and Helena Wulff, 70–88. Stockholm: Stockholm University Press, 2018. DOI: https://doi.org/10.16993/bat.g. License: CC-BY.

to a broader project of cultural renovation".[2] Reformists within the New Culture Movement, such as Hu Shi, Chen Duxiu and Lu Xun, promoted "modern" Chinese literature written in the vernacular. This entailed re-evaluations of language, content, genres, forms, narrative strategies and aesthetic ideals, often inspired by western literature, philosophy, science etc.

Although some ideas promoted by anti-traditionalists within the New Culture Movement had roots in domestic literary culture, what may be called a "reformist discourse on literary revolution", with regard to the development of modern Chinese literature in the era of the May Fourth Movement,[3] dominated in literary histories

---

[2] David Der-Wei Wang, "Chinese Literature from 1841-1937", in *The Cambridge History of Chinese Literature: Volume II: From 1375*, ed. Kang-i Sun Chang and Stephen Owen (Cambridge: Cambridge University Press, 2010), 469.

[3] In its most narrow sense, the term referred to the May Fourth Incident, i.e. the student demonstrations that broke out in Peking on May Fourth, 1919, against Japanese imperialism and the Versailles Peace Treaty after World War I, which ceded the German concessions in Shandong to Japan. In its broader sense, the May Fourth Movement now refers to the demonstrations on May Fourth, together with the intellectual currents, protests and debates leading up to them, and also to the continued debates, protests and demands for cultural, social and political reforms that spread across China and gained in impact after the demonstrations (Chow, *The May Fourth Movement*, 1-2). Chow sums up the main goals of the movement: "[...] the students and new intellectual leaders promoted an anti-Japanese campaign and a vast modernization movement to build a new China through intellectual and social reforms" (Chow, *The May Fourth Movement*, 1). The May Fourth Movement in this broader sense was a sociopolitical, intellectual and cultural reform movement. They rejected traditional (Confucian) ethics, philosophy etc., demanded reforms of language and literature, as well as political institutions and were strongly inspired by western ideas, while at the same time the participants held several political orientations, such as socialism, anarchism and liberalism (Chow, *The May Fourth Movement*, 1). The major events related to the movement took place in 1917-1921 (Chow, *The May Fourth Movement*, 6). See also Merle Goldman and Leo Ou-Fan Lee, eds., *An Intellectual History of Modern China* (Cambridge: Cambridge University Press, 2002) and others. The cultural legacy of this movement is still a matter of great controversy among scholars within the field of Chinese literature.

in the People's Republic of China after 1949.⁴ This "mainstream narrative" was modified several times due to changing socio-political circumstances in China, entailing political re-evaluations of authors and their works.⁵ After 1978, the influence of Late Qing fiction on the development of modern Chinese literature was recognised, and manifestos/literary experiments by reformists prior to the May Fourth era (i.e. not sharing the political views of later leftist reformists), such as Liang Qichao, were included into the reformist discourses on literature and language leading up to the New Culture Movement.⁶

It is of course impossible to exhaust the subject of language reform and the development of modern literature in China in this chapter.⁷ My aim is to trace a few influential voices of reformists/writers in the early twentieth century to show how their calls for reform of language and literature were embodied in a single liter-

---

⁴ The views of the Communist Party of China on traditional Chinese culture conflicted with those of the Nationalist party, which retreated to Taiwan after 1949, where the preservation of traditional Chinese culture and language became of essence; thus the May Fourth reformists/writers were regarded less favourably. In recent times, the concept of "sinophone" literature is creating heated debates. Jing Tsu, on the issue of "national" versus "sinophone" literature claims that: "Diaspora, rather than pointing at an unspecific desire that can easily be mapped anywhere onto the idea of China, generates tensions not only between nations but also between dispersed Sinophone communities vying to protect their hard-won capital of distinction", Jing Tsu, "Epilogue", in *The Cambridge History of Chinese Literature: Volume II: From 1375*, ed. Kang-i Sun Chang and Stephen Owen (Cambridge: Cambridge University Press, 2010), 714. For more on the debates on the concept of sinophone literature, see Irmy Schweiger's chapter in this volume.

⁵ For more on politics involved when writing histories of modern Chinese literature and postcolonial critique of mainstream narratives, see Irmy Schweiger's chapter in this volume.

⁶ Li Guiqi 李桂起 and Jiang Qi 姜启, "Xiaoshuo tishi juan" 小说体式卷 [Section on Forms of Fiction], in *Zhongguo jinbainian wenxue tishi liubianshi* 中国近百年文学体式流变史 [History of the Evolution of Literary Forms in China in the Past Century], edited by Feng Guanglian 冯光廉 (Beijing: Renmin wenxue chubanshe人民文学出版社, 1999), 87-88.

⁷ For an overview of the development of modern Chinese literature in China, see for instance David Wang, "Chinese Literature from 1841-1937", 413-529.

ary work. I begin by brief accounts of manifestos calling for fiction written in the vernacular by Liang Qichao, Hu Shi and Chen Duxiu. Then I show how their reformist discourse on language and literature confronts literary tradition *within a work of fiction*, through the conflict between the juxtaposed classical, literary language narrative and the modern, written vernacular narrative in Lu Xun's "A Madman's Diary". A short introduction to the "classical, literary language" and "written vernacular" is required before discussing the manifestos and Lu Xun's short story.

The Classical, Literary Language and the Written Vernacular

In China since ancient times, oral and the written traditions have interacted in a multitude of ways and contributed to the development of both high and popular literary forms.[8] The written language designated for education, administration and high literature, such as poetry and non-fictional prose, was the classical, literary language *wenyan* (文言). The First Emperor of the Qin Dynasty (221–207 BCE) mandated the unification of the writing system. This became a milestone in the development of a standardised, written, literary language used in the imperial administration,[9] to bridge the difficulties in communication with officials in different parts of the empire speaking in different dialects and strengthen the Emperor's control. For centuries, the educated elite

---

[8] As Børdahl and Wan have pointed out: "How oral and written traditions interact in Chinese popular literature is a question of almost incredible breadth and complexity, [...] the topic could easily include studies of the earliest Chinese folk songs as found in *The Book of Odes*, Shi Jing (1000–600BC)[...]", Vibeke Børdahl and Margaret B. Wan, eds., *The Interplay of the Oral and the Written in Chinese Popular Literature* (Copenhagen: NIAS press, 2010), 1. Børdahl and Wan also cite Ruth Finnegan's claim in *Literacy and Orality* (1988) that rather than distinguishing "orality" and "literacy" as two separate modes, they may be regarded as "a continuum", in which they "mutually interact and affect each other", *The Interplay*, 1.

[9] Ping Chen, *Modern Chinese: History and Sociolinguistics* (Cambridge: Cambridge University Press, 1999), 67.

taught their sons to read and write in this literary language, as they memorised the Confucian classics, the histories and the philosophers' works, and imitated the most esteemed writers' poetry and prose, in order to pass the imperial civil service examination to obtain office (an examination system abolished in 1905).

The written vernacular, later referred to as *baihua* (白话), "vernacular literary language", had roots in folk songs and ballads, early translations of Buddhist narratives, oral story-telling in the Tang and Song dynasties etc. The written vernacular became the major medium for fiction writing and matured with famous novels published in the sixteenth century, such as *The Water Margin*, *Journey to the West* and others.[10] The written vernacular was closer to contemporary spoken languages and had low status. Ping Chen writes:

> Due to the conservatism prevalent among the ruling class and the literati, *wenyan* was considered refined and elegant, thus ideal for high-culture functions, while *baihua* was despised as coarse and vulgar, suitable only for low-culture functions.[11]

Popular genres written in the vernacular, such as fiction, had low status. During the Han dynasty (206 BCE–220 CE), when Confucianism became state ideology, the term today translated into English as "fiction", namely *xiaoshuo* (小说), which literally means "small talk", was explicated by Han dynasty historian Ban Gu (32–92):

> The school of small talk originates from officials of low ranking. It is created out of the talk of the streets and the gossip of the alleys, and what has been overheard on roadsides and spoken on pathways.
> 小说家者流，盖出于稗官。街谈巷语，道听涂说者之所造也。[12]

---

[10] For an overview of the development of the written vernacular in China, see for instance Liangyan Ge, *Out of the Margins: The Rise of Chinese Vernacular Fiction* (Honolulu: University of Hawai'i Press, 2001) and others.

[11] Chen, *Modern Chinese*, 69.

[12] Ban Gu 班固, *Hanshu* 汉书 [History of the Han Dynasty], (Beijing: Zhonghua shuju 中华书局, [1962] 1975), vol. 5, 1745.

Although the literati enjoyed collecting, reading and writing *xiaoshuo* themselves, they officially did not recognise fiction written in the vernacular as part of high literature up to the early twentieth century. By then, the *wenyan* was more removed from the spoken languages, intelligible only for the educated elite. For many reformists, the classical, literary language was a "dead language" not spoken by people[13] and unsuited for conveying "enlightened" discourse: this required a living, spoken language in literature. Liang Qichao, Hu Shi and Chen Duxiu published manifestos calling for the reform of literature and literature in contemporary written vernacular.

Liang Qichao's Call for the Reform of Fiction

Liang Qichao (1873–1929), a young reformist exiled in Japan for a decade (after the failed "Hundred days of reform" in 1898), studied western and Japanese ideas, traveled to several countries and launched journals advocating political reforms. Since ancient times in the mainstream Confucian tradition, literature was supposed to fulfill a didactic purpose, summed up in the famous slogan "Literature is a vehicle of the Way" (文以載道),[14] the "way" implying "the Confucian way". For Liang, literature could be a "vehicle" for something more than Confucian ethics, spread new ideas on politics, society and culture. However, the main part the population had limited reading skills. Poetry and non-fictional prose, high-literary "vehicles" for moral education, were written in *wenyan* for the educated elite. On the contrary, fiction written in the vernacular flourished, easier to read and popular among the general reading public. Liang, also impressed by the political novels in Europe and Japan, believed that fiction could be an effective vehicle for reformist discourses in China, but fiction had low status among intellectuals, thus a re-evaluation both of fiction and of the written language was required.

---

[13] Chow, *May Fourth Movement*, 271.
[14] A slogan originating in statements by neo-Confucian Zhou Dunyi 周敦颐 (1017–1073), cited and translated by James J. Y. Liu, *Chinese Theories of Literature* (Chicago: University of Chicago Press, 1975), 114.

In 1902, Liang started the magazine *The New Novel* (*Xin xiaoshuo* 新小说) and published his manifesto "On the Relationship between Fiction and the Government of the People" starting with the famous words: "If one wants to renew the people of a nation, one must first renew the fiction of that nation" (欲新一国之民，不可不先新一国之小说).[15] He goes on to claim that changes in morality, religion, politics, social customs etc. all require the reform of fiction: fiction can "change people's minds" (新人心) and "remold people's characters" (新人格), "because fiction has unimaginable powers to govern the way of mankind" (小说有不可思议之力支配人道故).[16] Moreover, fiction is easy to understand and fun to read, can deeply move us and provide insight into our own emotions as well as those of others; it leads us to "the world beyond oneself and one's world" (身外之身，世界外之世界).[17] Liang also claimed that: "In writing, the vulgar language [vernacular] is more effective than the literary [classical] language" (在文字中，则文言不如其俗语).[18]

Liang's manifesto was timely, in the midst of rapidly growing urban culture and increasing demands for popular literature it contributed to the elevation of fiction among the educated

---

[15] Liang Qichao 梁启超, "Lun xiaoshuo yu qunzhi zhi guanxi" 论小说与群治 之关系 [On the Relationship Between Fiction and the Government of the People], in *Liang Qichao wenji* 梁启超文集 [The Collected Works by Liang Qichao], (Beijing: Beijing Yanshan chubanshe 北京燕山出版社, 1997), 282. For an English translation of Liang's manifesto, see Gek Nai Cheng's translation in Kirk A. Denton, ed., *Modern Chinese Literary Thought: Writings on Literature, 1893–1945* (Stanford: Stanford University Press, 1996), 73–81.

[16] Liang, "Lun xiaoshuo", 282. According to Liang, fiction has "four powers" (四种力), that can change the individual reader, and by extension the norms and values of an entire culture and society. These are: gradual and subconscious "intoxication" (熏) and complete "immersion" (浸) of readers' minds; "provocation" (刺) of strong emotional response; and "transcendence" (提) of one's own body and mind, thereby making readers completely forget themselves "as if transforming themselves – entering into the book and becoming the main character" (若自化其身焉 —入于书中，而为其书之主人翁), Liang, 283–285.

[17] Liang, "Lun xiaoshuo", 282–3.

[18] Liang, "Lun xiaoshuo", 284.

elite.¹⁹ No longer seen as simple entertainment, fiction could fulfill a traditional, didactic purpose of literature. David Wang stated that: "the conviction that fiction could and should serve as the foremost medium of enlightened discourse has apparently been endorsed by elite and mainstream literary historians ever since".²⁰ Further calls for language reform came with Hu Shi's and Chen Duxiu's manifestos and the New Culture Movement.

Hu Shi's and Chen Duxiu's Calls for a "Revolution" in Literature and Language

In 1915 in Shanghai, Chen Duxiu (1879–1942), later one of the founders of the Communist Party of China (CPC), started a journal which became pivotal for the New Culture Movement, advocating science, democracy and "literary revolution" (文学革命). In *New Youth* (新青年), Chen introduced western literature and published translations of western novels. In January 1917, Hu Shi (1891–1962), at the time a student in the US, published "Humble Suggestions for the Reform of Chinese Literature" in *New Youth*. In the article, Hu urged writers to stop imitating ancient masters and avoid using allusions, parallelism and old clichés, while on the contrary, "not avoid using vulgar [vernacular] words and expressions" (不避俗字俗语).²¹ His article has been regarded as

---

¹⁹ Liang and his predecessors (Yan Fu, Xia Zengyou and others) shared in what Wang calls "the story of the boom in late Qing literature", including several factors pivotal for the rise of "a new popular reading culture", such as the growth of urban culture, print industry, public media, popular literature etc. David Wang stated, "Without these material factors by which the cultural and social environment had been conditioned, Liang's advocacy of a new form of literature would not have had such an overwhelming effect" (Wang, "Chinese Literature", 441).
²⁰ Wang, "Chinese Literature", 441.
²¹ These are five of the eight famous suggestions in Hu Shi 胡适, "Wenxue gailiang chuyi 文学改良刍议 [Humble Suggestions for the Reform of Chinese Literature], *Xin qingnian* 新青年 [*New Youth*], vol. 2, no. 5 (1917), (Dongjing: Jigu shuyuan 汲古书院, 1970–1971), vol. 2, 467. For an English translation of Hu's article, see Denton, *Modern Chinese Literary Thought*, 123-139.

the "first trumpet call of the literary revolution",[22] although Liang Qichao and others had earlier advocated literary reform.[23] In the subsequent issue of *New Youth*, Chen Duxiu published "On the Literary Revolution", writing:

1. To overthrow the painted, powdered, and obsequious literature of the aristocratic few, and to create the plain, simple, and expressive literature of the people;
2. To overthrow the stereotyped and over-ornamental literature of classicism, and to create the fresh and sincere literature of realism;
3. To overthrow the pedantic, unintelligible, and obscurantist literature of the hermit and the recluse, and to create the plain speaking and popular literature of society in general.[24]
   曰，推倒雕琢的、阿谀的贵族文学，建设平易的、抒情的国民文学；曰，推倒陈腐的、铺张的古典文学，建设新鲜的、立诚的写实文学；曰，推倒迂晦的、艰涩的山林文学，建设明了的、通俗的社会文学。[25]

Hu's and Chen's ideas met with opposition from the conservative camp, but the May Fourth Movement put additional pressure on the authorities to make the vernacular become the standard written language.[26] In his article, Chen also dared Chinese writers to

---

[22] Chow, *May Fourth Movement*, 275.
[23] David Wang states: "What distinguishes Hu Shi lies in his vision of the relation of the vernacular to a total literary and cultural renewal. While his Qing predecessors considered vernacular language an efficient tool to enlighten the public, they did not do away with the classical language as a sign system of cultural continuity and intellectual fecundity" (Wang, "Chinese Literature", 468).
[24] Chen Duxiu "Wenxue geminglun" [On the Literary Revolution] in English translation by Chow, *May Fourth Movement*, 276. For an English translation of Chen Duxiu's article, see Timothy Wong's in Denton, *Modern Chinese Literary Thought*, 140–145.
[25] Chen Duxiu陈独秀, "Wenxue geminglun" 文学革命论 [On the Literary Revolution], *Xin qingnian* 新青年 [*New Youth*], vol. 2, no. 6 (1917), (Dongjing: Jigu shuyuan 汲古书院, 1970–1971), vol. 2, 563.
[26] Ping Chen, *Modern Chinese*, 74. Hu Shi's and Chen Duxiu's articles had certain impact on debates, but several factors contributed to the

become "a Chinese Hugo, Zola, Goethe, Hauptman, Dickens, or Wilde."[27] Many writers at the time drew inspiration from western literature, such as Lu Xun, whose short stories published in *New Youth* reinforced Hu's and Chen's calls for "literary revolution".

The Language of Tradition versus the Language of Reform in "A Madman's Diary"

In May 1918, Lu Xun (1881–1936) published "A Madman's Diary", which "is considered the first 'modern' Chinese short story ever published", in *New Youth*.[28] Lu Xun, being critical of some superstitious medical practices in China (his own father being the treated with ineffective methods before dying), went to study western medicine in Japan.[29] Thinking that the teaching of

---

  replacement of the classical, literary language: the abolishment of the civil service examination in 1905; the fall of the Qing Dynasty and establishment of the Republic of China in 1912; rising nationalism; the May Fourth Movement etc., see Ping Chen, 70–75.
[27] Chen Duxiu, "Wenxue geminglun", 566. In 1918, Hu Shi published an article in *New Youth* advocating "A literature written in the national language [written vernacular], a national language for literature" (国语的文学,文学的国语), Hu Shi 胡适, "Jianshe de wenxue geminglun" 建设的文学革命论 [Construction of Literary revolution], *Xin qingnian* 新青年 [*New Youth*], vol. 4, no. 4 (1918), (Dongjing: Jigu shuyuan 汲古书院, 1970–1971), vol. 4, 345.
[28] Shu-mei Shih, *The Lure of the Modern: Writing Modernism in Semicolonial China, 1917–1937* (Berkeley: University of California Press, 2001), 85. Shih states: "Not that China did not have its own forms of short vernacular fiction (*xiaoshuo*), but the modern short story form, as it has been used since the May Fourth period, was modeled explicitly after its western counterpart, where more emphasis is given to the economy of plot and character conflict, and where supposedly 'modern' issues are dealt with" (Shih, 85, f. 43). According to David Wang, the first "modern" Chinese short story written in the vernacular could be Chen Hengzhe's "One Day" (一日), written by a Chinese student in the US about the daily lives of female college students, published in 1917 in *US Student Quarterly*, David Wang, "Chinese Literature", 479.
[29] Lu Xun 鲁迅, "Zixu" [Author's Preface] 自序 to *Nahan* 呐喊 [Call to Arms], in *Lu Xun quanji* 鲁迅全集 (Beijing: Renmin wenxue chubanshe 人民文学出版社, 1973), vol. 1, 270. For an English translation of this

western medical science in Japan had had an effect on the Japanese Reformation, he believed that as a doctor, he could provide effective cures to illnesses in China for patients like his father, while at the same time "promote a belief in reformation among my fellow countrymen" (促进了国人对于维新的信仰).³⁰ Lu Xun claimed to have changed his mind after seeing newsreel slides in Japan about the Russo-Japanese war, showing a Chinese "spy" being executed by the Japanese, while his countrymen stood passively by.³¹ He decided to study literature, since medical science cured people's bodies, not their attitudes:

> The most important thing, therefore, was to change their spirit; and since at that time I felt that literature was the best means to this end, I decided to promote a literary movement.³²
> 第一要著，是在改变他们的精神，而善于改变精神的是，我那时以为当然要推文艺，于是想提倡文艺运动了。³³

Lu Xun, just as Hu Shi, Chen Duxiu, and Liang Qichao, for all their anti-traditionalist views, adhered to a traditional, didactic view of the function of literature.³⁴ Lu Xun rejected traditional Chinese culture and promoted learning from the west.³⁵ With the

---

preface, see the Yangs' in Denton, *Modern Chinese Literary Thought*, 238–42.
30 Lu Xun, "Zixu", 271.
31 Lu Xun, "Zixu", 271.
32 Lu Xun, "*Preface to* Call to Arms", a translation of Lu Xun's preface to the collection of stories in *Call to Arms* by the Yangs in Denton, *Modern Chinese Literary Thought*, 240.
33 Lu Xun, "Zixu", 271.
34 Reformists within the May Fourth Movement embraced different ideas, several writers advocated literature for literature's sake and other ideas; see for instance David Wang, "Chinese Literature" and others.
35 Lu Xun translated many literary works and expressed views on cosmopolitanism and the idea of "World Citizens" (a concept introduced to China by Liang Qichao): "Some people say: 'We intend to grow within the boundaries of our traditional culture; otherwise how can we be Chinese?' Thus, I fear for the exclusion of China from the global society of World Citizens", Lu Xun, "Suigan lu 36" [Collection of Random Thoughts 36] published in *New Youth* in 1918, cited and translated by Fugui Zhang and Ren Chuangong, "The Spread of Cosmopolitanism in China and Lu Xun's Understanding of the 'World Citizen'", *Frontiers of*

publication of "A Madman's Diary", he became a leading voice within the New Culture Movement. This short story was inspired by Gogol's "The Diary of a Madman" (1835) and likewise tells the story of a madman in the form of his diary.[36] The young man in question is tormented by what he thinks are mortal threats from everyone surrounding him – people on the street, neighbours, his doctor and even his brother. His deranged mind takes a bleak view of Chinese history:

> Everything requires careful consideration if one is to understand it. In ancient times, as I recollect, people often ate human beings, but I am rather hazy about it. I tried to look this up, but my history has no chronology and scrawled all over each page are the words "Confucian Virtue and Morality". Since I could not sleep anyway, I read intently half the night until I began to see words between the lines. The whole book was filled with the two words – "Eat people!"[37]

> 凡事总须研究，才会明白。古来时常吃人，我也还会记得， 可是不甚清楚。我翻开历史一查， 这历史没有年代，歪歪斜斜的每叶上都写着 "仁义道德" 几个字。我横竖睡不着，仔细看了半夜， 才从字缝里看出字来，满本都写着两个字是 "吃人"！[38]

Lu Xun intended an allegorical reading of the story as a critique of society and Confucian ethics.[39] The diary is written in a first-

---

Literary Studies in China 6, no. 4 (2012): 564. However, Lu Xun's ideas about cosmopolitanism changed during his lifetime, also discussed by Zhang and Ren.

[36] There are numerous studies of the influence of foreign literature on Lu Xun's works; in English, see for instance Patrick Hanan, "The Technique of Lu Hsün's Fiction", *Harvard Journal of Asiatic Studies* 34 (1974): 53–96.

[37] Lu Xun, "A Madman's Diary", translated by the Yangs in Joseph S. M. Lau and Howard Goldblatt (eds.), *The Columbia Anthology of Modern Chinese Literature: Second edition* (New York: Columbia University Press, 2007), 10.

[38] Lu Xun 鲁迅, "Kuangren riji" 狂人日记 [A Madman's Diary], *Xin qingnian* 新青年 [*New Youth*], 4, no. 5 (1918), (Dongjing: Jigu shuyuan 汲古书院, 1970–1971), vol. 4, 485–486.

[39] Lu Xun, "Lu Xun lun wenxue yu yishu" [Lu Xun on Literature and Arts], cited by Ming Dong Gu, "Lu Xun, Jameson and Multiple Polysemia",

person voice and we get to see the world through the narrator's, the madman's, eyes. While the madman's thoughts are absurd to the point of being hilarious, the reader gradually comes to think that perhaps he is a kind of "poet-prophet" type of literary character. He is the only sane person in what in his mind is a seriously dysfunctional Chinese traditional society. He is a rebel against society and conventions.

The diary is written in contemporary vernacular and ends in the madman's utter despair and call to "save the children" (救救孩子) from becoming "man eaters".[40] However, the diary has a preface written in *wenyan* that has already let the reader know how the story ends. The narrator of this preface claims to have decided to publish the diary, written by a friend during a period of mental illness, since it might be of value for medical research. The young man in question has by then recovered and been appointed to an office in the government administration. However, having

---

Canadian Review of Comparative Literature December (2001): 450. Gu says: "Scholars generally agree on the basic theme of the story. Through a madman's mouth, the author voices his opinion of Chinese history and society", i.e. his fierce critique of Confucian virtue and morality (Gu, 446). However, Gu applies a semiotic/psychological model to uncover deeper layers of possible interpretations of conscious or unconscious messages in the story. Gu adds: "Since 'A Madman's Diary' marks the birth of modern Chinese fiction, I suggest that the modernity of this story lies in the author's conscious use of the unconscious not only as the thematic concern but also as its mode of narration" (Gu, 446).

[40] Lu Xun, "Kuangren riji", 493. Lu Xun's criticism of traditional society in his fictional works profited greatly from the shocking effect of using the metaphor of "man eating". Among his main targets were superstitious medical cures. He also wrote a short story called "Medicine" (药), in which a father buys a bun soaked in blood from an executed revolutionary to cure his son's tuberculosis. This of course has no effect; the son is dead, just as the revolutionary who possibly could have changed society and superstitious customs. Mo Yan, Nobel laureate in literature 2012, wrote "The Elixir" (灵药) in 2000, a short story staged in China after the revolution had taken place. On the advice of a local doctor, a man procures human bile to cure his mother's blindness. He cuts up the gallbladder of an executed landowner/class enemy and obtains the "elixir", but his mother dies from the shock of learning what the medicine consisted of. The story *may* be read as a response to "Medicine": the revolution did not wipe out superstitious practices or political persecutions.

read the diary, the reader realises that the recovery described in the preface rather indicates that the rebel has given in to societal pressures. The madman has regained his "sanity" only in the sense of accepting the Confucian virtue and morality, done his filial duty and become a government official in this traditional socio-political system, contributing to its legitimatisation and persistence, and if so, that is the tragedy, or irony, of his "recovery".

The preface written in the classical, literary language and the diary written in the modern vernacular interact and undermine each other, thus the story embodies the contemporary struggle between literary tradition and traditional morals, and the reformists' "modern", anti-traditionalist ideas within the realm of language in a work of fiction. The "madman", the person questioning "man-eating"– that is, the metaphor for "Confucian Virtue and Morality" – uses the vernacular as his medium. The friend in the preface speaking on behalf of the "sanity" or rationality of traditional society and Confucian ethics uses the normative classical, literary language. It is a battle between thoughts, worldviews, morals and values expressed in "different" mediums.[41] The classical, literary language expresses and safeguards traditional society and Confucian morals, while the vernacular language breaks off from tradition both in content and expression, and becomes the language of rebels/reformists, the written language for demands for change, reform and revolution. This shows the different functions and alliances of *wenyan* and *baihua* at the time from the viewpoint of these reformists. In that sense, "A Madman's Diary" embodies *within* a single literary work of fiction the power struggle between the "traditional" classical, literary language and the "modern" written vernacular in China in the early twentieth century. Lu Xun subsequently published several stories written in the vernacular. The written vernacular in time became the main written language of fiction in China. The substitution of the classical, literary language by the contemporary, written vernacular in

---

[41] On the affinities between *wenyan* and *baihua*, see Patrick Hanan, *The Chinese Vernacular Story* (Cambridge and London: Harvard University Press, 1981).

China in education and administration in the 1920s in China is in many ways connected with the New Culture Movement.⁴²

Lu Xun's rejection of Confucianism and traditional Chinese culture, his promotion of western ideas, and his criticism of the Chinese national spirit were controversial in his lifetime, China at the time being semi-colonised by western and Japanese imperialists. The evaluations of Lu Xun and his literary works have changed over time, in response to socio-political and cultural changes in China, oscillating between the two extremes of seeing Lu Xun as a patriot trying to save his country through western learning versus a destroyer of the indigenous Chinese culture and civilisation.⁴³ The Cultural Revolution (1966–76) entailed a complete rejection of Confucianism and traditional culture and entailed a deification of Lu Xun by the leadership of the CPC. However, the present CPC leadership's promotion of Chinese cultural identity entails a revival of traditional Chinese culture and Confucianism, thus Lu Xun's works have become a burden.⁴⁴ In western and

---

⁴² Ping Chen, *Modern Chinese*, 70–82. Establishing a standardised, modern vernacular entailed a complicated, political process; see Ping Chen and others. Many May Fourth writers were educated abroad and their "heavily Europeanized and Japanized (i.e. translated) vernacular might in effect be as alien to the ordinary reader as *wenyan*", according to Shih, *The Lure of the Modern*, 71. For a list of loan words, transliterations etc. at the time, see Lydia He Liu, *Translingual Practice: Literature, National Culture, and Translated Modernity – China, 1900–1937* (Stanford: Stanford University Press, 1995). May Fourth writers calling for vernacular literature for the people instead of the "aristocratic few", themselves came under attack by leftists for being Europeanised elitists.

⁴³ For changing evaluations of Lu Xun's work in China and political implications, see for instance Fugui Zhang, "Three Paradigms in Lu Xun Research and Contemporary Value Options", *Social Sciences in China* (English edition) vol. 35, no. 3 (2014): 100–118 and others. As Zhang points out, evaluations rely on the "richness and complexity of Lu Xun's spiritual world", but also on "the value criteria of the evaluator", "Three Paradigms", 114. See also for instance Kang Liu, "Politics, Critical Paradigms: Reflections on Modern Chinese Literature Studies", *Modern China* vol. 19, no.1 (1993): 13–40.

⁴⁴ In 2006, huge commemorations of Lu Xun's death 70 years earlier by the government did not take place as many had expected. The 100-year anniversary of the May Fourth Movement falls on 4 May 2019, and official

Taiwanese academia, the critique against Lu Xun and his works have gained strength from postcolonial criticism,[45] while in the Chinese Mainland some scholars regard him as a patron of critical thinking.[46] A hundred years after the publication of "A Madman's Diary", Lu Xun's fiction is part of the literary canon in China and of world literature, but the ideas expressed in his fiction remain provocative and are still subject to controversy among researchers across the globe. His fiction still has relevance in present-day debates among researchers, critics and readers.[47]

Bibliography

Ban Gu 班固. *Hanshu* 汉书 [History of the Han Dynasty]. Beijing: Zhonghua shuju中华书局, [1962] 1975, Vol. 5.

Børdahl, Vibeke and Margaret B. Wan, eds. *The Interplay of the Oral and the Written in Chinese Popular Literature*. Copenhagen: NIAS press, 2010.

Chang, Kang-i Sun and Stephen Owen, eds. *The Cambridge History of Chinese Literature. Vol. 2, From 1375*. Cambridge: Cambridge University Press, 2010.

Chen Duxiu陈独秀. "Wenxue geminglun" 文学革命论 [On the Literary Revolution]. *Xin qingnian* 新青年 [*New Youth*] vol. 2, no. 6 (1917). Dongjing: Jigu shuyuan 汲古书院, 1970–1971, vol. 2, 563–66.

---

celebrations (or the lack of them) will reflect the present leadership's view of its legacy.
[45] Shu-mei Shih states, "Lu Xun's Occidentalism is complete", *The Lure of the Modern*, 84.
[46] See for instance Liqun Qian, "The Historical Fate of Lu Xun in Today's China", in *Frontiers of Literary Studies in China*, vol. 7, no. 4 (2013): 529–40, a polemical article in which Qian hails Lu Xun's critical thinking and then uses this as a pretext for overt criticism of Taiwanese society, politics, education etc.
[47] According to Zhang, in 2000–12, there were 9,988 articles on Lu Xun published just in the Chinese Mainland, "Three paradigms", 105.

Chen, Ping. *Modern Chinese: History and Sociolinguistics*. Cambridge: Cambridge University Press, 1999.

Chow, Tse-tsung. *The May Fourth Movement: Intellectual Revolution in Modern China*. Stanford, Ca.: Stanford University Press, [1960] 1967.

Denton, Kirk A., ed. *Modern Chinese Literary Thought: Writings on Literature, 1893–1945*. Stanford, Ca.: Stanford University Press, 1996.

Ge, Liangyan. *Out of the Margins: The Rise of Chinese Vernacular Fiction*. Honolulu: University of Hawai'i Press, 2001.

Goldman, Merle and Leo Ou-Fan Lee, eds. *An Intellectual History of Modern China*. Cambridge: Cambridge University Press, 2002.

Gu, Ming Dong. "Lu Xun, Jameson and Multiple Polysemia". *Canadian Review of Comparative Literature* December (2001): 434–53.

Hanan, Patrick. *The Chinese Vernacular Story*. Cambridge and London: Harvard University Press, 1981.

Hanan, Patrick. "The Technique of Lu Hsün's Fiction". *Harvard Journal of Asiatic Studies*. vol. 34 (1974): 53–96.

Hu Shi 胡适. "Jianshe de wenxue geminglun" 建设的文学革命论 [Construction of Literary revolution]. *Xin qingnian* 新青年 [*New Youth*] vol. 4, no. 4 (1918). Dongjing: Jigu shuyuan 汲古书院, 1970–1971, vol. 4, 343–60.

Hu Shi 胡适. "Wenxue gailiang chuyi" 文学改良刍议 [Humble Suggestions for the Reform of Chinese Literature]. *Xin qingnian* 新青年 [*New Youth*] vol. 2, no. 5 (1917). Dongjing: Jigu shuyuan 汲古书院, 1970–1971, vol. 2, 467–77.

Lau, Joseph S. M. and Howard Goldblatt, eds. *The Columbia Anthology of Modern Chinese Literature: Second edition*. New York: Columbia University Press, 2007.

Li Guiqi 李桂起 and Jiang Qi 姜启. "Xiaoshuo tishi juan" 小说体式卷 [Section on Forms of Fiction]. In *Zhongguo jinbainian wenxue tishi liubianshi* 中国近百年文学体式流变史 [History of the Evolution of Literary Forms in China in the Past Century], edited by Feng Guanglian 冯光廉. Beijing: Renmin wenxue chubanshe 人民文学出版社, 1999, 1–323.

Liang Qichao 梁启超. "Lun xiaoshuo yu qunzhi zhi guanxi" 论小说与 群治 之关系 [On the Relationship Between Fiction and the Government of the People]. In *Liang Qichao wenji* 梁启超文集 [The Collected Works by Liang Qichao]. Beijing: Beijing Yanshan chubanshe 北京燕山出版社, 1997, 282–87.

Liu, James J. Y. *Chinese Theories of Literature*. Chicago: University of Chicago Press, 1975.

Liu, Kang. "Politics, Critical Paradigms: Reflections on Modern Chinese Literature Studies". *Modern China* 19, no. 1 (1993): 13–40.

Liu, Lydia He, *Translingual Practice: Literature, National Culture, and Translated Modernity – China, 1900–1937*. Stanford, Ca.: Stanford University Press, 1995.

Lu Xun 鲁迅. "Kuangren riji" 狂人日记 [A Madman's Diary]. *Xin qingnian* 新青年 [*New Youth*] vol. 4. no. 5 (1918). Dongjing: Jigu shuyuan 汲古书院, 1970–1971, vol. 4, 483–93.

Lu Xun 鲁迅. "Zixu" [Author's Preface] 自序 to *Nahan* 呐喊 [Call to Arms]. In *Lu Xun quanji* 鲁迅全集. Beijing: Renmin wenxue chubanshe 人民文学出版社, 1973, vol. 1, 269–276.

Qian, Liqun. "The Historical Fate of Lu Xun in Today's China". In *Frontiers of Literary Studies in China* 7, no. 4 (2013): 529–540. DOI: https://doi.org/10.3868/s010-002-013-0034-0.

Shi, Shu-mei. *The Lure of the Modern: Writing Modernism in Semicolonial China, 1917–1937*. Berkeley: University of California Press, 2001.

Tsu, Jing. "Epilogue: Sinophone Writings and the Chinese Diaspora". In *The Cambridge History of Chinese Literature: Volume II: From 1375*, edited by Kang-i Sun Chang and Stephen Owen, 706–714. Cambridge: Cambridge University Press, 2010.

Wang, David Der-Wei. "Chinese Literature from 1841–1937". In *The Cambridge History of Chinese Literature: Volume II: From*

1375, edited by Kang-i Sun Chang and Stephen Owen, 413–529. Cambridge: Cambridge University Press, 2010.

Zhang, Fugui. "Three Paradigms in Lu Xun Research and Contemporary Value Options". *Social Sciences in China* (English edition) vol. 35, no. 3 (2014): 100–118.

Zhang, Fugui, and Ren Chuangong. "The Spread of Cosmopolitanism in China and Lu Xun's Understanding of the 'World Citizen'". *Frontiers of Literary Studies in China* 6, no. 4 (2012): 553–69.

8. Reflections on Gender and Small Languages in World Literature Scholarship: Methods of Inclusions and Exclusions[1]

Katarina Leppänen
History of Ideas, University of Gothenburg

An overarching question in my research as a scholar working in small languages in the Nordic countries concerns how world literature studies can promote localised and gendered knowledge. Firstly, gendered perspectives informed by feminist literary studies are, as I will argue, often totally absent or activated only as a political context rather than as an analytical literary category. Secondly, smaller languages seem to evaporate in highly globalised scholarly practices. Is world literature a field with specific analytical tools, designed in a manner that is incommensurable with the aims and methods of feminist analysis where conjunctions of social, economic and political powers intersect in texts? This way of understanding texts as political could, following Gayatri Spivak, be termed "a socially grounded view of comparative literature and

---

[1] This chapter is a considerably abbreviated and rewritten version of the article by Jenny Bergenmar and Katarina Leppänen, "Gender and Vernaculars in Digital Humanities and World Literature", *NORA: Nordic Journal of Feminist and Gender Research*, 25, no. 4 (2017).

How to cite this book chapter:
Leppänen, Katarina. "Reflections on Gender and Small Languages in World Literature Scholarship: Methods of Inclusions and Exclusions". In *World Literatures: Exploring the Cosmopolitan-Vernacular Exchange*, edited by Stefan Helgesson, Annika Mörte Alling, Yvonne Lindqvist, and Helena Wulff, 89–99. Stockholm: Stockholm University Press, 2018. DOI: https://doi.org/10.16993/bat.h. License: CC-BY.

world literature".[2] In two recent projects in transnational literary history focusing on women writers, such as the HERA project *Travelling Texts (1790–1914). Transnational Reception of Women's Writing at the Fringes of Europe* and *Swedish Women Writers on Export in the Nineteenth Century*, the latter based at my home department at Gothenburg University, neither world literature nor digital humanities provide unconditionally useful research methods or theories, because they lack sufficient tools for multilingual analysis in diverse sources.[3] Although world literature scholars at times challenge the western canon, the forgotten writers in these projects may not be seen as a priority since they are western (even if they are not canonical).

This chapter will approach world literature through three themes that have been central to my research: quality, representation and transfer/translation. In the following I will let these concepts introduce some key aspects of my approach to the research programme.

Quality

Unqualified use of the idea of literary quality as an element inherent in the text runs countercurrent to the understanding of literature presented here. Quality has to be politically, culturally and socially grounded. As intellectual historian Mikela Lundahl writes in an article on canon and democracy, for every canonical text there are countless excluded, forgotten and silenced texts. Her point is that these texts, the ones yet to be recovered, potentially become valuable because they *shed new light on the emergence of our aesthetic ideals*.[4]

---

[2] Gayatri Chakravorty Spivak and David Damrosch, "Comparative Literature/World Literature: A Discussion", in *World Literature in Theory*, ed. David Damrosch (Chichester: Wiley Blackwell, 2014), 363.
[3] See further Bergenmar and Leppänen, "Gender and Vernaculars".
[4] Mikela Lundahl, "Kanon och demokrati", in *Kanon ifrågasatt: Kanoniseringsprocesser och makten över vetandet*, eds. Katarina Leppänen and Mikela Lundahl (Möklinta: Gidlunds, 2009), 17.

Lundahl highlights the multiple effects that minor or peripheral texts may have on our understanding of canon and quality: There are yet undiscovered texts that could, hopefully, be included in the canon, and, even more importantly, the non-canonical texts are highly relevant for understanding canon formation *per se*.

However, Zhang Longxi, for example, argues in an ardent defence of world literature studies, that the field offers a unique opportunity for nations to present "canonical works because they are by definition the best and most exemplary works of different literary traditions".[5] Zhang rejects outright any reason other than the aesthetic (as if this were a neutral unit of measurement) to include literature in the world literature canon. He does acknowledge the existence of a critical discussion on western canon, embraces the idea of a geographically expanding canon that can include non-western texts, yet no other expansion is neither expected nor desirable. Postcolonial literary studies are almost totally rejected as simply "political" and as making unwarranted claims of ethical superiority, "women and minority writers ... cannot become canonical simply because they have been overlooked or neglected in the past".[6] Zhang's position may be extreme, yet, as Castillo's argument shows in the next section, quality arguments have not only been central since Goethe's *Weltliteratur*, but are still unproblematically used. Zhang's article is published in the very first volume of the *Journal of World Literature*, an issue that also hosts an article by Mads Rosendahl Thomsen. Rosendahl Thomsen's perspective is rather different from Zhang's when he highlights the importance of "current topics that are already making a significant impact on the future shape of international circulation of literary works, as well as the continuous canonization of works that circulate as world literature of the past".[7] He mentions migration and networked identities, digital interfaces, climate change, and the posthuman horizon, suggesting that the

---

[5] Longxi Zhang, "Canon and World Literature", *Journal of World Literature* 1, no. 1 (2016), 122.
[6] Zhang, "Canon and World Literature", 125, 121.
[7] Mads Rosendahl Thomsen, "Grand Challenges! Great Literature?" *Journal of World Literature*, 1, no. 1 (2016), 97.

subject matter is also a measure of quality. Gender is, however, not listed as a current topic that would significantly influence world literature or world literary history. Perhaps this phenomenon can be understood through Damrosch's exposition of the displacement of texts in relation to the canon. The hypercanon, Damrosch argues, consists of "major" authors (one imagines a Shakespeare or a Joyce), the countercanon consists of the new postcolonial/world authors (one imagines a Rushdie or a Pamuk). The shadowcanon is, however, the most interesting category when it comes to gender because it consists of "the old 'minor' authors who fade increasingly into the background".[8] No women authors are mentioned explicitly as having been left in the shadows, but considering their position as minors in relation to the old canon, this can at least partly explain the position of women authors and the absence of gender theories in world literature studies. Thus, national recovery projects of lost or forgotten authors, including women writers, need to be stepped up to the world literature scale.

Comparative literature, as an academic field, David Damrosch states in an article in *PMLA*, is haunted by a "specter of amateurism" due to the impossibility of any one person to grasp the world's languages and cultures.[9] One may, of course, claim that there is a risk of a different kind of "amateurism" when it comes to the presumed canonical works, that is, of a near total contextual insensitivity. By this I mean that in an eagerness to make claims regarding a text's universal appeal or thematics, its worldliness, the spatial and temporal uniqueness may be lost. While in some sense "objective" (as in a given aesthetic yardstick for the canonical, or a superior method of large-scale text mining in digital humanities), such methods risk making the achieved results rather meaningless. Matthew Jockers, for example, includes gender as an analytical category in *Macroanalysis* and finds that "female authors are far more likely to write about women, and they use the female pronouns her and she far more often than

---

[8] David Damrosch, "World Literature in a Postcolonial, Hypercanonical Age", in *Comparative Literature in an Age of Globalization*, ed. Haun Saussy (Baltimore: Johns Hopkins University Press), 45.

[9] David Damrosch, "Comparative Literature", *PMLA* 118, no. 2 (2003), 326.

their male counterparts".[10] Interesting indeed, but hardly cutting-edge research results, if such findings are not theorised and contextualised. That is, such findings risk cementing hierarchical and already widely spread misogynist understandings of "women who only write about women", if not followed by questions of "why", "how" and "where". There is a whole corpus of feminist literary theory analysing, exploring and explaining the rise of the novel, the domestic themes and the female characters, and the political meanings and implications of such texts, that large-scale digital humanities and world literary studies need to relate to.

Representation

"Silences enter the process of historical production at four crucial moments", writes anthropologist and postcolonial scholar Michel Rolph Trouillot, "the moment of fact creation (the making of sources), the moment of fact assembly (the making of archives) the moment of fact retrieval (the making of narratives); and the moment of retrospective significance (the making of history in the final instance)".[11] Following Trouillot, one is tempted to ask the question of absence of gender in world literature, historically, theoretically and numerically. His observation speaks, of course, both to canonisation and representation.

The compilation of readers and companions is a central issue because, in effect, such compilations create and construct world literature studies as a university subject by making a selection of texts available in a collected volume, in a given language. A look at the larger English language companions shows that gender hardly figures at all as an analytical category. Neither is gender a category of analysis in any prominent readers, nor in major methodological handbooks. It is, of course, not a novel insight that there are more men than women in world literature – anything else would be astounding. But just as astounding is the near total

---

[10] Matthew Jockers, *Macroanalysis: Digital Methods and Literary History* (Urbana, Chicago & Springfield: University of Illinois Press, 2013), 93.

[11] Michel-Rolph Trouillot, *Silencing the Past: Power and the Production of History* (Boston: Beacon Press, 1995), 26.

absence of gender and/or feminism, with the exception of those with special focus on women.[12]

The issue is addressed critically by Debra A. Castillo in her article "Gender and Sexuality in World Literature" in the *Routledge Companion to World Literature* (2012). Castillo's survey concludes that roughly 20 per cent of the included works are written by women. Women appear in specific sections of the anthologies, primarily in the sections of women authors, indigenous authors or among the non-western authors. "Suggestively", Castillo writes, "the particular selection of all three of these non-Western sections implicitly ask us to think of how genre is associated with race as well as with gender, highlighting, perhaps, more vernacular, more personally charged, more overtly ideological forms…".[13] The selection in other sections is, unsurprisingly, based on "enduring aesthetic principles", Castillo concludes.[14] It is as if, when elevated to a world scale, the social dimensions of texts have to either be diminished (universalisable texts), or become the sole or primary frame of interpretation.

Although Castillo does not use the word, this is of course an argument based on literary quality, something women through history have had a hard time achieving or proving. Tellingly, the *Routledge Companion to World Literature* where Castillo's analysis appears, only indexes "gender" as appearing in Castillo's own article. Feminism, by comparison, is not listed at all. *World Literature in Theory* (2014) has no index but none of the chosen articles focus gender or feminism, while *What is World Literature?* has an overly generous interpretation of "gender and politics", listing at times the very mentioning of women in the book.

An interesting literary history project with a different approach to representation is the *History of the Literary Cultures of*

---

[12] See, for example, Deborah Weagel, *Women and Contemporary World Literature: Power, Fragmentation and Metaphor* (New York: Peter Lang, 2009).

[13] Debra Castillo, "Gender and sexuality in world literature", in *Routledge Companion to World Literature*, eds. Theo D'haen, David Damrosch and Djelal Kadir (London: Routledge, 2012), 401.

[14] Castillo, "Gender and sexuality", 401.

the East-Central Europe: Junctures and Dis-junctures in the Nineteenth and Twentieth Centuries (2004–2010). In its attempt to apply a comprehensive transnational approach to the vast cultural and literary region that stretches from the Baltic countries to Albania, from Ukraine to the Czech Republic, it offers a prismatic, multicultural, and multimedia model of literary history, an "experiment in writing literary history that acknowledges ruptures as well as transnational connections".[15] Commencing from a spectrum of themes, languages, genres and geographies, the volumes constantly construct and reconstruct the region, though its literary cultures. The effect of such an approach to this region that is truly multi-everything – language, religion, nation, politics – opens for reading culture in several directions simultaneously. What can be left out in such an approach are the restrictions posed by national borders, as nation itself does not become a dominant frame of interpretation, even though nation is never totally unimportant, given the role literary culture played in the very formation of nations. Of course, at the periphery of this periphery, other border zones are neglected, for reasons related to scope and aim.

Translation/transfer

There is an interesting tension between specialist knowledge (for example of different national literatures such as Marcel Cornis-Pope's and John Neubauer's project above that engages 120 scholars) and the generalist tendencies. David Damrosch, a generalist sensitive to the virtues of specialism, argues that "the generalist should feel the same ethical responsibility towards specialized scholarship that a translator has towards a text's original language".[16] Gayatri Spivak, a strong advocate for specialism reflects on how the plurality of languages and literatures can be secured at our universities only by genuine and in-depth knowledge of both literature and culture. She deplores Damrosch's idea of achieving

---

[15] Marcel Cornis-Pope, "Literary History in Transnational Mode: The Challenges of Writing a History of East-Central European Literatures", *Comparative Literature Studies*, 50, no. 2 (2013): 204.

[16] Damrosch, "Comparative Literature", 202.

more generalist skills, "more languages and more language studies", by accepting a "sliding scale" of knowledge and using, among other things, a diverse student body in the classroom as a resource.[17] Instead, comparative studies and world literature studies require high standards of language skills, cultural orientation and skills for reading "in the most robust sense".[18]

Translation studies have become an essential part of comparative literature, with its discussions of the translatability or untranslatability of ideas, cultures and texts. Emily Apter "activate[s] untranslatability as a theoretical fulcrum of comparative literature" that has bearings on all aspects of large scale or comparative studies, from "world literatures", "the translation of philosophy and theory" to "ethical, cosmological and theological dimensions of worldliness".[19] Apter rejects, firstly, ideas about cultural equivalence and substitutionality and, secondly, nationally and ethically branded differences.[20] Translation can never be understood simply as a conversion of one language to another, it must rather be seen as an intricate intellectual challenge, an endeavour through which world literature scholars can deprovincialise the canon and draw "on translation to deliver surprising cognitive landscapes hailing from inaccessible linguistic folds".[21] The idea of the translation as an intellectual activity that fundamentally changes the texts stands in stark contrast to how translations are used in the writing of literary history with computational methods, and also in the study of world literature, Apter contends. To be able to study world literature, translations are a necessary medium, since few scholars or students master more than a few languages sufficiently well.

For me, coming from intellectual history rather than a literary discipline, Apter's contestation of translation and her devotion to

---

[17] Spivak and Damrosch, "Comparative Literature/World Literature", 368–69.
[18] Spivak and Damrosch, "Comparative Literature/World Literature", 376.
[19] Emily Apter, *Against World Literature: On the Politics of Untranslatability* (London: Verso, 2013), 3–4.
[20] Apter, *Against World Literature*, 2.
[21] Apter, *Against World Literature*, 2.

the messiness of translation is appealing for several reasons. The question of small languages is perhaps obvious as translation is a requirement of reaching an audience of any considerable size. Conceptual translations are part of translation in general but hold a deeper significance when it comes to political and national(-ist) concepts such as gender, nation and people, to name a few. A future task is to investigate such conceptualisations in the Nordic-Baltic region. From the viewpoint of translationality and transferability, renewed focus can be given to the regional. How is the translation of literature from one small peripheral language to another small peripheral language part of the nation formation?

When social dimensions of texts, such as genres, genders and languages, are discussed, there are several feminist theoretical challenges that could inform world literary studies. Margaret Higonnet contends that to include gender in literary analysis is "to trace historical shifts and cultural differences for which the scholarship is still evolving".[22] The social context of both text and text production must be seen as culturally and politically embedded and as developing differently across cultures. Gender studies can, furthermore, offer a shift in "understanding a self that is complex, many-layered, projected and performed in a constant shifting process".[23] A consequence of such a re-thinking of identity as neither solid nor permanent makes it much less interesting to group or categorise texts according to apparently permanent or essentialising categories (such as nation, language, gender, indigenous), which, as Castillo shows, is still being done. In this chapter, I have pointed out some challenges I see in combining the world literature field with my research interests in small languages and gender.

The research programme *Cosmopolitan and Vernacular Dynamics in World Literatures* approaches world literatures as a field of exchange between the global and the local by investigating the fundamental inter-dependency of, and generative tension between, cosmopolitan and vernacular trajectories in literary

---

[22] Margaret Higonnet, "Introduction", *Comparative Critical Studies* 6 (2009), 135.
[23] Higonnet, "Introduction", 137.

cultures. In this dynamic, world literary scholarship holds an unfulfilled promise where translation becomes the most consequential sites of negotiation between the cosmopolitan and the vernacular. Studying literature in more than 15 languages, the contestation is that world literature is that which comprise both cosmopolitan and vernacular dimensions, rather than a world literature canon. Although the project displays few explicitly feminist theoretical trajectories it opens for understanding the social and political aspects of literary culture. I especially hope that the research programme will open for a deepened interest in the social and political implications of unreflected references to the canon, to universality and to translation, regarding both localised linguistic expression and embodied gendered experiences.

Bibliography

Apter, Emily. *Against World Literature: On the Politics of Untranslatability*. London: Verso, 2013.

Bergenmar, Jenny and Leppänen, Katarina. "Gender and Vernacular in Digital Humanities and World Literature". *NORA: Nordic Journal of Feminist and Gender Research* 25:4 (2017): 232–46.

Castillo, Debra. "Gender and Sexuality in World Literature". In *The Routledge Companion to World Literature*, edited by Theo D'haen, David Damrosch and Djelal Kadir, 393–403. London: Routledge, 2012.

Cornis-Pope, Marcel and Neubauer, John. *History of the Literary Cultures of the East-Central Europe: Junctures and Dis-junctures in the Nineteenth and Twentieth Centuries*. Vol. 1–4. Amsterdam and Philadelphia: John Benjamins, 2004–2010.

Cornis-Pope, Marcel. "Literary History in Transnational Mode: The Challenges of Writing a History of East-Central European Literatures". *Comparative Literature Studies* 50:2 (2013): 204–210.

Damrosch, David. "Comparative literature". *PMLA* 118, no. 2 (2003): 326–33.

———. *What Is World Literature?* Princeton and Oxford: Princeton University Press, 2003.

Damrosch, David. "World Literature in a Postcolonial, Hypercanonical Age". In *Comparative Literature in an Age of Globalization*, edited by Haun Saussy, 43–53. Baltimore: Johns Hopkins University Press, 2006.

Higonnet, Margaret. "Introduction". *Comparative Critical Studies* 6 (2009): 135–48.

Jockers, Matthew. *Macroanalysis: Digital Methods and Literary History*. Urbana, Chicago & Springfield: University of Illinois Press, 2013.

Longxi, Zhang. "Canon and World Literature". *Journal of World Literature* 1, no. 1 (2016): 119–27.

Lundahl, Mikela. "Kanon och demokrati". In *Kanon ifrågasatt: Kanoniseringsprocesser och makten över vetandet*, edited by Katarina Leppänen and Mikela Lundahl, 13–50. Möklinta: Gidlunds, 2009.

Rosendahl Thomsen, Mads. "Grand Challenges! Great Literature?" *Journal of World Literature* 1, no. 1 (2016): 97–106.

Spivak, Gayatri Chakravorty and David Damrosch. "Comparative Literature/World Literature: A Discussion". In *World Literature in Theory*, edited by David Damrosch, 363–88. Chichester: Wiley Blackwell, 2014.

Trouillot, Michel-Rolph. *Silencing the Past: Power and the Production of History*. Boston: Beacon Press, 1995.

Weagel, Deborah. *Women and Contemporary World Literature: Power, Fragmentation and Metaphor*. New York: Peter Lang, 2009.

PART 2:
NEITHER HERE NOR THERE? LOCATIONS AND ORIENTATIONS IN CONTEMPORARY LITERATURE

9. Introduction to Part 2
Helena Wulff

How are worldly locations and orientations registered in literature? The terms "locations" and "orientations" appear, at first, to have very different qualities: a location operates as a fixed, spatial dimension whereas an orientation implies movement across both spatial and more abstract dimensions, such as ideology or identity. Yet orientation might also imply a form of vector and could be related to "disorientation". This section posits that the two terms, "locations" and "orientations", might, rather, be productively read as co-constitutive. That is to say, the ways literature locates itself reveals various orientations that may reinforce or, indeed, destabilise that very location. Alternatively, literary orientations, towards say, a home, a diaspora, the world, might reveal surprising aspects about how literature registers its locatedness. There is also Homi Bhabha's (2004) concept of "the location of culture" connected to questions of national affiliation, hybridty and limiality and referring to how cultural production is the most creative when it is the most ambivalent. We wager that in attending to the centrifugal and centripetal movements back and forth between location and orientation we might mobilise insights into the ways in which the cosmopolitan-vernacular exchange operates in world literatures.

In her chapter, **Ashleigh Harris** exemplifies the dynamics between African location and global orientation by way of a close reading of the short story "How to Eat a Forest" by the Kenyan

---

How to cite this book chapter:
Wulff, Helena. "Introduction to Part 2". In *World Literatures: Exploring the Cosmopolitan-Vernacular Exchange*, edited by Stefan Helgesson, Annika Mörte Alling, Yvonne Lindqvist, and Helena Wulff, 103–106. Stockholm: Stockholm University Press, 2018. DOI: https://doi.org/10.16993/bat.i. License: CC-BY.

writer Billy Kahora. Harris considers the ways in which African environmentalist fiction orients itself both outwards (towards a global readership in the interests of mobilising an environmental politics) and inwards (towards the local scales upon which environmental depletion is most acutely felt). This has consequences for both the material production and distribution processes and the aesthetic forms of this fiction. Harris posits that the aesthetic and material innovations of Billy Kahora's multi-genre text are codetermining factors of his environmentalism. She argues that Kahora's interweaving of aesthetics and material production enables him to address both the global and local scales of what Rob Nixon calls "slow violence": that is, the global forces that are decimating African natural resources and are registered, first, in the lived scales of the everyday.

In their anthropological approach to world literatures, Helena Wulff and Paula Uimonen combine participant observation and interviews with close readings of different texts. Drawing on her study of diaspora writers, **Helena Wulff**'s chapter explores how they are located in Sweden, yet oriented both towards Sweden and the country of their origin. As is evident in Pooneh Rohi's novel *Araben* ("The Arab"), home can be a divided location and one's orientation towards these places might change over the course of time prompted by key events and stages in life. A young woman in the novel is from Iran, but she is so well integrated that people think she was adopted. At first, Sweden is her main location, but as the novel unfolds her orientation towards Iran becomes more important. At the same time, an older man leads his lonely life in Stockholm where he moved decades ago from Iran, and we come to understand that "the Arab" is actually Persian, but is taken to be an Arab in the Swedish context, highlighting his dislocation and feelings of homelessness. While his orientation to Iran is weaker than it used to be, he is not really oriented to Sweden either. Through their fiction and journalism, diaspora writers such as Pooneh Rohi can be said to cosmopolitanise Sweden from within.

In **Paula Uimonen**'s chapter, African women writers bring attention to two interrelated aspects of cosmopolitan-vernacular exchanges in world literature: as *women* writers, their work highlights the transnational tensions of feminism, and as *African* writers, their works exemplify the cultural construction of Africanness in a globalised world, a cosmopolitan orientation that is informed by and many times challenges the spatiotemporal ranking of Africa's place in the world, as exemplified by the Pan-African movement. With the performance poetry *Warrior Unleashed* by Zuhura Seng'enge as a point of departure, Uimonen discusses the cultural dynamics of location and orientation, from the perspective of contemporary African women writers in Tanzania. Rather than privileging African literature that circulates in the western publishing industry, this chapter focuses on the cultural circumstances of literary production within the continent. It offers a view where location is multilayered and orientation multidirectional, which is a way to capture interlocking spatiotemporal configurations in literary production.

Post 9/11 Muslim writing in English is the topic of **Adnan Mahmutović**'s chapter. Now the label Muslim writing has been used primarily for authors who are openly religious while writing on topics in relation to Islam and Muslim identity. However, this excludes the cosmopolitan heritage of Islam, as Mahmutović points out. While written in radically different voices, novels by authors like Mohsin Hamid, Michael Muhammad Knight and Mohja Kahf are built around the same concern: how do Muslims find a place while constantly having to move, in the post 9/11 world? The desire to be located drives characters, and yet there is an equivalent centrifugal force of orientation: orientation outward becomes the only way of actually locating oneself. This seemingly contradictory dynamic of location-through-orientation, or centripetality-through-centrifugality, translates from the characters to the novels themselves. In other words, one cannot but ask, where do novels such as *Taqwacores*, *The Reluctant Fundamentalist* and *The Girl in the Tangerine Scarf* want to be located and what are their orientations? Applying Alexander Beecroft's theory of the ecologies of world literature, Mahmutović argues that the dynamics between location and orientation makes it possible to include variegated Muslim fictions in English in ecologies as different as national, cosmopolitan and global.

Authored by **Bo G. Ekelund**, the final chapter in Part 2 takes us to the Caribbean and a discussion about the relationship between land, place and language strategies in fictional worlds there. As Ekelund contends, every literary work claims a territory, and in doing so it betrays an orientation. It can do so only by means of its literary language. As peripheral cosmopolitans, writers from the anglophone Caribbean have used the Caribbean vernaculars as a linguistic resource, a narrative object and a utopian thematic in order to reorganise the literary territory sustained by metropolitan and cosmopolitan markets. By looking at the English-language literature of the Caribbean from the perspective of cosmopolitan and vernacular orientations, Ekelund discusses the three modes that are informing the necessary strategies to claim place by means of language: language as personal style, as linguistic variety and as deliberate discourse. The chapter forms part of a larger study of the linguistic strategies that come into play when territory is claimed in a selection of 32 works of fiction written by authors from the anglophone Caribbean in two distinct periods: 1955–65 and 1985–95. Here, Ekelund begins to analyse the shifting orientations – towards centres and peripheries of the geopolitical world – realised by these literary works in their creation of fictional worlds.

Bibliography

Bhabha, Homi K. *The Location of Culture*. London: Routledge, 2004.

10. Locating Chronic Violence: Billy Kahora's "How to Eat a Forest"

Ashleigh Harris
Department of English, Uppsala University

The Chimurenga trust is an eclectic and pan-African publishing concern based in Cape Town. Founded in 2002 by Ntone Edjabe, a Cameroonian writer and artist, the Chimurenga trust articulates itself as "an innovative platform for free ideas and political reflection about Africa by Africans".[1] The outputs of the trust include the printed journal-style *Chimurenga Magazine*, a broadsheet paper *The Chronic*, which has an online equivalent, an "online radio station and pop-up studio", called the Pan African Space Station, amongst others. The innovation behind these forms is politically motivated, as the trust itself writes:

> The aim of these projects is not just to produce new knowledge, but rather to express the intensities of our world, to capture those forces and to take action. This has required a stretching of the boundaries, for unless we push form and content beyond what exists, then we merely reproduce the original form – the colonized form, if you will. It requires not only a new set of questions, but its own set of tools; new practices and methodologies that allow us to engage the lines of flight, of fragility, the precariousness, as well as joy, creativity and beauty that defines contemporary African life.[2]

---

[1] "About us", Chimurenga online, accessed 16 November 2016. http://www.chimurenga.co.za/about-us
[2] "About us", Chimurenga online.

How to cite this book chapter:
Harris, Ashleigh. "Locating Chronic Violence: Billy Kahora's "How to Eat a Forest"". In *World Literatures: Exploring the Cosmopolitan-Vernacular Exchange*, edited by Stefan Helgesson, Annika Mörte Alling, Yvonne Lindqvist, and Helena Wulff, 107–118. Stockholm: Stockholm University Press, 2018. DOI: https://doi.org/10.16993/bat.j. License: CC-BY.

Here we have, then, a publication politics that orients itself by virtue of its locatedness in Africa. This orientation certainly prioritises, but is not limited to, its Pan-African locatedness. For example, the March 2015 edition of *The Chronic* is produced, the trust writes, in "Cape Town, Nairobi, Johannesburg, Lagos, Luanda, Abidjan, Barbados, Mombasa, Katanga, Kampala, Kinshasa, Dar es Salaam, Malabo, Tripoli, and Slemani" and, like all editions of the paper, is distributed globally. The imagined boundaries of sub-Saharan Africa are also challenged in the July 2015 edition of *The Chronic*, which not only deconstructs the imaginary lines between the Maghreb and the sub-continent, but is also published entirely in Arabic. Moving further abroad, PASS pop-up studios have been located in Amsterdam, Lagos, Helsinki, New York, London and Paris, one edition of the *Chimurenga Magazine* was translated into Swedish, and two versions of *The Chronic* have been translated into German.[3]

The theme of the March 2015 edition of *The Chronic* is cartographies, described on the front cover as "a tool of imperialism". This theme fits our focus here of reading location and orientation as co-constitutive terms. As the editors of *The Chronic* ask:

> what if maps were made by Africans for their own use, to understand and make visible their own realities or imaginaries? How does it shift the perception we have of ourselves and how we make life on this continent?[4]

The spatial articulation of location via cartography, then, reveals an orientation. Unlike Eileen Julien's notion of extroverted African writing, which orients itself outwards to a non-local readership,[5] what we have here is a literature of and for Africa. That is to say, this literature concerns a specific location and is orientated

---

[3] *Chimurenga 11* entitled "Conversations with Poets Who Refuse to Speak" (2007) was published in Swedish by *Glänta* as "Chimurenga" as their second volume of 2010. "Read the Chimurenga Chronic in German", Chimurenga online. Accessed 13 April 2017. http://chimurengachronic.co.za/read-the-chimurenga-chronic-in-german/.
[4] *The Chronic Online*, March 2015. Accessed 13 April 2017. http://chimurengachronic.co.za/in-print/archive/the-chronic-march-2015/.
[5] Eileen Julien, "The Extroverted African Novel", in *The Novel, Vol. 1 – History, Geography, and Culture,* ed. Franco Moretti (Princeton: Princeton University Press, 2006), 668.

towards a specific readership. As such this edition of *The Chronic* maps an *extraverted*, rather than an extroverted orientation;[6] that is to say it orients itself in Africa and of (rather than for) the world. In this chapter I illustrate the dynamic between African location and global orientation in one short story from this edition of *The Chronic*: "How to Eat a Forest" by Kenyan writer, Billy Kahora. Kahora's engagement with deforestation in Kenya employs such an extraverted narrative strategy, one which addresses global economic and environmental forces from the scale of the contesting everyday lives of those making a living off or depending for their survival on deforestation in Kenya's Mau Forests.

"How to Eat a Forest" begins with a journalistic narration of a series of interviews that Kahora conducted in his capacity as a reporter for an environmentalist magazine *EcoForum* with members of the Ogiek tribe.[7] The Ogiek are an indigenous minority who inhabit – and have been considered by many national and international stake-holders to be the custodians of – the now-threatened Mau Forest. As Kahora's interviews begin to uncover some uncomfortable truths about the Ogiek's complicity in the destruction of the Mau forest, his narrative fractures into multiple genres: the piece becomes part fiction, part political critique, part hand-drawn sketches on a map of the forest, part email exchange, and part intertextual descriptions of a photo essay by Geert van Kesteren in *Granta's* "The View from Africa" edition.

Kahora's story is divided into three sections, each of which is prefaced with a quote from Achille Mbembe's "At the Edge of the World: Boundaries, Territoriality, and Sovereignty".[8] This academic intertext operates as a prompt to us literary readers to make use of Mbembe's paper as a theoretical tool to extract the meanings of this complex story. In reading Mbembe's theoretical

---

[6] I follow Jean-Francois Bayart's use of the term in "Africa in the World: A History of Extraversion", where he concludes with the important reminder that "More than ever, the discourse on Africa's marginality is a nonsense". Jean-Francois Bayart. "Africa in the World: A History of Extraversion", *African Affairs* 99 (2000): 267.
[7] Billy Kahora, "How to Eat a Forest", *The Chronic* (2015): 28–35.
[8] Achille Mbembe, "At the Edge of the World: Boundaries, Territoriality, and Sovereignty in Africa", trans. Steven Rendall, *Public Culture* 12, no.1 (2000): 259–84.

intervention alongside Kahora's story we reorient the literary terms that as a matter of rote circumvent Africa towards a distinctly pan-African location. It would be easy, for example, to describe Kahora's innovations as simply "post-modern": the story is metafictional, intertextual, multi-modal and genre-breaking. Yet, such a description would fail to pick-up on the extent to which these strategies are vernacularised by Kahora and how they operate as imprints of the key ideas running through Mbembe's more broadly regional theoretical discussion of boundaries, territoriality and sovereignty in Africa.

I note just one thread of Mbembe's paper relevant to this discussion. Mbembe opens his paper with the same problematic Rob Nixon describes as slow violence;[9] Mbembe writes that between the "slowly evolving" "temporalities of long and very long duration" and those that are "less slowly evolving [...] rapid and virtually instantaneous deviations"[10] the faster the temporality, the easier events are "to detect".[11] Mbembe's claim is that both these quick, visible and slow, invisible temporalities are entangled. I would argue that this means that the representation of long, slow, environmental violence, is itself deeply entangled with the everyday in which it becomes lived and visible. The material location of chronic environmental change betrays a global orientation that bears witness to much longer temporalities. The strategies that Kahora uses to tell his story, multi-generic, intertextual and metafictive as they are, are a strategy to connect these two scales of temporality. Indeed, just as Mbembe's paper takes up the spatial dimensions of entanglement (localities are inextricably tethered to the global), so too, does Kahora's text bind the geographical scales of everyday practice in the Mau Forests and the global complicities that are the substratum of those practices.

---

[9] Rob Nixon, *Slow Violence and the Environmentalism of the Poor* (Cambridge, MA: Harvard University Press, 2011).

[10] Mbembe, "At the Edge of the World", 259–60, paraphrasing Braudel. Fernand Braudel, *Civilization and Capitalism, The Fifteenth to the Eighteenth Century*, vol. 3, *The Perspective of the World*, trans. Siân Reynolds (New York: Harper and Row, 1984), 18.

[11] Mbembe, "At the Edge of the World," 260, paraphrasing Braudel *Civilization and Capitalism*, 18.

The attention to the everyday is perfectly suited to the journalistic prose that opens the first section of the story. This section, also called "How to Eat a Forest", provides an account of the 1990 history of the Mau Forest complex and describes the competing claims made on this land by different groups (including local tribes, international and national NGOs, and the government). The attention to locality is vividly apparent in the prose itself. For example, we read:

> In the west the land brokers found land-hungry Kipsigis, Sikii, and Luhya people who were mostly teachers, small-scale farmers, small businessmen and shopkeepers looking for land. But the visitors from Maasailand, who were actually selling a bountiful future, were a curious medley, the kind of disparate mishmash of fortune seekers found on any frontier that is up for grabs.[12]

Even as this attention to detail seems in line with the reportage that opens the story, the tone turns to something more akin to storytelling at certain points, with sentences like: "These travellers of fortune went among the Kalenjin and Kissii small landholders and told amazing tales of *kitiya,* land that is untilled and virgin and up for sale, cheap".[13] As we read about what Kahora calls "one of the largest land grabs in Kenyan history",[14] we start to see his tale giving local detail to Mbembe's broader argument about territory being "the privileged space of the exercise of sovereignty and of self-determination, and as such the ideal framework of the imposition of authority".[15] As Kahora shows us, maps of the Mau forest had less to do with depicting the landscape as it was, and more to do with drawing the lines of territory for economic gain and the rights of plunder. He writes:

> The premise was simple and devastating: the crooked lawyers and surveyors arbitrarily changed the representation on a map to a magnification that stretched into the nearby Mau South Forest. [...] Small parcels of land multiplied into their tens as land surveyors

---

[12] Kahora, "How to Eat a Forest", 28.
[13] Kahora, "How to Eat a Forest", 28.
[14] Kahora, "How to Eat a Forest", 28.
[15] Mbembe, "At the Edge of the World", 263.

were instructed to redraw the map of the original piece of land and eat up the forest.[16]

In a last-ditch attempt to put an end to this devastation of the forest, a new self-determination emerges in which the Narok Ogiek community are constructed by various stakeholders as the authentic guardians of the forest. "The Ogiek," writes Kahora,

> [...] seemed to have emerged into the national psyche around 1994, after the United Nations declared an International Day for Indigenous People. Non-governmental organisations were set up in Narok by individuals, until then popularly known as Ndorobos, to start fighting for their rights. The leaders of this movement took up their new name, the Ogiek (meaning "caretaker of all animals and plants") and claimed a unique and conservation-friendly relationship with the forest.[17]

As the international NGOs leap to support the Ogiek community in their custodianship of the forest, Kahora's text starts a new section entitled "Practising forest, selling shambas". Here, he narrates a tale of meeting an Ogiek man, Samuel Kamikil, "who, [the narrator is] told, knows how the forest was eaten".[18] This section blends interview, story-telling and even hand-drawn maps and sketches over a copy of a map from a text book (see figure 1), thereby disrupting the prosaic clarity of the largely dominant reportage style of section one.

The Ogiek man being interviewed by Kahora calls himself Samuel, but it turns out he is actually Salaton Ole Nadunguenkop (a Maasai name). Samuel/Salaton tells a nostalgic story of "an idyllic time when Ogiek clans lived in harmony and migrated to and fro within the Mau forest".[19] He narrates his own childhood in similar terms and in a similar tone, speaking of how his family lived according to the patterns of bees' migrations. This nostalgic version of the Ogiek past is quickly undermined by the character Setek, a treasurer of a local NGO called "Friends of

---

[16] Kahora, "How to Eat a Forest", 28.
[17] Kahora, "How to Eat a Forest", 29.
[18] Kahora, "How to Eat a Forest", 29.
[19] Kahora, "How to Eat a Forest", 30.

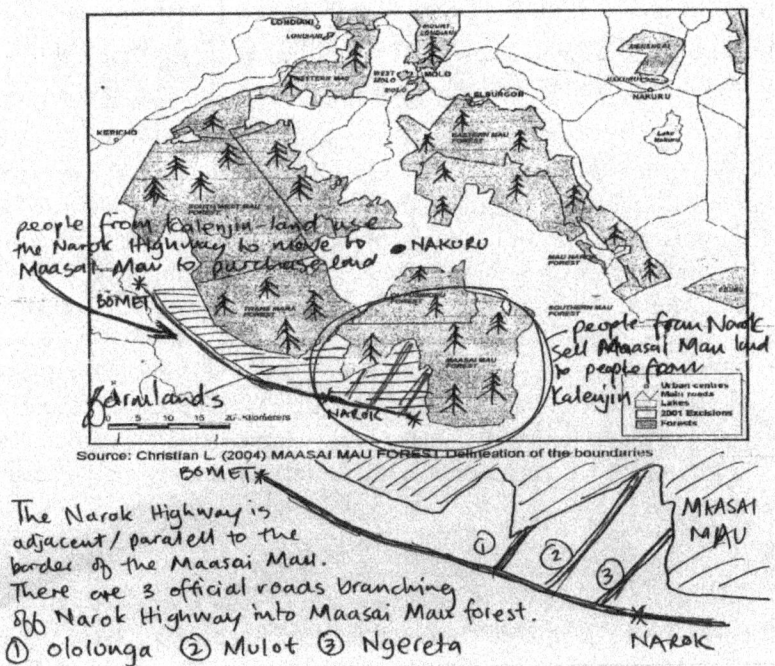

Figure 1. Kahora "How to Eat a Forest", 31. Copyright: Billy Kahora. License: CC BY, granted by the author, Billy Kahora. Image scanned by Ashleigh Harris.

the Mau Forest", who informs Kahora that "[t]his man you are calling Kamikil I know him very well. He is Ole Nadunguenkop. He has sold a lot of the forest".[20] Kahora then writes that "Ole Nadunguenkop is the first living signpost we meet of an Ogiek schizophrenia that wavers between the Ogiek as conservationist and the Ogiek as land broker".[21] And, indeed, this schizophrenia is depicted in the literary style of this section of the story itself. Both reportage and story-like, both narrative and image, code-switching between Maasai Swahili, Nairobi Swahili and English, and formatted (in the printed broadsheet version) as a

---

[20] Kahora, "How to Eat a Forest", 30.
[21] Kahora, "How to Eat a Forest", 31.

piece interwoven with other texts across various pages,[22] the story's material and literary form both reflect its thematic of schizophrenia. And this makes sense when we read:

> Like Samuel Kamikil/ Salaton Ole Nadunguenkop, many Ogiek we eventually encounter seem to be two things, an interface between the ideal and the real: Samuel Kamikil, who claims to be dispossessed and landless, is a forest dweller and hunter and gatherer who lives on honey; and Salaton Ole Nadunguenkop, who is a Mau forest broker, is a landowner and drives a Subaru. After Kamili/ Ole Nadunguenkop we encounter the interface between Ndorobos, who in reinventing themselves into Ogieks became one of the last indigenous Kenyan peoples, long-suffering and landless, and, on the other hand, the members of large rich Ogiek landowning families who are lawyers, professors, human rights activists and NGO heads, and who are dabbling in eating forest.[23]

As the title of section three indicates, "How to be indigenous – a workshop, a photo essay and an email",[24] the stylistic fragmentation noted above is further exacerbated in this final part of the story, which becomes a play of multi-modal pastiche and develops a scathing critique of various factors that continue to deplete the Mau Forests. The section is particularly scathing towards global development discourse (and the cultural paraphernalia that buttresses it), its simplification of the environmental situation of the Mau Forests and, hence, its complicity in the chronic situation of environmental decimation that this story notes. This third section refers to a photo essay by Geert van Kesteren in the literary

---

[22] In the print edition of *The Chronic*, the story begins on p. 28, where the lower part of the broadsheet format is a continuation of Dalle Ibrahim's contribution "Bordering on Borana". This same set-up continues on p. 29, though here the text shares a page with the continuation of Ngola Chome's "Pwani si Kenya", printed in red ink. Pages 30 and 31 are dedicated entirely to Kahora's story, with the inclusion of the two images included in the story. A new contribution by António Tomás, "Living dangerously in Petroluanda" follows on pp. 32–33. Kahora's story then continues, underneath Tomás's on the lower half of pp. 34–35, where it ends.
[23] Kahora, "How to Eat a Forest," 31.
[24] Kahora, "How to Eat a Forest", 31.

magazine *Granta 92: A View from Africa*.²⁵ The original visual narrative of the Ogiek is not captioned, which Kahora ironically corrects in his story. As we read through Kahora's captioning of van Kesteren's photographs, we are encouraged (if we are to make any sense of the intertext) to 'read' Van Kesteren's visual essay alongside Kahora's comment on it (much as we were encouraged to read Mbembe's essay alongside the story). After each caption provided by Kahora, the narrator asks questions that challenge the integrity of Van Kesteren's camera. We read, for example, "A man tears into animal flesh with his hands. Is this lunch?"; "Four men sit at the edge of a cave. Is this where they live?"; and, "A young man in animal hides and with chalked face holds up a little dead yellow bird. Is he going to eat it?"²⁶ The unanswered questions develop a sardonic tone that illustrates the problem of a European photographer promoting a project of authenticating an African tribe as the indigenous protectors of the forest, an indigenisation that is posited from the outside. Indeed, as Van Kesteren writes in a brief note on his photo essay, "[t]he Ogiek people have lived inside [the Mau Forest], and in harmony with it, for thousands of years".²⁷ Kahora's tone not only critiques mythologising developmental discourses, but also what Amatoritsero Ede calls the "self-anthropologizing rhetorical style" of extroverted African fiction.²⁸

The email exchange that concludes Kahora's (inconclusive) story, in which a Dutch NGO, quizzed by Kahora for its complicity with Ogiek land-brokers, responds by ignoring Kahora's local knowledge and perspective in an extraordinarily patronising dismissal of his concerns, highlights how difficult it is for Kahora

---

²⁵ Geert van Kesteren, "The Ogiek", *Granta* 92 (2005): 97–126.
²⁶ Kahora, "How to Eat a Forest", 34.
²⁷ Van Kesteren, "The Ogiek", 100.
²⁸ Amatoritsero Ede, "Narrative Moment and Self-Anthropologizing Discourse", *Research in African Literatures* 46, no. 3 (2015): 112. Interestingly, Kahora's tone is reminiscent of Kahora's colleague and countryman Binyavanga Wainaina's acerbic and satirical essay in an essay collected in precisely the same edition of *Granta* as Van Kesteren's photo essay, "How to write about Africa?" Wainaina's essay immediately precedes van Kesteren's.

to tell his version of Ogiek complicity in the destruction of the forest when faced with European NGO's investment in convenient myths about indigeneity. We are led to believe that Kahora is quoting a real correspondence, which, once again, challenges the reader's sense of how to interpret this 'story'. Yet this is ultimately a literary strategy to draw our attention to the very problem of discourse faced by a writer like Kahora. "The view from Africa", to cite *Granta's* edition critiqued here, is only acceptable to western audiences if it is, indeed, a view refracted through – dare I say refined by – a non-African lens.

These strategies of self-reflexivity and irony are vernacularised by Kahora not via an autochthonous aesthetic, bound to the Maasai or to the Ogiek. Instead, Kahora vernacularises this postmodern aesthetic by relocating and reorienting the so-called 'view from Africa'. This is a vernacular of the extraverted present. It seeks to articulate the global entanglements at play in the politics of the Mau forests and their environmental future.

Mbembe concludes "At the edge of the world: Boundaries, territoriality, and sovereignty" with the observation that,

> [in] the regions of the world situated on the margins of major contemporary technological transformations, the material deconstruction of existing territorial frameworks goes hand in hand with the establishment of an economy of coercion whose objective is to destroy 'superfluous' populations and to exploit raw materials.[29]

Writing against such coercion is a feat that requires more than a non-complicit publishing house, it requires a self-aware aesthetic that constantly draws reader's attention to their own complicity in this representational problem. This, in my view, is what Billy Kahora's story achieves. Its environmental politics is articulated as a combination of its aesthetic innovations and the material innovations of the chronicle it appears in, a chronicle that allows for and encourages such formal experimentation and innovation. As such, Kahora's aesthetics and the materiality of his text enables him to address both the global and local scales – and the

---

[29] Mbembe, "At the Edge of the World", 284.

dynamics between the two – of the attrition of the Mau Forest and to provide a temporality of urgency to the chronic conditions of environmental change.

Bibliography

Adesokan, Akin. "New African Writing and the Question of Audience". *Research in African Literatures* 43, no.3 (2012): 1–20.

Bayart, J. F. "Africa in the World: A History of Extraversion". *African Affairs* 99 (2000): 217–67.

Braudel, Ferdinand. *Civilization and Capitalism, The Fifteenth to the Eighteenth Century*, vol. 3, *The Perspective of the World*, translated by Siân Reynolds. New York: Harper and Row, 1984.

Chimurenga online. "About us". Accessed November 16, 2016: http://chimurengachronic.co.za/about/.

Chimurenga online. "Read the Chimurenga Chronic in German". Accessed April 13, 2017. http://chimurengachronic.co.za/read-the-chimurenga-chronic-in-german/.

Ede, Amatoritsero. "Narrative Moment and Self-Anthropologizing Discourse". *Research in African Literatures* 46, no. 3 (2015): 112–29.

Harris, Ashleigh. "An Awkward Silence: Reflections on Theory and Africa". *Kunapipi: A Journal of Postcolonial Writing* 34, no. 1 (2012): 28–41.

———. "Awkward Form and Writing the African Present". *The Johannesburg Salon*, 7 (2014): 3–8.

Julien, Eileen. "The Extroverted African Novel". In *The Novel, Vol. 1 – History, Geography, and Culture*, edited by Franco Moretti, 667–700. Princeton: Princeton University Press, 2006.

Kahora, Billy. "How to Eat a Forest". *The Chronic* (2015): 28–35.

Mbembe, J-Achille. "At the Edge of the World: Boundaries, Territoriality, and Sovereignty in Africa". Translated by Steven Rendall. *Public Culture* 12, no.1 (2000): 259–84.

Nixon, Rob. *Slow Violence and the Environmentalism of the Poor.* Cambridge: Harvard University Press, 2011.

Van Kesteren, Geert. "The Ogiek". *Granta* 92 (2005): 97–126.

Wainaina, Binyavanga. "How to Write About Africa". *Granta* 92 (2005): 91–96.

11. Diasporic Divides: Location and Orientations of "Home" in Pooneh Rohi's *Araben*

Helena Wulff
Social Anthropology, Stockholm University

Sweden used to be a country where an ethnically inclusive policy was a matter of national pride.[1] Not so any more. This generous stance ended abruptly in 2015 when 160,000 refugees arrived from war-torn Syria, but also from North Africa, Afghanistan and Iraq. There were those who argued that the infrastructure of housing, health care and schooling built by the Swedish welfare system over decades would collapse with the many "newly arrived" (*nyanlända*). A change in attitude towards people with a "foreign" background became palpable. Yet to some Swedes, experiences of exclusion, even racism, were nothing new. As evident in fiction and journalism by a young generation of diaspora writers in Sweden, such experiences have been commonplace for a long time. With their location in Sweden, their orientation is at the same time to their, or their parents', countries of origin, such as Iran. This orientation entails that the work of these writers can be identified as instances of literary cosmopolitanism from within. A case in point is the acclaimed debut novel *Araben* "The Arab" by

---

[1] Helena Wulff, "Diversifying from Within: Diaspora Writings in Sweden", in *The Composition of Anthropology: How Anthropological Texts Are Written*, eds. Morten Nielsen and Nigel Rapport (London: Routledge, forthcoming).

How to cite this book chapter:
Wulff, Helena. "Diasporic Divides: Location and Orientations of 'Home' in Pooneh Rohi's *Araben*". In *World Literatures: Exploring the Cosmopolitan-Vernacular Exchange*, edited by Stefan Helgesson, Annika Mörte Alling, Yvonne Lindqvist, and Helena Wulff, 119–128. Stockholm: Stockholm University Press, 2018. DOI: https://doi.org/10.16993/bat.k. License: CC-BY.

Pooneh Rohi, first published in 2013.[2] Applying a literary anthropological approach, this chapter focusses on the ways in which home is a deeply divided location in this novel. This is literary anthropology that combines sociological ideas of diaspora with anthropological notions of culture and diversity in relation to a literary text. Methodologically, the chapter draws not only on textual analysis, but also on an in-depth interview with Pooneh Rohi.

Araben opens with the story about a man who, because of his physical looks, is assumed to be an Arab in Stockholm. But he is actually Persian, and from Iran, where he many years ago was working as a civil engineer, a background which is not acknowledged in the Swedish setting, where he only sometimes gets an odd job. The Arab leads a lonely life in the city of Stockholm, covered in snow and smelling of ice. He feels like "a margin of error that is included in the calculation, like cars that are put together in a faulty manner are included in the budget of a car factory, a necessity for profit or if you like the survival of humanity" ("en felmarginal som ingår i beräkningarna, som felmonterade bilar i budgeten på en bilfabrik, en nödvändighet för profiten eller om man så vill mänsklighetens fortlevnad"). In the morning, as he is watching the white landscape outside the window on the commuter train, he is thinking to himself that he is like "a waste product" ("en avfallsprodukt"): "He is a failure, something that never happened, a slip up or a divine mistake" ("Han är ett misslyckande, ett någonting som aldrig blev, en tabbe eller en gudomlig flopp").[3]

The day before, he had received a battered letter with many stamps. It had come over the mountains all the way from Iran with the news that his friend who had stayed on there had died. This evokes the memory of past events that he at one point decided to put away at the back of his mind. Now they appear forcefully: "The memory of the other country. Of the last night in the country that once was his home". ("Minnet av det andra landet. Av den sista natten i det land som en gång var hans hem".)[4]

---

[2] Pooneh Rohi, *Araben* (Stockholm: Ordfront, 2014).
[3] Rohi, *Araben*, 7.
[4] Rohi, *Araben*, 21.

As Sweden does not seem to be the Arab's home either, in a sense he remains homeless in his heart. Soon another protagonist also from Iran, a young woman, is introduced into the novel, and two parallel stories start to unfold. Contrary to the Arab's story, told in the third person, the one about the young woman is in the first person. With a Swedish boyfriend and successful in her university studies, she has learnt the codes and is integrated in Swedish life, so much so that she is taken to have been adopted as a child. Together with her boyfriend, she is planning to buy a flat with a wooden floor and high ceiling. She visits her mother who spends most time on her own, joyless, while keeping an Iranian way of life. But the young woman hardly remembers her childhood in Iran. It is just a distant memory from the past, at least in the beginning of the book. Eventually "her longing for that rain, that salty scent from the sea" ("längtan efter det där regnet, den där salta fuktiga luften från havet") grows, as well as significantly her longing for "that part of the room that is invisible in the mirror" ("den där delen av rummet som inte syns i spegeln").[5] Yet she is more at home in Sweden than the Arab. Moving towards the end of the novel, the two parallel stories weave together with an encounter between the young woman and the Arab. It turns out that they have met at cafés for all of ten years and that they are related: they are father and daughter, although not on the best of terms. The novels ends with the young woman being offered a position as PhD student at the university, but she breaks up with her Swedish boyfriend because of cultural differences.

The notion of home tends to be associated with a cherished place, a shelter that provides comfort and belonging, a place to return to. This meaning of home is emphasised through exile and emigration. Here Ireland, with its endemic emigration, offers a useful comparative case in point. As Irish journalist Fintan O'Toole has noted about the predicament of the Irish diaspora "*home* itself comes into focus only when one is away from home", it is "usually made powerful by the act of leaving it" and "home is much more than a dwelling place. It is also a whole set

---

[5] Rohi, *Araben*, 77.

of connections and affections, the web of mutual recognition that we spin around ourselves and that gives us a place in the world".[6] For the Arab in the novel, all this is brutally brought back when he receives the letter with news about the death of his friend. But also to him, home is a divided place. With increasing migration and other types of movement and travel across space follow the widespread experience of being at home, more or less and in different ways, in *two* places, perhaps more so in one of them during certain stages in life. This is what it was like for the young woman, who ended up feeling more Iranian and less Swedish, as the novel progressed, than she did in the beginning: importantly, the orientation towards one's locations might change over the course of time.

Another writer who recently made a name in Sweden is the poet Athena Farrokhzad, also with roots in Iran. Her poetry collection *Vitsvit* (2013) (*White Blight*, 2015) has been an inspiration for Pooneh Rohi. This comes across in her short opinion piece in *Dagens Nyheter* one year after the publication of *Araben*.[7] In the opinion piece she develops further the topic from the novel by discussing the idea of home and homelessness, also in relation to exclusion. The online piece was illustrated with a large picture of brown-eyed Rohi with her black curly hair gathered in a topknot, next to the title "And you call me stranger" ("Och ni kallar mig främling").[8] In the piece she refers to Athena Farrokhzad when she says that writing in Swedish is what puts bread on the table. It is also the language that is worth the price of betraying a mother, and that:

> I am an involuntary Swede. I have no choice. This is my country, this is my language ... Without Sweden I am homeless ... And yet

---

[6] Fintan O'Toole, "Perpetual Motion", in *Arguing at the Crossroads: Essays on a Changing Ireland*, ed. Paul Brennan and Catherine de Saint Phalle (Dublin: New Island Books, 1997), 86.

[7] Athena Farrokhzad, *Vitsvit* (Stockholm: Albert Bonniers Förlag, 2013); Athena Farrokhzad, *White Blight* (Brooklyn, NY: Argos Books, 2015).

[8] Pooneh Rohi, "Och ni kallar mig främling", *Dagens Nyheter*, 10 April 2014.

you call me stranger every time you talk about those you actually should call by their real name: racists.⁹

(Jag är en ofrivillig svensk. Jag har inget val. Detta är mitt land, detta är mitt språk....Utan Sverige är jag hemlös... Och ändå kallar ni mig för främling varje gång ni talar om dem som ni i stället borde kalla vid deras rätta namn: rasister.)

Key in Rohi's opinion piece is thus the contradiction between how she is identified as "a stranger" ("en främling") because she "looks different" ("ser annorlunda ut"), yet has no other home than Sweden, whether she likes to or not. When I met Pooneh Rohi for an interview, she talked about this as a form of racialisation:

> Racialisation concerns everyone who looks different. The first generation and those who were born here. There will absolutely be a movement. Many of us came about twenty years ago. It will be a very political movement of people who share this identification. Our parents were treated incredibly badly. We did not suffer so much. Now their children, us, who have the language, we have the codes, we are now in the social elite, we are educated.
>
> (Rasifiering gäller alla som ser annorlunda ut. Den första generationen och de som föddes här. Det kommer absolut en rörelse. Många av oss kom för ungefär tjugo år sen. Det kommer bli en väldigt politisk rörelse med människor som delar den här identifikationen. Våra föräldrar behandlades oerhört illa. Vi råkade inte lika illa ut. Nu har deras barn, vi, vi har språket, vi har koderna. Vi är nu i den sociala eliten, vi är utbildade.)¹⁰

This is in line with the notion that a young middle-class generation of Iranian background now are "continuing" the careers their parents had to give up in Iran, as many of them only could get menial jobs in Sweden.

Just like the young woman in *Araben*, Pooneh Rohi came to Sweden from Iran as a child. She grew up in a middle-class home in Stockholm. Her father was a physicist and her mother taught literature in school. It was as an Erasmus exchange student in comparative literature at University of Sheffield that she discovered postcolonial

---

⁹ Rohi, "Och ni kallar mig främling".
¹⁰ Interview with Pooneh Rohi, 2 May 2014 in Stockholm.

literature, and suddenly her own feelings of dislocation made sense as a part of a larger scheme. She was not alone. In the interview with Rohi, I asked about the writing process, how and why she wrote *Araben*. She said that she had been writing short stories – very short stories – since she was a teenager. They could be just half a page long. That was how it started with *Araben*. It originated as a short story that she later combined with a number of other short stories. This topic was different than anything else she had written. With this topic, she was able to keep her focus rather than taking off in other directions like she used to do, as this topic engaged her more. She was totally consumed by it. It took seven years to write *Araben*, which had been useful for Rohi, she explained, as this long time span had made it possible for her to combine the young person she used to be with the one who is somewhat older. The novel features two sides of herself. Coming across Willy Kyrklund's montage novel *Tvåsam* (1949) ("Two Together") was a turning point for Rohi.[11] She found that novel excellent not least in its poetic style and went on to write her undergraduate essay in comparative literature about it. It is likely that the precise economical style of *Tvåsam* also made an impression on Rohi, who at the time of the interview, was working on a PhD dissertation in linguistics, and thus had a special interest in significant linguistic details. So *Araben* can be said to have been influenced both by the poetic precise prose and the montage format (which was regarded as falling outside standard literary genres) of *Tvåsam* that creates an allegorical level.[12] During the interview, Rohi mentioned Willy Kyrklund's Finnish-Swedish background. After having finished school, he moved to Sweden from Finland, an experience which was reflected in his literary work in terms of feelings of alienation and melancholia that incidentally appear in *The Arab* as well. It is likely that Rohi feels an affinity with Kyrklund also because of this: the fact that he, too, had moved to Sweden from another country. He incidentally also had an interest in Iran.

If Kyrklund was a "writer who had immigrated" ("invandrad författare"), Rohi is identified as an immigrant writer in

---

[11] Willy Kyrklund, *Tvåsam*, (Stockholm: Bonniers, 1949).
[12] See also Arne Florin, "Om Willy Kyrklunds genrer och genreblandningar" (diss., Stockholm University, 1992).

literary journalism such as reviews. As Iranian immigrants are also referred to as forming a diaspora, which is a term they tend to prefer, it is relevant to have a look at the terminology here. Both "immigrant" and "migrant" literature are standard notions, as is "diaspora" literature. Yet there is an awareness in comparative literature that the notion of "immigrant" or "migrant" literature might not actually correspond to the level of the authors' integration or Swedishness, nor to their literary topics. Many authors in Sweden who were born in another country or whose parents were, identify as Swedish authors.[13] When it comes to the designation "diaspora" literature, *Araben* does fit in here. In a wider perspective, diaspora literature draws attention to issues ranging from the nation-state to ideas of home and homeland.[14] Yet as sociologist Rogers Brubaker has pointed out in an influential statement: "rather than speak of 'a diaspora' or 'the diaspora' as an entity, a bounded group, an ethnodemographic or ethnocultural fact, it may be more fruitful, and certainly more precise, to speak of diasporic stances, projects, claims, idioms, practices".[15]

When Rohi had finished *Araben*, she sent it to about fifteen publishers – all she could find on the internet. All but two sent her standard rejection letters. These two liked her way of writing, but noted that the novel was just not ready yet. Ordfront in Stockholm was willing to publish the manuscript as it stood,

---

[13] See Satu Gröndahl, "Identity Politics and the Construction of Minor Literatures: Multicultural Swedish Literature at the Turn of the Millenium", *multiethnica* 30 (2007): 21–29; Magnus Nilsson, "Swedish 'Immigrant Literature' and the Construction of Ethnicity", *TijdSchrift voor Skandinavistiek*, 31, no. 1 (2010): 199–218; and Lars Wendelius, *Den dubbla identiteten: Immigrant- och minoritetslitteratur på svenska 1970–2000* (Uppsala: Centrum för Multietnisk forskning, 2002) among others.

[14] Considering the usage of the notion of diaspora in academia, anthropologists Steven Vertovec and Robin Cohen (1999) have suggested four types: social form, consciousness, mode of cultural production and political orientation. Vertovec, Steven and Robin Cohen, "Introduction", in *Migration, Diasporas and Transnationalism*, ed. Steven Vertovec and Robin Cohen. xiii–xxviii (Cheltenham: Edward Elgar), 1999.

[15] Rogers Brubaker, "The 'diaspora' diaspora", *Ethnic and Racial Studies* 28, no. 1 (2005): 13.

and eventually did publish the novel, but after she had followed the editor's advice to "fill it out".[16] Rohi realised she could use many very short stories about exile that she already had and add two more chapters: one about the Arab and one about the young woman. The book was a success. It was reviewed very positively in major newspapers and literary journals, and Pooneh Rohi was interviewed in *Babel*, the literary program on Swedish Television. Eva Johansson wrote a review in *Svenska Dagbladet* where she praised Rohi's remarkable way of making her as a reader recognise herself in something that she has never experienced.[17]

To conclude, this analysis of home as a divided location in the novel *The Arab* has exemplified shifting orientations to the two locations Stockholm and Iran over time, especially at different events and stages in life for the two protagonists. It was the notion of diaspora that brought out the idea of home as a divided location, also in terms of a simultaneous sense of homelessness. Yet it may actually be the case that the two locations in the novel could be connected and understood as two sides of the same home, at least for the young woman. The interview with Pooneh Rohi and her opinion piece moreover made her political engagement in relation to racialisation obvious. She was concerned about the consequences of "looking different", which comes back in the novel. Writing *Araben* had been something of a revelation to her, a way to sort out her situation. She really was not sure that she would write another book. With *Araben* she had "ticked off" this topic that she had been absorbed by. There might not be another topic that she would get into this deeply for such a long time. In fact, writing fiction full-time is not the life she desires.[18] This might change later on, of course, but for now it seems as if Pooneh Rohi is joining a quickly growing group of young writers in Sweden who publish one debut novel on experiences of exclusion that is very well received – and that is it. They do not become fiction writers, but pursue other careers. In 2016, Rohi did a reading of sections from *Araben* at an event

---

[16] Interview with Rohi, 2014.
[17] Eva Johansson, "Araben: Rohi fångar exilens sorg och smärta", *Svenska Dagbladet*, 28 January 2014.
[18] Interview with Rohi, 2014.

about the relation between Jews and Muslims organised by the Association for Jewish Culture in Sweden at Berns in Stockholm.[19] And incidentally, later that year, the feminist magazine *Bang* published a new short story by Rohi, characteristically succinct in its style, titled "The Bicycle Accident" ("Cykelolyckan").[20] It was written in response to the recent influx of Syrian refugees to Sweden I mentioned in the opening of this chapter. It remains to be seen if this short story is the beginning of another book, after all.

On a final wider analytical note, in *An Accented Cinema* (2001) media scholar Hamid Naficy from Iran writes about the growing film genre that is about expatriation in the west by Third World filmmakers.[21] He refers to these films as "accented", combining cinematic and diasporic traditions, thereby revealing new perspectives to a mainstream public.

This is precisely what diaspora writings do in Sweden. And while the writers, such as Pooneh Rohi, discuss changing orientations of home as a divided location through fiction and journalism, they are cosmopolitanising Sweden from within. This also entails that vernacular features of Swedish society now include diasporic stances.

Bibliography

Brubaker, Rogers. "The 'diaspora' diaspora". *Ethnic and Racial Studies* 28, no.1 (2005): 1–19.

Farrokhzad, Athena. *Vitsvit*. Stockholm: Albert Bonniers Förlag, 2013.

———. *White Blight*. Brooklyn, NY: Argos Books, 2015.

---

[19] This took place 8 February 2016 at Berns in Stockholm; see http://urskola.se/Produkter/188177-UR-Samtiden-Judisk-var-relationen-mellan-judar-och-muslimer-Araben-av-Pooneh-Rohi.

[20] Ponneh Rohi, "Cykelolyckan", *Bang* 1 (2016), accessed 10 September 2017, http://www.bang.se.

[21] Hamid Naficy, *An Accented Cinema: Exilic and Diasporic Filmmaking* (Princeton: Princeton University Press, 2001).

Florin, Arne. "Om Willy Kyrklunds genrer och genreblandningar". Diss., Stockholm University, 1992.

Gröndahl, Satu. "Identity Politics and the Construction of Minor Literatures: Multicultural Swedish Literature at the Turn of the Millenium". *multiethnica* 30 (2007): 21–29.

Johansson, Eva. "Araben: Rohi fångar exilens sorg och smärta". *Svenska Dagbladet*, 28 January 2014.

Kyrklund, Willy. *Tvåsam*. Stockholm: Bonniers, 1949.

Naficy, Hamid. *An Accented Cinema: Exilic and Diasporic Filmmaking*. Princeton: Princeton University Press, 2001.

Nilsson, Magnus. "Swedish 'Immigrant Literature' and the Construction of Ethnicity". *TijdSchrift voor Skandinavistiek* 31, no. 1 (2007): 199–218.

O'Toole, Fintan. "Perpetual Motion". In *Arguing at the Crossroads: Essays on a Changing Ireland*, edited by Paul Brennan and Catherine de Saint Phalle, 77–97. Dublin: New Island Books, 1997.

Rohi, Pooneh. *Araben*. Stockholm: Ordfront, 2013.

———. "Och ni kallar mig främling". *Dagens Nyheter*, 10 April 2014.

———. "Cykelolyckan". *Bang* 1 (2016). Accessed 10 September 2017. http://www.bang.se.

Vertovec, Steven and Robin Cohen. "Introduction". In *Migration, Diasporas and Transnationalism*, edited by Steven Vertovec and Robin Cohen, xiii–xxviii. Cheltenham: Edward Elgar, 1999.

Wulff, Helena. "Diversifying from Within: Diaspora Writings in Sweden". In *The Composition of Anthropology: How Anthropological Texts are Written*, edited by Morten Nielsen and Nigel Rapport, 122–36. London: Routledge. Forthcoming.

12. Zuhura the African Lioness: Performance Poetry, Digital Media and the Transnational Tangle in World Literature

Paula Uimonen
Social Anthropology, Stockholm University

African lions
African lionesses
African warriors
African children
African brothers
African sisters

It is time to rise
Let them see you rise
Let them see you rise

The poet Zuhura Seng'enge concludes her performance with these lines from her poem *Warrior Unleashed*. She holds the microphone steadily in her hand as she articulates the words with theatrical emphasis, slowly moving closer to the audience, her steps in rhythm with the instrumental music that punctuates her words. As she repeats the last line after a dramatic pause, "Let them see you rise", carefully enunciating each word, Zuhura nods her head towards the audience, a gesture expressing complicity as well as collective agency. As soon as she ends, with a polite "Thank you very much", the audience breaks out in loud cheers and

---

How to cite this book chapter:
Uimonen, Paula. "Zuhura the African Lioness: Performance Poetry, Digital Media and the Transnational Tangle in World Literature". In *World Literatures: Exploring the Cosmopolitan-Vernacular Exchange*, edited by Stefan Helgesson, Annika Mörte Alling, Yvonne Lindqvist, and Helena Wulff, 129–139. Stockholm: Stockholm University Press, 2018. DOI: https://doi.org/10.16993/bat.l. License: CC-BY.

applause. The launch of Zuhura's first poetry collection, *Warrior Unleashed*, is clearly a success. Staged at the Soma Book Café in Dar es Salaam on 15 July 2016, the event has attracted a small audience of friends, many of them artists: poets, writers, musicians and dancers. The program stretches over three hours, alternating between Zuhura's poetry performances as well as music, dance, rapping and poetry readings by other young artists, some of them performing in public for the first time. The audience is predominantly Tanzanian, with a few *mzungu* (white person), including myself, a Swedish anthropologist doing fieldwork on women writers in Tanzania (see www.womenwriters.one).

In this chapter, I discuss the multilayered location and multidirectional orientation of Zuhura's performance poetry in terms of *transnational tangle* in world literature. On social media, Zuhura calls herself *Zuhura the African Lioness*, a multilayered cultural identity that captures a sense of belonging to the world at large as well as a specific place in it. Similarly, Zuhura's cultural perspective is multidirectional: she looks at the world from an African perspective, but she also engages with Africa from a global perspective. Rather than viewing the cosmopolitan/vernacular or global/local in world literature in terms of binary opposites, it is worth looking more closely at the interactions and entanglements that take place in between, in what I call the transnational tangle, thus building on anthropological theories on cosmopolitanism, globalisation and digital media[1] as well as world-making in literature.[2] As an analytical tool, the transnational tangle seeks to capture the multifaceted complexity of location and orientation in an interconnected world where the intricate entanglements of

---

[1] Ulf Hannerz, "The global ecumene as a network of networks", in *Conceptualizing Society,* ed. Adam Kuper (London: Routledge, 1992), 34–55; Ulf Hannerz, "Cosmopolitanism", in *Companion to the Anthropology of Politics,* ed. Joan Vincent and Daniel Nugent (Oxford: Blackwell, 2007), 69–85; Paula Uimonen, *Digital Drama: Teaching and Learning Art and Media in Tanzania* (New York: Routledge, 2012).

[2] Peng Cheah, "What Is a World? On World Literature as World-Making Activity", *Daedalus* 137, no. 3 (2008): 26–38; Peng Cheah, "World against Globe: Toward a Normative Conception of World Literature", *New Literary History* 45, no. 3 (2014): 303–29.

the local and the global defy the structural binarism of "either/or," instead pointing to "both/and".

The aesthetics of Zuhura's performance poetry is illustrative of a transnational tangle in literary production that mixes genres of various spatiotemporal origin, creatively blending literature, orature, music and theatre. In this genre, the sounds of poetic articulation are just as important as the words themselves, while the artist's voice is augmented through music, thus merging literature, orature and music. Similarly, performance poetry collapses distinctions between literature and theatre. Although it is true that all literary readings are performative acts,[3] in the case of performance poetry, it is intrinsic to the genre. Interestingly, while anthropologist Hastrup uses poetry (language) as a point of comparison with theatre (acting), in performance poetry these art forms merge, thus combining the *magic of performance* in theatre[4] with *imaginary literary world-making*.[5] Indeed, it is in interaction with the audience that performance poetry functions best, an embodied art form that relies on language as well as acting, on a stage that serves as a site of passage where possible experiences are created and secret worlds are revealed.[6] By merging various genres, Zuhura's performance poetry constitutes a transnational tangle of *both* local/vernacular *and* global/cosmopolitan aesthetics that is far more multifaceted than the sum of its various parts.

Zuhura started exploring performance poetry in 2014, while in her second year at the University of Dar es Salaam.[7] She saw a poster for a *La Poetista* event and although she felt scared she went for a first rehearsal. It was the first time she memorised a poem. The organisers were very helpful, coaching her along and encouraging her to "be the poem". Zuhura practiced at home,

---

[3] Helena Wulff, "Literary Readings as Performance. On the Career of Contemporary Writers in the New Ireland", *Anthropological Journal of European Cultures*, 17 (2008): 98–113.
[4] Kirsten Hastrup, "Theatre as a Site of Passage. Some Reflections on the Magic of Acting", in *Ritual, Performance, Media*, ed. Felicia Hughes-Freeland (New York: Routledge, 1998), 42.
[5] Cheah, "What is a World".
[6] Hastrup, "Theatre as a Site of Passage".
[7] Interview with Zuhura Seng'enge in Dar es Salaam on 21 July 2016.

in front of the mirror and her sister. When she went back for a second rehearsal, she was told "you're a natural". She then performed at a large event at the Goethe Institute to a mostly non-Tanzanian, expatriate audience. Afterwards she was invited to perform at Open Mic events in Dar, to mostly Tanzanian audiences. Her confidence grew and nowadays she only does readings at poetry readings; otherwise she performs her poetry with live or recorded music.

While performance poetry comes across as a very contemporary art form, Zuhura's passion for poetry is rooted in a vernacular literary tradition, which she aims to revitalise. When asked what she hopes to achieve through her writing, Zuhura explained that she wants to bring back poetry in Tanzania as a respected literary genre.[8] She recalled how poetry used to be valued more than any other art form. Nowadays film and music are more popular and literature is seen as ancient, especially poetry, Zuhura lamented.

Zuhura's ambition to "bring back respect for poetry" is instructive of her cultural rootedness in a vernacular literary tradition, while her efforts to do so convey a cosmopolitan sensibility. As a Tanzanian artist, Zuhura values the national cultural heritage, like the national poet Shabaan Roberts, whose role in the Tanzanian independence movement is still celebrated. But while Shabaan Roberts is praised for writing in Kiswahili,[9] Zuhura writes mainly in English. In the *Warrior Unleashed* collection, only three poems are in Kiswahili: *Uzuri wako* (your beauty), *Ndoto kubwa* (big dream) and *Home Sweet Home*, which has a title in English. Most of the poems are in English, and one is bilingual. This is not to suggest that the content is delocalised. The bilingual poem *What Binds Us* is a tribute to the nation, emphasising the national unity of Tanzanians as "one people". Zuhura herself has grown up with three languages, her tribal language Kisambaa, Kiswahili and English. Zuhura prefers to write in English, which is also the language that she mostly reads in.

---

[8] Interview with Zhura Seng'enge in Dar es Salaam on 4 July 2016.
[9] Ngugi wa Thiong'o, *Decolonising the Mind: The Politics of Language in African Literature* (London: James Currey, 1986).

English is a common language in the small circle of writers that Zuhura interacts with, an important social world and professional network, which is bilingual in its interaction. While Kiswahili is highly valued by these writers, it is also considered limiting when it comes to reaching a broader audience, since few works get translated into other languages. English thus offers a transnational lingua franca that mediates intercultural interaction, indicative of a cosmopolitan openness to and interest in cultural diversity.[10]

In her efforts to revive poetry in Tanzania, Zuhura draws upon digitally mediated transnational resources. She reinvents traditional literature through digital media (CD, computer-recorded music, digital light and sound equipment) and a global lingua franca (English), thus repositioning and rethinking national cultural production in the wider context of transnational interactions, mediated through social and mobile media. Zuhura's first poetry collection, *Warrior Unleashed,* was released on CD, not in print. Over time, she has produced videos, and her second poetry collection was released online.[11]

Zuhura's performance poetry sheds light on the complex entanglements in world literature, a *transnational tangle of cultural blending*. Rather than seeing the cosmopolitan/global/transnational and the vernacular/local/national as opposite ends of a spectrum, thus emphasising binary categories, it is worth exploring the space in between. "Tangle" visualises the complexities of this in-betweenness. A tangle is closely related to "network", which has a long history in the anthropology of globalisation, dating back to Hannerz's conceptualisation of the global ecumene as a network of networks.[12] Thinking of the social organisation of culture in world society in terms of a network of networks is particularly useful in relation to the Internet, which is generally defined as a network of networks.[13] While networks point to transnational connections of

---

[10] Hannerz, "Cosmopolitanism".
[11] Paula Uimonen, "Digital Infrastructure in World Literature", *Anthropology and Humanism*, forthcoming.
[12] Hannerz, "The Global Ecumene".
[13] Uimonen, *Digital Drama*.

exchange and interaction, transnational tangle captures and structures the multifaceted complexity of these connections.

Zuhura's performance poetry exemplifies the multilayered location and multidirectional orientation of a transnational tangle. She refers to herself as an African Lioness, rather than a more local form of identity, yet her African identity encapsulates many layers of belonging. Zuhura's cultural identity ranges from the very local to the global: ethnic (Sambaa), national (Tanzanian), regional (African) and global (cosmopolitan). In *Warrior Unleashed*, these multiple layers are expressed in various poems, switching between different languages and cultural contexts. In a poem of gratitude to her family, *Home Sweet Home*, Zuhura's eulogy expands from her own family to all families that support their children, just like her opening poem *Cheers to the Women* pays tribute to women in a variety of roles, in different settings. Zuhura's multilayered cultural perspective becomes even more poignant in poems that are explicitly focused on Africanness, shifting between the local and the global, the vernacular and the cosmopolitan. *Beautiful Land* praises the "great things in Africa" the "beautiful things", to counter how "when you talk about Africa, the first thing that comes to a person's mind is the suffering, the pain, the bad things, the blah blah, the ugly things", as Zuhura explained to the audience before performing the poem, thus addressing negative stereotypes so common in external portrayals of Africa.

When introducing *Me and My Brown Skin,* Zuhura remarked "So, if you are African, if you are not African, if you have a brown skin, if you don't have a brown skin, as long as you love your skin, this is for you". She proceeded with the opening line of the poem: "I asked God for a blessing and he blessed me with a brown skin", articulated in a smooth seductive voice, accompanied by jazzy tunes. The poem was inspired by some friends doing a movement on skin bleaching and the song *Brown Skin* by the African-American artist India Ari that Zuhura had seen on YouTube. In tackling the politics of race crafting in an African context,[14] the

---

[14] Jemima Pierre, *The Predicament of Blackness: Postcolonial Ghana and the Politics of Race* (Chicago: University of Chicago Press, 2013).

poem addresses Africa's place in the world,[15] in racialised global hierarchies. But through the magic of performance poetry, another world is made possible, as Zuhura evokes an imaginary world where people love their skin, no matter the colour.

While this poem could be interpreted from the vantage point of her location (Tanzania/Africa), it is clear that Zuhura's orientation is transcultural, looking at the world from an African perspective and looking at Africa from a global perspective. Using her own brown skin to accentuate the poem, stroking her arm for emphasis, Zuhura's take on race and gender spans from personal embodiment to a worldwide imaginary. Not only does her poetry insist on the miraculous beauty of brown skin as opposed to a global political-aesthetic ideal of whiteness, but by insisting on worldwide inclusion, addressing Africans and non-Africans regardless of skin colour, she propagates harmonious co-existence and mutual respect, the kind of openness to cultural diversity that is the hallmark of cosmopolitanism.

It is through literature and digital media that Zuhura is able to express her multilayered cultural self and it is these forms of cultural mediation that also inspire and influence her multidirectional cultural expression. To date, Zuhura has never travelled outside of Africa and the first and only time she was on a plane was in 2015 when she attended a writers' workshop in Kampala, Uganda. Yet she has been exposed to cultural influences from other parts of the world since she was a child, especially through literature. Most of the literature she has read has been in English, by British or North American writers. In school she also read African literature, canonical works by writers like Chinua Achebe and Ngũgĩ wa Thiong'o, but she cannot remember reading anything by African women writers, possibly a poem, but not as compulsory reading. Nowadays she reads contemporary African writers like Chimamanda Ngozi Adichie as well as fellow poets and writers.

---

[15] James Ferguson, *Global Shadows: Africa in the Neoliberal World Order* (Durham: Duke University Press, 2006).

Zuhura is an avid Internet user. Since she started with Facebook in 2012, she has acquired over 1,300 friends in her primary account and over 500 likes on another page. She also has a blog, a YouTube channel and a Twitter account. On the blog *Zuhura Seng'enge's Poetry and Short Stories* she posts some of her poems and stories, along with information about events.[16] On her YouTube channel, she posts short videos from her live performances.[17] On Twitter, Zuhura has over 150 followers and uses the account to post short messages about her work and local literary events.[18] In 2016, Zuhura also started a WhatsApp group called *Writers & Editors of 21stC*. Contrary to its generic name, the group consists of writers in Tanzania, mostly in Dar es Salaam, who share information about events, workshops and literary competitions as well as jokes about writing, in English and Kiswahili.[19]

For Zuhura, social media offers a chance to share and exchange with writers in Africa and outside Africa, a resource for learning and inspiration from "so many people", in her own words a "really big library". This sense of being connected with the world has less to do with the number of actual connections than the feeling of being interrelated with people around the world, thus illustrating how digital media can inspire a sense of membership in world society even in the peripheries of the global network society.[20]

Digital media can augment the world-making aesthetics of world literature. As argued by Cheah,[21] world literature can be seen as a world-making activity, especially in relation to the cultural process of imagining the world as one. This comes close to an anthropological appreciation of world society in terms of the world as we know it, the global ecumene.[22] Through literary

---

[16] http://zuhurasaad22.blogspot.com/, accessed on 28 April 2018.
[17] ZuhuratheAfricanLioness: https://www.youtube.com/channel/UCOi5lN74CDXnS5aFVYOB8fQ, accessed on 28 April 2018.
[18] Zuhura Seng'enge: @Zu_thelioness, accessed on 28 April 2018.
[19] I have been a member of this group since July 2016.
[20] Ferguson, *Global Shadows*; Uimonen, *Digital Drama*.
[21] Cheah, "What Is a World?".
[22] Hannerz, "The Global Ecumene".

production, different imaginary worlds are created, and through literary circulation, different people can engage with these imaginary worlds. As writers in different parts of the world connect with other writers as well as readers through digital media, literary world-making is expanded well beyond printed texts.

Digital media offers an interesting infrastructure of world literature that somehow challenges the global inequalities of literary production and circulation.[23] Critical scholars have underlined the reproduction of global inequalities in world literary circuits, even defining world literature as the literature of the capitalist world system.[24] Following Cheah, this emphasis on material conditions, social relations and political economic structures tends to ignore the aesthetic dimensions of literature, while conflating the categories world (imaginary) and globe (spatio-geographical).[25] Digital media brings forth this conceptual shortcoming, while partially addressing it. On the one hand, digital media can inspire a cosmopolitan sense of the world as one, which transcends social and material boundaries. Through social media, Zuhura can express her poetry to a worldwide audience, thus using her literary talent to contribute to the making of imaginary worlds. In March 2017, Zuhura even released some of her poems for free download on the site www.mkito.com, because the site makes it "easier to spread news about what you do to many people all over".[26] On the other hand, digital infrastructure is intrinsically bound up with a global capitalist system that reproduces, at times even reinforces global racial hierarchies.[27] When the *African Lioness* called on her brothers and sisters to rise, she used performance poetry to create an imaginary world that is more just and equal for all of humanity. But once the performance was concluded, Zuhura and her friends

---

[23] Uimonen, "Digital Infrastructure in World Literature".
[24] Warwick Research Collective (WReC), *Combined and Uneven Development. Towards a New Theory of World-Literature* (Liverpool: Liverpool University Press, 2015).
[25] Cheah, "World against Globe".
[26] Facebook chat with Zuhura on 17 March 2017.
[27] Paula Uimonen, "'Number not Reachable'. Mobile Infrastructure and Global Racial Hierarchy in Africa", *Journal des Anthropologues* 142–143 (2015): 29–47.

in Dar faced a social reality in which most people cannot afford to buy a CD, or a book for that matter, and where the spectacular launch of the digitally mediated *Warrior Unleashed* was preceded by a few hours of power outage.

This study uses an anthropological approach that pays attention to women's literary production as well as the cultural context framing their work, thus offering a more nuanced understanding of the making of world literature. Such a holistic approach can be used to deconstruct some of the prevailing binaries in world literature studies and reconstruct a more culturally sensitive approach that allows for greater complexity.

In this text I have used *transnational tangle* to capture multifaceted cultural complexity in world literature, emphasising multilayered location and multidirectional orientation in contemporary literary production. Far from being bounded and static entities, location and orientation offer entry points into the cultural dynamics of transnational entanglements in world literature, the intricacies of which deserve further scrutiny. As glimpsed from Zuhura's performance poetry, young contemporary women writers in places like Tanzania draw on a variety of transnational resources, including digital media, to tell their stories in the world, of the world, and for the world in the making.

Bibliography

Cheah, Peng. "What Is a World? On World Literature as World-Making Activity". *Daedalus* 137, no. 3 (2008): 26–38.

———. "World against Globe: Toward a Normative Conception of World Literature". *New Literary History* 45, no. 3 (2014): 303–29.

Ferguson, James. *Global Shadows: Africa in the Neoliberal World Order*. Durham: Duke University Press, 2006.

Hannerz, Ulf. "The Global Ecumene as a Network of Networks". In *Conceptualizing Society*, edited by Adam Kuper, 34–55. London: Routledge, 1992.

———. "Cosmopolitanism". In *Companion to the Anthropology of Politics*, edited by Joan Vincent and Daniel Nugent, 69–85. Oxford: Blackwell, 2007.

Hastrup, Kirsten. "Theatre as a Site of Passage. Some Reflections on the Magic of Acting". In *Ritual, Performance, Media*, edited by Felicia Hughes-Freeland, 29–45. New York: Routledge, 1998.

Ngũgĩ Wa Thiong'o. *Decolonising the Mind: The Politics of Language in African Literature*. London: James Currey, 1986.

Pierre, Jemima. *The Predicament of Blackness: Postcolonial Ghana and the Politics of Race*. Chicago: The University of Chicago Press, 2013.

Uimonen, Paula. *Digital Drama. Teaching and Learning Art and Media in Tanzania*. New York: Routledge, 2012. http://innovativeethnographies.net/digitaldrama.

———. "'Number not Reachable.' Mobile Infrastructure and Global Racial Hierarchy in Africa". *Journal des Anthropologues* 142–143 (2015): 29–47.

———. "Digital Infrastructure in World Literature". *Anthropology and Humanism*, forthcoming.

Warwick Research Collective (WReC). *Combined and Uneven Development. Towards a New Theory of World-Literature*. Liverpool: Liverpool University Press, 2015.

Wulff, Helena. "Literary Readings as Performance: On the Career of Contemporary Writers in the New Ireland". *Anthropological Journal of European Cultures* 17 (2008): 98–113.

13. Literary Ecologies and Post-9/11 Muslim Writing

Adnan Mahmutović
English, Stockholm University

This chapter seeks to outline some of the main topics and methodologies in the larger project that is a study of post-9/11 American Muslim writing in terms of Alexander Beecroft's *literary ecologies*.[1] Such an analysis requires an examination of the form and content of literary texts as well as their dissemination and reception, that is, the ways in which readers pull together authors and their works into *a* literature within the field of world literature. If Beecroft is correct in claiming that *a* literature is made mainly through the ways readers make connections between works – as well as authorial intentions in cases where writers aim at producing a particular type of literature it is possible to speak of American Muslim writing as *a* literature that belongs to different literary ecologies, for instance different national literatures. What is more, due to its reduced size, it is possible to speak of it as a form of vernacular literature (in a modified sense of the word I will explain later), but it is also possible to see it in terms of a cosmopolitan literature given its dissemination, translatability and accessibility. Since a large proportion of contemporary writers work in/towards what Beecroft calls the emerging global ecology, American Muslim writing may not only find itself pulled in

---

[1] Alexander Beecroft, *An Ecology of World Literature: From Antiquity to the Present Day* (London: Verso, 2015). See also the discussion of Beecroft in the general introduction to this volume.

How to cite this book chapter:
Mahmutović, Adnan. "Literary Ecologies and Post-9/11 Muslim Writing". In *World Literatures: Exploring the Cosmopolitan-Vernacular Exchange*, edited by Stefan Helgesson, Annika Mörte Alling, Yvonne Lindqvist, and Helena Wulff, 140–149. Stockholm: Stockholm University Press, 2018. DOI: https://doi.org/10.16993/bat.m. License: CC-BY.

several directions through the workings of literary markets and diverse audiences, but will also deliberately, through form and content, orient itself towards different ecologies. This is the main feature I see as defining American Muslim writing, namely its plural location and orientation. It is at the same time firmly located in American national literature but it constantly orients itself towards other national literatures and a global literary ecology.

The label "American Muslim" pulls together often very idiosyncratic works on the basis of interrelated sets of concerns as well as the fact that it is tied to and strongly defined by the American literary markets. To only locate certain writing in a national literary ecology and deem it a niche writing would, for American Muslim writing effectively stage *a forgetting of the cosmopolitan heritage of Islam*, which informs this writing and de facto produces its particular dynamic between location and orientation. Indeed, American Muslim writing is a product not only of our time but strongly informed by the continuous, fourteen-centuries-long form of what Alex MacGillivray calls "archaic globalization",[2] which includes the history of Muslim colonialism and its economic and cultural impact on the world. What is more, we must not forget the notion of the Muslim *Ummah* as an early form of cosmopolitan consciousness, which I see strongly affects both the location and orientation of American Muslim writing. Indeed, by positing itself as a global project, Islam not only achieved a transcontinental reach centuries before European colonialism and industrialisation but continues to be an essential part of current globalisation processes and its effects are felt in world literatures, especially the types of literature produced by those for whom Muslim identity is at stake.

The practically non-existent use of the label "Muslim", in contrast to for instance national or ethnic tags, in more global marketing is not incidental. In the post-9/11 period, it may not provide social capital that can boost international success. At the same time, dealing with Muslim-related, often controversial subjects

---

[2] Alex MacGillivray, *A Brief History of Globalization* (London: Robinson, 2006): 15.

such as terrorism does boost sales and international distribution.[3] In contrast to globally popular ways of disseminating categories and discussing literature, the tag "Muslim" does not appear much in critical reception (including reviews and interviews). A notable exception is for instance Rehana Ahmed's work.[4]

American Muslim writing, produced after 11 September 2001 in the USA, draws attention to complex orientations towards different literary ecologies. Here we find authors such as Mohsin Hamid, Michael Muhammad Knight, Khaled Hosseini, Mohja Kahf, Leila Lalami, Kamran Pasha, and a few others. These diverse works, often produced as some form of response to the post-9/11 historical developments, stage a particular dialectic between the cosmopolitan notions of flexible world citizen and location within national borders.[5] American Muslim writing in this reading contains two movements elaborated in the critical dialogue between Richard Gray and Michael Rothberg: "centripetal" globalisation and a complementary centrifugal mapping that charts "the prosthetic reach of [the US] empire into other worlds".[6] In contrast to the pervasive domestication of change in post-9/11 American literary ecology, which is not only visible in a lack of *formal* innovation but also in a failure to engage the *global* dimensions of that change, American Muslim writing does not exhibit Gray's "imaginative paralysis".[7] What is more, the fact that this writing

---

[3] Besides Mohsin Hamid's and Khaled Hosseini's work, we see this all over the world even with writers such as Tabish Khair's *How to Fight Islamic Fundamentalism from the Missionary Position* (Interlink Publishing Group, 2013) and *Just Another Jihadi Jane* (Interlink Publishing Group, 2016). Works by for instance Leila Aboulela, which are more character-driven, subtle stories of identity crises, do not reach the required heghts of global literary markets to make any significant impact on the different ecologies.

[4] Rehana Ahmed, Peter Morey, and Amina Yaqin, *Culture, Diaspora and Modernity in Muslim Writing* (New York and London: Routledge, 2012).

[5] Aihwa Ong, *Flexible Citizenship: The Cultural Logic of Transnationality* (London: Durham University Press, 1999).

[6] Michael Rothberg, "A Failure of the Imagination: Diagnosing the Post-9/11 Novel: A Response to Richard Gray", *American Literary History* 21, no. 1 (2009): 153.

[7] Richard Gray, "Open Doors, Closed Minds: American Prose Writing at a Time of Crisis", *American Literary History* 21, no. 1 (2008): 128–51.

is read across multiple ethnoscapes, to use Arjun Appadurai's term,[8] and that it often inspires change in different demographics, is an example of an ongoing oscillation between stable location and a strong need for global orientation.

I now want to show the use of Beecroft's ecological model as a way of highlighting the abovementioned, and crucial, features of American Muslim writing. Beecroft's model is useful because literature must "be understood as being in an ecological relationship to other phenomena – political, economic, sociocultural, religious – as well as to the other languages and literatures with which it is in contact".[9] An ecological lens helps us understand processes "of survival and recognition".[10] In his identification of basic types of ecologies – epichoric, panchoric, cosmopolitan, national, vernacular, global – Beecroft looks at the following factors: the linguistic situation, economy, the political world, religion, cultural politics and technologies of distribution. What we gain from seeing American Muslim writing in terms of literary ecologies is an expanded sense of diversity and crosspollination that explain certain defining features that pull together sets of works into a category which yields itself to analysis. While a more thorough investigation is needed to explore how all these factors shape *a* literature, in this short overview, I will only touch upon some elements that are crucial for my analysis and do so by using specifics of Hamid and Muhammad Knight's work.

Linguistically speaking, though American Muslim writing is in English and thus affected by the literary history of this language, Beecroft is correct in claiming that one should look at "how many other languages exist as viable media for literary expression" and whether or not an author had a choice to write in that or another language.[11] When it comes to American Muslim writing, while the authors do not seem to have had much of a choice (due to education, native-language proficiency etc.), there are several

---

[8] Arjun Appadurai, *Modernity at Large: Cultural Dimensions of Globalization* (Minneapolis: University of Minnesota Press, 1996).
[9] Beecroft, *An Ecology*, 19.
[10] Beecroft, *An Ecology*, 20.
[11] Beecroft, *An Ecology*, 25.

other languages at play within the English language itself, as for instance Arabic, Urdu, Farsi, etc. because the authors have, either though ethnic or religious connections, access to and, in fact, a need to let these other languages seep into the prose itself. Arabic is particularly significant because it, according to Beecroft, "perhaps uniquely, remains extant as a literary cosmopolis today".[12] In other words, the cosmopolitan or global orientation of American Muslim writing is, language-wise, created not solely because English is a global lingua franca, but because of the previously mentioned cosmopolitan character of Islamic ideology and global spread. Arabic is de facto a default language of Islamic practice and the official language of Muslim Ummah, so that any prose that deals with it as an issue at stake will inevitably be coloured by its (at least) liturgic use.

Regarding the political world, it is indeed the nation that provides the strongest pull in American Muslim writing, but the fact of global politics with regard to the notion of Muslim-ness is omnipresent even if only implicitly. There is, in other words, at least an implicit demand for orientation towards global concerns. The same applies to the question of economy and the extent to which literature is "implicated … in political, religious, and other symbolic networks".[13] There is no doubt that American Muslim writing is commercialised exactly because it is, or can be, easily implicated in various symbolic networks. *The Reluctant Fundamentalist* is *the* case in point.[14] Despite the importance of religion, we cannot, and should not, go into the degree of religious practice of the authors in questions, but there is no doubt that the religion of Islam, due to its continuous controversial political status, not only in the western hemisphere but also much of Asia, Africa and Australia, plays an enormous role in the way American Muslim writing is produced and received. Even in *The Reluctant Fundamentalist*, where religion is not even mentioned, it is implied to the extent that the narrative produces a sense of

---

[12] Beecroft, *An Ecology*, 143.
[13] Beecroft, *An Ecology*, 26.
[14] Mohsin Hamid, *The Reluctant Fundamentalist* (London: Penguin Books, 2007).

unbearable absence of it, and in this way, it is nevertheless, perhaps even more strikingly, present.

When it comes to the cultural politics, the variety of Muslim writing shows that there is no one thing that defines them, but the presence of such politics is undeniable.[15] Each of the mentioned authors is given certain cultural capital and used for different political purposes. Hamid is given the status of literary fiction, while Hosseini is easily slotted into the category of airport literature. The unique case of Muhammad Knight is necessarily sorted as underground literature, too raw to be sold as intellectually challenging. Kahf, in contrast, is a de facto Muslim-female voice, which shapes the reception in terms of a great deal of prejudiced expectations. The politics is closely tied to the technologies of distribution, because the print culture of our modern publishing seems to be hard to digest without perpetual creation and distribution of online content, E-books, audio books, TV and Radio interviews, readings and lectures recorded by audiences and posted on YouTube and social media.[16]

Looking more closely at for instance Muhammad Knight's *Taqwacores* will show specifically how American Muslim writing is characterised by the dynamic between location and orientation both in terms of its content and the abovementioned ways of belonging to certain literary ecologies. It is the story of a house in Buffalo inhabited by Muslim youth from all major Islamic traditions, from Sunnis and Shias to mystics and even modern punk Muslims. The very fact of its identification as *The Catcher in the Rye* for young Muslims firmly situates it in the ecology of American national literature and the original way of distributing it, like it were some bootleg edition (DIY zine) or a pirated copy, indeed reinforces certain American cultural stereotypes of underground writing. It spread through niche venues, creating not only readers, but also followers, movements, and only much later, a film.

In many ways, it is an American story about young people trying to find their way (as Muslims) in America. There is music and

---

[15] Beecroft, *An Ecology*, 26.
[16] Beecroft, *An Ecology*, 27.

drinking and cohabiting. The world outside is barely acknowledged. Besides the fact that they have visitors, the story is almost absolutely confined to the locality of their house. Despite the centrality and particularity of the house, the place appears transnational. It is not a home even though it evokes a desire for being located. It is a petri dish of variegated religious dogma and global youth culture. As such, this house in Buffalo, rather than a place in any country with Muslim majority, is a staggering metaphor for the diversity in the cosmopolitan house of Islam, the Ummah. Knight uses the typical metaphor of a microcosm containing the macrocosm to present intra-religious dynamics. The local is therefore ultimately global. This metaphoric character of the house effectively situates Islam in the US as part and parcel of the nation and, despite the sense of national claustrophobia, creates a centrifugal orientation towards the imagined global community of Ummah. But what keeps the youth together is the fact that they are American and not that they are Muslim. In fact, the impossibility of co-habitation of different kinds of Muslims in the house is suggestive of the impossibility of a homogenous Ummah, which remains an idea(l) of a cosmopolis.

If it were not for this orientation out, the novel would have a somewhat vernacular character. I am using vernacular here not simply to denote language but a certain way of shape-taking of a new type of literature. Given its peculiarity the novel reads like a niche work within the American literary ecology. It establishes an aesthetic which one can imagine as something that could become a form of a communal genre, or a genre for a particular streak in American-Muslim communities. Indeed, we have seen this in the very development of the Muslim punk scene as one of the many responses to the novel.

What also produces a dynamic between some form of vernacular (within nation) and cosmopolitan literary ecology, is the use of language, which makes the reader see beyond the national ecology. The English of *Taqwacores* is often skilfully broken up and stitched together with liturgic Arabic to the point of appearing as some form of global-vernacular that would more easily be spoken and understood by Muslims around the globe than general American readership. The opening sentence –"Bismillahir, Rahmanir *and so on*"[17] – would, for a Muslim reader, speak volumes. This is, no doubt, rather basic code switching, but stylistically, unlike many other works written by Muslims or with Muslim characters, the Qur'anic phrase is used as if it were entirely natural in English, the way phrases like "once upon a time" or "in the beginning there was" are frequently used. A Muslim reader would know that the Bismillah-opening is obligatory for any type of honest and halal work, used naturally without thinking, shows the character and intent of the narrator (automatically reliable), that the narrator speaks to a community (note that the "foreign" words are not typically italicised). It is the second part – "*and so on*" that is in italics like it were foreign to the first phrase. This "*and so on*" also appears disrespectful because the narrator refuses to repeat the entire phrase, as Muslims always do, but this speaking-by-rote of the phrase is implied. It is the very relaxed, or natural, way of code-switching that makes the language appear at the same time both very local (to the house) and global, because it speaks to Muslims all over the world.

It is, in some way a cosmopolitan or global language which creates rich signification for Muslims regardless of their ethnicity, nationality, particularity of religious practice and dogma, etc. It is not some vernacular developed in isolation, but a language produced in the meeting of two cosmopolitan languages, English and Arabic. The fact that a global Muslim audience would be able to appreciate this work in terms of its use of language produces a rather unique situation within and across literary ecologies. While a vernacular would, according to Beecroft, prevent wider distribution of the work, the novel's outward orientation makes us revise this analysis. Disregarding its potentially controversial content and language, this novel would be highly accessible to a Muslim readership around the globe while at the same also quite obscure for most global audiences. In other words, it appears both local and global given a particular type audience, and yet, because of

---

[17] Michael Muhammad Knight, *Taqwacores* (New York: Soft Skull Press, 2004): 5.

that, very local when considering what usually makes literature that is read widely across different ethnoscapes etc.

In addition, regarding dissemination, it is not only the movement of the text itself that defines it, but ultimately the *taqwacore* effect: the creation of Muslim punk bands and other such alternative music scene among Muslim youth. In other words, the content of the novel, though fictional, inspired a great deal of transnational movement among Muslims.[18] The increased demand led to distribution by the publishers Alternative Tentacles and then Autonomedia. Asra Nomani has credited the novel as the source of the idea for woman-led prayer, which took place on 18 March 2005 with Amina Wadud acting as imam.[19]

In this overview, I have tried to show how American Muslim writing, seen through the lens of Beecroft's model is inherently defined by a complex oscillation between location (nation) and orientation (cosmopolitanism, globe). As such, American Muslim writing shows both the utility of Beecroft's model for world literature today and opens a critical space for its possible revision.

Bibliography

Ahmed, Rehana, Peter Morey, and Amina Yaqin. *Culture, Diaspora and Modernity in Muslim Writing*. New York: Routledge, 2012.

Appadurai, Arjun. *Modernity at Large: Cultural Dimensions of Globalization*. Minneapolis: University of Minnesota Press, 1996.

Beecroft, Alexander. *An Ecology of World Literature: From Antiquity to the Present Day*. London: Verso, 2015.

Fiscella, Anthony T. "From Muslim Punks to Taqwacore: An Incomplete History of Punk Islam". *Contemporary Islam* 6, no. 3 (2012): 255–81.

---

[18] Mark LeVine, *Heavy Metal Islam: Rock, Resistance, and the Struggle for the Soul of Islam* (New York: Broadway Books, 2008); Anthony T. Fiscella, "From Muslim Punks to Taqwacore: An Incomplete History of Punk Islam", *Contemporary Islam* 6, no. 3 (2012): 255–81.

[19] Michael Muhammad Knight, *Blue-eyed Devil: A Road Odyssey Through Islamic America* (New York: Autonomedia, 2006): 206.

Gray, Richard. "Open Doors, Closed Minds: American Prose Writing at a Time of Crisis". *American Literary History* 21, no. 1 (2008): 128–51.

Hamid, Mohsin. *The Reluctant Fundamentalist*. London: Penguin Books, 2007.

Kahf, Mohja. *The Girl in the Tangerine Scarf*. New York: Carroll & Graf Publishers. 2006.

Khair, Tabish. *How to Fight Islamic Fundamentalism from the Missionary Position*. Interlink Publishing Group, 2013.

———. *Just Another Jihadi Jane*. Interlink Publishing Group, 2016.

Muhammad Knight, Michael. *Blue-eyed Devil: A Road Odyssey Through Islamic America*. New York: Autonomedia, 2006, 2006.

———. *Taqwacores*. New York: Soft Skull Press, 2004.

LeVine, Mark. *Heavy Metal Islam: Rock, Resistance, and the Struggle for the Soul of Islam*. New York: Broadway Books, 2008.

MacGillivray, Alex. *A Brief History of Globalization*. London: Robinson, 2006.

Ong, Aihwa. *Flexible Citizenship: The Cultural Logic of Transnationality*. London: Durham University Press, 1999.

Rothberg, Michael. "A Failure of the Imagination: Diagnosing the Post-9/11 Novel: A Response to Richard Gray". *American Literary History* 21, no. 1 (2009): 152–58.

14. Worldly Vernaculars in the Anglophone Caribbean

Bo G. Ekelund
English, Stockholm University

Writers of the extended Caribbean have been caught in a particularly awkward bind determined by the spatial distribution of linguistic, economic, and cultural resources: in the absence of a developed local publishing industry, many moved to metropolitan locations in order to make themselves authors; in the absence of indigenous non-colonial official languages, they have had the choice of celebrating creole vernaculars or submitting to the literary forms of imperial English (British or US), French, Spanish or Dutch; in the absence of a large enough Caribbean audience, they have had to play the games of either "strategic exoticism" or of differently conceived forms of authenticity.

Various artistic and critical discourses of empowerment have emerged from this bind: *négritude*, *creolité*, *antillanité*, nation language and tidalectics, as forms of resistance to colonial and imperial structures and affirmation of independence. Thus, Caribbean writing has defined itself by opposites such as the archipelagic and the continental, the creolised and the spuriously "pure", interculturation and acculturation. Operating under these and other labels we see the boundary-work by which writers seek to "reshape the boundaries of their cultural universe", to borrow

---

How to cite this book chapter:
Ekelund, Bo G. "Worldly Vernaculars in the Anglophone Caribbean". In *World Literatures: Exploring the Cosmopolitan-Vernacular Exchange*, edited by Stefan Helgesson, Annika Mörte Alling, Yvonne Lindqvist, and Helena Wulff, 150–161. Stockholm: Stockholm University Press, 2018. DOI: https://doi.org/10.16993/bat.n. License: CC-BY.

Sheldon Pollock's phrase.[1] However, rather than "renouncing the larger world for the smaller place", like the writers of Pollock's first wave of vernacular literary cultures, Caribbean authors have drawn on cosmopolitan and vernacular forms as the means of a double or ambivalent affiliation.[2] I will suggest in the following that we need to study the two modes – the cosmopolitan and the vernacular – as informing (and being informed by) the necessary strategies to claim place by means of literary language: place as one of the particularities that literature cannot but render readable.

Such particularities of place are tied to, but not reducible to the *positions* – in literary space – claimed by or attributed to writers; while these positions are located in social space, they are invariably also expressed as places. Different strategies of cosmopolitanisation and vernacularisation are then inevitably associated with definite forms of claiming place, and vice versa. What is clearly called for, to my mind, is a rigorous analysis of the particulars of such affiliations with and disavowals of place. In this exploratory essay, I will offer one example to suggest what such an analysis might entail.

There are few exhibits of rivalling literary approaches to the Caribbean more famous than the opposition between Edward Kamau Brathwaite and Derek Walcott.[3] Patricia Ismond's tersely titled "Walcott vs. Brathwaite" summed up some of the "stock attitudes" that had already thickened around the two poets at that time, 1971: "the poet of the people", on the one hand, the

---

[1] Sheldon Pollock, "Cosmopolitan and Vernacular in History", in *Cosmopolitanism*, ed. Carol A. Breckenridge et al. (Durham: Duke University Press, 2002), 16.

[2] Pollock, "Cosmopolitan", 16.

[3] There is a large number of scholarly works that take this pair as their focus. Apart from the articles by Patricia Ismond and Bill Ashcroft, which I will deal with in more detail, see especially Charles W. Pollard, *New World Modernisms* (Charlottesville: U of Virgina P, 2004) and Lorna Burns, "Prophetic Visions of the Past", in *The Routledge Companion to Anglophone Caribbean Writing*, ed. Alison Donnell and Michael A. Bucknor (London: Routledge, 2011), 181–90.

Eurocentric "poet's poet", on the other.[4] Brathwaite's reconstruction of a historical experience that is collective is pitted against Walcott's scrutiny of an individual experience that is historical, and even as Ismond finds their projects "complementary", their attitudes towards the concrete places that figure in their poems are finally determined by an unbridgeable distance between cultural abstractions: orientations towards a "West" or an "Africa" that are made of imagination, mythology, religion, experience, metaphysics, and tradition rather than land, territories, borders, roads, infrastructure. The nature of such abstractions from the particularity of place was no doubt partly an effect of the terms that the political moment supplied, but it is also symptomatic of a generalised neglect of toponymical particulars on the part of critics and scholars.[5]

It is instructive – and germane to my argument – to see how that same level of abstraction along with the same neglect recurs in a recent piece by Bill Ashcroft. He sees no conflict represented by the two poets, Brathwaite and Walcott, but instead holds them up as joint figures of an archipelagic utopia. The opposition that Ismond took for granted in 1971, irreconcilably pitched between folk and humanist, nation and cosmopolitan, is transmuted by Ashcroft into a single if archipelagic dream, into one impulse

---

[4] Patricia Ismond, "Walcott vs. Brathwaite", *Caribbean Quarterly* 17, no. 3–4 (1971): 54.

[5] It should be noted that Ismond has paid substantial and rewarding attention to the concrete details of Walcott's poetic use of place in a later book, *Abandoning Dead Metaphors: The Caribbean Phase of Derek Walcott's Poetry* (Kingston: University of the West Indies Press, 2001). To fully substantiate my claim about a neglect of toponymical particulars would require more space than I have here. However, one interesting and influential exhibit I can offer is Sarah Upstone's *Spatial Politics in the Postcolonial Novel* (Farnham: Ashgate, 2009), which investigates "spatial locales" but does so in order to loosen them from particular geographies, so as to avoid the "colonial myth of spatial order" (19). "For literary post-space", as Upstone would have it, "it is ultimately the text itself that becomes the most suggestive space" (182). In a book dealing to a large extent with Guyanese writer Wilson Harris and including a chapter on "Postcolonial Cities" there is, perhaps unsurprisingly, no mention of Georgetown or Albouystown.

towards transformation, mediated by utopia as "archipelagic thinking".[6] No question of different audiences is broached here, nor of any ambivalence concerning the sources of the poetic strategies: the eccentric use that Ashcroft makes of Ernst Bloch's utopian dialectics removes all historical and material resistance from the places and poets he enlists for his vision of the Caribbean as a "utopian 'Front' space".[7] On the few occasions when the actualities of the region's place in a global space-time come into the open, they are swiftly put back in the bottle by the genie of utopian wishes, with "archipelagic thought" as the stopper. For example, Ashcroft acknowledges that these islands were essential for capitalist production, but then assures us that "islands resist their function as nodes for territorialising global capital because they are open in ways that the continent cannot be".[8] In a way that I take to be perfectly consonant with this easy gesture dispensing with capital, history, and territory, Ashcroft's reading of Walcott's "The Schooner *Flight*" omits every single verse that lays claim to territory on its own, unmediated terms, finding in it only the flight towards utopia as "the third space between the African past with its tragic legacy of the Middle Passage, and the call of the imperial home".[9] If the Caribbean is immediately and fully translated into utopia, as it is here, it has only a symbolic function, in contrast to the historical particularity which is given to Africa and the metropolis, abstractions though they may be.

I do not hold up these two articles as charting some larger trajectory in the scholarship on Caribbean poetry. My point is rather that whether the two modes of orienting oneself in the world that we started with are present in some discernible, euphemised form (Ismond) or dissolved as having no longer any theoretical relevance (Ashcroft), the reckoning of the two poetic projects is conducted with little concern for actual places, either of origin, production or residence. The African past or the imperial home,

---

[6] Bill Ashcroft, "Archipelago of Dreams: Utopianism in Caribbean Literature", *Textual Practice* 30, no. 1 (2016): 93.
[7] Ashcroft, "Archipelagic", 105.
[8] Ashcroft, "Archipelagic", 92.
[9] Ashcroft, "Archipelagic", 97.

the western or African traditions, can be mobilised not as class or geographical signifiers so much as moral or political abstractions.

The geographic particularity that slips away from those abstract terms is one that needs to be reinstated. The critical point I raise is simple: something is missing from any article on Brathwaite and Walcott that does not mention Barbados and St Lucia, and from any reading of "The Schooner *Flight*" that doesn't mention Carenage or Laventille, Wrightson Road or Frederick Street.[10] The neglect of place is an omission from any literary analysis, but especially one concerned with the cosmopolitan and the vernacular, since the two terms cannot be divorced from habitation and mobility, location and orientation.

Placing Brathwaite and Walcott within the framework of the cosmopolitan and the vernacular as strategies for claiming place implies more than noting place names in their work. First of all, it entails a reconsideration of the terms themselves as indicating different types of relationship between location and orientation, while recognising that these relationships can be expressed in a variety of linguistic forms and stylistic levels. The "larger world" and "the smaller place" figure both as locations and possible orientations, while the renunciation of one or the other may use strategies that derive from the pole that is renounced.

To take a rather obvious example, it is plausible to identify the thrust of Brathwaite's first trilogy, *The Arrivants,* as "speaking in towards [society]" in Brathwaite's own words, distinguishing that attitude from that of the "humanist poet" who is "often speaking away from that society".[11] As a poetic work that sought the core of Caribbean culture in its African roots, its main concern was the African Caribbean. Developing a lyrical language in ways consonant with his own analysis of creolisation and nation language, Brathwaite "speaks in towards" the Caribbean with a language derived from the community of speakers rather than from

---

[10] Derek Walcott, "The Schooner *Flight*", *Collected Poems: 1948–1984* (New York: Farrar, Straus & Giroux, 1986), 345–61.

[11] Brathwaite quoted in Mervyn Morris, "Walcott and the Audience for Poetry", in *Critical Perspectives on Derek Walcott,* ed. Robert D. Hamner (Boulder: Rienner, 1997), 178.

an established canon of writing.¹² On the face of it, this would all appear to place that work on the vernacular side of the spectrum. However, if *The Arrivants* turns towards the smaller place, it does so carrying a larger world on its shoulders. It is to "New York London" Uncle Tom rambles.¹³ Is the "nigger's home", the poem asks, found in "Paris Brixton Kingston / Rome?"¹⁴ A veteran coming to church "knows Burma Malaya and has been / to Singapore", while trumpets and saxophones build bridges between Nairobi, Harlem and Havanna.¹⁵ But the real opening onto a larger world comes in the "Masks" part of the trilogy, with its trek across the African continent from Axum in the east to Elmina on Ghana's coast, evoked in an abundance of place names. All of these places, as contrasted with New York, Brixton and Havanna, are identified and located in the Glossary of the Oxford one-volume edition of the trilogy. The use of a glossary, of course, is a tell-tale sign in literatures whose audience is split.¹⁶ In this case, however, a Caribbean audience would be equally helped by having Akropong placed on the map, as a European or North American one. While Ashcroft would have us read Brathwaite's poetry as leaving all origins behind, insisting on arrivals only, a reader of *The Arrivants* will remember the hypnotic intensity of that movement from one city to another, feet marking the ground of the "seven kingdoms". Whether these place claims manage to turn "every periphery into a center" or whether they take place within a larger world structured in spatial dominance is a larger question and must be left for later.¹⁷ A consideration of Brathwaite's poetry within the

---

[12] See Edward Kamau Brathwaite, "Nation Language", in *The Routledge Language and Cultural Theory Reader*, ed. Lucy Burke et al. (London: Routledge, 2000), 310–16.
[13] Kamau Brathwaite, *The Arrivants* (Oxford: Oxford University Press, 1973), 22.
[14] Brathwaite, *Arrivants*, 77.
[15] Brathwaite, *Arrivants*, 162, 174
[16] See Isidore Okpewho's discussion of Achebe and Ngugi: "On the Concept: 'Commonwealth Literature'", in *Meditations on African Literature*, ed. Dubem Okafor (Westport: Greenwood Publishing Group, 2001), 38.
[17] The quoted phrase is from Édouard Glissant, *Poetics of Relation* (Ann Arbor: University of Michigan Press, 1997), 29.

cosmopolitan/vernacular problematic, however, will have to register those claims, and reflect on their effect. The "small place" of the Caribbean is not a foregrounded location that determines an overall orientation, but its various instantiations are added with no particular emphasis to the catalogue of place names mapping out a pan-African and diasporic world.

The case of Walcott, for all its differences, demonstrates the same need for attention to the complex mediation of location and orientation. As a structural parallel to *The Arrivants*, at a later point in Walcott's oeuvre, *Omeros* features a middle section that stages a visionary return to Africa, but unlike Brathwaite, Walcott's evocation does almost entirely without place names.[18] No doubt the authority of first-hand experience, of travel and habitation, plays some part in Brathwaite's confident use of African place names, an assertiveness displayed in *Omeros* instead in references to Boston, Lisbon, Toronto, or Genoa. These eccentric references serve to accentuate the central claim to place in *Omeros*, which is the reversible equation of the Caribbean with the Mediterranean, the sands of St Lucia's beaches and the shores of Ilium. This relation between the places of the "larger world" and the sites which make up the supposedly restricted local environment also stand as exemplary for a renegotiation of spatial terms. As locations, the cities of the global north support an orientation towards the island "periphery" – now the centre, but only by means of a carefully orchestrated constellation of spatial references and with the reader's necessary complicity.

How is that complicity elicited? This question is central to a larger argument about place claims. A full answer would entail an account of a totality of spatial claims, subtended by a world of places, or, more correctly, by a world of "site effects".[19] Knowing that we must defer such an account, it is still imperative that

---

[18] The exception is one mention of the Congo river, and the phrase "the Bight of Benin, [...] the margin of Guinea", repeated once: Derek Walcott, *Omeros* (New York: Farrar, 1990), 149. The parallel is discussed by Jahan Ramazani in his chapter on *Omeros* in *The Hybrid Muse* (Chicago: University of Chicago Press, 2001), 51.

[19] The term is Pierre Bourdieu's, *"effets de lieu"*: "Site Effects", in *The Weight of the World* (Stanford: Stanford UP, 1999), 123–29.

claims to place be analysed with an awareness of that complex and reversible dynamic of location and orientation, always articulated with the choices of the more or less cosmopolitan, the more or less vernacular. These choices concern distances that are social and geographical at the same time. The complicity of the reader who is distant to the places claimed is differently engaged than that of the proximate reader. Literary toponymy has that crude dimension; a place name implies two reactions – this place is theirs; or, this place is mine – followed by one of two versions of the same question: How is it made available to me? How is it made foreign to me? The cosmopolitan and the vernacular, the larger world and the smaller place help determine the responses.

One of Walcott's early poems, "A Sea-Chantey", will illustrate how the larger world and the smaller place dialectically contain one another in its place claims, even when the toponyms all belong to the latter.[20] Its first lines form just the beginning of a long art sentence that develops a single image of masts, but for my purposes the first part will suffice:

> Anguilla, Adina
> Antigua, Cannelles
> Andreuille, all the l's
> Voyelles of the liquid Antilles,
> The names tremble like needles
> Of anchored frigates[21]

For both John Thieme and Patricia Ismond, Walcott can here be seen to conjure up a local scene by means of onomatopoeia, the "liquid sounds of water" (Ismond) scooped up from the verbal resources of local names.[22] As Edward Baugh has pointed out, the incantation of names alternate between places and women: "the l's are also *elles*".[23] However, the female names are also distinctly

---

[20] Walcott, "A Sea-Chantey", *Collected*, 44–46.
[21] Walcott, "Sea-Chantey", 44.
[22] John Thieme, *Derek Walcott* (Manchester: Manchester University Press, 1999), 35; Ismond, *Abandoning*, 34.
[23] Edward Baugh, *Derek Walcott* (Cambridge, Cambridge University Press, 2006), 42

local to the Caribbean: Andreuille will return as Walcott's muse and early love in *Another Life*[24] and Adina is the female figure invoked by Trinidadian poet Harold Telemaque as the symbolic reference for all island life that is hidden from the tourist gaze.[25] Onomastics and toponymy converge: these are our names; these are their names. The liquid Antilles are called upon to build up the extended metaphor from the phonetic depths to the spires of masts and bell towers. But that exchangeability of sounds and visual perceptions is presided over by the allusion to Rimbaud's canonical meditation on synaesthesis, the sonnet "*Voyelles*". Moreover, the reader happens upon the first lines only after an epigraph from Baudelaire, in French. And before we will reach the final toponymical reassertion of "Anguilla, Antigua, / Virgin of Guadeloupe, / and stone-white Grenada", we will have been routed via Ezra Pound's "Pisan Cantos" by means of a quoted phrase that in itself embeds an allusion to François Villon.[26] In short, the "small world" is affirmed by means of the "cosmopolitan" allusions; that is, "their" place is made available to the distant reader by means of his or her access to familiar literary conventions. As for the Antillean reader, such a subject position is being constructed by poems such as these: to say that Anguilla, Antigua, Guadeloupe, Grenada refer to "my place" is to affirm the boundary-work that makes all of the Caribbean available to that composite complicity.

Walcott's allusions to canonical authors from a selective European tradition and Brathwaite's use of a glossary constitute different ways of making their writerly place claims readable within particular existing horizons of expectation. The readability of any content depends on the double coding of all

---

[24] Maria Cristina Fumagalli, *The Flight of the Vernacular: Seamus Heaney, Derek Walcott and the Impress of Dante* (Amsterdam: Rodopi, 2001), 72–73.

[25] Harold Telemaque, "Adina", in *The Poetry of the Negro 1746–1949* ed. Langston Hughes and Arna Bontemps (Garden City: Doubleday, 1951), 350–51.

[26] The line is "*Repos donnez à cils*". See the editor Richard Sieburth's note to Ezra Pound's "Pisan Cantos" in *New Selected Poems and Translations* (New York: New Directions, 2010), 335.

literary claims: that the thing claimed be recognised as worthy of literary form and that the form of the claim be recognised as literary. That is why the formula dividing poetry into speaking in towards society or speaking away from society falters, especially when applied to locations. To bring a place into literary existence, to have it recognised, involves, for the Caribbean poet, multiple sites of recognition. Taking one of them to be the "small place" of our initial pair, both Brathwaite and Walcott engage in constructing a pan-African or a pan-Caribbean, Antillean reader rather than "speaking in towards" any single location. With regard to the "larger world", both poets count, as Charles Pollard has persuasively argued, on the recognition of modernist conventions.[27]

In conclusion, my brief consideration of the notorious case of "Brathwaite vs Walcott" has insisted on the rather simple point that an analysis of their positions in literary space must also reckon with the particularities of place with which their position-takings were bound up. Their literary place claims attain a distinct significance when we consider linguistic, stylistic and other literary choices within the polarity of the cosmopolitan and the vernacular. Taking the heuristic pair of the smaller place and larger world as my starting point, I found it necessary to pry them loose from the conceptual pair cosmopolitan/vernacular, in order to show how particular locations in the Caribbean enter Brathwaite's and Walcott's poetry in a variety of ways. They may be oriented toward a larger world or articulated as already part of that larger world, as in *The Arrivants*. They may constitute a centre towards which the particular places that mark the larger world are oriented, as in *Omeros*. Finally, they may be toponymically autonomous, placed in no external relationship to the places of the larger world, standing, apparently, as self-oriented locations. As the example of "A Sea-Chantey" showed, the latter place claim may be made by means of cosmopolitan formal features, which means that our two pairs in fact form a full matrix rather than synonymous couples: the smaller place may be claimed with

---

[27] Pollard, *New World*.

cosmopolitan means or in the vernacular; the larger world may be invested with cosmopolitan expressivity or with vernacular forms.

The worldly vernaculars of the Caribbean turn their toponyms into literary places. Our inclination, as literary scholars, to recognise the results of the transformation is never in doubt. With some conceptual effort, we may be able to register the particulars of the world that is thus transformed.

Bibliography

Ashcroft, Bill. "Archipelago of Dreams: Utopianism in Caribbean Literature". *Textual Practice* 30, no.1 (2016): 89–112.

Baugh, Edward. *Derek Walcott*. Cambridge, Cambridge University Press, 2006.

Brathwaite, Edward Kamau. *The Arrivants: A New World Trilogy*. Oxford: Oxford University Press, 1973.

———. "Nation Language". In *The Routledge Language and Cultural Theory Reader*, edited by Lucy Burke, Tony Crowley and Alan Girvin, 310–16. London: Routledge, 2000.

Burns, Lorna. "Prophetic Visions of the Past: *The Arrivants* and *Another Life*. In *The Routledge Companion to Anglophone Caribbean Writing*, edited by Alison Donnell and Michael A. Bucknor, 181–90. London: Routledge, 2011.

Fumagalli, Maria Cristina. *The Flight of the Vernacular: Seamus Heaney, Derek Walcott and the Impress of Dante*. Amsterdam: Rodopi, 2001.

Glissant, Édouard. *Poetics of Relation*. Ann Arbor: University of Michigan Press, 1997.

Ismond, Patricia. "Walcott vs. Brathwaite", *Caribbean Quarterly* 17, no. 3–4 (1971): 54–71.

Ismond, Patricia. *Abandoning Dead Metaphors: The Caribbean Phase of Derek Walcott's Poetry*. Kingston: University of the West Indies Press, 2001.

Okpewho, Isidore. "On the Concept: 'Commonwealth Literature.'" *Meditations on African Literature*, edited by Dubem Okafor, 35–43. Westport: Greenwood Publishing Group, 2001.

Pollard, Charles W. *New World Modernisms: T.S. Eliot, Derek Walcott, and Kamau Brathwaite*. Charlottesville: University of Virginia Press, 2004.

Pollock, Sheldon. "Cosmopolitan and Vernacular in History". In *Cosmopolitanism*, edited by Carol A. Breckenridge, Sheldon Pollock, Homi K. Bhabha and Dipesh Chakrabarty, 15–53. Durham: Duke University Press, 2002.

Pound, Ezra. *New Selected Poems and Translations*, edited by Richard Sieburth. New York: New Directions, 2010.

Ramazani, Jahan. *The Hybrid Muse: Postcolonial Poetry in English*. Chicago: University of Chicago Press, 2001.

Telemaque, Harold. "Adina". In *The Poetry of the Negro 1746–1949*, edited by Langston Hughes and Arna Bontemps, 350–51. Garden City: Doubleday, 1951.

Thieme, John. *Derek Walcott*. Manchester: Manchester University Press, 1999.

Upstone, Sarah. *Spatial Politics in the Postcolonial Novel*. Farnham: Ashgate, 2009.

Walcott, Derek. *Collected Poems 1948–1984*. New York: Farrar, Straus & Giroux, 1986.

———. *Omeros*. New York: Farrar, Straus & Giroux, 1990.

PART 3:
WORLD ENOUGH, AND TIME: WORLD-MAKING AND LITERARY PRACTICE

15. Introduction to Part 3
Stefan Helgesson

The contributions in this section of the book distinguish themselves by the attention they pay to a range of material, linguistic and formal practices that constitute the domain of literature and its capacity to intervene in the shaping of cosmopolitan and vernacular world imaginaries. A central assumption here is that "world" must not be taken as a transparent, self-evident backdrop to circulation or narrativisation, but rather as a relational mode between self and other, or between communites and external spaces or entities of varying scales. The "world as such" is never available to any individual consciousness, but is constantly being imagined, often in such pervasive and socially entrenched ways (news media or facebook, for example) that the notion is mistaken for the thing itself. This is where literary history presents us with a storehouse of world-making practices that, in Debjani Ganguly's words, are "attuned to the actual work of language, narrative, form, and genre", and thereby provide alternatives "to thinking the world purely as extension".[1]

Contrary to Ganguly's (and Pheng Cheah's, for that matter) scepticism towards sociological modes of enquiry, however, we see the relationship between an immanent reading of literary world-making and an investigation of material and extratextual

---

[1] Debjani Ganguly, *This Thing Called the World: The Contemporary Novel as Global Form* (Durham: Duke University Press, 2016), 80.

How to cite this book chapter:
Helgesson, Stefan. "Introduction to Part 3". In *World Literatures: Exploring the Cosmopolitan-Vernacular Exchange*, edited by Stefan Helgesson, Annika Mörte Alling, Yvonne Lindqvist, and Helena Wulff, 165–170. Stockholm: Stockholm University Press, 2018. DOI: https://doi.org/10.16993/bat.o. License: CC-BY.

dimensions of literature as complementary, not as mutually exclusive. The word "practice" has a usefully wide referential scope which include narratological and stylistic aspects of the text, as well as extratextual practices such as editing, archiving or marketing. The material demands and possibilities of print technology in a given historical moment will contribute to shaping generic forms such as travel writing, little magazines or documentary modernist collage. These genres, in turn, participate in specific negotiations between language communities, and between cosmopolitan and vernacular world imaginaries, the theorisation of which can contribute to a more cogent understanding of how literature forges world-relations – be they existential, political, or aesthetic.

To establish a few of the terms of such theorisation, **Stefan Helgesson**'s chapter, "Literary World-Making under Apartheid", begins by providing an overview of some world-conceptions, both in contemporary world literature debates and in the philosophy of Hannah Arendt. Using Eric Hayot's distinction between two meanings of "world" as either a self-contained entity or as the totality of everything, Helgesson argues in favour of a multiple-level understanding of literary world-making. The literary work itself can be read as constructing an aesthetic world which intimates the world in a more totalising sense. At an extratextual level, communities of writers, editors and readers also engage in world-making – with literature as a unifying element and by way of vehicular forms, such as the journal. Helgesson's empirical case is the South African literary journal *Staffrider* (1978–1996). Normally read in an exclusively local, national and political context, Helgesson argues instead that *Staffrider*'s local and vernacular valence derives to no small degree from its commitment to "literature" as a putatively cosmopolitan and multilingual realm both exceeding and evading the repressive constraints of apartheid.

In "Documentary Modernism", **Irina Rasmussen** looks at alternative genres of inter-war modernism, such as the anthology, the scrapbook and the photographic reportage. Her focus, too, is on collaborative endeavours rather than individual authorships, cases in point being Nancy Cunard's *Negro: An*

Anthology, L. S. Gumby's *The Harlem Scrapbook* and James Agee's and Walker Evans's *Let Us Now Praise Famous Men*. These interventionist works, typically using the assemblage as form and method, all intervene in the shaping of the global imaginary of their time. In Rasmussen's reading, documentary modernism can therefore be read not only as sharing a drive towards establishing a cosmopolitan, word-historical outlook, but also as establishing institutional practices with a cosmopolitical and emancipatory bent.

Moving back in time and into the inner workings of narrative, **Annika Mörte Alling**'s chapter on French realism traces the characteristic trajectory of protagonists in Stendhal's, Balzac's and Flaubert's novels from the province to the cosmopolitan metropolis of Paris. Intriguingly, this movement is presented as having been prepared imaginatively already by reading. The desire for a larger world is, in other words, not a given, nor are the limits and extension of that world. Instead, they must be actively imagined. In this way, the novels themselves *stage* the capacity of fiction to open new dimensions and facets of the world. By demonstrating in this way how cosmopolitan desires are generated, they also ironise the cosmopolitan prestige and authority subsequently attached to the novels as canonical instances of "world literature".

France and cosmopolitanism loom large also in **Anna Ljunggren**'s essay, although from a Russian vantage point. If Dostoevsky famously berated the Russian infatuation with western Europe and Parisian modernity in particular, several generations of Russian exile writers have made the transition to western cultures, with the notable cases Vladimir Nabokov, Joseph Brodsky, Andreï Makine and Mikhail Shishkin being highlighted in this chapter. Of these, all except Shishkin have also shifted language, which complicate questions of belonging – both culturally and in terms of literary identity. Contrary to most contemporary debates on cosmopolitanism, which grapple with postcolonial inequities, Ljunggren points out that the Russian discourse on cosmopolitanism is based rather on a long-standing "inner dichotomy" in Russian culture between an openness towards the west, and a withdrawal into its cultural heartland. During the isolationism of the Soviet era, this produced a powerful conception of an "imaginary West" and of exile as a heroic identity. Today, exile is no longer a central concern for writers like Makine and Shishkin – instead, Ljunggren argues, we are witnessing the emergence of a poetics of transculturalism.

Approaching Russia from the opposite direction – from the outside in – **Mattias Viktorin**'s chapter investigates the emergence, beginning in the late nineteenth century, of a transnational, multilingual corpus of works dealing with the Siberian prison island Sakhalin. This is world-making in an inverted sense: a cosmopolitan literary realm constructing a world out of a highly specific, "remote" location. Although this sub-genre of writing was initiated in Russian by writers such as Tolstoy and Chekhov, it proliferated elsewhere as well – including Britain, Finland, Norway and Sweden – confirming thereby the link between institutions of publishing and the construction of world imaginaries. Using an anthropological approach, Viktorin shows how the notions of exile and prison have merged in the "setting apart" of an existentially extreme world in these works which tend towards a form of fictionalised ethnography. The setting apart results, however, not only in an othering of Siberia, but also in explorations of how the world emerged in and through Siberia.

Helena Bodin's chapter deals similarly with the construction of a specific and secluded world – the harems of Constantinople – by an external gaze, in this instance the Swedish writer Elsa Lindberg-Dovlette. Focusing on the textual mechanics of narration, Bodin shows how the characters' varying access to direct speech and focalisation, as well as the narrative world's degree of connectedness to other worlds can effectively be used to gauge the mode and substance of world-making in specific works of literature. In the case of Lindberg-Dovlette, who was married to a Persian diplomat, the harem becomes narrativised as an exclusively female space, clearly bounded but nonetheless transcultural. The paradox, as Bodin demonstrates, is that the women who belong to a harem are confined to it, separated from the outer world by walls and gates, yet women from the outside could always access the harem. Added to that, the harem as a cultural space in Lindberg-Dovlette's fictions is distinctly hybrid, combining Parisian fashion, European languages and Ottoman traditions. The governesses accessing the harem function in this way as cultural brokers.

The polar opposite of the chronotope of the harem would probably be the western fantasy of the South Sea paradise, a timeless haven replete with promises of leisure and sexual license. **Anette Nyqvist** unpacks this fantasy by way of a very specific case, namely the Swedish traveller Carl-Emil Pettersson, who eventually would serve as inspiration for Pippi Longstocking's father in Astrid Lindgren's famous stories from the 1940s. "Travel" is the operative term in Nyqvist's essay, in several respects: as an activity, as an element in the imaginative making of the world, as the elusive object of a genre of writing, and as the movement of narratives across places, languages and media. The "travelling story" of her title, therefore, refers therefore both to travel writing's capacity to make stories travel, and to the transposition of the figure of Pettersson from factual to fictional discourse, as well as from news media to books and television. In this extended chain of remediation, elements of racism and othering are likewise reproduced but also, eventually, challenged.

This carries over, finally, to **Per Ståhlberg**'s discussion of the differentiated mediation of an "Indian" imaginary in different circuits of literary production and distribution. Two best-selling novels, both of them in English and both published in 2008, are shown here to speak to distinct audiences, producing thereby contrasting conceptions of contemporary India. Following Francesca Orsini's identification of international, national and regional literatures in (or of) India, Ståhlberg shows how Arvind Adiga's Booker Prize-winning *The White Tiger* incorporates a cosmopolitan mode of address in its narrative discourse, directing the story to outsiders, whereas Chetan Bhagat's *The Three Mistakes of My Life* not only directs its discourse to an insider but also cultivates a more congenial and quotidian image of India. The dark pessimism of *The White Tiger* places it a remove from the preferred national image of an upbeat high-tech player in the global economy. However, the neat distinction between national and international falls apart if one considers how *The Three Mistakes* circulates among an

Indian diaspora, and how *The White Tiger* is also read and recognised in India. Ståhlberg confirms in this way how the outcome of the cosmopolitan-vernacular dynamic is hard to predict and never uniform.

Bibliography

Ganguly, Debjani. *This Thing Called the World: The Contemporary Novel as Global Form*. Durham: Duke University Press, 2016.

16. Literary World-Making under Apartheid: *Staffrider* and the Location of Print Culture

Stefan Helgesson
English, Stockholm University

The fields of (literary) postcolonial studies and world literature stand in an uneasy relationship to each other, not least because of their divergent approaches to literary value.[1] If postcolonial scholars endeavour to reevaluate the devalued and bring that which has been marginalised, repressed or silenced to public attention, world literature has focused on that which is *already* valued. By looking at works that have "gained in translation", at processes of international canonisation or at the hierarchy of the "world republic of letters", important contributions to world literary scholarship have had a tautological tendency: they have confirmed what we already know, namely that some centres of publication and reception (Paris, New York, London) are more influential than others

---

[1] For examples of these debates, see Pascale Casanova, "Literature as a World", *New Left Review* 31 (2005): 71–90; Peter Hitchcock, *The Long Space: Transnationalism and Postcolonial Form* (Stanford: Stanford University Press, 2010); Stefan Helgesson, "Postcolonialism and World Literature: Rethinking the Boundaries", *Interventions* 16, no. 4 (2014): 483–500; Aamir Mufti, *Forget English! Orientalisms and World Literatures* (Cambridge: Harvard University Press, 2016); Mads Rosendahl Thomsen, *Mapping World Literature: International Canonization and Translation Literatures* (London: Continuum, 2008).

How to cite this book chapter:
Helgesson, Stefan. "Literary World-Making under Apartheid: *Staffrider* and the Location of Print Culture". In *World Literatures: Exploring the Cosmopolitan-Vernacular Exchange*, edited by Stefan Helgesson, Annika Mörte Alling, Yvonne Lindqvist, and Helena Wulff, 171–184. Stockholm: Stockholm University Press, 2018. DOI: https://doi.org/10.16993/bat.p. License: CC-BY.

(Lagos, Warsaw, Jakarta), and that only the work of a select few writers achieves global prominence.[2]

Understanding the complex ways in which literary value accumulates and is consolidated is no trivial matter. On the contrary, criticism of "the canon" has often downplayed two things. The first is that canonicity is not a voluntaristic matter. One does not dismantle a canon simply by presenting a new list of writers and works that *ought* to be valued. The second is that each critical intervention will in itself count as a bid in the unpredictable, drawn-out construction of canonicity. (And it is, as J. M. Coetzee once observed, not least when under attack that the canonical status of a particular work is confirmed.[3]) Indeed, it makes more sense to tie the question of canonicity to how different interpretive communities each will attach value to certain sets of works – be they Shakespeare's plays, Kendrick Lamar's hiphop lyrics or Sudanese poetry. Such a perspective will show that the conflict has less to do with canonicity per se than with social inequalities between interpretive communities.[4]

The specific problem broached in this chapter, however, has to do with the relevance of the "world" perspective in relation to literary value. Or more to the point: Can the cosmopolitan paradigm of world literature advance our understanding of local, vernacular constructions of literary value? Are there, in other words, productive points of intersection between the concerns of world literature studies and postcolonialism that can advance our understanding of literary world-making? The short answer is yes, although this brief piece can only begin to explain why. My empirical case is the South African literary journal *Staffrider* (especially its March 1979 issue), and my theoretical point of entry is

---

[2] See e. g. David Damrosch, *What Is World Literature?* (Princeton: Princeton University Press, 2003); Pascale Casanova, *La république mondiale des lettres* (Paris: Seuil, 1999).
[3] J. M. Coetzee, "What Is a Classic?", *Current Writing* 5, no. 2 (1993): 20.
[4] For more on critiques – and defences – of canonicity, see John Guillory, *Cultural Capital: The Problem of Literary Canon Formation* (Chicago: Chicago University Press, 1993); Harold Bloom, *The Western Canon: The Books and School of the Ages* (New York: Harcourt Brace, 1994); Thomsen, *Mapping*.

the concept of "world-making". The specific choice of the 1979 issue is abitrary, but my focus on the the early period of *Staffrider* is not, given the journal's experimental editorial practice at the time – as I soon shall explain. The effectiveness of *Staffrider* as a world-making enterprise, often in direct conflict with state power, can, I claim, be attributed to a cultivation of literary value that harnessed formal, linguistic and canonical resources of a wider literary world for local ends. Hence, properly accounting for its significance in the history of South African literature requires that we move beyond its immediate location and moment, and adopt a broader and deeper analytical framework that recognises the relative autonomony of literature as an aspect of its world-making capacity. In its generality, this may seem like a harmless claim, but its interest lies in *how* such a harnessing of resources is done – and also how this may adjust or even challenge the received South African understanding of *Staffrider*'s importance.

First a few words on "world" and "world-making". As Eric Hayot usefully points out, there are two different, even opposed, uses of the term "world" in current world literature scholarship. The first is exemplified by the approaches of Pascale Casanova and Franco Moretti. Here, "'world' refers not to the actual world but to the total enworldedness, or world-constituting force, of a system."[5] The second, by contrast, does in fact invoke the actual world by taking upon itself the duty to expand literary study across linguistic and geographical boundaries. This is, essentially, the approach that has been cultivated by David Damrosch, but also by other scholars such as Anders Pettersson, Gunilla Lindberg-Wada and Alexander Beecroft.[6]

The "world", then, can be an enclosed, self-supporting entity. Or it can denote the ungraspable totality of the actual world – by

---

[5] Eric Hayot, *On Literary Worlds* (Oxford: Oxford University Press, 2012), 31.
[6] Alexander Beecroft, *An Ecology of World Literature* (London: Verso, 2015); Damrosch, *World Literature*; Gunilla Lindberg-Wada, ed., *Literary Genres: An Intercultural Approach* (Berlin: De Gruyter, 2006); Anders Pettersson, ed., *Notions of Literature Across Times and Cultures* (Berlin: De Gruyter, 2006).

which is normally meant the planet Earth and everything that it contains. This conceptual tension between "world" as a part within a bigger whole and "world" as that bigger whole itself must however be understood precisely as a tension between positions on a sliding semantic scale, and not as an absolute difference. This is because the actual world exceeds our conceptual, perceptual and cognitive grasp. The actual world – even if we restrict ourselves to a specific realm such as literature – will always be *more* than an individual consciousness can fathom. It is for that reason that Moretti famously stated that "[r]eading 'more' is always a good thing, but not the solution", and that therefore "world literature is not an object, it's a *problem*".[7] But that is also why the problem needs to be reformulated again and again, lest we otherwise fall back on habit and risk mistaking our partial conception of the world with the actual world.[8]

What happens, then, if we think of "world" and "literature" in terms of *world-making*? The term has previously been elaborated by, among others, Nelson Goodman, Mario Valdés and Pheng Cheah, and it directs our attention to an *activity* rather than something given.[9] The world of world-making is not simply "there", it is in process. It is obviously not the same as the actual world in its entirety, but nor is it exclusively a self-enclosed system. Rather, the world of world-making refers more openly to

---

[7] Franco Moretti, "Conjectures on World Literature", *New Left Review* 1 (2000): 55.

[8] A striking historical instance of a deliberately partial yet planet-wide world-conception would be "the Third World", coined first in French as *le tiers monde* in the 1950s, and then gaining currency in the 1960s phase of decolonisation – specifically as a contrast to the binary world-conception of the Cold War.

[9] Nelson Goodman, *Ways of Worldmaking* (Indianapolis: Hackett, 1978); Mario J. Valdés, *World-Making: The Literary Truth-Claim and the Interpretation of Texts* (Toronto: Toronto University Press, 1992); Pheng Cheah, *What Is a World? Postcolonial Literature and World Literature* (Durham: Duke University Press, 2016). See also Nathalie Karagiannis and Peter Wagner, eds., *Varieties of World-Making* (Cambridge: Cambridge University Press, 2007) and Vera Nünning, Ansgar Nünning and Birgit Neumann, eds., *Cultural Ways of Worldmaking: Media and Narrative* (Berlin: De Gruyter, 2010).

the domain of human activity and to the world as a relational modality.

One way to make sense of this is to introduce a threefold distinction between *planet, globe* and *world*. The planet, as Gayatri Spivak once wrote, is "in the species of alterity, belonging to another system".[10] It exceeds the human realm. The globe, by contrast, is an abstraction that conceives of the planet Earth according to the needs and protocols of – in particular – finance capital, thereby imposing the same system of exchange everywhere. As Spivak puts it, "[n]o one lives there".[11] The world, finally, is a term that could be reserved precisely for the human domain. Here we may draw on Hannah Arendt, who used the world-concept to denote that which humans construct as a common, public world:

> the term "public" signifies the world itself, in so far as it is common to all of us and distinguished from our privately owned place in it. This world, however, is not identical with the earth or with nature, as the limited space for the movement of men and the general condition of organic life. It is related, rather, to the human artifact, the fabrication of human hands, as well as to affairs which go on among those who inhabit the man-made world together. To live together in the world means essentially that a world of things is between those who have it in common, as a table is located between those who sit around it; the world, like every in-between, relates and separates men at the same time.[12]

But besides its public, in-between nature, the world in this sense also has a privileged relationship with time. In Arendt's understanding, it bestows "a measure of permanence and durability upon the futility of mortal life and the fleeting character of human time".[13] This is the understanding that has been developed in particular by Pheng Cheah, for whom "world" is a temporal rather than spatial category: "[a] world only is and we are only worldly

---

[10] Gayatri Spivak, *Death of a Discipline* (New York: Columbia University Press, 2003), 72.
[11] Spivak, *Discipline*, 72.
[12] Hannah Arendt, *The Human Condition* (Chicago: University of Chicago Press, 1958 [1998]), 52.
[13] Arendt, *Human Condition*, 8.

beings if there is already time. The unity and permanence of a world are thus premised on the persistence of time."[14] If we read Cheah and Arendt together, it becomes evident that "world" – in this sense – is completely dependent on the collective, diachronic activity of humans. No individual can make a world alone, but no world will exist and persist without a succession of individual makers and collaboration between them.

Literature is from that point of view a particular and peculiar instance of world-making. Thanks to their durability and withdrawal from sheer utility, Arendt sees works of art as being "the most intensely worldly of all tangible things".[15] Yet literature, understood as verbal art, is a strangely intangible art form. Or rather, its tangibility – as print, script or as soundwaves – could be seen merely as the enabler of intangible semantic and affective qualities of language. *Language* is nonetheless one of the strongest and most pervasive instruments of human world-making. Language is always "in-between". It is never private or individual, but exists only through a community of speakers. Language (understood as a set of specific semiotic practices) is also much more durable than the individual: it is there before the individual is born and will – normally – persist long after the death of the individual speaker. Literature can thereby be seen as harnessing the world-making force of language by creating – to use Hayot's term – an "aesthetic world".[16]

Such an aesthetic world is, self-evidently, not the same as the world in the sense of the unfathomable totality of everything. An aesthetic world forms part of the human world in Arendt's sense, and is – in so far as we are speaking of literature – bound to the particular language or combination of languages in which it is composed and, more pointedly, to the medium through which it is presented. This importance of language and medium is in fact ignored by Cheah and Hayot alike, and yet it is central to understanding the world-making capacity (and limitations) of literature. When Hayot observes that worldedness "emerges as the unconscious of the work, as the establishing rules that constitute

---

[14] Cheah, *What Is a World?*, 2.
[15] Arendt, *Human Condition*, 167.
[16] Hayot, *Literary Worlds*, 54.

the work as a whole", I would therefore add that language and medium are among the most fundamental aspects of that unconscious.[17] As such, they have a formative impact on literature's worldledness that far exceeds momentary political exigencies.

To test this claim, let us look a bit closer at our case in point, *Staffrider*. Launched in 1978, *Staffrider* represented a new departure for South African literary culture. It is most famous for its "populist" ethos, eschewing not only "elite" standards of literary taste but also true and tried editorial practices – in its early years, the magazine devolved editorial responsibility for selection on community-based writers' groups. It would keep appearing until 1996, but it was most innovative in its first ten years, making a mark on South African literature that few, if any, other journals have made. It "both challenged and transformed the social image and meaning of literature in South Africa", in the wording of an early assessment by Michael Vaughan.[18] David Maughan-Brown would later add that it had been particularly successful "in shaking up literary critical assumptions and expectations and putting important theoretical issues, such as the relationship between individual authorship and community cultural production, firmly on the South African cultural agenda".[19]

If this interventionist populism – which was also roundly criticised from both liberal and Marxist vantage points – hints at *Staffrider*'s importance, it is just as crucial to recognise that it did not just spring up organically like a tree from the ground. The world-making force of *Staffrider* had structural, cultural and political preconditions. It was published by Ravan Press, the flagship radical publisher in South Africa in the 1970s, supported in part by external donors.[20] The magazine emerged on the back of intensified political mobilisation against the apartheid state, especially following the Soweto uprising in 1976. Above all, it

---

[17] Hayot, *Literary Worlds*, 54.
[18] Michael Vaughan, "Literature and Populism in South Africa: Reflections on the Ideology of *Staffrider*", in Georg M. Gugelberger, ed., *Marxism and African Literature* (London: James Currey, 1985), 195.
[19] David Maughan-Brown, "The Anthology as Reliquary?", *Current Writing* 1, no.1 (1989): 3.
[20] Peter D. McDonald, *The Literature Police: Apartheid Censorship and Its Cultural Consequences* (Oxford: Oxford University Press, 2009), 135.

published work by "community" writers side by side with a vast array of already established writers and critics such as Miriam Tlali, Es'kia Mphahlele, Nadine Gordimer, J. M. Coetzee, Njabulo Ndebele, Mtutuzeli Matshoba, Peter Wilhelm and Richard Rive. In so far as "politics" and "literature" can be regarded as distinct from each other, *Staffrider*'s effectiveness derived in no small degree from viewing literature and the aesthetic not in isolation from, but as situated *within* a heavily politicised and repressive context. As its founding editor Mike Kirkwood would write retrospectively about the early years:

> The oddest thing about *Staffrider* was always this: that it was a *literary* magazine. Yet it was. Of course, one could turn this statement around and say that the odd thing about most of its contributors was that they were *writers*. Yet they were. It happened, at that time in South Africa, that literature became overburdened with a number of other social and political functions. While only a narrow view of literature would exclude these functions from among those literature can perform, it is true that existing literary forms must undergo a considerable development before they begin to be adequate to these "new" functions [...]. By the same token, it happened that an unusual number of people found they could best participate in the making of new society, or best pursue their more personal aspirations, by *writing*.[21]

Kirkwood's point is borne out if we look closer at our chosen example, the March 1979 issue (which also happened to be one of the issues that were banned by the authorities). What we find here, organised in characteristically unhierarchical fashion, is a substantial collection of poems, short stories, reviews and drawings, plus a hands-on "workshop" piece by Es'kia Mphahlele on the craft of writing short stories. The cover image sports a fantasy creature, half-bird, half-human, ready to take flight, whereas the drawings inside the magazine almost all depict individuals – mostly faces – in bare or unspecified environments.

---

[21] Mike Kirkwood, "Remembering *Staffrider*", in *Ten Years of* Staffrider, ed. Andries Oliphant and Ivan Vladislavić, *Staffrider* 7, no. 3–4 (1988): 3.

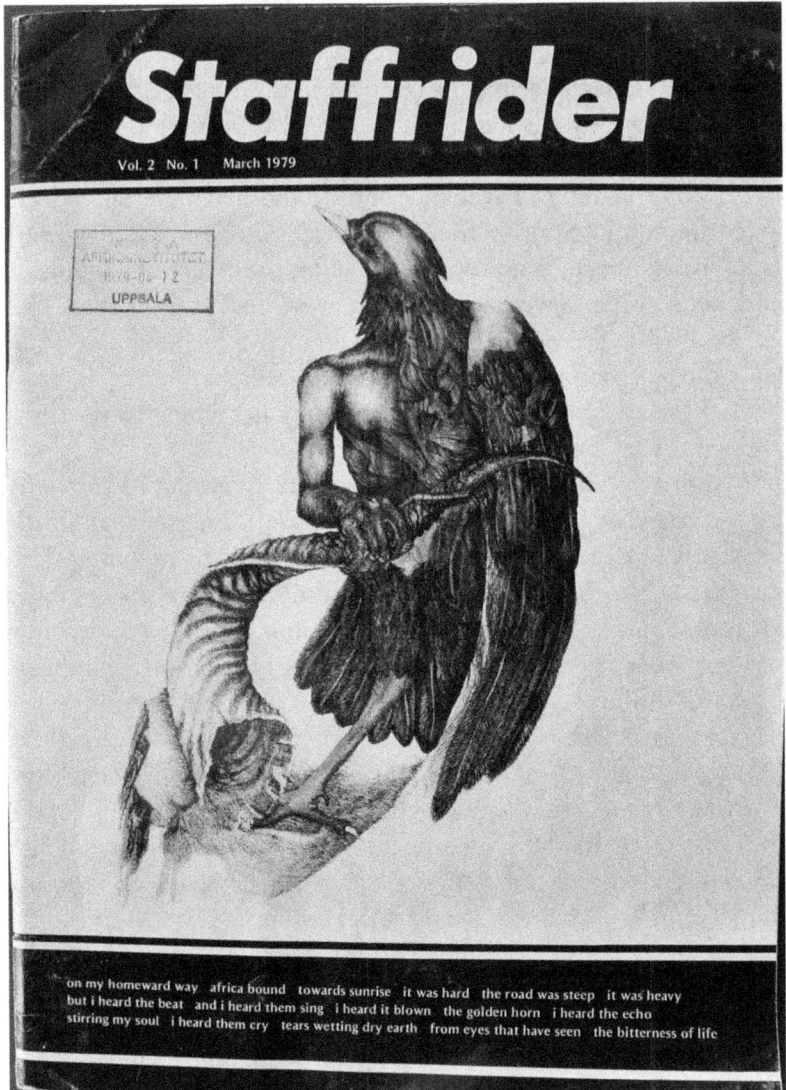

Figure 2. Cover from *Staffrider* 1, 1979. Artist: Harry Moyaga. Copyright: Unknown. License: CC BY. Repeated but unsuccessful attempts have been made to identify and contact the copyright holder. If the rights holder contacts the author, this situation will be rectified. Image taken by Stefan Helgesson.

The content of this *Staffrider* issue is in other words almost exclusively literary and aesthetic. Its 60 pages contain no commercial advertising (a striking contrast to the South African 1950s journal *Drum*, for instance) but is instead filled with the work of both established and emergent writers. Most sections are organised according to the provenance of the published material. Indeed, an entire map of South Africa is sketched out as work by writers from Rustenburg, Kimberley, Katlehong, Soweto, Sharpeville, Sebokeng, Cape Town, and so on, is presented on the pages. This is, notably, an *alternative* map of the country which highlights not least the townships created by apartheid policies, rather than the official "white" geography of the country (to which Cape Town and Kimberley belonged).

A similarly discrepant sense of locality is produced not only by the frequent inclusion of words marked as vernacular in the English-language texts, but also by a number of poems in languages such as Sotho, Xhosa and Zulu. With English being by far the dominant language in the journal, it is notable how often writers incorporate especially Afrikaans terms ("nie-blankes", "baas", "skollies", "knobkieries") – often precisely to confirm the negative association of Afrikaans with state power at this time. Phrases in African languages occur more commonly in the poetry, as in Magoleng wa Selepe's well known "My Name". Here, the meaning of the name Nomgqibelo Ncamisile Mnqhibisa is both the point of the entire poem – "Look what they have done to my name [...] to this man it is trash [...] I end up being / Maria ..." – and at the same time withheld from readers who don't know an Nguni language (Xhosa or Zulu).[22]

This is arguably the point at which something we might call "strategic vernacularism" is most effectively deployed in this issue of *Staffrider*. If the frequent invocation of place names, township settings and demotic registers of language all contribute to creating irreducibly local bonds between the magazine and its South

---

[22] *Staffrider* 1 (1979), 7. The name is in Xhosa. "Nomgqibelo" bears reference to "Saturday", and "Ncamisile" means "kissed". "Mnqhibisa" is apparently just a surname with no particular meaning. Heartfelt thanks for Uhuru Phalafala for her help in deciphering the words.

African readers, Selepe's poem exploits this multilingual ethos in such a way as to highlight a *rift between worlds*. It rejects, effectively, the world-making force of the English language – at least on the terms of "white" power – and endorses instead the resonance and temporal depth of not just the Xhosa name but of the entire Xhosa world that it metonymically invokes.

But rather than simply reaffirming the vernacular tendency in *Staffrider*, what needs to be foregrounded here is how this vernacularism derives much of its force from the journal's cultivation of a *literary* ethos that is not reducible to locality or to a supposedly national culture, but is a mode of cosmopolitanism in its own right. In Mphahlele's guide to writing short stories, he presents a long list of writers whom he regards as indispensable models for the budding writer. Among these can be noted Ernest Hemingway, Richard Wright, Anton Chekhov, Nikolai Gogol, James Joyce, Ama Ata Aidoo, Chinua Achebe, Luís Bernardo Honwana, Nadine Gordimer and Can Themba.[23] Similarly, in a review of a new edition of Sol Plaatje's classic novel *Mhudi*, the critic Mshengu reads it in relation to, among other things, Chinua Achebe's novel *Things Fall Apart* and Modikwe Dikobe's *The Marabi Dance*.[24] In the poetry, imaginary geographies consisting particularly of Africa/Afrika, but also of Mecca, India, Holland, Vietnam, Cuba and Australia – the latter in an allusion to the Nobel Prize-winning author Patrick White – are established.[25]

These examples alone indicate that the local literary value of *Staffrider* is in no way isolated from a wider world, either in a literary or a geographical sense. Its mode of address and means of production and distribution are pressured by the exigencies of its time and place; its economic base is partly derived from international support; its symbolic, intellectual and formal resources are drawn from a historical and cosmopolitan repository of genres, names, styles and narrative techniques that could be defined as a "world" of literature with its own, inconsistently distributed affordances. If we look at what enables *Staffrider*'s existence on

---

[23] *Staffrider* 1 (1979), 50.
[24] *Staffrider* 1 (1979), 55.
[25] *Staffrider* 1 (1979), 48, 49.

even more fundamental levels – such as the reliance on English as a vehicular language, the print medium, the use of the Latin alphabet, the generic conventions of lyric poetry and the short story – it becomes evident how it is entangled in a *longue durée* of literary and literate culture that derives from no single place, but has been formed historically across centuries and is implicated transnationally in the politics of its Cold War moment. In this way, *Staffrider*'s contribution to making the world differently in the late-apartheid temporality of crisis is itself made possible by longer, and deeply ambiguous, histories of world-making.

To conclude, *Staffrider* presents us with a strong instance of the construction of local literary value under adverse circumstances. With respect to an Arendtian understanding of "world" as that which is constructed collectively by humans, it contributed to *alternative* forms of world-making that interlocked with the world-destroying forces of racialised state power at the time. This was done, however, by cultivating a dialectic between the intensely local and expansively cosmopolitan dimensions of literature, the impact of which was attributable to the convergence of national anti-apartheid activism, alternative publishing structures and a coalition of widely but differentially networked writers and editors. This allowed the magazine to work in canonical and non-canonical registers at one and the same time – or rather, it causes us to question the explanatory value of opposing the canonical and non-canonical, as has been common in critical commentary on *Staffrider*. It is in this respect that the concept of "world-making" provides another way of accounting for its location in the cosmopolitan-vernacular nexus. The vernacular figure of the "staffrider" clinging illegally on trains, a "*skelm* of sorts" moving between worlds, therfore turns out to be an apt metaphor for its world-literary positioning as well.[26]

---

[26] *Staffrider* 1 (1978), 2.

Bibliography

Arendt, Hannah. *The Human Condition*. 1958. Chicago: University of Chicago Press, 1998.

Beecroft, Alexander. *An Ecology of World Literature*. London: Verso, 2015.

Bloom, Harold. *The Western Canon: The Books and School of the Ages*. New York: Harcourt Brace, 1994.

Casanova, Pascale. *La république mondiale des lettres*. Paris: Seuil, 1999.

———. "Literature as a World". *New Left Review* 31 (2005): 71–90.

Cheah, Pheng. *What Is a World? Postcolonial Literature and World Literature*. Durham: Duke University Press, 2016.

Coetzee, J. M. "What Is a Classic?". *Current Writing* 5, no. 2 (1993): 7–24.

Damrosch, David. *What Is World Literature?* Princeton: Princeton University Press, 2003.

Goodman, Nelson. *Ways of Worldmaking*. Indianapolis: Hackett, 1978.

Guillory, John. *Cultural Capital: The Problem of Literary Canon Formation*. Chicago: Chicago University Press, 1993.

Hayot, Eric. *On Literary Worlds*. Oxford: Oxford University Press, 2012.

Helgesson, Stefan. "Postcolonialism and World Literature: Rethinking the Boundaries". *Interventions* 16, no. 4 (2014): 483–500.

Hitchcock, Peter. *The Long Space: Transnationalism and Postcolonial Form*. Stanford: Stanford University Press, 2010.

Karagiannis, Nathalie and Peter Wagner, eds. *Varieties of World-Making*. Cambridge: Cambridge University Press, 2007.

Kirkwood, Mike. "Remembering *Staffrider*". In *Ten Years of* Staffrider, edited by Andries Oliphant and Ivan Vladislavić, *Staffrider* 7, no. 3–4 (1988): 1–9.

Lindberg-Wada, Gunilla, ed. *Literary Genres: An Intercultural Approach*. Berlin: De Gruyter, 2006.

Maughan-Brown, David. "The Anthology as Reliquary?". *Current Writing* 1, no.1 (1989): 3–21.

McDonald, Peter D. *The Literature Police: Apartheid Censorship and Its Cultural Consequences*. Oxford: Oxford University Press, 2009.

Moretti, Franco. "Conjectures on World Literature". *New Left Review* 1 (2000): 54–68.

Mufti, Aamir R. *Forget English! Orientalisms and World Literatures*. Cambridge: Harvard University Press, 2016.

Nünning, Vera, Ansgar Nünning and Birgit Neumann, eds. *Cultural Ways of Worldmaking: Media and Narrative*. Berlin: De Gruyter, 2010.

Pettersson, Anders, ed. *Notions of Literature Across Times and Cultures*. Berlin: De Gruyter, 2006.

Spivak, Gayatri Chakravorty. *Death of a Discipline*. New York: Columbia University Press, 2003.

Staffrider 1 (1978).

Staffrider 1 (1979).

Thomsen, Mads Rosendahl. *Mapping World Literature: International Canonization and Transnational Literatures*. London: Continuum, 2008.

Valdés, Mario J. *World-Making: The Literary Truth-Claim and the Interpretation of Texts*. Toronto: Toronto University Press, 1992.

Vaughan, Michael. "Literature and Populism in South Africa: Reflections on the Ideology of *Staffrider*". In *Marxism and African Literature*, edited by Georg M. Gugelberger, 195–220. London: James Currey, 1985.

17. Documentary Modernism: Worldly Sympathies, Ideal Collectivities and Dissenting Individualism

Irina Rasmussen
English, Stockholm University

An important intellectual debate in modernism concerns the uneasy coexistence of cosmopolitan and nationalist orientations toward the world. From the rise of nationalism in the nineteenth century, attempts to reconcile cosmopolitanism and nationalism, which can be considered as two contending "vehicles of universalism",[1] pre-conditioned the cultures of modernity to future neuroses, like a primal scene. The resurgence of cosmopolitanism in the early twenty-first century – when the concept is invoked in relation to economic globalisation and in discussions about world literature understood to foster a desire for universal justice – might suggest that cosmopolitanism has always been a reaction against nationalism and a symptom of the nation-state's weakening. Perhaps surprisingly, historical analysis suggests otherwise: Nationalism is a more recent phenomenon than cosmopolitanism and a relatively late contender in the arena of world politics.

---

[1] Pheng Cheah, "Introduction Part II: The Cosmopolitical Today", in *Cosmopolitics: Thinking and Feeling Beyond the Nation*, ed. Pheng Cheah and Bruce Robbins (London: University of Minnesota Press, 1998), 22.

How to cite this book chapter:
Rasmussen, Irina. "Documentary Modernism: Worldly Sympathies, Ideal Collectivities and Dissenting Individualism". In *World Literatures: Exploring the Cosmopolitan-Vernacular Exchange*, edited by Stefan Helgesson, Annika Mörte Alling, Yvonne Lindqvist, and Helena Wulff, 185–198. Stockholm: Stockholm University Press, 2018. DOI: https://doi.org/10.16993/bat.q. License: CC-BY.

Pheng Cheah questions the view that cosmopolitanism emerged as a response to nationalism, arguing that in actuality modern subjects were cosmopolitans before they became nationals. He points out that cosmopolitanism was "a central concept of the eighteenth-century French philosophies"; the term was derived from "the Greek words for 'world' and 'citizen', by way of the *espirit cosmopolite* of Renaissance humanism", and it came to designate "an intellectual ethics, a universal humanism that transcends regional particularism".[2] In other words, before cosmopolitanism reconstituted itself as a challenge to nationalism in the age of nation-states, it was used in opposition to various regionalisms and related identitarian tendencies to categorise peoples "territorially, culturally, linguistically, or even racially".[3] So, the relationship between cosmopolitanism and its contenders, whether conflicting or complementary, was always significant in terms of its influence on the concurrent mappings of the world dynamics.

The emergence of a fully articulated "doctrine of nationalism"[4] in the age of nation-states transforms cosmopolitanism more specifically into an ideological counterweight to *exclusionary* nationalism and discourses of cultural superiority that promote, overtly or indirectly, colonialism, imperialism and regionalism. To illuminate these two competing ideological conceptions of the world in modernity, I suggest approaching the nexus of cosmopolitanism and nationalism as it is actualised in a range of aesthetic documentary projects from the 1920s and 30s. I argue that these highly designed documentary modernist projects implement cosmopolitan practices of collection, assemblage and reportage in order to remap the world in formations conductive to universal social justice. My intention is, first, to show how the modernist production of cosmopolitan value in aestheticised documentary cultural forms energises the sociopolitical imaginary of the period and, secondly, to suggest how aesthetic modernisms' response to the cosmopolitics of the interwar period anticipates contemporary

---

[2] Cheah, "Introduction", 22.
[3] Cheah, "Introduction", 22.
[4] Cheah, "Introduction", 22.

debates in the early twenty-first century about globalisation and world literature.

Cosmopolitan practices

Competing national and global outlooks distinguish the decidedly collaborative modernist projects of the 1920s and '30s I am bringing together under the rubric of *documentary modernism* in order to foreground the complementary aesthetic and political qualities of imaginative, creative documentarian works. Focusing on three kinds of projects – an anthology, a photographic reportage, and a scrapbook historiography – helps to clarify how documentary modernism negotiates between the rock of nationalism and the whirlpool of cosmopolitanism. By attending to how each project transcends generic and political borders, we can better understand documentary modernism in terms of its cosmopolitan value and its methods of collaborating and curating vernacular expressions as practised globalism.

Documentary modernist projects often emerged from the artistic networks established around little magazines and small presses. Writers, editors, translators, activists and public intellectuals in the interwar period turned to a novel kind of collaborative network practice. They made a concerted effort to collect artefactual materials that recorded local realities and contributed to a more nuanced understanding of the diverse process of modernisation. These efforts resulted in diverse works of documentary modernism – generic forms that included literary and ethnographic anthologies, photographic and cinematic reportages and other forms of social and historiographic undertakings – all of which experimented with assemblage and developed aesthetic practices of recording life and social history. Importantly, these collaborative acts of critical making constituted themselves as a creative, intellectual and socially conscious genre. The participants' disciplinary backgrounds varied significantly, as did their agendas and the media they worked in to achieve their aims. These projects, however different in subject, form and impact, nevertheless, developed a distinct approach to documenting world events: they strategically reappraised geopolitics, remapped the centre-and-periphery dynamics and re-interpreted cultural geographies, typically in novel ways. In the process, they forged innovative genealogies of a dynamic world of culture. All of these projects raised questions about how best to strike a balance between global and national citizenship while addressing, fairly and justly, the asymmetrical distribution of material, cultural and political resources within hegemonic socioeconomic formations.

Because documentary modernism encompasses a great diversity of forms and materials, it is impossible to present a comprehensive analysis of this creative genre. Therefore, I will be focusing on three distinct documentary compilations with artistic and historiographic aims. These documentary modernist projects include: an interventionist anthology (Nancy Cunard's *Negro*), a scrapbook project of vernacular historiography (L. S. Gumby's *Harlem Scrapbooks*) and a narrativised photographic reportage (James Agee and Walker Evans's *Let Us Now Praise Famous Men*). A close analysis of each reveals that the task of curating art and social history by assemblage allowed the authors of these projects to move conceptually and imaginatively in multiple directions simultaneously. While they shared interventionist objectives, the unique materials of each project generate specific critical, aesthetic and curating practices and shape particular kinds of global cosmopolitanism.

The notion of national belonging is opened to revision in multiple ways in Nancy Cunard's monumental, 855-page-long anthology of black cultural achievements, *Negro: An Anthology* (1934). *Negro* was compiled internationally, by contributors from multiple geographical locations around the world, whose efforts exemplify a collective modernist effort to forge a world-cultural perspective. One example of *Negro*'s achievement is its multiple entries on world music and dance, written by critics, historians, and musician, that show how careful consideration of black artists and performers' contributions alters the landscapes of existing forms. George Antheil's essay, "The Negro on the Spiritual, or A Method of Negro Music", for instance, charts contemporary musical styles through complex pathways of African diasporas. Antheil argues that black music "survived and built up an incredible machinery" that shaped not only contemporary jazz but also fire-ritual dances on the islands off the coast of the American South, work-songs, children songs and the spirituals. He notes the influence of black music in the way "The *Rumba* of Cuba and the *Beguine* of Martinique, although Spanish in dress, have Negro hearts and certainly nothing but Negro bodies".[5] By locating influential sources for syncopation, jazz and dance in multiple locations, Antheil's genealogy avoids the trap of promoting an expressive logic of cultural analysis. That is, his account discourages efforts to link cultural expressions to a singular place of origins. Instead, Antheil draws attention to the way in which cultural expressions travel and transform, and in doing so, he effectively remaps the geocultural vectors of classical music, jazz and modern dance.

Working with different kinds of records, Alexander Gumby's *Harlem Scrapbooks*[6] compiles local materials about the impact of the Harlem Renaissance within the neighbourhood of Harlem and the city of New York, while recording the movement's global imaginary and its national and worldwide influence and appeal. By blending cultural historiography and sentimental history, Gumby's project develops a crossover form of vernacular historiography that defies generic categorisation, straddling the varied fields of artistic and intellectual production as well as social and personal histories. For instance, Scrapbook 43, "Langston Hughes: Poet, author and play-writer", the volume in Gumby's collection that documents Hughes's literary career, opens with early reviews of his poetry, the 1926 full publication of Hughes's *The Weary Blues* in *Poetry: A Magazine of Verse*, edited by H. Monroe (vol. XXIX, Nov. 1926, Number 11), and individually published poems from that award-winning collection in *Palm* (October 1926), *The Crisis* (March 1925), *Opportunity* (May 1925 and October 1926) and *The Nation* (February 16, 1927),

---

[5] Nancy Cunard, *Negro: An Anthology*, edited and abridged, with an introduction by Hugh Ford (New York: Frederick Ungar Publishing, 1970), 215.

[6] The scrapbooks are archived as: *Alexander Gumby Collection of Negroiana*, [ca. 1800]–1981, in Rare Book & Manuscript Library Collection, at Butler Library, Columbia University.

to mention a few. These are interspersed with pages of newspaper reviews of Hughes' poetry and plays, photos of Hughes's public readings in Harlem, alongside with journal articles and news columns by Hughes. This assembled news flow is interrupted midway through the scrapbook with a personal memento on a verso page, a photograph of the poet with an inscription to Gumby: "Sincerely is so commonplace – Langston".[7] Hughes's ironic coupling of "commonplace" with "sincerely" creates an intimate break, which perhaps amused Gumby in the way Hughes' inscription signalled the poet's veiled recognition of Gumby's own sincerity as a collector of the commonplace. Gumby's blending of vernacular and public forms of expression fits his purpose to create an archive of the *unwritten history*, of black experience mostly in Harlem, New York City. Effectively, the project's scope and the multi-dimensionality of its records transform the scrapbook format, which might appear to be idiosyncratic, into a curatorial project with clear political, conservationist and aesthetic implications that need foregrounding.

While Cunard's and Gumby's undertakings can be seen as actualising modernism's global reach and outlook, James Agee and Walker Evans's coverage of the Depression-era American South in *Let Us Now Praise Famous Men* (1936; 1941) exemplifies the global imaginary of a localist modernism.[8] Composed as a crossover, creative, non-fictional and photographic reportage of Depression-era America, this collaboration between Agee, a writer known for his literary work, journalism and film criticism, and Evans, a photographer known for developing an influential modernist style of documentary photography, experiments with a new kind of social writing by combining elegiac narrative with vernacular photography. Set in Alabama, the reporting follows

---

[7] *Alexander Gumby Collection of Negroina, [ca. 1800]–1981.* MS #0527. CMI Box 71. "Scrapbook 43: Langston Hughes: Poet, author and playwriter (1 volume)". Rare Book and Manuscript Library, Butler Library, Columbia University.

[8] See Eric White's discussion of localist modernism as guided by the slogan that "The Locality Is the Only Universal", in his *Transatlantic Avant-Gardes: Little Magazines and Localist Modernism* (Edinburgh: Edinburgh UP, 213), 9–14.

families of tenant cotton-farmers and traces their symbolic attachments to and dependence on the land and cotton-picking. It highlights the social plight and abject poverty of the cotton-farmers by broadening the perspective to rural living around the globe. By presenting rural existence agonistically as a world of both beauty and suffering, the reportage approximates in language and image the capacity the tenants' existence has for asserting and obviating the beauty of the world simultaneously. Rather than treating farming in the Heideggerian terms of "turn[ing] the earth into the world",[9] Agee and Evans's reporting elicits the logic the Kantian amphiboly.[10] It reveals the grandeur and the "grand deception of phenomena", capturing the attraction of things while illuminating "an obstruction to the apprehension of things in themselves".[11] In short, finding beauty within a harsh world the reporters struggle to apprehend, these modernist documentarians continuously attune themselves and their method to the material conditions of terrible rural poverty. Agee and Evans' medium of modernist reporting exemplifies the world-making potential of modernist form to redress local injustices in global terms.

Documentary modernism and world literature

Aesthetically, critics have described the crossovers between literary modernisms and the 1930s' documentary forms as conveying

---

[9] Emily Apter, *Against World Literature: On the Politics of Untranslatability* (London: Verso, 2013), 19.
[10] While semantically the word "amphiboly", which means encompassing two opposite meanings at once, is close to "equivocation" and "ambiguity", etymologically, originating in Greek, the word's association with "something about language's very essence" in Aristotle's writings has evolved into "a theory of equivocal symptoms in language" (Apter 25). Another "troubling aspect of amphiboly" is that it produces the "effect of intelligibility within nonsense" and "makes an error of meaning acceptable even as it arouses conscious suspicion of something off-kilter or terribly wrong in language" (Apter 26).
[11] Apter 26. Apter refers to Kant's discussion of the constraints of language and its instability on our immediate experience of the sensible, that is, "our ignorance of the conditions proper to the sensible" in his *The Amphiboly of Concepts of Reflection* (Apter 26).

an aesthetics of interruption in their sharp redrawing of boundaries between literary and propagandistic forms. While Jeff Allred's *American Modernism and Depression Documentary* (2009), a study of the Depression-era documentary photo-texts, represents the consolidation of the modernist documentary as a response to the Great Depression, Allred concludes that, in institutional terms, collecting and assemblage as aesthetic practices led to the institutionalisation of modernism and neutralisation of its interventionist aims.[12] Even Jeremy Braddock's *Collecting as Modernist Practice*, a study of the complex intersection between aesthetic and collecting practices such as "archiving, ethnography, museum display, [and] anthologization",[13] concludes that modernist collection acted towards the end of the period only "as a provisional institution".[14] Emphasising how "canon-defining anthologies"[15] and "the increased authority of the Museum of Modern Art (est. 1929)" emerged as the sanctifying mode of collection, Braddock contrasts that mode with socially interventionist modes of collecting, arguing that the latter "could no longer serve as the basis for the institutionalisation of modernism (provisional or otherwise)".[16]

In response to such studies, the question I want to pose is: What if we extend out critical outlook beyond the frameworks of institutionalisation? Doing so, I argue, enables us to better appreciate the impressive scope and scale of documentary modernism. This socially conscious genre reaches out to the future, aesthetically, by melding social and aesthetic aims, and does so conceptually, by initiating debates that continue today in world-literature studies about literary cosmopolitics and also in the new modernist studies about the institutionalised narrative of modernism. What links documentary modernism to these contemporary discourses are:

---

[12] Jeff Allred, *American Modernism and Depression Documentary* (Oxford: Oxford University Press, 2009).

[13] Jeremy Braddock, *Collecting as Modernist Practice* (Baltimore: Johns Hopkins University Press, 2013), 2.

[14] Braddock 27.

[15] Braddock 2.

[16] Braddock 212.

(1) a shared cosmopolitan drive to establish a world-historical, global perspective; and (2) an effort to develop alternative kinds of institutionalising practices that combine cosmopolitics with emancipatory critical practices. The projects' interventionist aim of remedying the asymmetric relations among cultures motivates their crossing of real, medial and symbolic divides. In contrast with institutionalised accounts of modernism in terms of a relatively definitive canon and narratives suggesting that aesthetic modernism is disconnected from social concerns (which became dominant in the 1950s and required excision and homogenisation), this study argues that documentary modernism combines aesthetic and social concerns to produce a socially engaged aesthetics that imagines art as a form of social agency in the wider world.

The critical script of institutionalised modernism also risks obscuring how these modernist works travel geographically and culturally, how they reach broader audiences and how they attempt to create a new cultural platform in opposition to the hierarchical division of the world into spheres of influence. In the 1930s, proponents of realism and defenders of artistic modernism debated about the merits of Expressionism. One of the key issues concerned how far artistic and cultural artefacts could circulate within social groups given the constraints imposed by their tone and content. In Georg Lukács's response to Ernst Bloch, who defended Expressionism's practice of drawing on folk art and ordinary people's experiences, Lukács countered that artistic strength could only be measured by the benchmarks of cultural heritage:

> [T]he cultural heritage has a living relationship to the real life of the people ... it is characterised by a dynamic, progressive movement in which the active forces of popular tradition ... are buoyed up, preserved, transcended and further developed. For a writer to possess a living relationship to the cultural heritage means being a son of the people.[17]

---

[17] Georg Lukács, "Realism in the Balance", in *Aesthetics and Politics* (London: Verso, 2007), 54.

For Lukács, the true folk component in art was found in its alignment with and continuation of national art, which was irreconcilable with lower-order sensibilities such as drawing on the doodles "of children and prisoners, on the disturbing works of the mentally sick, and on primitive art":[18]

> Popular art does not imply an ideologically indiscriminate, "arty" appreciation of "primitive" products of connoisseurs. Truly popular art has nothing in common with any of that. For if it did, any swank who collects stained glass or negro sculpture, any snob who celebrates insanity as the emancipation of mankind from the fetters of the mechanistic mind, could claim to be a champion of popular art.[19]

He concludes that the efforts to "collect old folk products indiscriminately" ultimately appeal to what he calls "[r]etrograde traditionalism, such as regional art" and thus fall short of the real aim he posits for modern art, namely, the intertwined political and aesthetic project of creating works that "grow out of the life and history of their people … [as] an organic product of the development of their nation".[20]

Opposing national consciousness that unifies the imaginary to regionalism that fragments the totality, Lukács dismisses modernism's assembling practices as attempts to heap "lifeless objects in which one can rummage around at will, picking out whatever one happens to need at the moment",[21] a practice, in his view, completely detrimental to the development of a properly historical consciousness. Lukács's model of historical understanding differs significantly from Walter Benjamin's valorisation of assemblage as the kind of historiography that opens the opportunity to counteract triumphalist narratives of modernity, progress and civilisation.[22] Benjamin conceives of individual, found objects as

---

[18] Lukács 54.
[19] Lukács 53.
[20] Lukács 53–54.
[21] Lukács 54.
[22] Quoting Hegel's redefinition of historical analysis as, "Seek for food and clothing first; then shall the Kingdom of God be granted to you", Benjamin envisions a historical materialist analysis as focused on "the

arbitrators between the past and the future because to a historiographer of the vernacular they exist simultaneously within multiple temporalities.

Most significantly, in contrast to homogenising histories, assemblages function as material manifestations of multiple histories and cultural geographies and can be understood as forms of "dispossessive collectivism", a term that informs Bruce Robbins's and Emily Apter's understanding of world-literary forms.[23] The aesthetic expression informed by dispossessive collectivism stands in contrast to an aesthetic stance that promotes our "self-interest" and sense of cultural ownership.[24] And, significantly for my analysis of the cosmopolitanism-nationalism bind of modernism, the critical project of imagining "a dispossessive ethics of reading", which sensitises us to the notion that the world is really "an unownable estate",[25] promotes the sensibility akin to the modernist documentarians who resist the idea that art belongs nationally.

The materiality of assemblages facilitates a closer look, firstly, into what function these artistic practices assign to the arts and, secondly, into what models of history, culture and the world emerge through the curatorial practices of blending art, ethnography, history, journalism and cultural geography. An aesthetic and cultural sensibility they share is the possibility of folding multiple

---

crude and material things without which no refined and spiritual things could exist"; his is a historiography that draws not on "a vision of spoils that fall to the victor" but on past existence that resonates with the present "as confidence, courage, humour, cunning, and fortitude"; see Walter Benjamin, "On the Concept of History", in *Selected Writings*, vol. 4, 1938–1940, trans. E. Jephcott et al., ed. H. Eiland and M. W. Jennings (London: The Belknap Press of Harvard University Press, 2003), 390.

[23] Apter 329. Emily Apter discusses forms of dispossessive collectivism as important for conceptions of *world literature*. She references Bruce Robbins's coinage, "dispossessive collectivism", in his essay, "Uses of World Literature", in *The Routledge Companion to World Literature*, ed. Theo D'haen, David Damrosch and Djelal Kadir (New York: Routledge, 2012), 391.

[24] Apter 329. Apter refers here to Bruce Robbins's critique of modernism as not really "encourage[ing] an ethical relation with the entire world" but experimenting primarily with art's estranging, alienating function.

[25] Apter 329.

temporalities, cultural frames, localities and geographical places. Recent discussions of art's world-making potential[26] advance a similar notion of the world as plastic and malleable, constituted by multiple frames and subtended by shapes it acquires in the works of art, not least. Caroline Levine illuminates this interaction between the world and art in the way artworks connect disparate elements to "give shape to worlds".[27] By flaunting its awareness of being an artifice, an artistic project creates an aesthetic model of the world. The world-making work of such models, as Levine perceptively shows, serves the purpose of making sense of existence. "The work of models", Levine explains, is "to move across scales": to either make a graspable version of a vastly complex reality or to imagine possible complicating consequences and scenarios of a particular event.[28] In either case, "models shift scales", designed to make us see what cannot be grasped and seen for "they sharpen and alter what can be known and imagined".[29]

In documentary modernism, reporting, curating and creating become complimentary world-re-creating practices that inform the projects' utopian politics and aesthetics of interruption. Cunard's interventionist world-oriented anthology, Agee and Evans's reportage on the rural poor towards the backdrop of poverty across America and around the globe, and Gumby's vernacular historiography of black modernity – are all world-oriented forms that escape generic and institutional constraints. What unites these collaborative, multimodal projects is that they reappraise the dynamics between cosmopolitanism and nationalism by configuring a dynamics of interconnectedness between local temporalities and global histories, and by this, they project, I claim, a new cultural dynamics.

---

[26] See for instance, Pheng Cheah's *What Is a World?* (2016) and Mark Seltzer's *The Official World* (2016).
[27] Caroline Levine, "How to Make Worlds", in *Public Books*, January 11 (2016).
[28] Levine, "How to Make Worlds".
[29] Levine, "How to Make Worlds".

If modernism is known for its stylistic and formal inconsistencies, documentary modernist projects display how these inconsistencies open themselves to hybrid forms of artistic and journalistic composition. The resulting multimedial aesthetic forms exemplify the archival impulse to examine a particular context – a figure, an object, a history, or an event – so as to challenge a monolithic view of national culture. What unites them is the shared desire to break the established moulds of historiography and cultural bias. To place this discussion within the emergent discourse of *world literature* is to follow the cues in the works themselves and to account for the broader effects of the new cultural imaginary that shapes this period.

Bibliography

Allred, Jeff. *American Modernism and Depression Documentary*. Oxford: Oxford University Press, 2009.

Apter, Emily. *Against World Literature: On the Politics of Untranslatability*. London: Verso, 2013.

Benjamin, Walter. "On the Concept of History". In *Selected Writings*, vol. 4, 1938–1940, translated by E. Jephcott et al., edited by H. Eiland and M. W. Jennings. London: The Belknap Press of Harvard University Press, 2003.

Braddock, Jeremy. *Collecting as Modernist Practice*. Baltimore: Johns Hopkins University Press, 2013.

Cheng, Pheng and Bruce Robbins, eds. *Cosmopolitics: Thinking and Feeling beyond the Nation*. London: Minnesota Press, 1998.

Cunard, Nancy. *Negro: An Anthology*. Edited and abridged. With an introduction by Hugh Ford. New York: Frederick Ungar Publishing, 1970.

Levine, Caroline. "How to Make Worlds". *Public Books*, 11 January 2016.

Lukács, Georg. "Realism in the Balance". *Aesthetics and Politics*. London: Verso, 2007.

Robbins, Bruce. "Uses of World Literature". In *The Routledge Companion to World Literature*, edited by Theo D'haen, David Damrosch and Djelal Kadir. New York: Routledge, 2012.

White, Eric B. *Transatlantic Avant-Gardes: Little Magazines and Localist Modernism*. Edinburgh: Edinburgh University Press, 2013.

18. In Conquest of the World and of Modernity: Movements from the Countryside to Paris in Novels by Stendhal, Balzac and Flaubert

Annika Mörte Alling
French, Lund University

The works of Stendhal, Balzac and Flaubert have travelled across continents, survived through the centuries and have been abundantly translated, re-issued and read worldwide. This could be seen as proof of their quality and canonical position. Still, if we put them on the reading lists of our university courses, it should not simply be with reference to their status as classics and adherence to a western, European canon; we need to be able to explain to our students *why* we put these authors there, *how* they are relevant to us now and important to the literature that came after, and not only in a European context. Consequently, researchers also should deal with these questions; we need to study what makes the nineteenth-century French novels interesting today, in a global perspective.[1]

---

[1] A few studies have been published in the last six years that place these authors in a larger perspective. Jennifer Yee's *The Colonial Comedy: Imperialism in the French Realist Novel* (Oxford: Oxford University Press, 2016) treats colonial elements in Balzac, Flaubert and Zola. See also Christie McDonald and Susan Suleiman, ed., *The French Global. A New Approach to Literary History* (New York: Columbia University Press, 2011).

How to cite this book chapter:
Mörte Alling, Annika. "In Conquest of the World and of Modernity: Movements from the Countryside to Paris in Novels by Stendhal, Balzac and Flaubert". In *World Literatures: Exploring the Cosmopolitan-Vernacular Exchange*, edited by Stefan Helgesson, Annika Mörte Alling, Yvonne Lindqvist, and Helena Wulff, 199–210. Stockholm: Stockholm University Press, 2018. DOI: https://doi.org/10.16993/bat.r. License: CC-BY.

One means of doing so is to examine how these works have been received and valued in different parts of the world, in the past up to the present. In the case of canonical authors such as these, comparative transhistorical examinations are in fact possible. There are already reception studies of for instance Stendhal in China, Japan, Sweden and the United States, and to compare them would mean a new more global contribution to Stendhalian research (this is my objective in another study).[2] Such a reception analysis, however, needs to be combined with close readings of the novels, an approach that is often neglected in world literature studies. Even if "distant reading"[3] is often necessary when we are interested in literature on a global scale, we need to analyse the texts closely to discover the local, vernacular elements *in the novels*, those that relate, for instance, to the characters, their emotions and experiences of the world. In fact, it may be necessary to examine these elements to understand why we can enjoy, relate to and feel involved in a literary text in different times and places.

In this chapter one important element or theme in the nineteenth-century French novel will be discussed, namely the movement from small, rural contexts to the modern, cosmopolitan city, ultimately Paris. It will be analysed briefly in three novels, representing different types of realism: *Le Rouge et le Noir* by Stendhal (1830), *Illusions Perdues* by Honoré de Balzac (1843) and *Madame Bovary* by Gustave Flaubert (1857). This quick overview should only be seen as an introductory reflection; a

---

[2] For China, see Qian Kong, *La traduction et la reception de Stendhal en Chine 1922–2013*, Honoré de Champion (to be published). For Japan: Julie Brock, ed., *Réception et créativité. Le cas de Stendhal dans la littérature japonaise moderne et contemporaine*, Berne: Peter Lang, 2011, 2013, vol. 1 and 2. For Sweden: Annika Mörte Alling, *La réception de Stendhal en Suède*, in *L'Image du Nord chez Stendhal et les Romantiques IV. Études comparées. Textes réunis par Kajsa Andersson*, vol 4. Örebro: Örebro university, 2007, 13–42. For the USA: Maud S. Walther, *La présence de Stendhal aux États-Unis 1818–1920* (Aran: Éditions du Grand Chêne, 1974).

[3] Franco Moretti, "Conjectures on World Literature", *New Left Review* 1 (2000): 57–58.

coming study will analyse the theme more profoundly and also include examples from other novels, mainly by Balzac and Zola.

Even if several aspects of the displacement from the countryside to the metropolis have been studied before, for instance the role of Paris in the nineteenth-century novel and that of the countryside in Balzac's and Stendhal's work, there is more to say about the subject, notably in relation to world literature studies.[4] I will focus here on the main characters' initial situations in the countryside and on how they are affected emotionally by the force that drives them to transgress their confined locations, in direction of Paris, the "Capital of the Nineteenth-Century",[5] and the new modern world. As we shall see, the literature that the protagonists read plays an important role in this transgression. Let us keep in mind the question of the global perspective and see what can be concluded at the end; how can a close reading of a literary text reveal its relevance to many people, across time and space?

The immediate starting point of Stendhal's *Le Rouge et le Noir* is the small provincial town of Verrières in Franche-Comté, at first sight very attractive with its white beautiful houses, the river Doubs, and the snow-covered mountaintops of the Jura. The observer of this idyllic setting is a first-time visitor from Paris. In reality, Verrières is quite an "intolerable" place though, the narrator informs us, since it is dominated by "the most offensive despotism" ("le plus ennuyeux *despotisme*"), as is life in small towns in general.[6]

---

[4] See for instance Christopher Prendergast's important *Paris and the Nineteenth Century* (Oxford: Wiley-Blackwell, 1995). For the role of the countryside in Balzac's novels, see Nicole Mozet's *La ville de province dans l'œuvre de Balzac* (Paris: Sedes, 1982) and the more recent study by Andrew Watts, *Preserving the Provinces – Small Town and Countryside in the Work of Honoré de Balzac* (Oxford: Peter Lang, 2007). The countryside in Stendhal has been studied by for instance Cécile Meynard in *Stendhal et la province* (Paris: Honoré Champion, 2005).

[5] Walter Benjamin, *The Capital of the Nineteenth Century, The Arcades Project* (Cambridge: Harvard University Press, 1999).

[6] Stendhal, *The Red and the Black*, trans. Horace B. Samuel (New York: E.P. Dutton and Co., 1916), 29, http://www.gutenberg.org/ebooks/44747; Stendhal, *Le Rouge et le Noir* (Paris: Gallimard, 1972), 22.

It is in this intolerable milieu that we later meet the protagonist, young Julien Sorel, who is represented as an exceptional character, being in the wrong place, doing absolutely the wrong thing. He is reading a book, on a roof by the sawmill, where he ought to have been working, too deeply concentrated to hear his father's angry calls. Père Sorel hits him violently twice, making him bleed profusely. In fact, no other activity is more odious to this old man, himself illiterate: "So that's it, is it, lazy bones! always going to read your damned books are you [...]?"[7] ("—Eh bien, paresseux! tu liras donc toujours tes maudits livres [...]?"[8]

Julien is pale, weak and has delicate traits and tears in his eyes (mostly because of the loss of his "beloved" book that fell down from the roof).[9] He clearly stands out in this harsh countryside milieu – also inhabited by his two violent brothers – and his inferiority invites us to feel sorry for him. This representation of the hero, and perhaps also his symbolically superior position on the rooftop, tell us on whose side the author is.

The book Julien is reading is the *Memorial de Sainte-Helene*, which constitutes his "coran", together with Rousseau's *Confessions* and the *Bulletins de la Grande Armée*.[10] From these books he gets his vision of the world and a desire to succeed, to make a fortune, which above all means leaving Verrières – since "everything that he saw there froze his imagination" ("[t]out ce qu'il y voyait glaçait son imagination") – and being "presented one day to the pretty women of Paris" ("présenté aux jolies femmes de Paris").[11]

Julien's readings not only inspire him to trangress the limit of the countryside and other geographical and social limits, they also give him the strength and power to achieve these transgressions. By learning to recite the Bible by heart he gets a position as tutor to M. de Rênal's children, and then a place in Abbé Pirard's seminary in Besançon. After that he gets to work as secretary for the

---

[7] Stendhal, *The Red and the Black*, 53.
[8] Stendhal, *Le Rouge et le Noir*, 32.
[9] Stendhal, *The Red and the Black*, 44.
[10] Stendhal, *Le Rouge et le Noir*, 35.
[11] Stendhal, *The Red and the Black*, 69; Stendhal, *Le Rouge et le Noir*, 39.

Marquis de La Mole in Paris and even to be the lover of the beautiful Parisian lady Mathilde de La Mole, thus realising one of his most important desires.

The movement from the province to Paris is important in novels by Balzac too, as is well known. Paris is the centre for art, literature and politics and the most obvious destination for the individuals determined to succeed, like Rastignac and Lucien Chardon. Madame de Bargeton in *Illusions Perdues* exhorts Lucien to leave Angoulême and start a new life in Paris :

> There, beloved, is the life for a man who has anything in him. [...] Paris, besides, is the capital of the intellectual world, the stage on which you will succeed; overleap the gulf that separates us quickly. You must not allow your ideas to grow rancid in the provinces; put yourself into communication at once with the great men who represent the nineteenth century.[12]

> Là, cher, est la vie de gens supérieurs. [...] D'ailleurs Paris, capitale du monde intellectuel, est le théâtre de vos succès! franchissez promptement l'espace qui vous en sépare! Ne laissez pas vos idées se rancir en province, communiquez promptement avec les grands hommes qui représenteront le XIXe siècle.[13]

As in Stendhal, the displacement from the countryside is charged with symbolic and emotional significance. The protagonists are in search of a kind of general fulfilment, of a self-realisation, of an understanding of the new modern world that Paris symbolises and includes. Reading literature is an important means for trying to understand this new world, and it also offers comfort and meaning in itself, not least in the countryside, which is often an intellectually as well as emotionally confined place. Reading Schiller, Gœthe, Lord Byron, Walter Scott, Lamartine and André Chenier, among others, is a unique source of happiness for Lucien and his friend David Séchard in the otherwise austere and passionless

---

[12] Honoré de Balzac, *Lost Illusions*, trans. Ellen Marriage (2004), http://www.gutenberg.org/ebooks/13159, 323–324.
[13] Honoré de Balzac, *Illusions perdues* (Paris: Gallimard, Folio classique, 1974), 159.

environment, dominated by David's father (as unwilling to understand the point of this activity as Père Sorel). Absorbed by these texts, they forget about the sorrows of the countryside, cry together and plan for a future of fame and success: "Incessantly they worked with the unwearied vitality of youth; comrades in poverty, comrades in the consuming love of art and science, till they forgot the hard life of the present, for their minds were wholly bent on laying the foundations of future fame" ("dévorés par l'amour de l'art [...], ils oubliaient la misère présente en s'occupant à jeter les fondements de leur renommée").[14] For Lucien, this future means glory as a writer – in Paris, as Madame de Bargeton helps to convince him in the longer citation above. Madame de Bargeton herself is an even more passionate reader than Lucien, suffering greatly from the monotony of the countryside. She adores Lord Byron and Jean-Jacques Rousseau, and longs strongly for a life in Paris. Despite initial doubts, she is able to realise this desire and travels to the capital together with Lucien in the beginning of the novel's second part.

In *Madame Bovary* too, the countryside, Normandy in this case, is represented as a narrow-minded world that in no way satisfies the desires of the main character. An important difference from Stendhal's and Balzac's novels is that Emma is herself *part of* this ordinariness and part of the monotony she complains about. She is not an exception, but in much behaving like most women of the countryside suffering from ennui, for instance reading romantic novels about love. As Julien, Lucien and David, she finds a certain comfort in her reading – it is one of the few activities she can indulge in where she is – and obtains her vision of reality from books such as *Paul et Virginie* and *Ivanhoe* by Walter Scott.

Unfortunately, Emma is unable to adapt her desires to reality, suffering from a pathological version of "bovarysme", a term defined by the philosopher Jules de Gaultier in 1902, as "the faculty of man to conceive of himself as other than he is, and to conceive of the world as other than it is" ("la faculté qu'a l'homme de se concevoir autre qu'il n'est et de concevoir le monde autre").[15]

---

[14] Balzac, *Lost Illusions*, 61; *Illusions perdues*, 53.

[15] Jules de Gaultier, *Le Bovarysme – Essai sur le pouvoir d'imaginer* (Paris: Société du Mercure de France, 1902), 10 (English translation mine).

In fact, Emma wants more from her life than the village people surrounding her, and so much more than her husband Charles Bovary, who "taught nothing, knew nothing, wished nothing" ("n'enseignait rien, celui-là, ne savait rien, ne souhaitait rien").[16] In this respect, Emma too can be regarded as an exceptional character, despite Flaubert's intentions to make her ordinary and to write a novel about "nothing".[17] It is not the substance of her dreams that is extraordinary – Flaubert underlines their ordinariness with great irony – but her strong belief in them and her power to trangress limits to try to realise them, limits that no one else in the Normandy countryside would think possible or even desirable to transgress. After her marriage to Charles she moves to Tostes, later to the bigger town Yonville, and then tries to get closer to the city of her dreams, by reading about Parisian life in magazines and novels by Honoré de Balzac and George Sand. She even buys a map of the capital and walks up and down the streets with her fingertip. Emma never reaches Paris, but often visits the bigger town Rouen and adopts certain habits of a metropolitan woman; she wears expensive dresses in Parisian style and takes lovers, Rodolphe and later Léon.

In view of Emma's strong desires and her determination to realise her dreams, one cannot help wondering if she would have been able to realise her Parisian dream in more modern times, had she read different books and been able to move more freely as a woman, like Thérèse Désqueyroux, the eponymous heroine of François Mauriac's novel from 1927. After all, Thérèse succeeds in liberating herself from her suffocating situation and marriage in the province of Les Landes, goes to Paris in the end with her mind set to begin a new life there, even to take courses at the

---

[16] Gustave Flaubert, *Madame Bovary*, trans. Eleanor Marx-Aveling (2006) https://www.gutenberg.org/files/2413/2413-h/2413-h.htm, Chapter 7; Gustave Flaubert, *Madame Bovary* (Paris: Gallimard, 1972), 72.

[17] During the period when he was working with *Madame Bovary*, Flaubert wrote to Louise Colet that he wanted to create a book about "nothing", almost without subject, whose strength would be in its style, since he meant that the most beautiful works were those without content. (Letter to Louise Colet 16 January 1852, in Gustave Flaubert, *Correspondance* Paris: Gallimard, 1998, 156.)

university. In fact, without the adaptation problem, Bovarysme is a positive capacity, a constructive force, that makes us challenge conventions, strive forward and discover new things. This is what Jules de Gaultier concluded in the later part of his book *Le Bovarysme* from 1902.[18]

It is of course difficult to draw conclusions from the very brief observations in this chapter. It is also important to point out that the negative conception of the countryside context as a source of frustration and confinement is only the view of the main characters; it is by no means represented in the novels uniformly. We noted the narrator's descriptions of beautiful Verrières in the beginning of Stendhal's novel. It is obvious too that not all countryside inhabitants behave as Père Sorel and his rival, certainly not the kind-hearted Mme de Rênal. In Balzac's novels, as Andrew Watts has shown, countryside behaviour and people are condemned, as well as celebrated.[19] Even in *Madame Bovary* a positive view of the province is represented, that of Charles, who is quite content with what it has to offer. Regarding the conception of Paris in the novels mentioned here, this is of course quite complex too. Paris becomes many different things, even from the perspective of a single character in the process of discovering a new sense of the self and the world. The dynamics between local and cosmopolitan contexts could even be studied within the Parisian world of one single novel (here the novels of Zola would definitely also be interesting material). Finally, it should be noted that the

---

[18] In other words, Jules de Gaultier is cited incorrectly in most encyclopedias and dictionaries; what is seen as his definition of Bovarysme is taken from the initial discussion about Emma Bovary, which later in his voluminous book takes a different turn. He then modifies his definition and concludes that Bovarysme is a necessary human capacity and that Emma's case is a *pathological version* of this capacity. For a more detailed discussion, see Annika Mörte Alling, "Le bovarysme et le désir triangulaire. Deux théories sur l'être humain appliquées à la littérature" in *Jules de Gaultier Le Bovarysme La psychologie dans l'œuvre de Flaubert. Suivi d'une série d'études réunies et coordonnées par Per Buvik*, ed. Per Buvik (Paris: Éditions du Sandre, 2007), 231–50.

[19] Watts, *Preserving the Provinces*, 24.

functions of the literary texts read by the protagonists are various and diverse, as Joëlle Gleize has shown.[20]

However, this multiplication of perspectives does not prevent us from getting the impression that the texts analysed reveal something important about how human beings *could* experience the movement from local to global spheres described above. Even one single character represented as exceptional and unstable in its views can transmit important experiences to us. The indirect nature of the relation between fiction and reality, so often underlined by theorists, does not prevent this transmission of experience either.[21] Whether we are receptive of it or not probably has to do with emotions – the emotions expressed in a particular novel, perhaps in connection to the characters' experiences, as well as the emotions that the novel incites in us for various reasons. The context and life experiences of the reader play an important role of course, but one may wonder if a certain literary work cannot provoke the same type of emotions in different times and places. That is one of the reasons why world literary studies need to accord importance to close readings of literary examples: fictional literature has a high potential to gives us access to other people's emotions and experiences. Literature also provides a unique version of reality in that it can appear all-encompassing, in that it can embrace so many elements of the world at the same time, at so many different levels. It can give an impression of the world as

---

[20] Joëlle Gleize, *Le Double Miroir. Le livre dans les livres de Stendhal à Proust* (Paris: Hachette Supérieur, 1992). Gleize shows that books have many different functions in novels by Stendhal, Balzac and Flaubert, one of them being to represent reality, as objects among other objects that enhance the realistic effect. This function in particular is discussed in her study.

[21] See for instance Michael Riffaterre, "The Referential Fallacy", *Columbia Review* 57 (1978): 21–35. As Vincent Jouve affirms, even if the knowledge about the world that literature can mediate always is of a multiple and uncertain kind, most theorists agree that literature has a cognitive function, and that it helps us to understand the reality that surrounds us. ("Quelle exemplarité pour la fiction?", in *Littérature & exemplarité*, edited by Emmanuel Bouju et al., Rennes: Presses Universitaires de Rennes, 2007, 247).

"knowable" and "graspable", in Caroline Levine's words.[22] One single novel of Balzac – one single character even – can seem to contain the whole world.

In other words, by studying the movements of the above characters from the local to the global, from the familiar, limited context to larger and foreign spaces, we may learn something important about human beings in the process of transgressing limits and searching for meaning in an expanding world. Furthermore, the essential and sometimes creative role that literature plays for the characters in their movements makes us wonder if the authors are not trying to tell us something about the importance of reading literature to conceive of the world and of oneself as *other* and to be able to cross borders. There are many more examples of the creative type of reading in the French nineteenth-century novel.[23]

In the cases briefly analysed here, the reasons for the characters' need to move away from the rural contexts are not linked to war or poverty, but have to do with a desire of self-realisation and of approaching a modern world representing new possibilities for realising this desire. Other desires are encompassed by this existential project; to become successful, to belong somewhere, to find love and, simply, to be happy.

To know more precisely how the novels – each one in its specific manner – transmit these experiences, and if and how they can be interpreted as still "valid" for many people, empirical studies among readers from various sociocultural contexts would be

---

[22] In the article "How to make worlds" (*Public Books*, 11 January 2016, http://www.publicbooks.org), Caroline Levine discusses this world-making function of narratives in general and of artistic works of art, following the ideas of Martin Heidegger, Pheng Cheah and Mark Seltzer. As these theorists, Levine is critical of the large focus on the world as space in world literature research; we need to include other dimensions of the world in our studies, time for instance. We also need to include the literary texts themselves, since literature helps us grasp the world in time, as it "comes into being".

[23] Even if the literature read by the characters of the French nineteenth-century novel often influences them in a delusive manner, their reading is above all creative, as Gleize points out (*Le Double Miroir*, 114–115). However, she does not really analyse this creative function of the characters' reading.

necessary, as pointed out in the beginning. In other words, close readings of the texts need to be put in relation to studies of their translation and reception.

Bibliography

Alling Mörte, Annika. "La réception de Stendhal en Suède". In *L'Image du Nord chez Stendhal et les Romantiques IV. Études comparées*, edited by Kajsa Andersson, 13–42. Örebro: Örebro university, 2007.

———. "Le bovarysme et le désir triangulaire. Deux théories sur l'être humain appliquées à la littérature". In *Jules de Gaultier Le Bovarysme La psychologie dans l'œuvre de Flaubert. Suivi d'une série d'études réunies et coordonnées par Per Buvik*, edited by Per Buvik, 231–250. Paris: Éditions du Sandre, 2007.

Balzac, Honoré de. *Illusions perdues*. Paris: Gallimard, collection Folio classique, 1974.

———. *Lost Illusions*. Translated by Ellen Marriage. 2004. Accessed 20 August 2017. http://www.gutenberg.org/ebooks/13159.

Benjamin, Walter. *The Capital of the Nineteenth Century. The Arcades Project*. Cambridge: Harvard University Press, 1999.

Brock, Julie, ed. *Réception et créativité. Le cas de Stendhal dans la littérature japonaise moderne et contemporaine*, vol. 1 and 2. Berne: Peter Lang, 2011 and 2013.

Flaubert, Gustave. *Correspondance*. Paris: Gallimard, collection Folio classique, 1998.

———. *Madame Bovary*. Paris: Gallimard, collection Folio classique, 1972.

———. *Madame Bovary*. Translated by Eleanor Marx-Aveling. 2006. https://www.gutenberg.org/files/2413/2413-h/2413-h.htm.

Gaultier, Jules de. *Le Bovarysme*. Paris: Société du Mercure de France, 1902 (later with the undertitle *Essai sur le pouvoir d'imaginer*).

Gleize, Joëlle. *Le Double Miroir. Le livre dans les livres de Stendhal à Proust*. Paris: Hachette Supérieur, 1992.

Jouve, Vincent. "Quelle exemplarité pour la fiction?" In *Littérature & exemplarité*, edited by Bouju, Emmanuel, Gefen, Alexandre, Hautcœur, Macé, Marielle, 239–248. Rennes: Presses Universitaires de Rennes, 2007.

Kong, Qian. *La traduction et la reception de Stendhal en Chine 1922–2013*. Paris: Honoré Champion. Forthcoming.

Levine, Caroline. "How to make worlds". *Public Books*, 11 January (2016). http://www.publicbooks.org/how-to-make-worlds/.

McDonald, Christie and Suleiman, Susan, ed. *The French Global. A New Approach to Literary History*. New York: Columbia University Press, 2011.

Meynard, Cécile. *Stendhal et la province*. Paris: Honoré Champion, 2005.

Moretti, Franco. "Conjectures on World Literature". *New Left Review* 1 (2000): 57–58.

Mozet, Nicole. *La ville de province dans l'œuvre de Balzac*. Paris: Sedes, 1982.

Prendergast, Christopher. *Paris and the Nineteenth Century*. Oxford: Wiley-Blackwell, 1995.

Riffaterre, Michael. "The Referential Fallacy". *Columbia Review* 57 (1978): 21–35.

Stendhal. *Le Rouge et le Noir*. Paris: Gallimard, collection Folio, 1972.

———. *The Red and the Black, A Chronicle of 1830*. Translated by Horace B. Samuel. New York: E.P. Dutton and Co., 1916. http://www.gutenberg.org/ebooks/44747.

Walther, Maud S. *La présence de Stendhal aux États-Unis 1818–1920*. Aran: Éditions du Grand Chêne, 1974.

Watts, Andrew. *Preserving the Provinces Small Town and Countryside in the Work of Honoré de Balzac*. Oxford: Peter Lang, 2007.

Yee, Jennifer. *The Colonial Comedy: Imperialism in the French Realist Novel*. Oxford: Oxford University Press, 2016.

19. The Contemporary Russian Cosmopolitans

Anna Ljunggren
Slavic Languages, Stockholm University

In an entry from his journal *Diary of a Writer* from 1873, Dostoevsky offers readers some memories of his contemporary, the writer Alexander Herzen, who had died in exile in Paris three years earlier:

> He was a product of our aristocracy, *gentilhomme russe et citoyen du monde* above all, a type that appeared only in Russia and which could appear only in Russia. Herzen did not emigrate and did not lay the foundation for other Russian emigrés; no, he was simply born an emigré. They all, those people like him, were just born emigrés, even though the majority of them never left Russia. In one hundred and fifty years of the life of the Russian gentry that preceded him, with only a few exceptions, the last roots rotted and the last links with the Russian soil and the Russian truth were shaken loose.[1]

Dostoevsky depicts the Russian cosmopolitan with irony and venom; nonetheless his exposition grasps some significant traits of this cultural phenomenon, which "could appear only in Russia" in the post-Petrine period of its history ("one hundred and fifty years of the life of the Russian gentry" had passed by

---

[1] Fyodor Dostoevsky, "Old People", *A Writer's Diary* vol. 1 1873–76, trans. Kenneth Lantz. With an Introductory study by Gary Saul Morson (Evanson, Ill.: Northwestern University Press, 1994), 126.

How to cite this book chapter:
Ljunggren, Anna. "The Contemporary Russian Cosmopolitans". In *World Literatures: Exploring the Cosmopolitan-Vernacular Exchange*, edited by Stefan Helgesson, Annika Mörte Alling, Yvonne Lindqvist, and Helena Wulff, 211–228. Stockholm: Stockholm University Press, 2018. DOI: https://doi.org/10.16993/bat.s. License: CC-BY.

the time Dostoevsky wrote the piece). Dostoevsky's observations are built in two steps. First, he establishes a connection between exile and the internal westernisation of Russia, and secondly, a connection between cosmopolitanism and westernisation. In other words, Russian cosmopolitanism is not all-embracing: it has been historically "wedded" to the west, and has treated Europe as a metaphor for enlightenment and universalism.[2] Its opposite is "Russia as Asia", which stands for Russia as unenlightened, backward, despotic – that is, as vernacular in a bad sense. The opposition between the internalised west and authentic and archaic Russianness constitutes what is regarded in semiotics as the "inner dichotomy" specific to Russian culture.[3] The tension between these opposites has taken the form of literary and philosophical disputes, clashes between cultural and political doctrines and ideas (as in Dostoevsky's times between slavophiles and westernisers). It is important to stress that these two aspects have coexisted historically and that their interaction has defined the dynamics of Russian culture for centuries, including the Soviet and Post-Soviet periods. The strong connection between cosmopolitanism and interior westernisation of Russian culture is what distinguishes the Russian cosmopolitan discourse from that of the present-day west, where cosmopolitanism is strongly linked to the postcolonial condition and is fuelled by its inequalities.

While the Soviet Union was culturally isolated from the west, it created its own version of cosmopolitanism. The philosopher,

---

[2] Boris Uspensky, "Europe as Metaphor and Metonymy (in Relation to the History of Russia)", in Boris Uspensky and Viktor Zhivov, *"Tsar and God" and Other Essays in Russian Cultural Semiotics* (Boston: Academic Studies Press, 2012), 175–90.

[3] Lotman opposes the "binary" culture of Russia to the "ternary" cultures of Western Europe: Juri Lotman, *Culture and Explosion. Semiotics, Communication and Cognition*, ed. Marina Grishakova (Berlin-New York: De Gruyter Mouton, 2009), 166–172; Jurii Lotman and Boris Uspensky,"Binary Models in the Dynamics of Russian Culture (to the End of the Eighteenth Century)", in Jurii Lotman and Boris Uspenskii, *The Semiotics of Russian Cultural History*, ed. Alexander D. Nakhimovsky and Alice Stone Nakhimovsky (Ithaca and London: Cornell University Press, 1985), 30–67.

art critic and curator Boris Groys argues that the USSR, in its endeavour to radically modernise cultural politics in "one isolated country" (to use Lenin's words about the October Revolution), formulated a doctrine of "Communist internationalism" that can be seen as a prefiguration of contemporary globalisation in the wide sense.[4] During the later period, Soviet "internationalism" became centripetal, primarily embracing the nationalities of the USSR led by Russia, and also including the countries of the socialist bloc. When the project to create "an isolated future" collapsed, Russia had to attempt to return to its pre-Soviet roots.[5]

The isolation of the USSR was not absolute. During the late 1960s and '70s, the question of emigration became a burning issue both culturally and politically. Even though "the third wave" of Russian emigration to the west was extremely restricted, its impact on cultural and intellectual life was overwhelming. Whether "to leave or to stay" was discussed behind closed doors in the kitchens of the Moscow and Leningrad intelligentsia. This dilemma prompted a debate about the significance of one's native environment for creative work, and it was probably the most recent cultural expression of the very dichotomy that the semioticians Lotman and Uspensky described around this time.

The American anthropologist Alexei Yurchak has spoken about the "imaginary West" as a collective image invested with metaphysical significance in the late Soviet period.[6] It was an imaginary "elsewhere" that, using M. Foucault's term, one could call a late Soviet "heterotopia".[7] It was a cosmopolitan aesthetic utopia with

---

[4] Boris Groys, "Zurück aus der Zukunft: Kunst aus Ost und West", in *Zurück aus der Zukunft: osteuropäische Kulturen im Zeitalter des Postkommunismus*, ed. Boris Groys et al. (Frankfurt am Main, 2005), 422–423.
[5] Groys, 423.
[6] Alexei Yurchak, *Everything Was Forever, Until It Was No More: The Last Soviet Generation* (Princeton, NJ: Princeton University Press, 2005), 126–207.
[7] Michel Foucault, "Des espaces autres", *Empan* 54 (2004/2): 12–19, accessed 16 March 2017, https://www.cairn.info/revue-empan-2004-2-page-12.htm.

metaphysical overtones, constructed on the remains of Russian modernism and its visions.

The prevalence of aesthetics in this "imaginary West" can in fact explain why, as the prominent poet Olga Sedakova put it, the real encounter with the west during Perestroika turned out to be a disappointment ("we did not expect everyday life, but an aesthetic, moral, philosophical Europe").[8] This disillusionment has recently led to the Russian intelligentsia's partial withdrawal from "Occidentalism", characteristic of the unofficial late-Soviet culture.

Exile Literature or Transcultural Literature?

When two key figures of the unofficial culture of the 1970s – first Brodsky and then Solzhenitsyn – were expelled from the USSR, the centrifugal trend of the unofficial part of Soviet culture gathered momentum. What followed upon their expulsion revealed the fundamental differences in cultural choices that could be made in exile. While Solzhenitsyn worked and saw himself as a Russian writer and political thinker in exile, Brodsky took a step into Anglo-American literature, both as a prose writer and – although not always as successfully – as a poet. It can be argued that exile is insufficient as a term covering diverging cultural paths.[9] It can also be argued that these choices and types of cultural orientation

---

[8] Olga Sedakova, A poetry reading and discussion at the Department of Slavic Languages and Literatures (Stockholm University), 23 April 2012, accessed 16 March 2017, https://www.youtube.com/watch?v=FrL7wp-uwFM.

[9] The terms "exilic", "diasporic" and "transnational" are used as synonyms in Azade Seyhan, *Writing Outside the Nation* (Princeton, NJ, and Oxford: Princeton University Press, 2001), 11. In the Russian cultural context, further distinction is required. See also Eva Hausbacher's argument for a reconceptualisation of "exile": Eva Hausbacher, *Poetik der Migration. Transnationale Schreibweisen in der zeitgenössischen russischen Literatur* (Tübingen, 2009), 9–18. See also Adrian Wanner, *Fictions of a New Translingual Diaspora* (Evanston, IL: Northwestern University Press, 2011), 4.

are predetermined by a preexisting dichotomy within Russian culture.

Chronologically, generations of the Russian emigration in the twentieth century are counted in "waves": Nabokov belongs to the first, which stretches in time and overlaps with the third wave, Brodsky to the third, and Makine and Shishkin to the fourth.

Nabokov stopped being "a Russian exile writer" when he moved to the United States in May 1940, abandoning his pseudonym Sirin and leaving his last novel written in Russian, *Solus Rex*, unfinished. Brodsky defied the fact that he was banned, which for him meant to thwart the limitations imposed by the official Soviet patriotism and its prohibitions. In the speech "The Condition We Call Exile" (1988) he speaks instead of its "very strong, very clear metaphysical dimension".[10]

The political climate of today allows for much more flexibility. Writers of the younger generation, such as Mikhail Shishkin, who resides in Switzerland and writes in Russian, simply do not find the question about his being or not being an exile writer relevant. Andreï Makine (also writing under the pseudonym Gabriel Osmonde) has taken a different path; he chose to write exclusively in French and has recently been elected into the French Academy, which consecrated him as a French writer.

The term "transcultural" seems to be the most appropriate to describe complex mobility in the contemporary world.[11] It stresses the dynamics of transition between two cultural spaces. If we

---

[10] Joseph Brodsky, "The Condition We Call Exile", New York Review of Books, 21 January 1988, accessed 17 March 2017, http://www.bisla.sk/english/wp-content/uploads/2015/01/Joseph-Brodsky-The-Condition-We-Call-Exile.pdf.

[11] The term "transcultural" used here, is synonymous to "transnational" or "migrant", all in circulation at present. One reason why "transcultural" is preferable in the Russian context is that the Russian culture excedes the limits of Russia proper. Another is that it is more congruent with the question of poetics. One more important consideration here is how the authors define themselves: one should exercise caution with respect to terminology in order to avoid labels that might be rejected by authors themselves. In this respect also, because of its neutrality, "transcultural" seems to be preferable.

admit that transcultural literature has vernacular "difference" as a prerequisite, it becomes possible to see its similarity with anthropological discourse, which, according to French anthropologist Marc Augé, is based on difference and universality at the same time.[12] Even Appadurai defines contemporary cultural dynamics in terms of "tension between cultural homogenization and cultural heterogenization".[13] Transcultural literature mediates the native experience into a new cultural context, often by means of the language of this new cultural sphere.[14]

The process of mediation can be irreversible. One such trend was the "branding" of the Soviet Russian experience (Soviet exoticism) – as in Makine's novels, rejected in Russia for their "constructed" Russianness built on clichés.[15] To the traditional Russian images, such as snow and steppes, some Soviet ones were added; on a larger scale, defined historical narratives of WWII or the Siege of Leningrad were introduced to the French reader as the background for a love story in *Heaven and Earth of Jacques Dorme* (*La terre et le ciel de Jacques Dorme* [2003]) and *The Life of an Unknown Man* (*La vie d'un homme inconnu* [2009]). One

---

[12] Marc Augé states that anthropology is based on a triple experience: plurality, difference ("alterité") and identity: Marc Augé, *Pour une anthropologie des mondes contemporains* (Paris: Aubier, 1994), 81. Augé describes a crisis of difference in a shrinking world of globalisation as a reduction of the cultural value of difference, which is no longer concept of invested with prestige of exoticism (81). See also a discussion of the cosmopolitanism understood as openness to cultural diversity in David Damrosch, *What is World Literature?* (Princeton and Oxford: Princeton University Press, 2003), 120–21.

[13] Arjun Appadurai, "Disjuncture and Difference in the Global Cultural Economy", in *Theory. Culture. Society*, 1990, accessed 17 March 2017, http://www.arjunappadurai.org /articles/Appadurai Disjuncture_and _Difference_in_the_Global_Cultural_Economy.pdf.

[14] The deterritorialised vernacular becomes a sign in the complex cultural interactions of today. See the discussion of the semiotisation of "difference" in Homi K. Bhabba, "Cultural Diversity and Cultural Differences", accessed 21 March 2017, http://monumenttotransformation.org/atlas-of-transformation/html/c/cultural-diversity/cultural-diversity-and-cultural-differences-homi-k-bhabha.html.

[15] Adrian Wanner speaks of "constructed Russianness for foreign consumption": Wanner, *Out of Russia*, 3.

may ask on which side of the communication between western Europe and Russia these clichés originated. It seems that they are a product of cultural interaction and are akin to translation, not from language to language, but in a broader sense, from culture to culture. This effect is comparable to the impact which an anticipated translation may have on a text, as described by Rebecca Walkowitz in her *Born Translated*.[16] To draw an analogy with anthropology, it is as if a native would be telling an anthropologist his experience using the anthropologist's language and concepts.[17]

Towards a Poetics of Transcultural Literatures: Chronotope and Genre

Vladimir Nabokov, Joseph Brodsky, Andreï Makine and Mikhail Shishkin have the same mother tongue and country of origin, Russia. Their biographies share one fundamental feature – displacement[18] – and their work has been integrated into different host cultures: Anglo-American, French and Swiss-German. But are there common features in their writing, in spite of the differences, that can be called a poetics of transculturalism? The question of recurrent patterns is not a formal one. Rather, it concerns how transcultural writers represent, and thereby shape, the world. Research in this area is still limited, trying to catch up with a development that is unfolding before our eyes; yet the answer that the

---

[16] On "pre-emptive translation" see Rebecca Walkowitz, *Born Translated. The Contemporary Novel in an Age of World Literature* (New York: Columbia University Press, 2015), 11–17.

[17] Adrian Wanner observes that a transcultural autobiography is frequently perceived as an authentic ethnographic document: Wanner, *Out of Russia*, 10.

[18] Eva Hausbacher includes "displacement" as a common denominator in her discussion of transcultural poetics. It seems, however, that this concept should be applied to authors' biographies, not to their texts (Hausbacher, *Poetik der Migration*, 11–12, 136–45). Adrian Wanner comments on "constructed Russianness for foreign consumption" (Wanner, *Out of Russia*, 3). Displacement is used as a term by Homi K. Bhabba in relation to transcultural experience (Homi K. Bhabha, *The Location of Culture* (New York: Routledge, 1994), passim).

few works that exist on the subject are pointing to, is "yes".[19] This "yes", however, still requires both in-depth studies of individual authors as well as a comparative investigations on a wider scale.[20] In the growing body of works on individual writers, there are only a few that aim to present an overview of the phenomenon.[21]

Two issues characteristic of transcultural writing will be presented below. Firstly, patterns of spatio-temporal organisation will be outlined on the basis of the works of the authors chosen for this study. Secondly, the issue of the re-use of traditional genres will be addressed in connection with the phenomenon of "translingual autobiography".

A discussion of the poetics of a prosaic text can be based on what Mikhail Bakhtin called a "chronotope".[22] This notion represents the fusion of the categories of time and space into a "novelistic world". According to Bakhtin, both the type of protagonist and the genre of a text are related to its chronotope. The space of transcultural texts is frequently bipartite, being an instance of

---

[19] Eva Hausbacher's *Poetik des Migration* is a major contribution to the study of the poetics of Russian migrant literature; however, its scope is limited to contemporary writers of Russian extraction residing in Germany.

[20] Alain Ausoni discusses common features in bilingual autobiographies independently from the writer's country of origin (Alain Ausoni, "En d'autres mots: écriture translingue et autobiographie", in *L'Autobiographie entre autres. Écrire la vie aujourd'hui*, ed. Fabien Arribert-Narce and Alain Ausoni (Oxford and Bern: Peter Lang, 2013), 63–84). Wanner discusses a number of translingual diasporic Russian authors independently of their adopted language as a single phenomenon (Wanner, *Out of Russia*, 3–18).

[21] One can mention some works not focused on poetics which try to present a wide overview and discussion of the phenomenon, notably in Bhabha, *Location of Culture*; Steven Kellman, *The Translingual Imagination* (Lincoln and London: University of Nebraska Press, 2000); *Transcultural Identities in Contemporary Literature*, ed. Irene Gilsenan Nordin et al. (Amsterdam: Rodopi, 2013); see also Yoon Sun, "The Postcolonial Novel and Diaspora", in *The Cambridge Companion to the Postcolonial Novel*, ed. Ato Quayson (Cambridge University Press, 2015), 133–51.

[22] Mikhail Bakhtin, "Forms of Time and of the Chronotope in the Novel", *The Dialogic Imagination: Four Essays*, ed. Michael Holquist (Austin: University of Texas Press, 2008), 84–258.

what Eva Hausbacher calls the "duplication" ("Duplizität") that permeates transcultural writing.[23] Bipartite narratives can be created by means of a counterpoint technique or through a frame construction. Two countries, two cultures are here juxtaposed: Makine's stories oscillate between Paris and Siberia, Shishkin's between Moscow and Zurich.

Transition in space is related to shifts in time. Time can by divided into "now" and "before" following the pattern of "duplication". It can be both the time of retroactively related progression from old to new or a "dive" backwards in time, which Justine McConnell calls "kathabasis" in her study of South African literature.[24] Makine's already mentioned *The Life of an Unknown Man* is constructed as a two-step "descent": first into the protagonist's personal past – to meet his old love in St Petersburg, and then a step further into the big national narrative of Russian history – the siege of Leningrad during the Second World War.

The divided spaces are mediated by a protagonist who acts as a go-between: a traveller, a translator, or even a spy. Transition itself becomes the theme of transcultural texts, as in Brodsky's "Watermark" or Makine's *The Life of an Unknown Man*. The travels in these texts are connected to self-definition, or rather self-redefinition, and have overtones of initiation or rebirth.[25]

The difference between spaces can get neutralised in utopia: in Nabokov's *Ada,* his "most cosmopolitan and poetic novel",[26] protagonists belonging to a trilingual family of Russian descent are placed on a planet called Antiterra, where Russian, French and American toponyms intermingle and even rhyme. Nabokov's utopia in *Ada* is cumulative: it not only brings together toponyms in three languages, but also anachronistically fuses the different time periods of one century. Gabriel Osmonde (Andreï Makine's

---

[23] Hausbacher, *Poetik der Migration,* 117–18, 141.
[24] Justine McConnell, "Generation Telemachus: Dinaw Mengestu's *How to Read the Air*", in *Ancient Greek Myth in World Fiction since 1989,* ed. Justine McConnell and Edith Hall (London: Bloomsbury, 2016), 225–37.
[25] Ausoni, "En d'autres mots", 64, 73.
[26] Vladimir Nabokov, *Strong Opinions* (New York: Vintage International, 1990), 177.

pseudonym) situates the protagonist of his *Alternaissance* (2011), a Russian expatriate, in an experimental global community called the Diggers Foundation, whose centre is placed in the heterotopian "far away" of Australia.

It is the writing subject who creates continuity and bridges spatial and cultural gaps within "the third space" of the text itself.[27] The transcultural text frequently comments upon itself and the theme of writing. At the same time, there is a tendency to shift from an ethnic space and substitute it with a textual "space", i.e. a book within the book or picture within the book (ekphrasis). As a consequence, transcultural writing is saturated with quotes; Nabokov's *Ada* is but one example.

Turning to the question of genres, one might say that transcultural prose has not developed its own new genres, but has instead modified canonical ones, adjusting them to its own purposes. It has been observed that a favoured genre of transcultural writing is the autobiography that treats a transition, a "metamorphosis" into a new culture;[28] Makine compares the transition to a second literary language to a second birth.[29] Translingual autobiographies differ from their native counterparts: they perform an act of recreation and rewriting of one's biography in the language of a new cultural sphere.

A frequently cited example is Nabokov's *Conclusive Evidence/Speak, Memory* (1951), which was written in English, subsequently auto-translated into Russian under the title *Drugie berega* (1954) [Other Shores], and once again reappeared as *Speak, Memory: An Autobiography Revisited* (1966).[30] The

---

[27] Bhabba speaks of "survival cultures" and foregrounds the functional, performative aspect of their texts: Bhabba, *The Location of Culture*, 172.
[28] See for example, Wanner, *Out of Russia*, 10.
[29] Andreï Makine, *Cette France qu'on oublie d'aimer* (Paris: Flammarion, 2006), 61.
[30] Chapter Five of *Speak, Memory*, about the Nabokovs' Swiss-French governess, is the earliest part of the text preserved; it was written originally in French, signed Nabokoff-Sirine and published under the title "Mademoiselle O" in a quarterly *Mesures* 2 (P., 1936). The literary journal had on its editorial board Jean Poulhan, Henri Michaux and Giuseppe Ungaretti; before the war, it had published a wide range of

book ends with the Nabokov family's departure for America in May 1940. What remains unspoken in the retrospective narrative is the entirety of WWII: the gap in between distances Nabokov from Russia and western Europe, both distorted and bastardised in the course of history (as shown in his wartime dystopia, *Bend Sinister*). Nabokov places emphasis not on the loss but, conversely, on the continued atemporal existence of the past in memory and imagination – as in his *Speak, Memory*, or in the utopia of *Ada*, where "memory meets imagination halfway".[31] What follows in this progression is *Look at the Harlequins!* (1974), where Nabokov creates a fictional parody of his autobiography (his mask) and tests further the border between autobiography and fiction. His protagonist is the author of Nabokov's own novels under recognisable titles: *A Kingdom by the Sea* for *Lolita*, *Ardis* for *Ada* etc. The theme of time is dominant in all these works.

Writing in two different languages triggers divergence between the Russian and English versions as they interact with two different literary contexts: together, they form one two-faced Janus-like book, to use Georges Nivat's expression.[32] Nabokov returns to Russian as a translator, previously having abandoned it as his literary language. As Elizabeth Klosty Beaujour comments, for the bilingual author, the pains of metamorphosis are those

---

authors, French and foreign in French translation. Among them were Paul Claudel, André Gide, Paul Eluard, Jules Supervielle, as well as James Joyce, T.S. Eliot, Stefan George, Franz Kafka, F. G. Lorca and J. L. Borges; among Russians it published Pushkin, Tolstoy, Dostoevsky, even the Archpriest Avvakum, as well as Nabokov's contemporaries, a Russian philosopher Lev Shestov and a Symbolist writer Aleksei Remizov.

[31] Nabokov's words refer to Van Veen, the protagonist of *Ada*: "Memory met imagination halfway in the hammock of his boyhood's dawns". Vladimir Nabokov, *Ada or Ardor: A Family Chronicle* (New York: Penguin Classics, 2011), 52.

[32] Georges Nivat, "Speak, Memory", in *Garland Companion to Vladimir Nabokov*, ed. Vladimir Alexandrov (New York: Garland, 1995), 677, 680–82. See also Jane Grayson, *Nabokov Translated: A Comparison of Nabokov's Russian and English Prose* (Oxford: Oxford University Press, 1977).

of self-translation.[33] Nabokov's later multilingual novel *Ada* is indebted both linguistically and thematically to bilingual redactions of *Speak, Memory*.

Translingual autobiographies have an additional dimension: they are performative, i.e. they not only tell of the transition, but enact it.[34] A comparison between Brodsky's autobiographical essay "Watermark" and Boris Pasternak's "Safe Conduct" (1929–1930) can help to uncover this dimension. The title "Watermark", which is directly related to Venice, also has a second meaning, that of a sign of authenticity, which echoes the title of Pasternak's essay. "Safe Conduct", dedicated to the memory of Rainer Maria Rilke, contains chapters about Pasternak's student year in Marburg and a trip to Venice, and is a direct predecessor of Brodsky's piece. The key theme of "Safe Conduct" is the relationship between the poet and the powers of state at the onset of Stalin's terror and during the time of radical and catastrophic changes in the whole of society. The title functions as Pasternak's self-defence, an attempt to safeguard himself as a poet, to save and preserve his personal and cultural attachments, including his affiliation to western literature and art. Migration, in turn, puts the role of a writer in a new society to severe proof which Brodsky describes as loss of significance.[35] As stated by Wanner, a translingual biog-

---

[33] Elizabeth Klosty Beaujour argues that the process of translation is impeded by bilingualism, the use of each language triggering its own mode of writing (Elizabeth Klosty Beaujour. "Bilingualism", in *Garland Companion to Vladimir Nabokov*, 37–44; "Translation and Self-Translation". in *Garland Companion to Vladimir Nabokov*, 714–725). According to Klosty Beaujour, translation and auto-translation of *Speak, Memory* paved the way for Nabokov's later "intrinsically polyglot" *Ada* (Ibid. 722).

[34] Elisabeth Bruss connects her study of the evolution of autobiography to the linguistic theory of the speech act as formulated by John Searle and John Austin. She initiates a discussion of autobiography as illocutory (Searle) or performative (Austin) speech act: Elisabeth Bruss, "L'autobiographie considérée comme acte littéraire", *Poétique* 17 (1974): 14–26. Homi K. Bhabba even speaks of the "performative, deforming" transformation of modernity by postcolonial culture: Bhabha, *Location of Culture*, 241.

[35] Brodsky speaks of the writer's loss of significance: "The democracy into which he has arrived provides him with physical safety but renders him

raphy is "a radical act of assimilation".[36] Arguably it is equally an act of self-preservation in a new environment and is a claim of authenticity – and difference – as in Brodsky's "Watermark". In this sense all translingual biographies act as "safe-conducts" – passports, so to speak, into adoptive literatures.

Despite not having created its own genres, transcultural literature has its own arsenal of poetic means and an array of shared specific features. It has been re-using certain "favourite" traditional genres (such as autobiography or utopia), transforming them from within.

To conclude the discussion of transcultural poetics, one might add that the notion of poetics can be understood widely as not necessarily limited to textual patterns, but extended to cultural roles and patterns underlying biographical legends. Russian literature has its own transcultural heroes, whose writings and biographies both serve as a compass to writers of younger generations. These are Nabokov and Brodsky, who chronologically demarcate the period of Soviet isolation: Nabokov the beginning and Brodsky the end. The mythology of the writer in Russia, which had cast him as a demiurge at the end of the nineteenth century, and later on as a martyr, also exhibits a third type: that of the writer as unifier of an antagonised world, a crosser of boundaries who breaks free of the double isolation of the Soviet political system and of exile. That is why Nabokov's belated influence on contemporary literature, like Brodsky's, is still on the rise.

Bifurcating Paths: Cosmopolitan or Neo-Vernacular?

What we see in the writing of the "fourth wave" is a growing flexibility and variation in the choice of which language to use. Mikhail Shishkin lives in Switzerland, but the first publications of a number of his acclaimed novels appeared in Russian and in Russia. At the same time his *Montreux-Missolunghi-Astapovo, in the Steps of Byron and Tolstoy* (the complete original title in

---

socially insignificant. And the lack of significance is what no writer, exile or not, can take." (Brodsky, "The Condition we call Exile", 2).

[36] Wanner, *Out of Russia*, 5–6.

German being *Montreux – Missolunghi – Astapowo. Auf den Spuren von Byron und Tolstoj: Eine literarische Wanderung vom Genfersee ins Berner Oberland* (2002)) was written in Russian, was in part auto-translated and was first published in German. Translation in a wide sense even involves other media: Shishkin's short story "Nabokov's Inkspot" ("Kljaksa Nabokova", 2015) was reworked and staged as a play in German in Switzerland. The current situation allows writers to retain their link with Russia and combine it with a cosmopolitan lifestyle.

By contrast, Andreï Makine has taken a different path: as mentioned, he writes exclusively in French. He is a critic of globalism, which he equates with mass culture, and poses as a defender of traditional France from the impact of "egalitarisation".[37] However, Makine's praise of the spirit of French culture ("francité") does not come from its inside; it is at least in part a viewpoint of an admiring outsider defending French cultural idiocracy. The question about the cultural choices of the upcoming generation of Russian transcultural writers, bilingual children of the third and fourth wave, remains open for the future.

Another question that has not yet been sufficiently addressed in current research concerns how transcultural literature relates to world literature. The conception of world literature as based on the circulation of texts, with loss and acquisition of meaning occurring in the process of re-contextualisation, has entailed the indiscriminate treatment of transcultural writing as a part of this circulation.[38] An understanding of transcultural literature as world literature has also already been expressed: the question of how to place it remains.[39] Mads Rosendahl Thomsen has called migrant literature an important "cluster" within world literature and a mode of writing that "changes the way we think about the

---

[37] Makine, *Cette France*, 65.
[38] David Damrosch defines world literature as "a mode of circulation and reading". His discussions includes, however, examples from a transcultural Nabokov, his translations of *Eugene Onegin* and *Alice in Wonderland*: Damrosch, *What is World Literature?*, 157–58.
[39] The issue is addressed in Hausbacher, *Poetik der Migration*, 107–10; Heidi Rösch, "Migrationsliteratur als Neue Weltliteratur?", *Sprachkunst* 1 (Jg XXXV/2004): 89–109.

world".[40] Transcultural literature supersedes national literatures, it "performs" cosmopolitanism in reality. This version of cosmopolitanism is neither envisioned as a "concert" of cultures, nor is it an idealised heterotopian "elsewhere": it is the sum of cultural experiences acquired in direct contact. It appears that the circulation of people and the circulation of texts should be regarded as complementary to each other, as two distinctive flows in the accelerated "hypermodern" world.

Today there is a multiplicity of cultural choices. The questions and tensions of transcultural literature – a literature of difference and transition – arise on the path toward assimilation. Transcultural literature is not about effacing, but about embedding differences into new contexts, claiming a place both in the original and in the adopted cultures. Transcultural writing can be regarded as a mediator between national literatures. Biculturalism and multilingualism can no longer be associated with the periphery;[41] the paradox is that the cultural borders are moving into the centre of contemporary national cultures.

Bibliography

Appadurai, Arjun. "Disjuncture and Difference in the Global Cultural Economy".*Theory.Culture.Society,*1990, http://www.arjunappadurai.org/articles/Appadurai_Disjuncture_and_Difference_in_the_Global_Cultural_Economy.pdf. Accessed 17 March 2017.

Augé, Marc. *Pour une anthropologie des mondes contemporains*. Paris: Aubier, 1994.

Ausoni, Alain. "En d'autres mots: écriture translingue et autobiographie". In *L'Autobiographie entre autres. Écrire la vie aujourd'hui,*

---

[40] Mads Rosendahl Thomsen, *Mapping World Literature: International Canonization and Transnational Literatures* (London: Continuum, 2008), 97, 99.

[41] Boundaries of the the semiosphere are according to Lotman the "hottest spots" for semiotisation processes. Yuri M. Lotman, *Universe of the Mind: A Semiotic Theory of Culture* (London: Tauris, 1990), 136.

edited by Fabien Arribert-Narce and Alain Ausoni, 63–84. Oxford and Bern: Peter Lang, 2013.

Bakhtin, Mikhail. "Forms of Time and of the Chronotope in the Novel". *The Dialogic Imagination: Four Essays*, edited by Michael Holquist, 84–258. Austin: University of Texas Press, 2008.

Bhabha, Homi K. *The Location of Culture*. New York: Routledge, 1994.

———. "Cultural Diversity and Cultural Differences". Accessed 21 March 2017. http://monumenttotransformation.org/atlas-of-transformation/html/c/cultural-diversity/cultural-diversity-and-cultural-differences-homi-k-bhabha.html.

Brodsky, Joseph. "The Condition We Call Exile". *New York Review of Books*, 21 January 1988. Accessed 17 March 2017. http://www.bisla.sk/english/wp-content/uploads/2015/01/Joseph-Brodsky-The-Condition-We-Call-Exile.pdf.

Bruss, Elisabeth. "L'autobiographie considérée comme acte littéraire". *Poétique* 17 (1974): 14–26.

Damrosch, David. *What is World Literature?* Princeton and Oxford: Princeton University Press, 2003.

Dostoevsky, Fyodor. "Old People". *A Writer's Diary*, vol. 1. 1873–1876, trans. Kenneth Lantz. With an Introductory Study by Gary Saul Morson. Evanston: Northwestern University Press, 1994.

Grayson, Jane. *Nabokov Translated: A Comparison of Nabokov's Russian and English Prose*. Oxford: Oxford University Press, 1977.

Foucault, Michel. "Des espaces autres". 54 *Empan* (2/ 2004): 12–19. Accessed 16 March 2017. http:// www.cairn.info/revue-empan-2004-2-page-12.htm.

Gilsenan Nordin, Irene, Hansen, Julie, Zamorano Llena, Carmen, eds. *Transcultural Identities in Contemporary Literature*. Amsterdam: Rodopi, 2013.

Groys, Boris. "Zurück aus der Zukunft: Kunst aus Ost und West". In *Zurück aus der Zukunft: osteuropäische Kulturen im Zeitalter des*

Postkommunismus, edited by Boris Groys, Anne von der Heiden, Peter Weibel, 419–26. Frankfurt am Main: Suhrkamp, 2005.

Hausbacher, Eva. *Poetik der Migration. Transnationale Schreibweisen in der zeitgenössischen russischen Literatur*. Tübingen: Stauffenburg, 2009.

Kellman, Steven. *The Translingual Imagination*. Lincoln: University of Nebraska Press, 2000.

Klosty Beaujour, Elizabeth. Bilingualism". In *Garland Companion to Vladimir Nabokov*, edited by Vladimir Alexandrov, 37–43. New York: Garland, 1995.

———. "Translation and Self-Translation". In *Garland Companion to Vladimir Nabokov*, edited by Vladimir Alexandrov, 714–24. New York: Garland, 1995.

Lotman, Yuri. *Universe of the Mind: A Semiotic Teory of Culture*. London: Tauris. 1990.

———. *Culture and Explosion (Semiotics, Communication and Cognition)*, edited by Marina Grishakova, 166–72. Berlin: De Gruyter Mouton, 2009.

Lotman, Jurii, Uspenskij Boris. "Binary Models in the Dynamics of Russian Culture to the End of the Eighteenth Century". In Jurii Lotman and Boris Uspenskii, *The Semiotics of Russian Cultural History*. Introduction by Boris Gasparov, edited by Alexander D. Nakhimovsky and Alice Stone Nakhimovsky, 30–67. Ithaca and London: Cornell University Press, 1985.

McConnell, Justine. "Generation Telemachus: Dinaw Mengestu's How to Read the Air". In *Ancient Greek Myth in World Fiction since 1989*, edited by Justine McConnell and Edith Hall, 225–37. London: Bloomsbury, 2016.

Makine, Andreï. *Cette France qu'on oublie d'aimer*. Paris: Flammarion, 2006.

Nabokov, Vladimir. *Ada or Ardor: A Family Chronicle*. New York: Penguin Classics, 2011.

———. *Strong Opinions*. New York: Vintage International, 1990.

Nivat, Georges. "Speak, Memory". In *Garland Companion to Vladimir Nabokov*, edited by Vladimir Alexandrov, 674–85. New York: Garland, 1995.

Rösch, Heidi. "Migrationsliteratur als Neue Weltliteratur?" *Sprachkunst* 1 (Jg XXXV/2004): 90–109.

Sedakova, Olga. A poetry reading and discussion at the Department of Slavic Languages and Literatures (Stockholm University), 23 April 2012. Accessed 16 March 2017. https://www.youtube.com/watch?v=FrL7wp-uwFM.

Seyhan, Azade. *Writing Outside the Nation*. Princeton: Princeton University Press, 2001.

Thomsen, Mads Rosendahl. *Mapping World Literature: International Canonization and Transnational Literatures*. London: Continuum, 2008.

Uspensky, Boris. "Europe as Metaphor and Metonymy (in Relation to the History of Russia)". In *"Tsar and God" and Other Essays in Russian Cultural Semiotics*, Boris Uspensky and Viktor Zhivov, 175–90. Boston: Academic Studies Press, 2012.

Walkowitz, Rebecca. *Born Translated: The Contemporary Novel in an Age of World Literature*. New York: Columbia University Press, 2015.

Yoon Sun. "The Postcolonial Novel and Diaspora". In *The Cambridge Companion to the Postcolonial Novel*, edited by Ato Quayson. Cambridge: Cambridge University Press, 2015.

Wanner, Adrian. *Fictions of a New Translingual Diaspora*. Evanston: Northwestern University Press, 2011.

Yurchak, Alexei. *Everything Was Forever, Until It Was No More: The Last Soviet Generation*. Princeton: Princeton University Press, 2005.

20. A World Apart and the World at Large: Expressing Siberian Exile

Mattias Viktorin
Social Anthropology, Stockholm University

The publication in 1861–62 of Fyodor Dostoevsky's semi-biographical *Notes From a Dead House* inaugurated a new literary genre in Russia: narratives of exile and prison life, where Siberia was imagined as "a world apart" – separate from, yet somehow also mirroring, the domestic realities of Imperial Russia. Among the numerous texts that belong to this genre are Anton Chekhov's *The Island of Sakhalin* (1895), Pëtr Iakubovich's *In the World of the Outcasts* (1895–98), Leo Tolstoy's *Resurrection* (1899) and Vladimir Korolenko's "Siberian stories" (1880–1904).[1]

In my ongoing project, I seek to unmoor narratives of Siberian exile and prison life from this national literary tradition. Rather than relating the texts in focus to Russian literature or society,

[1] Fyodor Dostoevsky, *Notes from a Dead House*, trans. Richard Pevear and Larissa Volokhonsky (New York: Alfred A. Knopf, 2015 [1861–2]); Anton Chekhov, *The Island of Sakhalin*, trans. Luba and Michael Terpak (London: The Folio Society, 1989 [1895]); Pëtr Filippovich Iakubovich, *In the World of the Outcasts: Notes of a Former Penal Laborer*, 2 Volumes, trans. Andrew A. Gentes (London: Anthem Press, 2014 [1895–8]); Leo Tolstoy, *Resurrection*, trans. Louise Maude (Oxford: Oxford University Press, 1994 [1899]); Vladimir Korolenko, *Makar's Dream and Other Stories*, trans. Marian Fell (New York: Duffield and Company, 1916). On Korolenko's Siberian stories, see Radha Balasubramanian, "Harmonious Compositions: Korolenko's Siberian Stories", *Rocky Mountain Review of Language and Literature*, 44 (1990): 201–10.

How to cite this book chapter:
Viktorin, Mattias. "A World Apart and the World at Large: Expressing Siberian Exile". In *World Literatures: Exploring the Cosmopolitan-Vernacular Exchange*, edited by Stefan Helgesson, Annika Mörte Alling, Yvonne Lindqvist, and Helena Wulff, 229–245. Stockholm: Stockholm University Press, 2018. DOI: https://doi.org/10.16993/bat.t. License: CC-BY.

I approach them instead as parts of an extensive world literature on travel and exile.² I follow Pheng Cheah's view here of world literature as "literature that is *of* the world, not a body of timeless aesthetic objects or a commodity-like thing that circulates globally, but something that can play a fundamental role and be a force in the ongoing cartography and creation of the world", a perspective which admittedly risks excessive philosophical abstraction but is no less suggestive for my current purposes.³ In this way, narratives of Siberian exile also become anthropologically interesting, and what interests me in particular is what these texts could tell us about the concept of "world" itself.

This approach, which brings literature and anthropology together within a single framework, has led me to explore texts that conventionally fall outside the canon of Russian exile literature. As I started to approach narratives of Siberian exile in this way, Dostoevsky's book began to look much less like an unequivocal starting-point. Several earlier texts – and other *kinds* of texts – appeared equally indispensable. One representative example is Ewa Felińska's *Revelations of Siberia*.⁴ Written in Polish and translated in 1852 into English – ten years before the publication of *Notes from a Dead House* – her memoirs show that a nascent literature on Siberian exile existed well before the inauguration of the *national* tradition in Russia. Also, I explore texts on Siberia that transcend the vernacular, literary, temporal and geographical

---

² Peter Conrad, *Islands: A Trip through Time and Space* (London: Thames and Hudson, 2009); Christopher D'Addario, *Exile and Journey in Seventeenth-Century Literature* (Cambridge: Cambridge University Press, 2007); Edwards, Philip, *The Story of the Voyage: Sea-Narratives in Eighteenth-Century England* (Cambridge: Cambridge University Press, 1994); Jennifer Ingleheart, ed., *Two Thousand Years of Solitude: Exile After Ovid* (Oxford: Oxford University Press, 2011); Arne Melberg, *Resa och skriva. En guide till den moderna reselitteraturen* (Göteborg: Daidalos, 2005); Anders Olsson, *Ordens asyl. En inledning till den moderna exillitteraturen* (Stockholm: Albert Bonniers förlag, 2011).

³ Cheah, Pheng. "World against Globe: Toward a Normative Conception of World Literature," *New Literary History*, 45, no. 3 (2014): 326.

⁴ Ewa Felińska, *Revelations of Siberia. By A Banished Lady*, 2 Volumes, ed. by Colonel Lach Szyrma (London: Hurst and Blackett, 1854 [1852]).

boundaries of pre-revolutionary Russia.[5] Significant such examples include Ivar Hasselblatt's *Förvisad till Sibirien* (1917; Banished to Siberia), Elsa Brändström's *Bland krigsfångar i Ryssland och Sibirien* (1921; Among Prisoners of War in Russia and Siberia), Ester Blenda Nordström's *Byn i vulkanens skugga* (1930; The Village in the Shadow of the Volcano), James McConckey's *To A Distant Island* (1984) and Kristian Petri's *Resan till Sachalin* (1992; The Journey to Sakhalin).[6]

I draw on and synthesise insights from several different scholarly literatures. First, to provide historical context for the narratives I work with, there is the literature on Siberia and exile,[7] and on culture and society in Imperial Russia more broadly.[8] Next, the

---

[5] The fact that texts on Siberian exile written in various languages have circulated for a long time in English translations show that they belong to a world literary context. This makes them empirically relevant. Since I am not able to read Polish or Russian, the same fact also renders them methodologically accessible to me as objects of study.

[6] Ivar Wilhelm Hasselblatt, *Förvisad till Sibirien. Minnesanteckningar* (Stockholm: Albert Bonniers förlag, 1917); Elsa Brändström, *Bland krigsfångar i Ryssland och Sibirien 1914–1921* (Stockholm: Norstedt och söner, 1921); Ester Blenda Nordström, *Byn i vulkanens skugga* (Stockholm: Albert Bonniers förlag, 1930); James McConkey, *To A Distant Island* (New York: E. P. Dutton, 1984); Kristian Petri and Martin Sjöberg, *Resan till Sachalin* (Stockholm: Norstedts, 1992); cf. also Ian Frazier, *Travels in Siberia* (New York: Picador, 2010) and Rachel Polonsky, *Molotov's Magic Lantern: Travels in Russian History* (New York: Farrar, Straus and Giroux, 2010).

[7] See, e.g., Sarah Badcock, *A Prison Without Walls? Eastern Siberian Exile in the Last Years of Tsarism* (Oxford: Oxford University Press, 2016); Daniel Beer, *The House of the Dead: Siberian Exile under the Tsars* (London: Allen Lane, 2016); Andrew A. Gentes, *Exile to Siberia, 1590–1822* (New York: Palgrave Macmillan, 2008); Andrew A. Gentes, *Exile, Murder and Madness in Siberia, 1823–1861* (New York: Palgrave Macmillan, 2010); John J. Stephan, *Sakhalin: A History* (London: Clarendon Press, 1971); Alan Wood, *Russia's Frozen Frontier: A History of Siberia and the Russian Far East, 1581–1991* (London: Bloomsbury, 2011); Sarah Young, "Knowing Russia's Convicts: The Other in Narratives of Imprisonment and Exile of the Late Imperial Era", *Europe-Asia Studies*, 65 (2013): 1700–15.

[8] See, e.g., Daniel Beer, *Renovating Russia: The Human Sciences and the Fate of Liberal Modernity, 1880–1930* (Ithaca: Cornell University Press, 2008); Camilla Gray, *The Russian Experiment in Art, 1863–1922*

vast literature on the concept of exile,[9] together with historical, sociological and anthropological research on prisons and other forms of punishment,[10] help me explore in what ways the texts in focus also transcend the contexts of their appearance. And finally, the emergent field of world literature, particularly its focus on world-making, provides an analytical framework that facilitates an investigation of the concept of "world" at the intersection of anthropology and literature.[11]

When I speak of my primary sources as world literature, I have several different things in mind. First, I think it makes sense to characterise many of these narratives as belonging to a literature

---

(London: Thames and Hudson, 1986 [1962]); Ronald Hingley, *De ryska författarna och samhället, 1825–1904* (Stockholm: Bokförlaget Aldus/ Bonniers, 1967); David Jackson, *The Wanderers and Critical Realism in Nineteenth-Century Russian Painting* (Manchester: Manchester University Press, 2006).

[9] See Wendy Everett and Peter Wagstaff, eds., *Cultures of Exile: Images of Displacement* (New York: Berghahn Books, 2004); María-Inés Lagos-Pope, ed., *Exile in Literature* (London: Associated University Presses, 1988); Michael Seidel, *Exile and the Narrative Imagination* (New Haven: Yale University Press, 1986); Susan Rubin Suleiman, ed., *Exile and Creativity: Signposts, Travelers, Outsiders, Backward Glances* (Durham: Duke University Press, 1996); Mattias Viktorin, "Den förvisade människan. Bibliska exilberättelser och Gamla testamentets antropologi", *Lychnos* (2017): 27–49.

[10] See Jeremy Bentham, *The Panopticon Writings* (London: Verso, 1995 [1791]); Didier Fassin, *Prison Worlds: An Ethnography of the Carceral Condition* (Cambridge: Polity Press, 2017); Michel Foucault, *Discipline and Punish: The Birth of the Prison*, trans. Alan Sheridan (London: Penguin Books, 1991 [1975]); Erving Goffman, *Asylums: Essays on the Social Situation of Mental Patients and Other Inmates* (New York: Anchor Books, 1961); Victor Serge, *Men in Prison* (Oakland: PM Press, 2014 [1931]); Philip Smith, *Punishment and Culture* (Chicago: University of Chicago Press, 2008).

[11] See Pheng Cheah, *What Is a World? On Postcolonial Literature as World Literature* (Durham: Duke University Press, 2016); Eric Hayot, *On Literary Worlds* (Oxford: Oxford University Press, 2012); Mattias Viktorin, "Exil, värld och litterärt arbete. En socialantropologisk läsning av tre svenska skildringar från Sibirien", *Tidskrift för Litteraturvetenskap*, 1–2 (2018): 60–71.

which is *for* the world. This is so both in a sociological and an anthropological sense.

To begin with, most of the texts that I consider were not intended exclusively, or even primarily, for a Russian readership. They sought instead to reach out to fellow humans anywhere; they wanted, as it were, to address "the entire world" – which in practice often meant an elite circle of cosmopolitan readers in Europe, Russia and the United States. Naturally some of the writers in focus – Dostoevsky (1821–81), Chekhov (1860–1904), Iakubovitch (1860–1911) and others – wrote in Russian, and this of course limited the immediate reach of their books. But many others did not. The Polish aristocrat Ewa Felińska (1793– 1859), for example, wrote her exile memoirs in Polish, while Ivar Hasselblatt (1864–1948), a Finnish politician, told the story of his banishment to Siberia in Swedish. The nurse and philanthropist Elsa Brändström (1888–1948) – "the Angel of Siberia" – also authored a book in Swedish, based on her own extensive aid work in Russian and Siberian prisons during the First World War. The explorer and scientist Fridtjof Nansen (1861–1930) wrote his 1914 book on Siberia in Norwegian, but it also appeared in English translation that same year. Another explorer, the American George Kennan (1845–1924), and Henry Lansdell (1841–1919), a British missionary priest, both wrote in English on Siberian prisons and exile; and so did the Russian prince Peter Kropotkin (1842–1921) – while living in exile abroad.[12] Many authors also themselves belonged to a cosmopolitan community of intellectuals. London emerged in the nineteenth century as one important

---

[12] Felińska, *Revelations of Siberia*; Hasselblatt, *Förvisad till Sibirien*; Brändström, *Bland krigsfångar i Ryssland och Sibirien*; Fridtjof Nansen, *Gjennem Sibirien* (Kristiania: Jacob Dyvlads forlag, 1914); Fridtjof Nansen, *Through Siberia: The Land of the Future*, trans. Arthur G. Chater (Cambridge: Cambridge University Press, 2014); George Kennan, *Siberia and the Exile System*, 2 volumes (Cambridge: Cambridge University Press, 2012 [1891]); Henry Lansdell, *Through Siberia*, 2 volumes (London: Sampson Low, Marston, Searle, and Rivington, 1882); Peter Kropotkin, *In Russian and French Prisons* (New York: Schocken Books, 1971 [1887]); Peter Kropotkin, *Memoirs of a Revolutionist* (New York: Dover Publications, 1971 [1899]).

centre in this regard; here numerous books on the Siberian exile system were published.

The question of whom the exile texts speak to is significant also on a deeper anthropological level. In response to an imminent risk of disappearing into the void of death, it seems that people have always experienced an urge to somehow "leave a mark", lest the knowledge of their existence would forever vanish with them. "Oh that my words were now written! oh that they were printed in a book! / That they were graven with an iron pen and lead in the rock for ever!"[13] This quote from *The Book of Job*, written probably in the fifth or sixth century BCE, is arguably the paradigmatic such example, echoed on innumerable occasions throughout the succeeding history of literature.[14] According to the empire-wide census of 1897, there were some 300,000 exiles living in Siberia.[15] Of course, only a fraction of those people had the actual means to write and let alone publish their memoirs. Yet the primordial imperative to speak, to make one's voice heard, to bear witness, must have been shared by many of them. Indeed, Dostoevsky and Iakubovich describe, along with several other authors, how their fellow inmates – mostly unable to read or write – literally begged them to write down their life stories, to let the world know what life was like in "the world of the outcasts" (which was also the title Iakubovich used for his fictionalised autobiography). Mark Larrimore has observed how Job over the centuries has come to function as "a guarantor of individual consciousness, asserting a claim to being on behalf of those whose words failed. The isolated individual putting on Job's words", he suggests, "was not really alone".[16] Perhaps the lingering significance of Dostoevsky's book, which appears to have been rather well known in Siberian prisons

---

[13] "The Book of Job", 19: 23–24 (King James version).
[14] Robert Alter, The *Wisdom Books: Job, Proverbs, and Ecclesiastes. A Translation with Commentary* (New York: W. W. Norton & Company, 2010), 5.
[15] Beer, *The House of the Dead*, 28.
[16] Mark Larrimore, *The Book of Job: A Biography* (Princeton: Princeton University Press, 2013), 133.

toward the end of the nineteenth century, could be rethought in similar terms.

Narratives of Siberian exile also make up a literature which is *about* the world. It is of course first and foremost about a *particular* world: "a world apart" (Dostoevsky) or "a world of the outcasts" (Iakubovitch). To represent that world, however, proved more difficult than most authors had anticipated. Chekhov's *The Island of Sakhalin* may serve here as an illuminating example.[17]

Chekhov had travelled to the Russian Far East in 1890 to conduct research for a book on the infamous penal colony on Sakhalin Island. A prolific playwright and writer of short stories, Chekhov this time attempted a new "scientific style" characterised by empiricism, reliable observations, and statistics. "If I had written 'Sakhalin' in literary form, without figures", he later explained, "they'd say 'He's telling us fairy tales'. But numbers, statistics – they inspire respect. Any fool respects figures".[18] Yet to put his experiences into writing turned out to be challenging. In a letter to Suvorin, his publisher, Chekhov joked in frustration that "he would marry any 'girl' who could figure out how to organize all the statistical 'junk' he had accumulated on his research trip".[19] Chekhov, it seemed, had finally encountered a world that appeared to resist representation – scientific or literary.[20]

Once again, *The Book of Job* comes to mind. The "unrepresentability" of Siberia makes Chekhov's book, and several other Siberian texts too, resonate with a particular aspect of the Hebrew myth: its concern with "the limits of language and the power of representations that go beyond them".[21] Versions of this epistemological and literary challenge – of how to represent "the world" of Siberian exile and prison life – in fact still reverberate in debates on prison

---

[17] See Cathy Popkin, "Chekhov as Ethnographer: Epistemological Crises on Sakhalin Island", *Slavic Review*, 51 (1992): 36–51.
[18] Quoted in Popkin, "Chekhov as Ethnographer", 45, n. 14.
[19] Popkin, "Chekhov as Ethnographer", 44, n. 12.
[20] Lars Kleberg, *Tjechov och friheten. En litterär biografi* (Stockholm: Natur & Kultur, 2010), 106–27.
[21] Larrimore, *The Book of Job*, 30.

research. While in some contexts it remains common to present the prison as "a world apart", such "insular perspective, which views prison as a community closed in on itself and describes it as a subculture, has long been subject to debate in North American research, and has been taken up more recently in French writings".[22] In his book *Prison Worlds* (2017), the anthropologist Didier Fassin suggests an alternative approach. He characterises prison worlds as "simultaneously a reflection of society and the mirror in which it sees itself. They should therefore be thought of in ways that go beyond simply referring them to their buildings, their staff, and their regulations. We need to open the scope of our analysis to the extent that prison is open to the social space".[23]

One could argue that this perspective – the prison as open rather than closed to the social space – was immanent but mostly implicit in several of the narratives that I work with. While Chekhov and other authors set out to tell stories of Siberia as a "world apart", they nevertheless produced texts that in different ways transcended such an "insular perspective". Three features, common to several of the narratives, stand out. First, the books often include *conceptual discussions* about various aspects of "the exile experience", discussions that to different extents also approach the question of what it means to be human. For example, the authors tend to discuss the moral issues they encounter on a universal or anthropological scale, rather than referring them back exclusively to local or national contexts. Second, several authors have things to say about the native peoples of Siberia and of their ways of life, descriptions of various length that typically include *comparisons between "different worlds"* – e.g., the writer's home before exile; the world of prison or exile; and the world of a native people. Such comparisons are noteworthy because they invite an anthropological mode of thinking that evokes insights that do not fully coincide with any of those worlds, but transcend them. And third, the authors often make use of a particular style or *mode of writing* that one might characterise as "fictionalised ethnography". A brief

---

[22] Fassin, *Prison Worlds*, 11.
[23] Fassin, *Prison Worlds*, 13.

comparison with another style, satire, helps us see how exactly the ethnographic mode matters. Many Russian authors in the nineteenth century – including Gleb Uspensky (1840–1902) and Mikhail Saltykov (1826–1889) – worked within a satirical tradition.[24] Satire uses humour, irony and exaggeration to expose people and events in ways that make them look ridiculous. It thus appears inseparable from a certain place and moment in time; yet it also produces a sense of distance between the reader and the people or events represented. In contrast, the "fictionalised ethnography" adopted by Iakubovitch, Korolenko (1853–1921), Dmitry Mamin-Sibiryak (1952–1912), Fyodor Reshetnikov (1841–71) and others, has the potential to extend beyond the immediate context within which the events of the text take place.[25] An ethnographic writing style thereby elicits empathy and a sense of proximity – across cultural boundaries and across temporal distance. Korolenko, who had spent several years in exile, exemplifies this in a powerful way when in one of his "Siberian stories" he writes how Siberia teaches us to recognise even in a murderer a fellow human being.[26]

Understood as world literature, narratives of Siberian exile thus make up a heterogeneous corpus that in effect transcend both "methodological nationalism" and, although perhaps to a somewhat lesser degree, "sociological functionalism".[27] It does not fit

---

[24] See Gleb Uspenskij, *Den förlorade gatan*, trans. Carl Gustav Martinsson (Stockholm: Tidens förlag, 1951); Michail Saltykov, *Oskyldiga berättelser*, trans. Carl Gustav Martinsson (Stockholm: Tidens förlag, 1949). These are not exile narratives, but examples of satirical texts in Russian literature.

[25] See Dmitrij Mamin-Sibirjak, *Från Ural. Berättelser*, trans. Rafael Lindqvist (Stockholm: Albert Bonniers förlag, 1904); Dmitrij Mamin-Sibirjak, *Straffångar*, trans. Carl Gustav Martinsson (Stockholm: Tidens förlag, 1959); Fjodor Resjetnikov, *Pråmdragarna*, trans. E. von Sabsay and C. Sterzel (Stockholm: Tidens förlag, 1949).

[26] Vladimir Korolenko, "Flyktingen från Sachalin" (1885), in Korolenko, *Makars dröm och andra noveller*, trans. E. von Sabsay and C. Sterzel (Stockholm: Tidens förlag, 1947), 71.

[27] For a critique of "sociological functionalism", see Michel Foucault, *The Punitive Society: Lectures at the Collège de France, 1972–1973*, ed. Bernard E. Harcourt, trans. Graham Bruchell (New York: Palgrave Macmillan, 2015), 14. The key point in sociological functionalism is that

neatly within national or literary boundaries – not in terms of language, not politically, not sociologically. It is a literature, in other words, not only about the world of Siberia, nor merely of how Siberia reflected the domestic realities of Imperial Russia, but more specifically about *the world as it appeared in and through Siberia.*

Finally, narratives of Siberian exile make up a literature which is *of* the world. This of course is the case in the simple sense that the authors of Siberian exile and prison writing came from several different countries: from Finland, Norway, Russia, Sweden, the UK and the USA. But this literature is *of the world* also in a different, more intriguing, sense. Often characterised as "the end of the earth",[28] "the uttermost east"[29] and so on, Siberia might on the face of it appear as the very opposite of "the modern". Yet at the turn of the twentieth century, Siberia was in fact also related to the emergence of early modernism. It was a place where something larger was emerging – in relation to language, culture and shifting notions of the human. Chekhov's struggle with his Sakhalin book, for instance, exemplifies how "science" and "art" at that time tended to converge in particular ways – and such convergences were not limited to a Russian context. They were formative conditions of early modernism. Vincent Debaene has for instance explored in a recent book, *Far Afield* (2014), how

---

all sectors of society are interdependent, a premise that is placed under some pressure by these external narratives of Siberia. "Methodological nationalism" refers to the disciplinary practice of taking the nation-state as the point of departure and boundary for a given investigation. See Ulrich Beck, "The Cosmopolitan Condition: Why Methodological Nationalism Fails", in *Theory, Culture and Society* 24, no. 7–8 (2007): 286–90.

[28] Sharyl M. Corrado, "The 'End of the Earth': Sakhalin Island in the Russian Imperial Imagination", Ph.D. dissertation, University of Illinois at Urbana-Champaign, 2010.

[29] Charles H. Hawes, *In the Uttermost East. Being an Account of Investigations among the Natives and Russian Convicts of the Island of Sakhalin, with Notes of Travel in Korea, Siberia, and Manchuria* (London and New York: Harper & Brothers, 1904).

French anthropology emerged precisely in the epistemological space opened up at the intersection of literature and science.[30] Chekhov's attempt to move from literature toward the scientific was not, in other words, unique. Vasily Kandinsky (1866–1944), for example, attempted something similar but moved in the opposite direction. After completing an academic degree, which included a period of ethnographic fieldwork among indigenous Russian groups, Kandinsky felt that "ethnography is as much art as science".[31] Perhaps this insight was what led him to turn down an offer for a position at the University of Dorpat, to leave the academy, and to pursue a career as an exile artist in Munich.[32] Meanwhile, the journalist Vlas Doroshevich (1864–1922), in an attempt to write a book on Sakhalin that he hoped would succeed where he thought that Chekhov had failed, turned to literature to express what he thought that science, in his predecessor's book, had not been able to account for;[33] the political activist Iakubovitch wrote, as I mentioned above, his fictionalised account of his time in Siberian prisons in a style reminiscent of ethnography;[34] and finally, Lev Shternberg (1861–1927), also while in exile, developed in the 1890s a theoretical anthropology based on ethnographic field methods – twenty-five years before Bronislaw Malinowski went to the Trobriand Islands.[35]

---

[30] Vincent Debaene, *Far Afield: French Anthropology between Science and Literature*, trans. Justin Izzo (Chicago: The University of Chicago Press, 2014).

[31] Quoted in Peg Weiss, *Kandinsky and Old Russia: The Artist as Ethnographer and Shaman* (New Haven: Yale University Press, 1995), xiii.

[32] Peg Weiss, *Kandinsky in Munich: The Formative Jugendstil Years* (Princeton: Princeton University Press, 1979).

[33] Vlas Doroshevich, *Russia's Penal Colony in the Far East: A Translation of Vlas Doroshevich's "Sakhalin"*, trans. Andrew A. Gentes (London: Anthem Press, 2011).

[34] Iakubovich, *In the World of the Outcasts*.

[35] Lev Iakovlevich Shternberg, *The Social Organization of the Gilyak*. The American Museum of Natural History, Anthropological Papers, 82 (1999); Sergei Kan, *Lev Shternberg: Anthropologist, Russian Socialist, Jewish Activist* (Lincoln: University of Nebraska Press, 2009).

With a national literary framework in place, Dostoevsky arguably remains the unparalleled master, and *Notes from a Dead House* the single most important example of Siberian prison writing. But re-conceptualised as a world literature of anthropological importance, the heterogeneity of the exile narratives starts to speak to us rather differently. Something beyond "Russia" and "literature" begins to appear from behind the prison walls. It is the human world at large.

Bibliography

Alter, Robert. *The Wisdom Books: Job, Proverbs, and Ecclesiastes. A Translation with Commentary*. New York: W. W. Norton & Company, 2010.

Badcock, Sarah. *A Prison Without Walls? Eastern Siberian Exile in the Last Years of Tsarism*. Oxford: Oxford University Press, 2016.

Balasubramanian, Radha. "Harmonious Compositions: Korolenko's Siberian Stories". *Rocky Mountain Review of Language and Literature*, 44 (1990): 201–10.

Beck, Ulrich. "The Cosmopolitan Condition: Why Methodological Nationalism Fails". *Theory, Culture and Society* 24, no. 7-8 (2007): 286–90.

Beer, Daniel. *Renovating Russia: The Human Sciences and the Fate of Liberal Modernity, 1880–1930*. Ithaca: Cornell University Press, 2008.

———. *The House of the Dead: Siberian Exile under the Tsars*. London: Allen Lane, 2016.

Bentham, Jeremy. *The Panopticon Writings*. London: Verso, 1995.

Brändström, Elsa. *Bland krigsfångar i Ryssland och Sibirien 1914–1921*. Stockholm: Norstedt och söner, 1921.

Cheah, Pheng. "World against Globe: Toward a Normative Conception of World Literature". *New Literary History*, 45, no. 3, 2011: 303–29.

———. *What Is a World? On Postcolonial Literature as World Literature*. Durham: Duke University Press, 2016.

Chekhov, Anton. *The Island of Sakhalin*. Translated by Luba and Michael Terpak. London: The Folio Society, 1989.

Conrad, Peter. *Islands: A Trip through Time and Space*. London: Thames and Hudson, 2009.

Corrado, Sharyl M. "The 'End of the Earth': Sakhalin Island in the Russian Imperial Imagination", PhD dissertation, University of Illinois at Urbana-Champaign, 2010.

D'Addario, Christopher. *Exile and Journey in Seventeenth-Century Literature*. Cambridge: Cambridge University Press, 2007.

Debaene, Vincent. *Far Afield: French Anthropology between Science and Literature*. Translated by Justin Izzo. Chicago: University of Chicago Press, 2014.

Dorochevich, Vlas. *Russia's Penal Colony in the Far East: A Translation of Vlas Dorochevich's "Sakhalin"*. Translated by Andrew A. Gentes. London: Anthem Press, 2011.

Dostoevsky, Fyodor. *Notes from a Dead House*. Translated by Richard Pevear and Larissa Volokhonsky. New York: Alfred A. Knopf, 2015.

Edwards, Philip. *The Story of the Voyage: Sea-Narratives in Eighteenth-Century England*. Cambridge: Cambridge University Press, 1994.

Everett, Wendy and Peter Wagstaff, eds. *Cultures of Exile: Images of Displacement*. New York: Berghahn Books, 2004.

Fassin, Didier. *Prison Worlds: An Ethnography of the Carceral Condition*. Cambridge: Polity Press, 2017.

Feliñska, Ewa. *Revelations of Siberia. By A Banished Lady*, 2 Volumes, edited by Colonel Lach Szyrma. London: Hurst and Blackett, 1854.

Foucault, Michel. *Discipline and Punish: The Birth of the Prison*. London: Penguin Books, 1991.

———. *The Punitive Society: Lectures at the Collège de France, 1972–1973*, edited by Bernard E. Harcourt. Translated by Graham Bruchell. New York: Palgrave Macmillan, 2015.

Frazier, Ian. *Travels in Siberia*. New York: Picador, 2010.

Gentes, Andrew A. *Exile to Siberia, 1590–1822*. New York: Palgrave Macmillan, 2008.

———. *Exile, Murder and Madness in Siberia, 1823–1861*. New York: Palgrave Macmillan, 2010.

Goffman, Erving. *Asylums: Essays on the Social Situation of Mental Patients and Other Inmates*. New York: Anchor Books, 1961.

Gray, Camilla. *The Russian Experiment in Art, 1863–1922*. London: Thames and Hudson, 1986.

Hasselblatt, Ivar Wilhelm. *Förvisad till Sibirien. Minnesanteckningar*. Stockholm: Albert Bonniers förlag, 1917.

Hawes, Charles. *In the Uttermost East. Being an Account of Investigations among the Natives and Russian Convicts of the Island of Sakhalin, with Notes of Travel in Korea, Siberia, and Manchuria*. London and New York: Harper & Brothers, 1904.

Hayot, Eric. *On Literary Worlds*. Oxford: Oxford University Press, 2012.

Hingley, Ronald. *De ryska författarna och samhället, 1825–1904*. Stockholm: Bokförlaget Aldus/Bonniers, 1967.

Iakubovich, Pëtr Filippovich. *In the World of the Outcasts: Notes of a Former Penal Laborer*, 2 volumes. Translated by Andrew A. Gentes. London: Anthem Press, 2014.

Ingleheart, Jennifer, ed. *Two Thousand Years of Solitude: Exile After Ovid*. Oxford: Oxford University Press, 2011.

Jackson, David. *The Wanderers and Critical Realism in Nineteenth-Century Russian Painting*. Manchester: Manchester University Press, 2006.

Kan, Sergei. *Lev Shternberg: Anthropologist, Russian Socialist, Jewish Activist*. Lincoln: University of Nebraska Press, 2009.

Kennan, George. *Siberia and the Exile System*, 2 volumes. Cambridge: Cambridge University Press, 2012.

Kleberg, Lars. *Tjechov och friheten. En litterär biografi*. Stockholm: Natur & kultur, 2010.

Korolenko, Vladimir. *Makar's Dream and Other Stories*. Translated by Marian Fell. New York: Duffield and Company, 1916.

———. "Flyktingen från Sachalin". In Vladimir Korolenko, *Makars dröm och andra noveller*. Translated by E. von Sabsay and C. Sterzel. Stockholm: Tidens förlag, 1947.

Kropotkin, Peter. *In Russian and French Prisons*. New York: Schocken Books, 1971.

———. *Memoirs of a Revolutionist*. Mineola, New York: Dover Publications, 1971.

Lagos-Pope, María-Inés, ed. *Exile in Literature*. London: Associated University Presses, 1988.

Lansdell, Henry. *Through Siberia*, 2 volumes. London: Sampson Low, Marston, Searle, and Rivington, 1882.

Larrimore, Mark. *The Book of Job: A Biography*. Princeton: Princeton University Press, 2013.

Mamin-Sibirjak, Dmitrij. *Från Ural. Berättelser*. Translated by Rafael Lindqvist. Stockholm: Albert Bonniers förlag, 1904.

———. *Straffångar*. Translated by Carl Gustav Martinsson. Stockholm: Tidens förlag, 1959.

McConckey, James. *To A Distant Island*. New York: E.P. Dutton, 1984.

Melberg, Arne. *Resa och skriva. En guide till den moderna reselitteraturen*. Göteborg: Daidalos, 2005.

Nansen, Fridtjof. *Gjennem Sibirien*. Kristiania: Jacob Dyvlads forlag, 1914.

———. *Through Siberia: The Land of the Future*. Cambridge: Cambridge University Press, 2014.

Nordström, Ester Blenda. *Byn i vulkanens skugga*. Stockholm: Albert Bonniers förlag, 1930.

Olsson, Anders. *Ordens asyl. En inledning till den moderna exillitteraturen*. Stockholm: Albert Bonniers förlag, 2011.

Petri, Kristian and Martin Sjöberg. *Resan till Sachalin*. Stockholm: Norstedts, 1992.

Polonsky, Rachel. *Molotov's Magic Lantern: Travels in Russian History*. New York: Farrar, Straus and Giroux, 2010.

Popkin, Cathy. "Chekhov as Ethnographer: Epistemological Crises on Sakhalin Island". *Slavic Review*, 51 (1992): 36–51.

Resjetnikov, Fjodor. *Pråmdragarna*. Translated by E. von Sabsay and C. Sterzel. Stockholm: Tidens förlag, 1949.

Saltykov, Michail. *Oskyldiga berättelser*. Translated by Carl Gustav Martinsson. Stockholm: Tidens förlag, 1949.

Serge, Victor. *Men in Prison*. Oakland, CA: PM Press, 2014.

Shternberg, Lev Iakovlevich. *The Social Organization of the Gilyak*. The American Museum of Natural History, *Anthropological Papers*, 82 (1999).

Smith, Philip. *Punishment and Culture*. Chicago: University of Chicago Press, 2008.

Suleiman, Susan Rubin, ed. *Exile and Creativity: Signposts, Travelers, Outsiders, Backward Glances*. Durham: Duke University Press, 1996.

Tolstoy, Leo. *Resurrection*. Translated by Louse Maude. Oxford: Oxford University Press, 1994.

Uspenskij, Gleb. *Den förlorade gatan*. Translated by Carl Gustav Martinsson. Stockholm: Tidens förlag, 1951.

Viktorin, Mattias. "Den förvisade människan. Bibliska exilberättelser och Gamla testamentets antropologi. *Lychnos*, (2017): 27–49.

———. "Exil, värld och litterärt arbete. En socialantropologisk läsning av tre svenska skildringar från Sibirien". *Tidskrift för Litteraturvetenskap*, 1–2 (2018): 60–71.

Weiss, Peg. *Kandinsky in Munich: The Formative Jugendstil Years*. Princeton: Princeton University Press, 1979.

———. *Kandinsky and Old Russia: the Artist as Ethnographer and Shaman*. New Haven: Yale University Press, 1995.

Wood, Alan. *Russia's Frozen Frontier: A History of Siberia and the Russian Far East, 1581–1991*. London: Bloomsbury, 2011.

Young, Sarah. "Knowing Russia's Convicts: The Other in Narratives of Imprisonment and Exile of the Late Imperial Era". *Europe-Asia Studies*, 65 (2013): 1700–15.

21. Seclusion versus Accessibility: The Harems of Constantinople as Aesthetic Worlds in Stories by Elsa Lindberg-Dovlette

Helena Bodin
Comparative Literature, Stockholm University

At the turn of the twentieth century, the harem was still a secluded and concealed space, unknown to most westerners and therefore arousing their curiosity. Novels about life in a harem, such as Pierre Loti's *Les Désenchantées* (1906),[1] set in cosmopolitan Constantinople, were bestsellers and widely translated in the early twentieth century. Likewise, for several decades, descriptions of visits to Turkish harems had been essential elements in travelogues about Constantinople by female writers such as the Englishwoman E. C. C. Baillie and the Danish Elisabeth Jerichau Baumann,[2] while motifs from harems, painted by such artists as

---

[1] Pierre Loti, *Les Désenchantées: Roman des harems turcs contemporains* (Paris: Calmann-Lévy, 1906).

[2] E. C. C. Baillie, *A Sail to Smyrna: Or, an English Woman's Journal; Including Impressions of Constantinople, a Visit to a Turkish Harem, and a Railway Journey to Ephesus* ... (London: Longmans, Green, and Co., 1873), 165–99, as mentioned by Mary Roberts, *Intimate Outsiders: The Harem in Ottoman and Orientalist Art and Travel Literature* (Durham: Duke University Press, 2007), 62–63; Elisabeth Jerichau-Baumann, *Brogede rejsebilleder* (København: Forlagsbureauet, 1881), esp. 20–28, discussed by Elisabeth Oxfeldt, *Journeys from Scandinavia: Travelogues*

How to cite this book chapter:
Bodin, Helena. "Seclusion versus Accessibility: The Harems of Constantinople as Aesthetic Worlds in Stories by Elsa Lindberg-Dovlette". In *World Literatures: Exploring the Cosmopolitan-Vernacular Exchange*, edited by Stefan Helgesson, Annika Mörte Alling, Yvonne Lindqvist, and Helena Wulff, 246–260. Stockholm: Stockholm University Press, 2018. DOI: https://doi.org/10.16993/bat.u. License: CC-BY.

Osman Hamdi Bey and John Frederick Lewis, were extremely popular.

This chapter focuses on stories by the Swedish author Elsa Lindberg-Dovlette (1876–1944), in which life in the Ottoman harems of Constantinople in the early twentieth century is portrayed from the perspective of female insiders. These stories provide an example of the particular intersection of the Swedish and Turkish languages and cultures in Constantinople, as well as of Christian and Muslim beliefs, with special regard to the situation of women. As will be demonstrated, the "world-making" of these stories is informed by the limited and distorted perspective both from inside the harem and from behind the veil, but simultaneously also by the distinctive perspective of a young and – as it seems – emancipated Swedish woman, voluntarily living in a traditional Turkish harem. Although the notion of *harem* often activates a whole complex of ideas about veiled women, eunuchs, seclusion and polygamy, it does not necessarily imply polygamy but rather designates basically domestic spaces reserved for women in Muslim cultures, spaces found also in trains and boats.[3]

There are three such books by Lindberg-Dovlette on life in the harems of Constantinople. The first is a collection of eight short stories, *Kvinnor från minareternas stad* (1908; Women from the city of minarets), illustrated by portraits in India ink by Isaac Grünewald. The next is a novel, *Främling* (1924 and 1929; Stranger), of which the second edition is illustrated in bright colours by Einar Nerman, inspired by orientalist imaginings, which appeared in a series described by the publisher as gift novels "by the foremost Swedish women writers". Its sequel is also a novel, *Bakom stängda haremsdörrar* (1931; Behind the closed doors of the harem). The protagonists of the novels are two young women: the Swedish Astrid, who is renamed Anisa [Enise] when she marries a Turkish pasha and enters his harem, and the Turkish

---

of *Africa, Asia, and South America, 1840–2000* (Minneapolis: University of Minnesota Press, 2010), 31–57.

[3] Fadwa El Guindi, *Veil: Modesty, Privacy and Resistance* (Oxford: Berg, 1999), 3–12.

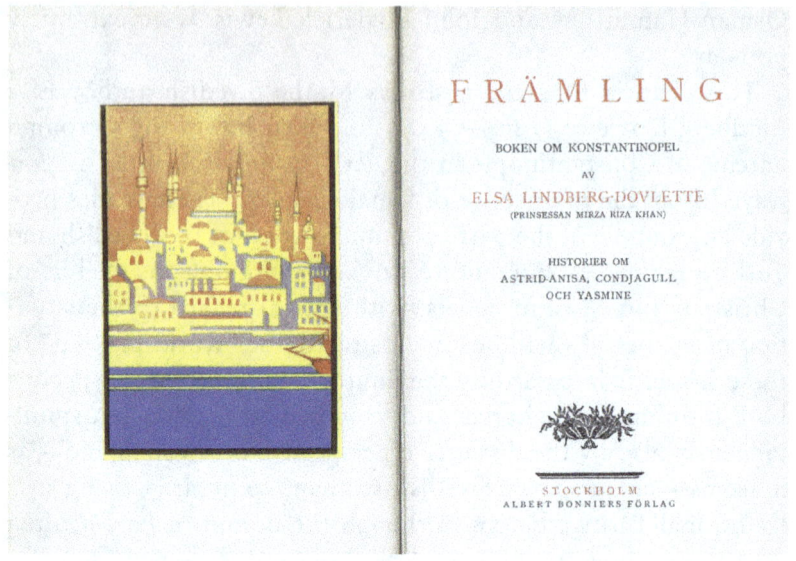

Figure 3. Title page of the second edition of Elsa Lindberg-Dovlette's *Främling* (1929; Stranger), illustrated by Einar Nerman. Copyright: Helena Bodin. License: CC BY.

Condjagull [Goncagül], who is raised in the same harem and is blind.

Lindberg-Dovlette renders various words, phrases and names in Turkish (transcribed into Roman letters according to Swedish pronunciation standards), together with translations into Swedish, occasionally with explanatory footnotes.[4] Such devices add a certain anthropological and documentary touch to these quite traditionally narrated, romantic stories of love, suffering, violence and death, which also owe something to fairy tales inspired by the Arabian Nights, especially because of their orientalising illustrations. Lindberg-Dovlette's knowledge of Turkish and of harem life has an autobiographical background: In 1902, she married a Persian diplomat and prince, Mirza Riza Khan Arfa (Arfaʿ-al-Dawla), and

---

[4] See Helena Bodin, "'Mai vite dale svenske'. Konstantinopels mångspråkighet i skandinavisk litteratur kring 1900", *Dragomanen* 19 (2017): 100–102.

lived in his harem in Constantinople as his sole wife, where she gave birth to two children. As a reminder of these circumstances, apparently, the covers and title pages of the novels are adorned with Persian and Arabic calligraphy. Her extraordinary life story attracted much public attention, and although she is generally forgotten today, she was a productive and appreciated journalist and writer in both Sweden and Finland.[5]

World-Making

By applying Eric Hayot's ideas as formulated in *On Literary Worlds* (2012), this chapter will examine aspects of character systems and connectedness as the strategies according to which Lindberg-Dovlette's stories create a distinctive aesthetic world. Drawing on Martin Heidegger in his *Der Ursprung des Kunstwerkes*, Hayot uses "world" (*Welt*) as a verb, indicating a process, an activity. His point is that there is a continuous *worlding* going on in literary works, thereby forming different aesthetic worlds: "Aesthetic worldedness is the form of the relation a work establishes between the world inside and the world outside the work".[6] These aesthetic worlds can be mapped and characterised from certain given aspects, including the examination of a work's *character system* by measuring the characters' "access to privileged narrative markers",[7] such as their access to direct speech and focalisation or their importance to the plot, while *connectedness* describes to what extent a particular aesthetic world is connected with or disconnected from other worlds. More generally, Hayot's approach implies the possibility of fruitfully reading and

---

[5] Henrika Zilliacus-Tikkanen, "Elsa Lindberg-Dovlette", in *När Könet började skriva: Kvinnor i finländsk press 1771–1900* (Helsingfors: Finska vetenskaps-Societeten, 2005), 138–44. For Elsa Lindberg-Dovlette's life and hyphenated identity, see Helena Bodin, "Haremslivet i Konstantinopel i berättelser av Elsa Lindberg-Dovlette", *Tijdschrift voor Skandinavistiek* 36 (2018): 2, 108–16.
[6] Eric Hayot, *On Literary Worlds* (Oxford: Oxford University Press, 2012), 45.
[7] Hayot, *On Literary Worlds*, 79.

interpreting "the world" as an immanent aspect of the literary text and not only as its external, contextual aspect.

Harems, and their representations in literature and art, often in connection with the topic of veiling, form an obvious and important part of studies of orientalism, inspired by the postcolonial perspective of Edward W. Said's seminal work of 1978.[8] Harems and veiling practices have been widely researched within various disciplines, such as history and anthropology, and, as an artistic or literary motif, in postcolonial and gender studies.[9] They have also been studied from the perspective of national cultures, where especially British orientalism has often been the focus.[10] Several important studies have been anthologised by Marilyn Booth in *Harem Histories* (2010).[11] Recently too, the Afghan photographer Sulaiman Edrissy has cross-dressed as a woman wearing a burka in order to explore in photographs the obscured view of the world from behind or inside the veil – a similar venture as that pursued by Lindberg-Dovlette in the early twentieth century, though by means of a different medium.[12] However, when studying older artefacts or literary texts such as Lindberg-Dovlette's stories, it is important to also consider John M. MacKenzie's criticism of Edward Said's concept of orientalism. As MacKenzie points out, the meaning and connotations of orientalism have differed with

---

[8] Edward W. Said, *Orientalism* (London: Routledge & Kegan Paul, 1978).

[9] See for example Leslie P. Peirce, *The Imperial Harem: Women and Sovereignty in the Ottoman Empire* (Oxford: Oxford University Press, 1993); Lila Abu-Lughod, *Veiled Sentiments: Honor and Poetry in a Bedouin Society* (Berkeley: University of California Press, 1999); El Guindi, *Veil*; Emily Apter, *Continental Drift: From National Characters to Virtual Subjects* (Chicago: University of Chicago Press, 1999); Reina Lewis, *Rethinking Orientalism: Women, Travel and the Ottoman Harem* (London: I. B. Tauris, 2004); Jennifer Heath, ed., *The Veil: Women Writers on Its History, Lore and Politics* (Berkeley: University of California Press, 2008).

[10] Roberts, *Intimate Outsiders*; Zeynep İnankur, Reina Lewis, and Mary Roberts, eds., *The Poetics and Politics of Place: Ottoman Istanbul and British Orientalism* (İstanbul: Pera Museum, 2011).

[11] Marilyn Booth, ed., *Harem Histories: Envisioning Places and Living Spaces* (Durham: Duke University Press, 2010).

[12] Sulaiman Edrissy, Burqa Web, http://imgur.com/a/Idjzf.

regard to space and time, and "contemporary attitudes and prejudices" should therefore not be read back into historical periods. He emphasises the importance of an appropriate historical and cultural contextualisation, and warns against "techniques of cultural cross-referencing" which risk missing complexities and tend to be ahistorical.[13] This is particularly true in relation to stories about harems and veiling practices, since they have never been homogeneous but have conveyed different meanings in different regions and eras. Veiling in the late twentieth century may have, for example, other reasons and connotations from at the beginning of the century.[14]

What interests me in Lindberg-Dovlette's stories is how the secluded milieus of harems in cosmopolitan early twentieth-century Constantinople are made accessible to western readers in their vernacular languages, not only in Swedish, but also in translation into Finnish, German, French and Dutch. Readers are thereby allowed to experience the limited view and reduced mobility of women in the harem as if from the inside. The stories are set during the reign of Abdülhamid II, before 1909, while the harems themselves were questioned, dissolved and finally forbidden in Turkey shortly afterwards under Atatürk in the 1920s. Also, this was the time when women were struggling for – and received – suffrage, in Sweden in 1919 and in Turkey in 1934. As we will see, these stories comment implicitly, but in particular cases also explicitly, on the political situation of women in both Turkey and Sweden. On yet another level, they reflect the obscured and distorted worldview of westerners producing and enjoying stories and paintings about harems. Issues of seeing – or rather issues of unseeing and blindness – connected with veiling practices, thematised in these stories and emphasised in some of the illustrations, will therefore be central to my analysis and discussion, while the concept of "seeing" will be operationalised as an analytical tool. Similar issues of seeing and perspective form the centre of attention in Mary Roberts's study of earlier travelogues by British women in

---

[13] John M. MacKenzie, *Orientalism: History, Theory and the Arts* (Manchester: Manchester University Press, 1995), 214, xxi, xvii.
[14] See further El Guindi, *Veil*, esp. at 3–12 and 177–86.

the chapter "Being Seen" in *Intimate Outsiders* (2007),[15] which will therefore be the starting point for my analysis, before introducing aspects of literary world-making as perceived by Hayot.

Observation and Confrontation

In contrast to men (except the husband), all women, including westerners, were allowed to enter the harem. Mary Roberts has found that women's travelogues generate a different kind of orientalist fantasy, experienced from inside the harem, from men's "voyeuristic images of the harem that emphasised the western viewer's fantasy of looking without being observed".[16] Her point is that western female visitors themselves became confronted by women in the harem and exposed to their straightforward opinions and active, interrogative stare. While the male gaze traditionally commanded the visual field, women could bear witness to fear, because of their sense of being watched and "simultaneously subject and object of the look".[17] By being observed by the women in the harem, the western woman was enabled "to see herself in the harem by being seen".[18]

At first glance, the conclusion drawn by Roberts seems to be valid also with regard to the stories by Elsa Lindberg-Dovlette. In the opening short story, for example, there is the young Turkish female narrator, who repeatedly addresses the reader personally as "my foreign friend" ("min främmande vän"),[19] thereby inviting the reader to take a walk through Constantinople: "Come with me, you, my foreign friend!" ("Kom med mig du, min främmande vän!")[20] But the reader is also told to be grateful that she does not have to dress in a veil, since the veil turns all faces pale and all

---

[15] Roberts, *Intimate Outsiders*, 80–91.
[16] Roberts, *Intimate Outsiders*, 82.
[17] Roberts, *Intimate Outsiders*, 86.
[18] Roberts, *Intimate Outsiders*, 90.
[19] Lindberg-Dovlette, *Kvinnor i minareternas stad* (Stockholm: Bonniers, 1908), 4. All translations from Lindberg-Dovlette's works are my own.
[20] Lindberg-Dovlette, *Kvinnor i minareternas stad*, 22.

eyes sad.[21] Also, the Swedish protagonist of the two later novels, Astrid, is amicably welcomed into the harem, on the one hand, by the blind Condjagull, but is treated on the other as a stranger by the evil and jealous Yasmine, her antagonist.[22] Furthermore, it is impossible for Astrid to feel comfortable wearing the veil: "To look out on the world through a thick black veil, that is like seeing everything through tears" ("Att se ut på världen genom en tät svart slöja, det är som att se på allt genom tårar").[23] In this way, both the reader and the Swedish protagonist are kindly invited to take part in daily harem life in Constantinople. But at the same time, the protagonist is treated and behaves like a stranger, who is observed and confronted by the women in the harem, and sometimes even makes protests or shows her own dislike of the restrictions imposed on women. The following analysis, where Hayot's ideas of character system and connectedness are examined, will show, however, that issues of seeing and perspective are even more complex in Lindberg-Dovlette's stories on Constantinople and its harems than in the cases described by Roberts. They are not only thematised by Lindberg-Dovlette but decisive for the total construction of this aesthetic world, characterised by seclusion, flickering light, darkness and various severe limitations on both vision and mobility.

Character System and Connectedness

The character system of Lindberg-Dovlette's stories constructs a women's world, where the female characters are the important ones as regards their allotted space for speaking and reflecting in dialogues and descriptions. Women are also the driving force when it comes to action. All kinds of actions – grounded in respectful honour, loving helpfulness, malicious incantations and open hatred – take place between women, as does that particular

---

[21] Lindberg-Dovlette, *Kvinnor i minareternas stad*, 23.
[22] Elsa Lindberg-Dovlette, *Bakom stängda haremsdörrar* (Stockholm: Bonniers, 1931), 95.
[23] Elsa Lindberg-Dovlette, *Främling. Boken om Konstantinopel. Historier om Astrid-Anisa, Condjagull och Yasmine* (Stockholm: Bonniers, 1929 [1924]), 127.

kind of eroticism and intimate depiction of feminine charms traditionally associated with harems.

The aesthetic world created by Lindberg-Dovlette is thus maintained by the female characters, by their actions, dialogues, reflections and desires. When it comes to the aspect of connectedness, however, the harem may seem to be disconnected from other, surrounding worlds, since the characters often reflect on how confining the barred harem windows and the veil are, how limited the field of vision becomes for the women in the harem, and how hard it is to move swiftly and sure-footedly when wearing a veil. Since the narrative point of view is theirs, it follows that the limitations to their field of vision crucially affect this aesthetic world. It becomes as narrow as the women's perspective is limited by the barred windows and the veil. This complication is also developed by the artist Isaac Grünewald in black India ink drawings, illustrating Lindberg-Dovlette's short stories, where concealing veils and sometimes window lattices are included as stylised parts of his portraits of the female protagonists. That the novels' Turkish protagonist Condjagull is born in the harem and gradually loses her sight only to become totally blind before the age of marrying, strengthens further this theme in a symbolic way.

Inside the harem, the view is limited because of the characteristic windows, which are covered by a type of wooden lattice that prevents women from being viewed from the outside and creates a special flickering light indoors. However, as the Swedish Astrid-Anisa observes, it is possible to look out through the lattice. But to do so, she has to press her forehead against the wooden slats, and then the view becomes cut into small pieces. She compares the distorted view to a jigsaw puzzle.[24]

Views from the harem are also limited because of the surrounding walls containing locked gates. In Lindberg-Dovlette's stories, these gates and doors always have more than one lock, of which the keys are carefully guarded. One of the short stories describes how the door to the harem may be transformed: Once the wedding contract is signed, the door closes, and thereafter, it is "no

---

[24] Lindberg-Dovlette, *Främling*, 155.

Figure 4. Vignette in India ink by Isaac Grünewald, illustrating Elsa Lindberg-Dovlette's short story "Skepp, som segla förbi" (Ships passing by) in *Kvinnor från minareternas stad* (1908; Women from the city of minarets), p. 116. License: public domain.

more the light harem door of childhood" ("icke barndomens lätta haremsdörr"), but a door belonging to the husband and master, a door with heavy hinges and many locks.[25]

If women need to go outside the harem, they have to be covered all over, according to law. As the female Turkish narrator in Lindberg-Dovlette's opening short story complains, it is not only a matter of being veiled but also of not being allowed by the police to stroll about the streets or to enjoy the beautiful light,

---

[25] Lindberg-Dovlette, *Kvinnor i minareternas stad*, 105.

colours and fresh air from the bridge. She has to move on straight ahead to her goal with her black veil turned down, preventing her from seeing clearly.[26] Another example may be found in the episode where Astrid-Anisa accompanies the blind Condjagull to her wedding. They travel in a carriage in which it is completely dark, like in a closed box, because of its covered windows. While the Swedish girl feels depressed in the darkness, the bride herself notices no difference between travelling in bright daylight or in a blacked-out carriage, because of her blindness, which especially in this case once again acquires symbolic significance.[27]

In spite of these difficulties, there are women in Lindberg-Dovlette's stories who deliberately leave the harem, trying to escape its enclosure. But when they change their minds and want to return to the harem, they are not let in. Their escape leads thus only to homelessness. Outside the harem, they face death, not because of sentences passed against them, but due to circumstances such as drowning or freezing to death. For the Swedish Astrid, this works however the other way round: She dies when she enters the harem and is renamed Anisa. Her husband declares, "Astrid is no more" ("Astrid finnes ej mer"), and she herself mourns Astrid as if dead – without being buried, Astrid has been obliterated.[28]

According to these examples, the aesthetic world of the harem in Lindberg-Dovlette's stories seems to be a disconnected one, enclosed by shutters, locked doors and turned-down veils. If a woman ventures nevertheless to use its openings in order to exit or enter, she is not transported into another world, as in the literary genre of fantasy, but most probably encounters death – physically or socially, through an irretrievable loss of identity. A potential opening in this aesthetic world does not therefore mean any new opportunity for the woman who tries it, but only her end.

Yet this aesthetic world does connect with the surrounding world: from the inside of the harem. Since Lindberg-Dovlette's stories are set in Constantinople in the early twentieth century,

---

[26] Lindberg-Dovlette, *Kvinnor i minareternas stad*, 19.
[27] Lindberg-Dovlette, *Bakom stängda haremsdörrar*, 127.
[28] Lindberg-Dovlette, *Främling*, 61 and 154.

they portray not only traditional Turkish ways of living, but also the heavy influence on life in the harems of western, particularly Parisian customs, fashion and education. For decades, there had been western governesses residing in harems who taught the girls reading, writing and how to speak French and English. Women in the harems played the piano and practised singing, dressed in Parisian fashions and furnished their bedrooms in the western style; they were also eager to have their portraits painted or be photographed – while all these activities have often been elaborated on in harem novels and travelogues. According to Lindberg-Dovlette's novels, it was of great importance for noble Turkish girls in the harems to be "*tjock à la franka*" [çok alafranga], translated in a footnote as "Just like in Europe" ("Alldeles som i Europa").[29] Hence there was a large English gilded bed in the blind girl's bedroom, even if she could not see it and never slept in it. The western influence on life in the harems also explains how Astrid-Anisa was able to communicate with her – both of them knew French.

The connections between the aesthetic world of the harem in Lindberg-Dovlette's stories and the surrounding world are consistently sustained by western governesses, who teach girls western European languages and arts (including fashion, design and furnishing) in the harems, not by moving about freely outside the harems or by opening their windows and doors. From an anthropological perspective, the governesses and teachers function in these cases as cultural brokers, while the inner world of the harem, rich in linguistic and artistic skills, may be likened to a cultural enclave – it neither connects with, nor influences the prevailing norms and values of the surrounding Ottoman society. The conflicts between western (Christian) and eastern (Muslim) practices are therefore numerous in Lindberg-Dovlette's stories and characterise their aesthetic world.[30]

---

[29] Lindberg-Dovlette, *Främling*, 208.
[30] For examples, see Bodin, "Haremslivet i Konstantinopel".

Conclusion

Inspired by Eric Hayot's thoughts on literary worlds and aspects of his idea of "worldedness" in literature, my analysis has demonstrated that Elsa Lindberg-Dovlette's stories set in the harems of Constantinople create an aesthetic world, wherein western readers can experience the special limited view and reduced mobility of the women living in them. This is accomplished by means of the character system of these stories, where women are the speaking, reflecting and acting protagonists, as well as by means of the special treatment of connectedness, where an outer, far-reaching disconnection with the surrounding world is complicated by inner, extensive connections with western Europe, its languages, arts and fashions. Although the harem in the aesthetic world created by Lindberg-Dovlette has certain connections with the surrounding world, women who pass through the walls of the harem – in either direction – risk their lives or identities. When the characters enter the harem or don the veil, it is not simply a matter of women observing each other from different perspectives, but rather of *seeing itself*, that is of the women's possibility to see and thereby partake in the surrounding world, that changes and becomes reduced, distorted and sorrowful. This makes Lindberg-Dovlette's stories different from the depictions of harems that Mary Roberts has studied in British women's travelogues.

In the aesthetic world of Lindberg-Dovlette, life conditions in the harem are portrayed from the twofold critical perspective of a Swedish woman. Although she has voluntarily become an insider, she laments the limitations imposed on her field of vision by the harem shutters and the veil, as well as the situation of Turkish women longing to enjoy mobility and open prospects. Elsa Lindberg-Dovlette's stories thereby offer a strong critique of the norms of harem life, but the strength of their argument lies not primarily in the discussions and reflections that are explicitly articulated by the female characters, but rather in their aesthetic world as a whole, constructed out of limited and distorted views. Above, I referred to Hayot's words that aesthetic "worldedness" implies a relation "between the world inside and the world outside the work". My conclusion on the aesthetic world of Lindberg-Dovlette is that it makes the seclusion of women in the harems of

Constantinople accessible to all readers of her stories, men and women alike.

Bibliography

Abu-Lughod, Lila. *Veiled Sentiments: Honor and Poetry in a Bedouin Society*. Updated edition. Berkeley: University of California Press, 1999 [1986].

Apter, Emily. *Continental Drift: From National Characters to Virtual Subjects*. Chicago: University of Chicago Press, 1999.

Baillie, E. C. C. *A Sail to Smyrna: Or, an English Woman's Journal; Including Impressions of Constantinople, a Visit to a Turkish Harem, and a Railway Journey to Ephesus...* London: Longmans, Green, and Co., 1873.

Bodin, Helena. "'Mai vite dale svenske'. Konstantinopels mångspråkighet i skandinavisk litteratur kring 1900". *Dragomanen* 19 (2017): 88–103.

———. "Haremslivet i Konstantinopel i berättelser av Elsa Lindberg-Dovlette". *Tijdschrift voor Skandinavistiek* 36 (2018): 2, 108–16.

Booth, Marilyn, ed. *Harem Histories: Envisioning Places and Living Spaces*. Durham: Duke University Press, 2010.

Edrissy, Sulaiman. Burqa Web. http://imgur.com/a/Idjzf.

El Guindi, Fadwa. *Veil: Modesty, Privacy and Resistance*. Oxford: Berg, 1999.

Hayot, Eric. *On Literary Worlds*. Oxford: Oxford University Press, 2012.

Heath, Jennifer, ed. *The Veil: Women Writers on Its History, Lore and Politics*. Berkeley: University of California Press, 2008.

İnankur, Zeynep, Reina Lewis and Mary Roberts, eds. *The Poetics and Politics of Place: Ottoman Istanbul and British Orientalism*. İstanbul: Pera Museum, 2011.

Jerichau-Baumann, Elisabeth. *Brogede rejsebilleder*. Kjøbenhavn: Forlagsbureauet, 1881.

Lewis, Reina. *Rethinking Orientalism: Women, Travel and the Ottoman Harem*. London: I. B. Tauris, 2004.

Lindberg-Dovlette, Elsa. *Kvinnor från minareternas stad*. Vignetter av Isaac Grünwald. Stockholm: Bonniers, 1908.

———. *Främling. Boken om Konstantinopel. Historier om Astrid-Anisa, Condjagull och Yasmine*. Colour illustrations by Einar Nerman. Stockholm: Bonniers, 1929 [1924].

———. *Bakom stängda haremsdörrar*. Stockholm: Bonniers, 1931.

Loti, Pierre. *Les Désenchantées: Roman des harems turcs contemporains*. Paris: Calman-Lévy, 1906.

MacKenzie, John M. *Orientalism: History, Theory and the Arts*. Manchester: Manchester University Press, 1995.

Oxfeldt, Elisabeth. *Journeys from Scandinavia: Travelogues of Africa, Asia, and South America, 1840–2000*. Minneapolis: University of Minnesota Press, 2010.

Peirce, Leslie P. *The Imperial Harem: Women and Sovereignty in the Ottoman Empire*. Oxford: Oxford University Press, 1993.

Roberts, Mary. *Intimate Outsiders: The Harem in Ottoman and Orientalist Art and Travel Literature*. Durham: Duke University Press, 2007.

Said, Edward W. *Orientalism*. London: Routledge, 1978.

Zilliacus-Tikkanen, Henrika. *När Könet började skriva: Kvinnor i finländsk press 1771–1900*. Helsingfors: Finska vetenskaps-Societeten, 2005.

22. The Travelling Story of Pettersson in the Pacific

Anette Nyqvist
Social Anthropology, Stockholm University

Some stories travel better than others. Consider the true story of Carl-Emil Pettersson, a young man who, at 17, leaves his home in rural Sweden and went to sea. He survives a ship-wreck in the Pacific, settles on the small island where is washed up, marries the local princess and strikes it rich in gold findings. That story is a well-travelled one.

The aim of this chapter is to show how the story of Pettersson's life not only endures extensive geographical and temporal travels but also, on its way through time and space, traverses multiple literary genres as well as forms of media. I use the story of Pettersson as an illustrative example of my suggestion that travelling stories play significant roles in processes of world-making. The world that the story of King Karl Pettersson I, in combination with its intriguing sequential narrative, assist in making is the persistent one of life in Oceania as "Paradise on Earth". This chapter points to the significant roles that media and narratives have in processes of world-making. It takes as its theoretical point of departure, Nelson Goodman's seminal work *Ways of Worldmaking*[1] and builds on how others point to the intricate relationship between narratives and media in processes of world-making.

---

[1] Nelson Goodman, *Ways of Worldmaking* (Indianapolis: Hackett, 1978).

How to cite this book chapter:
Nyqvist, Anette. "The Travelling Story of Pettersson in the Pacific". In *World Literatures: Exploring the Cosmopolitan-Vernacular Exchange*, edited by Stefan Helgesson, Annika Mörte Alling, Yvonne Lindqvist, and Helena Wulff, 261–274. Stockholm: Stockholm University Press, 2018. DOI: https://doi.org/10.16993/bat.v. License: CC-BY.

However, I here first turn to the literature on the world-making capacity of travel writing because, while this chapter points to the role that travelling stories have in processes of world-making, the larger project – through which the story of Pettersson suddenly came sailing – concerns the world-making capacity of travel writing.

Travel Stories and World-Making

Travel writing is a genre inherently difficult to define and classify. Travel stories, both oral and written, have been around for thousands of years and is one of the world's oldest and most widely dispersed forms of literature. It is a genre that has no national boundaries but, rather, claims to be cosmopolitan by definition.[2] As a particular corpus travel writing is a socially important literary genre and it has been far more influential in shaping perceptions of people and places than scholarly ethnographic publications.[3] Already during the tenth century travel narratives were seen as an important and influential literary genre outside the western world. The medieval Moroccan traveller and scholar Ibn Battuta is a point in case.[4] From a western perspective some of the earliest travel accounts are from the European explorers' reports of their discoveries and encounters in and of the world.[5] From Edward Said's *Orientalism* and on, we know that travel writing does not consist simply of factual accounts but, rather, often furthers exoticism and domination through textual (mis)representation.[6] Travel stories "reflect the conditions and

---

[2] William Dalrymple, "Home Truths Abroad", *The Guardian*, 19 September 2009; Tim Youngs, *The Cambridge Introduction to Travel Writing* (Cambridge: Cambridge University Press, 2013).

[3] Hussein M. Fahim, "European Travellers in Egypt: The Representation of the Host Culture," in *Travellers in Egypt*, ed. P. Starkey and J. Starkey (London: I. B. Tauris, 1998); Youngs, *The Cambridge Introduction*.

[4] Paul Zumthor and Catherine Peebles, "The Medieval Travel Narrative", *New Literary History* 25.4 (1994): 809–24; Youngs, *The Cambridge Introduction*.

[5] Maria Pretzler. *Pausanias. Travel Writing in Ancient Greece* (New York: Bloomsbury, 2013); Youngs *The Cambridge Introduction*.

[6] Edward Said, *Orientalism* (New York: Random House, 1978); Daniel

attitudes that exist in the traveller's home culture"[7] and, thus, "travellers have already been influenced, before they travel, by previous cultural representations that they have encountered".[8]

Travel stories from the large area now commonly called Oceania typically lump together the 30 000 islands scattered in the in the Pacific Ocean and turn them into an idea rather than a geographical location.[9] The consistent story that is told, by western travellers, from here is that life on the islands of Oceania is "Paradise on Earth". This notion was created as soon as western travellers went to the area and wrote home about it. This world-making, then, began with the travelogues of the eighteenth-century European explorers. The "South Seas" became the great frontier of romantic imagination as well as of modern science, and the allure of the area acquired utopian connotations.[10] One of the earliest written accounts is from 1768 when French explorer Louis Antoine de Bougainville spent ten days in what is now known as Tahiti and reports how he thought he "had been transported into the garden of Eden".[11] Bougainville soon learned that the island was not quite the paradise that he at first imagined, but his journal's depictions of an erotic paradise with its enticing pairing of native beauty and free love endured.[12] Such exoticised and romanticised stories of life in Oceania are consistently nurtured and reproduced.

In a general sense, it has been suggested that literary products are key elements in the configuration of the world itself.[13] Scholars

---

Martin Varisco, *Reading Orientalism: Said and the Unsaid* (Seattle: University of Washington Press. 2007).

[7] Youngs, *The Cambridge Introduction*, 165.
[8] Youngs, *The Cambridge Introduction*, 9.
[9] Anders Mathlein, *Senare i Söderhavet. Öar i drömmen och samtiden* (Stockholm: Carlssons bokförlag, 1994).
[10] Felipe Fernández-Armesto, "Reviews", *Journeys* 3, no. 2 (2002): 125–28.
[11] Louis-Antoine de Bougainville. *A Voyage round the World: Performed by Order of His Most Christian Majesty, in the Years 1766, 1767, 1768, and 1769.* Translated by J. R. Forester (London: J. Nourse Bookseller to His Majesty & T. Davies Bookseller to the Royal Academy, 1772), 228–29.
[12] Joyce Appleby, *Shores of Knowledge. New World Discoveries and the Scientific Imagination* (New York: W.W. Norton & Co. 2013), 192.
[13] Eduardo Archetti, *Exploring the Written. Anthropology and the Multiplicity of Writing* (Oslo: Scandinavian University Press, 1994).

of travel literature pose the question: "How does travel literature produce 'the rest of the world'?"[14] or, put differently, what role do travel stories play in processes of world-making? Peter Bishop answers that question with the assertion that: "Travel writing creates worlds, it does not simply discover them".[15] World-making thus starts, according to Goodman, from worlds already known; in other words: "the making is a remaking".[16]

This brings us straight to the roles that different forms of media and stories, or narratives, have in processes of world-making. Media play an important part here and the role of media, medialisation and the dynamics of pre- and remediation are seen as important factors that have shaped, and continue to shape, our ways of world making".[17] More specifically, inter- and transmedial adaptations and connections are key drivers in processes of world-making. This means that an assortment of different media, such as literary texts, newspaper articles, TV-programmes and more, together play significant parts in the making of worlds.[18] In conjunction with this, the complexity of narrative world-making deserves to be mentioned because the narrative is a powerful way of world-making. The main reason for this is that the narrative and storytelling – that is the procedures and processes through which happenings, occurrences, or incidents become meaningful events, stories, and story-worlds – not only generates possible worlds, narratives also exert performative power.[19]

---

[14] Mary Louise Pratt, *Imperial Eyes. Travel Writing and Transculturation* (London: Routledge, 1992).

[15] Peter Bishop, "The Geography of Hope and Despair: Peter Matthiessen's The Snow Leopard", *Critique* 26, no. 4 (1985): 204.

[16] Goodman, *Ways of Worldmaking*, 6.

[17] Ansgar Nünning and Vera Nünning, "Ways of Worldmaking as a Model for the Study of Culture: Theoretical Frameworks, Epistemological Underpinnings, New Horizons", in *Cultural Ways of Worldmaking. Media and Narratives*, eds. Nünning et al. (Berlin: de Gruyter, 2010), 4.

[18] Birgit Neumann and Martin Zierold, "Media as Ways of Worldmaking: Media-specific Structures and Intermedial Dynamics", in *Cultural Ways of Worldmaking: Media and Narratives*, ed. Nünning et al. (Berlin: de Gruyter, 2010), 103–18.

[19] Ansgar Nünning, "Making Events – Making Stories – Making Worlds: Ways of Worldmaking from a Narratological Point of View", in *Cultural*

The Story of Pettersson and Its Travels

Now to the well-travelled story of Carl-Emil Pettersson, how it contributes to the construction on life in Oceania as Paradise on Earth and why this particular travelling story has come to shape the notion of life in the South Seas for generations of Swedes.

Carl-Emil Pettersson, the story goes,[20] was born in October 1875 in the, then, small rural community of Sollentuna, just north of Stockholm. 17 years old he left home for work on board naval and merchant ships. Little was known of Pettersson after his departure in 1892 until one day, 15 years later, he showed up at his mother's door in Stockholm. Pettersson had during those years worked on merchant ships in the Bismarck Archipelago northeast of New Guinea in the western Pacific.[21] He had survived multiple dramatic ship wrecks and in 1905 he washed up on one of the Tabar Islands where he remained, acquired land and started a coconut palm plantation, became friends with the local chief, Lamry, and fell in love with his daughter, Singdo-Misse. After his brief visit in Stockholm Pettersson returns to Tabar and continues his life there. He marries Singdo-Misse and their first child is born 1910.[22]

Ways of Worldmaking: Media and Narratives, ed. Nünning et al. (Berlin: de Gruyter, 2010), 191–214.

[20] See for example: Unsigned article "Från signalmatros till negerprins och plantagekung", *Dagens Nyheter*, 17 September 1922; A handwritten note, signed J. Blees and dated May 24 1924 containing Petterson's biographical data. Note available in the archives of The Museum of World Culture, Gothenburg; "Svenska öden och äventyr i främmande land", *Allsvensk Samling*, 15 May 1924. Clipping available in the archives of The Museum of World Culture, Gothenburg and Joakim Langer and Hélena Regius, *Kung Kalle av Kurrekurreduttön. En resa i Efraim Långstrumps fotspår* (Stockholm: Forum, 2002).

[21] The region was at the time under German colonial rule.

[22] Hélena Regius, "Carl Emil Pettersson 1875–1937", in *Kung Kalle av Kurrekurreduttön. En resa i Efraim Långstrumps fotspår*, co-written with Joakim Langer (Stockholm: Forum, 2002), has thoroughly researched and accounted for the life story of Pettersson. In later editions (according to personal communication 29 March 2017) anthropologist Hélena Regius is referenced as being the author of this chapter in the book.

It is not until 1914 that the story of Carl Emil Pettersson becomes publically known in Sweden as the count, diplomat and author Birger Mörner (1867–1930) writes about it in a travel book. In 1913 Birger Mörner conducts his third trip to the South Seas and meets Pettersson and his family in their home on Tabar. Mörner's book about his travels in the eastern New Guinea and surrounding island, *Aráfis tropiska år*,[23] is published in 1914. Mörner – or rather his alter ego Aráfi – does not, however, pay much attention to Pettersson but dedicates a chapter to Petterson's wife, Singdo-Misse, and her stories. It is only at the very end of the chapter that Mörner mentions Pettersson in a short note.[24] The chapter is accompanied by a photograph of Carl Emil Pettersson and his wife, Singdo-Misse, both dressed in traditional Swedish costumes and surrounded by two of their children. In November 1914 Birger Mörner holds a public lecture in Stockholm about his travels and the largest daily newspaper, *Dagens Nyheter*, prints a report from the event. Carl Emil Pettersson's story is prominently featured, complete with Mörner's photo of the couple in Österåker-costumes, under the headline: "A Stockholm boy on the South Sea islands".[25] It tells the story of how "Kalle Pettersson" was shipwrecked in the South Sea, settled on the island of Tabar, married a local woman with whom he has several children and how he, because of his body and strength is called "The Strong Charley". The story of Pettersson, not least with the assistance of the photograph, gains a lot of attention in Sweden at the time and he becomes a national celebrity.[26]

Singdo-Misse dies 1921 soon after giving birth to the couple's ninth child and Pettersson travels to Sweden on a mission to find a second wife.[27] Chief Lamry of Tabar has by this time also passed away and Swedish media now write about Carl Emil Pettersson

---

[23] Birger Mörner, *Aráfis tropiska år* (Stockholm: P. A. Norstedts & söners förlag, 1914), 208–16. Book title in translation: "Aráfi's tropical years".
[24] Mörner, *Aráfis tropiska år*, 216.
[25] "En Stockholmspojke på Söderhavsöarna", *Dagens Nyheter*, 11 November 1914.
[26] Regius, "Carl Emil Pettersson," 117–21.
[27] Regius, "Carl Emil Pettersson", 117–21.

as royalty.²⁸ Several of the published stories of Pettersson's life on Tabar build on letters that Pettersson himself has written to editors and prominent figures in Sweden.²⁹ During the early 1920s there are plenty of stories of "Prince Pettersson", "King Carl I" and, since he does find a Swedish woman to marry – and bring back to Tabar – during his visit, she, Jessie Simpson from Gävle, becomes "Princess" and "Queen Pettersson" in the Swedish press.³⁰ By the 1930s Carl Emil Pettersson has become a media personality in Sweden. Events in his life on the islands in the western Pacific are printed as news in Swedish press and his life story is told and re-told in so-called women's magazines such as *Husmodern* and *Vecko-Journalen*.³¹ Over the years Swedish readers learn that Pettersson's coconut palm business is crumbling, that both he and his new wife have fallen ill in malaria and other tropical diseases, that Pettersson has found gold on his land on one of the Tabar islands, that he wants to sell his estate and business and move back to Sweden, that "Queen" Jessica has returned to Sweden for medical reasons, that she dies in Stockholm in May 1935 and that Carl Emil Pettersson, "King of Tabar", himself dies of a heart attack in Sydney, Australia May 1937.³² It is now that the travelling story of Pettersson in the Pacific takes a new turn.

Travelling to Fiction

Who does Carl Emil Pettersson resemble if not the incredibly strong, rich in gold, King of an island in the South Seas: Captain

---

²⁸ See for example: "Från signalmatros till negerprins och plantagekung", *Dagens Nyheter*, 17 September 1922; "Prins Pettersson av Fisher Island," *Dagens Nyheter*, 24 September 1922; "Svenska öden och äventyr i främmande land", *Allsvensk Samling*, 15 May 1924.
²⁹ Some of these letters are available in the archives of The Museum of World Culture, Gothenburg, filed as: "Documents concerning collection 35.27.1–12., s.c. malingans from Tabar."
³⁰ Regius, "Carl Emil Pettersson," 116–57, and Langer and Regius, "Kung Kalle", 187–88.
³¹ See especially: Thyra Ekegårdh, "Svenskan som blev drottning på en Söderhavsö", *Husmodern*, June 16, 1935.
³² Regius, "Carl Emil Pettersson", 152–65.

Ephraim Longstocking, Pippi Longstocking's seafaring father? Pippi Longstocking is, of course, the main character in Swedish author Astrid Lindgren's popular children's books about is the clever and independent girl in red braids and odd clothes who has superhuman strength, unlimited funds and lives by herself – with her horse and monkey – in a large house in a small town somewhere in Sweden. Her mother is "an angel in heaven" and her father is a seafaring Captain who, after a shipwreck in the Pacific washed ashore on a small island where he remained and eventually became King.[33]

It was a Swedish author, Joakim Langer, who in the year 2000 made the connection and "found" Pippi's father. In his basement Langer came upon a short newspaper clipping from 1935 stating that "King Karl I Pettersson sells his Kingdom".[34] Having, like most Swedes, grown up with the stories of Pippi Longstocking Langer immediately recognised the striking resemblances between Carl Emil Petterson and Ephraim Longstocking, Pippi's father.[35] Langer's theory is that Astrid Lindgren (1907–2002) must have read about, and been inspired by, Carl Emil Pettersson's life story in Swedish press and then, later, built her fictional character Ephraim Longstocking on Pettersson's story. Langer tries to get this confirmed from Lindgren herself but in early 2001 she is not healthy enough to recall or respond. He does reach Lindgren's sister, Stina, who confirms that she read about King Pettersson growing up.[36]

Astrid Lindgren created and developed the characters and adventures of Pippi Longstocking in 1941 as she told stories to

---

[33] Lindgren, Astrid. "Astrid Lindgren berättar om sig själv", in *En bok om Astrid Lindgren*, ed. M. Ørvig. (Stockholm: Rabén & Sjögren, 1977); Lundqvist, Ulla. *Århundradets barn. Fenomenet Pippi Långstrump och hennes förutsättningar* (Stockholm: Raben & Sjögren, 1979); Metcalf, Eva-Maria. "Tall Tale and spectacle in Pippi Longstocking," *Children's Literature Association Quarterly* 15, no. 3 (1990): 130–35.

[34] Joakim Langer, "Joakims berättelse", in *Kung Kalle av Kurrekurreduttön. En resa i Efraim Långstrumps fotspår*, co-written with Hélena Regius (Stockholm: Forum, 2002), 12.

[35] Langer, "Joakims berättelse", 11–24.

[36] Langer, "Joakims berättelse", 15; Regius, "Carl Emil Pettersson," 133.

cheer up her young daughter, who was suffering from pneumonia. Lindgren did not write down the stories of Pippi until 1944 when she herself became ill and had to be still.[37] After having been rejected by one publishing house, another publisher took on Lindgren and issued *Pippi Långstrump* late in 1945, soon to be followed by *Pippi goes aboard* in 1946 and *Pippi in the South Seas* in 1948.[38] Pippi's seafaring father Captain Ephraim Longstocking, King of Kurrekurredutt Isle in the South Seas, is more properly introduced to the readership in Lindgren's second and third books about Pippi. All in all Lindgren has published 15 books about Pippi Longstocking and, based on sales, these are the most popular of her work. The Pippi books have been translated into 70 languages and sold in 60 million copies worldwide.[39] Lindgren's Pippi adventures have been adapted into various TV-series and feature films both in Sweden and many other countries. Children all over the world and particularly in Sweden have, quite literally, grown up with the stories of Pippi Longstocking and come to well know her adventures, not least the ones where she sets off to look for – and find – her distant father Captain Ephraim Longstocking who is living on an island in the South Seas.[40]

The articles about Carl Emil Pettersson, as readers will have noticed, as well as, to some extent, Lindgren's books about Pippi in the South Seas are no exceptions from the exoticising and romanticising, stereotypical and outright racist descriptions and depictions of the people of, and life on, the islands in the western Pacific. Granted, the children's book from 1948, it should be noted, does not contain any reference to sexual license. But the notion of island life as idyllic, blissful and naturally opulent is

---

[37] Jens Andersen, *Denna dagen, ett liv: en biografi över Astrid Lindgren* (Stockholm: Norstedts, 2014); Margareta Strömstedt, *Astrid Lindgren: en levnadsteckning* (Stockholm: Raben & Sjögren, 2007).
[38] In translation: *Pippi Longstocking*, *Pippi goes aboard* and *Pippi in the South Seas*.
[39] astridlindgren.se, accessed April 1, 2017, http://www.astridlindgren.se.
[40] The TV-series *Pippi Långstrump*, aired in Sweden 1969 together with the major feature film *Pippi Långstrump på de sju haven* [transl. *Pippi Longstocking on the Seven Seas*) from 1970, were both critically acclaimed and immensely popular.

there, as well as the colonial, and racist, representations of "the natives". In the new 2015 edition of the first three Pippi books racist dialogue was edited out as was dialogue from the 2014 edition of the 1960s TV-series.[41]

Back to Langer's "discovery" of the real life model of Ephraim Longstocking. In 2001 he sets out on a search both for more information on Pettersson and for collaborators on a trip to Tabar island to look for traces of Pettersson. Langer gets in touch with anthropologist Hélena Regius who, as part of her research on Malangan art and ceremonies in Melanesia,[42] already had tracked down Pettersson's story and relatives in Australia, Papua New Guinea and Tabar Island.[43] Langer contacts media, find sponsors and collaborators and soon he two of his co-workers, Hélena Regius and a journalist travel to Tabar Islands to talk to relatives of Pettersson/Longstocking.[44] Upon their return, in April 2001, media scramble for the story of how the father of Pippi Longstocking is "found".[45] Langer and Regius are interviewed in national and international media,[46] they soon get a book deal and publish their book *Kung*

---

[41] Lotta Olsson, "'Negerkung' tas bort i nya Pippi", Dagens Nyheter, February 14, 2015; Kim Veerabuthooro Nordberg, "SVT rensar ut rasismen ur Pippi Långstrump", SVT Nyheter, 29 September 2014, accessed 1 April 2017: http://www.svt.se/kultur/svt-rensar-ut-rasismen-ur-pippi-langstrump.

[42] Intricate figures carved out of wood made for ceremonial use. Carl Emil Pettersson had, upon request, sent several malangans to Sweden. "The Pettersson malangans" have, on several occasions, been in exhibit at Swedish museums and are now kept in storage at The Museum of World Culture, Gothenburg.

[43] Hélena Regius, "Hélenas berättelse", in *Kung Kalle av Kurrekurreduttön. En resa i Efraim Långstrumps fotspår*, co-written with Hélena Regius (Stockholm: Forum, 2002), 25–35, and personal communication 29 March 2017.

[44] Joakim Langer, "Resan", in *Kung Kalle av Kurrekurreduttön. En resa i Efraim Långstrumps fotspår*, co-written with Hélena Regius (Stockholm: Forum, 2002), 39–59.

[45] Rolf Broberg, "Kurrekurreduttön i verkligheten", *Dagens Nyheter*, 29 April 2001; "Här är Pippis riktiga pappa. Carl E Pettersson var Kungen i Söderhavet", *TT/Aftonbladet*, 29 April 2001.

[46] Joakim Langer, "Vad hände sedan? 1937–2002", in *Kung Kalle av Kurrekurreduttön. En resa i Efraim Långstrumps fotspår*, co-written with Hélena Regius (Stockholm: Forum, 2002), 176.

Kalle av Kurrekurreduttön. En resa i Efraim Långstrumps fotspår,[47] Langer writes his own children's book on the theme: *Kapten Kalle på de sju haven*,[48] Regius and Langer tour the country and hold public lectures about the Pettersson/Longstrump story, they are contracted by a travel company and return to the Tabar Islands with a group of tourists, there is an exhibit at The Museum of Ethnography in Stockholm and Langer signs a feature film contract for the Pettersson/Longstocking story with a major filmmaker.[49]

Travelling Stories and the Making of Worlds

Carl Emil Pettersson's life in the Bismarck Archipelago northeast of New Guinea in the western Pacific became well known since his story, as I have here shown, was featured in a travel book in 1914 and then circulated in the Swedish print media between 1914 and 1937. Pettersson's life story was subsequently, through Astrid Lindgren's creation of Ephraim Longstocking, transposed into fiction and circulated once again, this time it travelled to even more forms of media such as TV-series and feature films. The story travelled to other geographical locations when Lindgren's books, as well as TV-series and feature films, were translated into other languages. With the connection of Carl Emil Pettersson to Ephraim Longstocking the story took a new journey and their joint story travelled through all forms of mass media in multiple languages and geographical settings, it travelled to non-fiction and fiction literature, and it travelled such diverse textual contexts as museum exhibits and travel catalogues.

The story of Pettersson/Longstocking and his life on an island in the Pacific has by now travelled for more than 100 years, all over the world and across literary genres and through various forms of media. Along the way there have been adaptations, adjustments and editing of the story but the idealised, romanticised and

---

[47] Langer and Regius, *Kung Kalle* (2002).
[48] Joakim Langer and Martin Trokenheim, *Kapten Kalle på de sju haven*, (Stockholm: Forum, 2002).
[49] Langer, "Vad hände sedan?", 180–85. The feature film is later "put on ice" and has yet to be made.

exoticised descriptions and depictions of life in Oceania remain intact and immovable throughout the travels.

And this well-travelled story keeps on moving – now it is at the core of a chapter in an anthology on literature and world-making published by Stockholm University Press. My point here, with the assistance of Carl-Emil Pettersson and Ephraim Longstocking, is to show that stories, or narratives, and various genres and forms of media play significant roles in processes of world-making.

Bibliography

Andersen, Jens. *Denna dagen, ett liv: en biografi över Astrid Lindgren*. Stockholm: Norstedts, 2014.

Appleby, Joyce. *Shores of Knowledge. New World Discoveries and the Scientific Imagination*. New York: W.W. Norton & Co., 2013.

Archetti, Eduardo. *Exploring the Written. Anthropology and the Multiplicity of Writing*. Oslo: Scandinavian University Press, 1994.

astridlindgren.se, accessed 1 April 2017, http://www.astridlindgren.se.

Bishop, Peter. "The Geography of Hope and Despair: Peter Matthiessen's The Snow Leopard," *Critique* 26, no. 4 (1985): 203–16.

Bougainville, Louis-Antoine de. *A Voyage round the World: Performed by Order of His Most Christian Majesty, in the Years 1766, 1767, 1768, and 1769*. Translated by J. R. Forester. London: J. Nourse Bookseller to His Majesty & T. Davies Bookseller to the Royal Academy, 1772.

Broberg, Rolf. "Kurrekurreduttön i verkligheten". *Dagens Nyheter*, 29 April 2001.

Dalrymple, William. "Home Truths Abroad". *The Guardian*, 19 September 2009.

"En Stockholmspojke på Söderhavsöarna". *Dagens Nyheter*, 11 November 1914.

Fahim, Hussein, M. "European Travellers in Egypt: The Representation of the Host Culture". In *Travellers in Egypt*, edited by P. Starkey and J. Starkey. London: I. B. Tauris, 1998.

Fernández-Armesto, Felipe. "Reviews". *Journeys* 3, no. 2 (2002): 125–28.

"Från signalmatros till negerprins och plantagekung". *Dagens Nyheter*, 17 September 1922.

Goodman, Nelson. *Ways of Worldmaking*. Indianapolis: Hackett, 1978.

"Här är Pippis riktiga pappa. Carl E Pettersson var Kungen i Söderhavet". *TT/Aftonbladet*, 20 April 2001.

Langer, Joakim and Hélena Regius. *Kung Kalle av Kurrekurreduttön – en resa i Efraim Långstrumps fotspår*. Stockholm: Forum, 2002.

Langer, Joakim and Martin Trokenheim, *Kapten Kalle på de sju haven*, Stockholm: Forum, 2002.

Lindgren, Astrid. "Astrid Lindgren berättar om sig själv". In *En bok om Astrid Lindgren*, edited by M. Ørvig. Stockholm: Rabén & Sjögren, 1977.

Lundqvist, Ulla. *Århundradets barn. Fenomenet Pippi Långstrump och hennes förutsättningar*. Stockholm: Raben & Sjögren, 1979.

Mathlein, Anders, *Senare i Söderhavet. Öar i drömmen och samtiden*. Stockholm: Carlssons bokförlag, 1994.

Metcalf, Eva-Maria. "Tall Tale and Spectacle in Pippi Longstocking," *Children's Literature Association Quarterly* 15, no. 3 (1990): 130–35.

Mörner, Birger. *Aráfis tropiska år*. Stockholm: P. A. Norstedts & söners förlag, 1914.

Neumann, Birgit and Martin Zierold. "Media as Ways of Worldmaking: Media-Specific Structures and Intermedial Dynamics". In *Cultural Ways of Worldmaking: Media and Narratives*, edited by Nünning et al., 103–18. Berlin: de Gruyter. 2010.

Nordberg, Kim Veerabuthooro. "SVT rensar ut rasismen ur Pippi Långstrump". *SVT Nyheter*, 29 September 2014, accessed 1 April 2017, http://www.svt.se/kultur/svt-rensar-ut-rasismen-ur-pippi-langstrump.

Nünning, Ansgar. "Making Events – Making Stories – Making Worlds: Ways of Worldmaking from a Narratological Point of

View". In *Cultural Ways of Worldmaking: Media and Narratives*, edited by Nünning et al., 191–214. Berlin: de Gruyter. 2010.

Nünning, Ansgar and Vera Nünning. "Ways of Worldmaking as a Model for the Study of Culture: Theoretical Frameworks, Epistemological Underpinnings, New Horizons". In *Cultural Ways of Worldmaking. Media and Narratives*, edited by Nünning et al., 1–25. Berlin: de Gruyter, 2010.

Olsson, Lotta. "'Negerkung' tas bort i nya Pippi". *Dagens Nyheter*, 14 February 2015.

Pratt, Mary Louise. *Imperial Eyes. Travel Writing and Transculturation.* London: Routledge, 1992.

Pretzler, Maria. *Pausanias. Travel Writing in Ancient Greece.* New York: Bloomsbury, 2013.

"Prins Pettersson av Fisher Island". *Dagens Nyheter*, 24 September 1922.

Said, Edward. *Orientalism.* New York: Random House, 1978.

Strömstedt, Margareta, *Astrid Lindgren: en levnadsteckning*, Stockholm: Raben & Sjögren, 2007.

"Svenska öden och äventyr i främmande land". *Allsvensk Samling*, 15 May 1924.

"Svenskan som blev drottning på en Söderhavsö". *Husmodern*, 16 June 1935.

Varisco, Daniel Martin, *Reading Orientalism. Said and the Unsaid.* Seattle: University of Washington Press, 2007.

Youngs, Tim. *The Cambridge Introduction to Travel Writing.* Cambridge: Cambridge University Press, 2013.

Zumthor, Paul and Catherine Peebles. "The Medieval Travel Narrative". *New Literary History* 25, no. 4 (1994): 809–24.

23. Indian Imaginaries in World Literature and Domestic Popular Culture

Per Ståhlberg
Media Studies, Södertörn University

At the turn of the millennium India became widely known as a "global superpower of the future". The image of a country rapidly transitioning from tradition and poverty to modernity and wealth was a dominant story, reported both internationally and domestically. Since then, these expectations have been both questioned and challenged, but they have also evolved as a recurrent theme in literature. Fiction writing centred on Indian society and its diaspora has been notably present in a global literary sphere since the last few decades but, importantly, also the Indian book market has more recently grown remarkably. Stories in English about urban Indian middle class realities are abundant both internationally and within India.[1]

In this chapter I will focus on two novels, both of them written in English by Indian authors and published in the same year, 2008: Aravind Adiga's *The White Tiger* and Chetan Bhagat's *The Three Mistakes of My Life*.[2] These are novels that relate closely to contemporary Indian society, or rather, to certain ideas of what a new Indian society, emerging around the first decade of the second millennium, is becoming. Both books could be read as commen-

---

[1] E. Dawson Varughese, *Reading New India: Post-Millennial Indian Fiction in English* (London: Bloomsbury, 2013).
[2] Aravind Adiga, *The White Tiger: A Novel* (London: Atlantic Books, 2008); Chetan Bhagat, *The Three Mistakes of My Life* (New Delhi: Rupa & Co, 2008).

How to cite this book chapter:
Ståhlberg, Per. "Indian Imaginaries in World Literature and Domestic Popular Culture". In *World Literatures: Exploring the Cosmopolitan-Vernacular Exchange*, edited by Stefan Helgesson, Annika Mörte Alling, Yvonne Lindqvist, and Helena Wulff, 275–286. Stockholm: Stockholm University Press, 2018. DOI: https://doi.org/10.16993/bat.w. License: CC-BY.

taries on what it means, in terms of desires, possibilities and constraints, to be young in today's India. Similarities and differences between them are in several ways instructive for discussing some conceptual issues within the scholarly field of world literature.[3]

Although they share several themes and narrative elements, one could claim that these books do not belong within a common literary field. Indian fiction, according to Francesca Orsini, is distributed across three distinct literatures. First, an *international* field of Indian literature in English, published by international publishing houses; second, a *national* field of English literature, usually limited to domestic recognition; third, several *regional* literatures in various vernacular languages that are rarely translated.[4] Suman Gupta has spelt out the difference between the first two Indian literatures, written in English:

> The Indian commercial fiction in English which circulates predominantly within the country can be regarded as reasonably distinct from the "literary fiction" which has a larger-than-India presence.[5]

Adiga's *The White Tiger* was awarded the Man Booker Prize of 2008, and obviously qualifies as belonging to the field of international literary Indian fiction, while Bhagat's *The Three Mistakes*, hugely successful domestically but hardly recognised outside India, would fall in the national category of commercial literature in English. The question, then, is to what extent these two novels narrate the contemporary Indian society differently.

---

[3] Adiga's book have been discussed frequently by scholars (while Bhagat's have rarely been noticed). See for example Ines Detmer, "New India? New Metropolis? Reading Aravind Adiga's The White Tiger as a 'condition-of-India Novel'", *Journal of Postcolonial Writing* 47.5 (2011): 535–545; Ana Cristina Mendes, "Exciting Tales of Exotic Dark India: Aravind Adiga's The White Tiger", *The Journal of Commonwealth Literature* 45, no. 2 (2010): 275–93; A. J. Sebastian, "Poor-Rich Divide in Aravind Adiga's The White Tiger", *Journal of Alternative Perspectives in the Social Sciences* 1, no. 2 (2009): 229–45.

[4] Francesca Orsini, "India in the Mirror of World Fiction", *New Left Review* 13 (2002): 75–88.

[5] Suman Gupta, "Indian 'commercial' fiction in English, the Publishing Industry, and Youth Culture", *Economic and Political Weekly* 46, no. 5 (2012): 46.

Two stories, in brief

The White Tiger is a story of Balram, a clever young man born into a poor low caste family in rural north India. He nurses a dream of escaping poverty and a future that is predetermined by a brutally hierarchical society. His first break comes when he manages to get a job as a driver in a landowning family. Together with his employers he moves to Gurgaon, the rapidly growing satellite city south of New Delhi, and encounters a world of new possibilities. In this middle class environment of luxury and corruption, Balram is a keen learner and soon realises how he could make his dreams come true. He kills his boss and steals a large amount of "black money" with which he escapes to Bangalore, the hub of IT business. There he starts a new life as a crafty entrepreneur in the transport business.

The Three Mistakes is about another young man, Govind. He lives in Ahmedabad, but on the old and less fortunate side of the river, which divides this modernising city into separate worlds. Govind loves mathematics but does not want to become an engineer as his mother wishes – he wants to be a businessman. Together with two best friends he opens a cricket shop in the compound of a Hindu temple. The goal is to build up a business profitable enough to be moved over to one of the posh shopping malls on the modern side of the river. The three friends almost succeed when a number of serious obstacles come in their way: first an earthquake, then a religious-political riot and finally a disastrous love affair. Govinds's dream finally ends with his suicide attempt.

Apart from the obvious theme about young men with ambitions of becoming businessmen, these two novels have several other elements and features in common – though often in contrasting shapes. I will not engage closely with the stories as such, but rather read the books from some distance (though not as distant as Franco Moretti suggests for reading world literature):[6] first by discussing the literary technique by which these stories are told, second, by looking at how the novels converge with other forms of cultural productions and, third, by asking how the stories relate

---

[6] Franco Moretti, "Conjectures on World Literature", *New Left Review* 1 (2000): 54–68.

to a contemporary Indian reality. My aim is to understand how vernacular and cosmopolitan tendencies are juxtaposed in various ways, thus constructing "world-making" narratives for separate audiences.

Framing the Indian story

To begin with, Adiga and Bhagat use similar techniques to narrate their core story within a frame tale: the protagonists themselves relate the events of their lives to a particular addressee. In Adiga's novel, this narration is conveyed in the form of letters that the self-taught entrepreneur Balram writes on his computer, addressed (but never sent) to the Chinese Prime Minister Wen Jiabao.[7]

In Bhagat's book, Govind tells his story to an author (a fictive Chetan Bhagat) sitting by the young man's hospital bedside after his suicide attempt. However, in this novel the listener-author is recounting what Govind tells him, in contrast to Balram who, in Adiga's book, is narrating in the first person.

In both novels the respective frame tales are essential to the vernacular and cosmopolitan dynamics of its story. In Adiga's case, it is of course no incident that Balram writes his letters to a Chinese addressee. In the image of a new global world order India and China are siblings and need to share experiences with each other – "*Hindi-Chini bhai-bhai*" as Balram phrase it. Now, he wants to give the Chinese prime minister a true picture of the new entrepreneurial India. One point with this frame tale is that it gives the author plenty of reasons to *explain* and reveal Indian particularities. The Chinese prime minister can't possibly know much about caste, religion or politics in India – Balram has to clarify. One could claim that the book is, with a liberal use of Rebecca Walkowitz's term, "born translated" for an international audience – though in a cultural, rather than linguistic, sense.[7]

The story in Chetan Bhagat's book is, on the other hand, told to a person who is familiar with the same place, share similar

---

[7] Rebecca L. Walkowitz, *Born Translated: The Contemporary Novel in an Age of World Literature* (New York: Columbia University Press, 2015).

ideas and tacit knowledge as the protagonist. The author (both the fictive persona and the real individual) has, like Govind, been a young student in Ahmedabad. General Indian peculiarities do not need to be explained; only the local setting, Ahmedabad, is explicitly introduced to a non-local reader.

Thus, by different uses of a common frame tale technique Adiga and Bhagat are constructing literary worlds that relate to readers in contrasting ways. *The Three Mistakes* is a novel that offers opportunities for identification. The main characters are sympathetic and their everyday life is full of activities and incidents – cricket, school exams and family troubles – recognisable to any young middle class Indian. *The White Tiger* does not have that appeal; it is a dark novel and most characters are unsympathetic or even cruel. Few readers would feel close to the cynical underdog Balram – and audiences who possibly might identify do not read novels in English. A dominant theme in this book is the relation between middle class families and their domestic servants. This portrayal is certainly not flattering, thus, Adiga is in a sense "disloyal" to Indian middle class readers.

This difference with regard to identification is also emphasised linguistically. Adiga does use typical words and concepts from Hindi, but selectively and always in italics, thus emphasising the cultural "otherness" of the story. In Bhagat's novel, on the other hand, the characters speak English as if it is natural to them and they do not express themselves in obviously Indianised English.[8] By contrast, Adiga is sometimes explicitly pointing out particular Indian English pronunciations and phrasing. Just as Aamir Mufti has observed with reference to Salman Rushdie's novels, Adiga attributes this form of speech to subaltern and illiterate people, rather than to the urban middle class who is more likely to speak such English.[9] It is the low-caste villager Balram, who has a peculiar Indian accent, not his employer.

---

[8] Rita Kothari and Rupert Snell, eds., *Chutnefying English: The Phenomenon of Hinglish* (New Delhi: Penguin Books India, 2011).

[9] Aamir R. Mufti, *Forget English! Orientalisms and World Literature* (Cambridge: Harvard University Press, 2016), 166.

Media convergence

A particular Indian discourse, established since decades, is concerned with a cleavage within the society: a traditional, rural, vernacular and religious Indian population is contrasted with a modern, urban, secular, English-speaking elite. The problematic relation between these "two Indias" is a recurrent theme in political and intellectual debate as well as in popular cultural productions. At the time when Adiga's and Bhagat's novels were published, an advertisement appearing in major television channels, both English and vernacular, was topical. It consisted of a video in black and white in which the legendary film actor Amitabh Bachchan was walking completely alone on a long bridge, a huge uncompleted construction reaching out over the sea with no land in sight. With a dark and powerful voice, the actor reads a poem:

> There are two Indias in this country.
> One India is straining at the leash, eager to spring forth and live up to all the adjectives that the world has been showering recently upon us.
> The other India is the leash.
> One India says, "Give me a chance and I'll prove myself". The other India says, "Prove yourself first and maybe then you'll have a chance".
> One India lives in the optimism of our hearts. The other India lurks in the skepticism of our minds [...].[10]

In *The White Tiger* this discourse is mirrored in Balram's desire to step out of "the Darkness" (tradition) into "the Light" (modernity) and in *The Three Mistakes* it is the Sabermati river dividing Ahmedabad into two worlds that represent this cleavage.

Looking at these two books from a little further distance it is also striking how both are associated with particular movies. *The Three Mistakes* has been made into a Bollywood film; it was

---

[10] The advertisement was part of a campaign, called India Poised, commissioned by the newspaper *The Times of India* and run during 2007, celebrating the 60th anniversary of independence. The poem was written by Gulzar, a well-known Urdu poet and film director.

released 2013 with the title *Kai Po Che!*.[11] Chetan Bhagat participated himself in writing the script, but one could indeed argue that already the novel contained most of the essential elements of a popular *Masala* movie, mixing romance, action, drama and comedy, and including archetypal characters of this film genre. The book even has a typical Bollywood film structure in which the narrative often takes a completely new direction after the compulsory half-way break in a three hour long production. Thus, the novel is written in a form in tune with Hindi cinema. In this sense it is *The Three Mistakes* which is "born translated", but for a vernacular, not a cosmopolitan, audience. Considering that most of Chetan Bhagat's novels have been adapted for the screen, he is a writer that blurs the boundaries of Francesca Orsini's taxonomy: he is published within the field of national English literature but has a much larger presence in vernacular popular culture.[12]

The White Tiger has not (yet) been adapted to film and it is not at all written in the style of a Bollywood production. Its relation to a particular movie is incidental. It was not only Aravind Adiga's book that attracted international attention to the "darkness" of a new global India in 2008. This was also the year when Danny Boyle's film *Slumdog Millionaire* premiered on cinema theaters around the world – it won eight Academy Awards (Oscars) in 2009.[13] The film is about a slum boy and his everyday struggle for existence in a brutal and unequal society, but whose experiences ultimately become a resource for escaping from that cruel world. Almost simultaneously *The White Tiger* and *Slumdog Millionaire* reminded the world that India is still a very unjust society, thus contributing in challenging the recently successful international "rebranding" of India as a modern democratic market economy. Not surprisingly, this attention stimulated heated debate within

---

[11] The film *Kai Po Che!* is directed by Abhichek Kapoor (2013). The title is a Gujarati expression used in kite flying competitions.

[12] Bhagat's novels are also translated into several vernacular languages.

[13] *Slumdog Millionaire* is based on another novel: *QA* by Vikas Swarup (London: Doubleday, 2005).

India about a representational "backlash"; these are not the success stories that should support India in the global economy.[14]

In this latter case of convergence between a novel and a film it becomes obvious that there is a certain friction between reality and fiction. This brings us to the next level of reading. That is, how do these two novels concretely relate to real events and persons in contemporary India?

Fiction and obtrusive realities

In both Adiga's and Bhagat's novels there is a powerful politician recurring in the background of the story. In *The White Tiger* this is "The Great Socialist", the Chief Minister whose powerful hands are everywhere, affecting Balram from the village school into the city. For a domestic reader, this character is unmistakably recognisable by appearance and deeds, because he is closely modelled on an (in)famous political former Chief Minister in the state of Bihar. This is of course a level of meaning that is lost to most international readers, but it is also not essential. The White Tiger is concerned with fictionalising reality in its general tendencies, not in the details. It does, however, reveal that the novel is double coded, not only aimed at an international audience.

The Three Mistakes has a more intricate relation to reality. The book narrates two horrible events that are not literary inventions.[15] The first is an earthquake that occurred on 26 January 2001, killing some 20 000 people in the state of Gujarat. The second, and in the novel more defining event, took place a year later, in February 2002, when a riot broke out in which 2 000 people, mainly Muslims, were killed by a mob. The Chief Minister of

---

[14] Assa Doron and Ursula Rao, "From the Edge of Power: The Cultural Politics of Disadvantage in South Asia", *Asian Studies Review* 33, no. 4 (2009): 419–28; Ana Cristina Mendes, "Showcasing India Unshining: Film Tourism in Danny Boyle's Slumdog Millionaire", *Third Text* 24, no. 4 (2010): 471–79; Anjana Mudambi, "Another Look at Orientalism: (An) Othering in Slumdog Millionaire", *Howard Journal of Communications* 24, no. 3 (2013): 275–92.

[15] This might sound strange in a commercial "feel-good"-novel, but is very consistent with the Bollywood form of the book.

Gujarat, at that time, was accused of not trying to stop – even to encourage – violence that later would be known as "the Gujarat massacre".[16] In the book, neither the name nor any descriptions of this politician is mentioned. Still, Bhagat tells a story of violence masterminded by activists in a nationalist political party, with blessings from political leaders high in command. One could have expected that this delicate theme would be toned down in the Bollywood version of the story. Not so. The film narrative is even modified so that the riot is emphasised – with a twist, however, that makes it possible to interpret some justification for those committing the killings. The domestic debate around the movie was confused: was *Kai Po Che* (and Chetan Bhagat) for or against the accused Chief Minister? Importantly, the film was screened and debated during the year preceding the Indian parliament election of 2014, in which the controversial politician would campaign as leader of the opposition. Today the same man, Narendra Modi, is the Prime Minister of India. Rarely is "commercial fiction" so intricately intertwined with vernacular realities of such ramification.

This has consequences, however. *The Three Mistakes* (or its film version) hardly stands for itself as a fictional narrative. The local reality is too obtrusive; it becomes a meta-frame for the whole story. The book is of course possible to read for an international audience without familiarity with the political controversies around "the Gujarat massacre" – but that would be a completely different reading.[17] In Adiga's novel it is, by contrast, rather the global reality that is obtrusive. That story is completely inscribed into a world scenario of rising economic power in Asia.

---

[16] For an anthropological account of the "Gujarat Massacre" see Parvis Ghassem-Fachandi, *Pogrom in Gujarat: Hindu Nationalism and Anti-Muslim Violence in India*. Princeton: Princeton University Press, 2012).

[17] The global reading audience may, however, encounter the Gujarat riots of 2002 in Arundhati Roy's recent novel *The Ministry of Utmost Happiness*, (London: Penguin 2017) in which they appear as a defining event of the story.

Concluding discussion

I have above discussed two books from the starting point that there are essential distinctions between two Indian English literatures: one international, "literary fiction" and one domestic, "commercial fiction". As I have tried to show, these differences are rather easy to find; in the framing of the stories, in the convergence with other media forms as well as in how they relate to actual political realities. In that sense this analyses would confirm the distinction that both Francesca Orsini and Suman Gupta identify between an international and a national Indian fiction written in English.

However, this presumption could also be challenged, not least on empirical grounds. *The White Tiger* is published, read and has a reputation within India – and it definitely has a commercial value – while *The Three Mistakes* circulates internationally, at least within a large Indian diaspora. Furthermore, it is very possible that other distinctions are more important than those between international and national texts, for example within fields of vernacular literary production.[18] In one of very few anthropological studies of literature in India, Sadana Rashmi draws the attention to a context in which distinctions between literary fields are completely irrelevant. That is where most books are traded in India: by vendors at railway stations, on pavements or at major road crossings in large cities. In these places, all sorts of Indian books are hawked, often in pirated editions, alongside international best-sellers by authors such as John Grisham, Paulo Coelho and Dan Brown.[19] Distinctions that one may find between fictional worlds of particular texts might soon blur when looking at the social reality where books are produced, sold, read, reviewed, debated or mixed up with other forms of cultural imaginaries. One example would be to see how distinctions are created and

---

[18] Suman Gupta, *Consumable Texts in Contemporary India: Uncultured Books and Bibliographical Sociology* (Houndmills: Palgrave Macmillan, 2015), 39–60.

[19] Rashmi Sadana, *English Heart, Hindi Heartland: The Political Life of Literature in India* (Berkeley: University of California Press, 2012): 3.

negotiated on book fairs and literature festivals that lately have been mushrooming in India. It is in this direction that I intend to work further on Indian writing within the field of world literature.

Bibliography

Adiga, Aravind. *The White Tiger*. London: Atlantic Books, 2008.

Bhagat, Chetan. *The Three Mistakes of My Life*. New Delhi: Rupa & Co, 2008.

Detmers, Ines. "New India? New Metropolis? Reading Aravind Adiga's The White Tiger as a 'condition-of-India Novel'". *Journal of Postcolonial Writing* 47, no. 5 (2011): 535–45.

Doron, Assa, and Ursula Rao. "From the Edge of Power: The Cultural Politics of Disadvantage in South Asia". *Asian Studies Review* 33, no. 4 (2009): 419–28.

Ghassem-Fachandi, Parvis. *Pogrom in Gujarat: Hindu Nationalism and Anti-Muslim Violence in India*. Princeton University Press, 2012.

Gupta, Suman. "Indian 'commercial'fiction in English, the Publishing Industry, and Youth Culture". *Economic and Political Weekly* 46, no. 5 (2012): 46–53.

Gupta, Suman. *Consumable Texts in Contemporary India: Uncultured Books and Bibliographical Sociology*. Houndmills: Palgrave Macmillan, 2015.

Kai Po Che! Directed by Abhishek Kapoor. Film. UTV Motion Pictures. 2013.

Kothari, Rita and Rupert Snell. *Chutnefying English: The Phenomenon of Hinglish*. New Delhi: Penguin Books India, 2011.

Mendes, Ana Cristina. "Exciting Tales of Exotic Dark India: Aravind Adiga's The White Tiger". *The Journal of Commonwealth Literature* 45, no. 2 (2010): 275–93.

———. "Showcasing India Unshining: Film Tourism in Danny Boyle's Slumdog Millionaire". *Third Text* 24, no. 4 (2010): 471–79.

Moretti, Franco. "Conjectures on World Literature". *New Left Review* 1 (2000): 54–68.

Mudambi, Anjana. "Another Look At Orientalism: (An)Othering in Slumdog Millionaire". *Howard Journal of Communications* 24.3 (2013): 275–92.

Mufti, Aamir R. *Forget English! Orientalisms and World Literature.* Cambridge: Harvard University Press, 2016.

Orsini, Francesca. "India in the Mirror of World Fiction". *New Left Review* 13 (2002): 75–88.

Roy, Arundhati. *The Ministry of Utmost Happiness.* London: Penguin, 2017.

Sadana, Rashmi. *English Heart, Hindi Heartland: The Political Life of Literature in India.* Berkeley: University of California Press, 2012.

Sebastian, A. J. "Poor-Rich Divide in Aravind Adiga's The White Tiger". *Journal of Alternative Perspectives in the Social Sciences* 1, no. 2 (2009): 229–45.

Slumdog Millionaire. Film. Directed by Danny Boyle. Fox Searchlight Pictures. 2008.

Swarup, Vikas. *Q&A.* London: Doubleday, 2005.

Varughese, Dawson E., *Reading New India: Post-Millennial Indian Fiction in English.* London: Bloomsbury, 2013.

Walkowitz, Rebecca L. *Born Translated: The Contemporary Novel in an Age of World Literature.* New York: Columbia University Press, 2015.

PART 4:
LOST AND FOUND: TRANSLATION AND CIRCULATION

24. Introduction to Part 4
Yvonne Lindqvist

What are the conditions and consequences of textual migrancy?

In response to this question, translation studies has become one of the most dynamic and wide-ranging transdisciplinary fields in the humanities of today – a fact reflected in the variety of theoretical frames and methodologies of the chapters in this section dealing mainly with multidirectional cosmopolitan and vernacular translation, circulation and reception of literature. The chapters scrutinise cosmopolitanising and vernacularising translation dynamics, i.e. literary migration on the global translation field from mainly dominated positions to the dominating in in the first case, and from dominating to dominated in the latter. The researchers clearly show that the processes of literary translation are implicated in struggles over cultural prestige and domination and that literary translation is one of the most strategic and consequential sites of negotiation between the cosmopolitan and the vernacular. The seven essays in the section are organised according to focus in translation dynamics starting with vernacularising translation into Swedish, Danish and Norwegian moving on to cosmopolitanising translation dynamics from Swedish into English and French, and concludes with cosmopolitanising mediation in Mozambican lusophone and East African literature. Five out of seven chapters explore Scandinavian and particularly Swedish literary translation dynamics. This distinguishes the present section from the other three in this book, demonstrating thereby the research programme's grounding in Sweden and also

---

How to cite this book chapter:
Lindqvist, Yvonne. "Introduction to Part 4". In *World Literatures: Exploring the Cosmopolitan-Vernacular Exchange*, edited by Stefan Helgesson, Annika Mörte Alling, Yvonne Lindqvist, and Helena Wulff, 289–294. Stockholm: Stockholm University Press, 2018. DOI: https://doi.org/10.16993/bat.x. License: CC-BY.

the potential gains of approaching world literature from within a given regional context (or a selection of such contexts).

Hence, in the chapter "Translation Bibliomigrancy", **Yvonne Lindqvist** presents the theoretical framework of her study of the meeting of Caribbean and Scandinavian literature by means of translation. Bibliomigrancy, i.e. the dynamics of cosmopolitanising and vernacularising translation processes in world literatures, is a central concept in the study as well as the *double consecration hypothesis,* according to which this literature needs to be consecrated primarily within respective dominant literary centre(s), and secondly within the Anglo-American literary culture before agents in Scandinavia even consider a translation into the Scandinavian languages. Contending that translation is a form of literary consecration the study traces translations *from* the Caribbean French, English and Spanish languages to the Scandinavian Swedish, Danish and Norwegian languages during the period 1990–2010. Given the construction of the studied literary cultures (mono-, duo- or pluri-centric), bibliomigrancy to the Scandinavian periphery will evince individual characteristics. The chapter discusses how cosmopolitanising and vernacularising translation dynamics influence bibliomigrancy and the hypothesised double consecration in the Scandinavian context.

The following chapter by **Cecilia Schwartz** suggests a methodological path to follow in order to find out more about attitudes towards Italian literature in contemporary Sweden. The focus is on four newly founded Swedish publishing houses specialised in Italian literature and their *selection* of titles as well as the *packaging* of the books – inscriptive and localising practices according to Venuti. In the study of the selection of Italian literature Schwartz proposes several analytical tools based on studies by Sapiro and Risterucci-Roudnicky (2008), for example a model for analysing the criteria used by the publishers when choosing titles for translation combining a vertical depoliticised-politicised axis with a horizontal axis from the particular (left) to the universal (right). By crossing these two axes, four different categories, in which the selected titles can be inserted and roughly classified, are distinguished. Schwartz's methodological path concludes with concrete signs of localising practices visible in the surroundings of the literary text, the paratext, particularly the editorial epitext and peritext.

Paul Tenngart's essay, which also has a methodological focus, looks at the translation processes from a reversed perspective – cosmopolitanising translation – and concerns British and American translations of Swedish working-class fiction from the 1930s. The Swedish versions of these novels are not only reshaped into another language, but also repackaged and recontextualised inevitably entailing significant changes of the works. Drawing on theories from book history and the sociology of translation Tenngart discusses and richly exemplifies nine different kinds of *transformations due to literary migration*. He explores changes in situation, format, language, hermeneutic distance and cultural context as necessary recodings that constitute the migration process and formal, generic and thematic changes, as well as changes in world perspectives – as secondary effects prompted by the inevitable recodings. He finds Emily Apter's notion of "untranslatablility" constructive to discuss the translators' struggles with domestic and everyday phenomena in the texts. The tendency discovered is that the translators make the narrative techniques less complex and more smoothly accessible, but the changes not only neutralise the narrative and the stylistic peculiarities of the Swedish authors, but also create new kinds of narratives from the stories at hand.

In her chapter on Nordic Noir, **Louise Nilsson** focuses on how Swedish translated crime fiction becomes visually framed – as a foreign literature – on a transnational book market and how this domestic literature intersects with the cosmopolitan mediascape. The main argument is that the perception of Swedish crime fiction as a local literature – often perceived as exotic – rests upon the shoulders of cultural history, popular culture as well as fine arts. In sum: a cosmopolitan cluster of shared ideas and values. The cover of Arne Dahl's *En midsommarnattsdröm – A Midsummer Night's Dream is* contextualised and in relation to the novel's content it is shown how the local place intersect with the cosmopolitan space. Drawing on Peter Davidson's arguments in *The Idea of the North*, she discusses how the perception of a north connects to various geographical locations. Nilsson's approach is qualitative and she employs discourse analysis as the theoretical and methodological point of departure, discussing subject positions, nodal points and social relations discernable on the cover. She also shows that snow, ravens and forest are all iconic symbols and imageries that hold special symbolic positions in the discursive field of the crime fiction genre. This aesthetic belongs though to a multilayered and faceted mediascape where visual expressions intertwine with the circulation of literature, allowing not only foreign literature to enter the transnational book market for world literatures but also contributing to forging new imaginaries of foreign places as well as narratives.

In "Swedes in French", **Andreas Hedberg** discusses world literature as a circulational concept and particularly how a peripheral literature is established on a central literary field. The objective of the study is to analyse the logics at work in the meeting of two literary systems, and to make a general contribution to the understanding of literary circulation as such. With a starting point in Hans Hertel's concepts *concentration* and *polarisation*, Hedberg demonstrates that the development of the modern book market has meant considerable changes in the mediation of Swedish fiction to the international market, not only when it comes to pace and itineraries, but also when it comes to intermediary languages and selection. The significant rise of the number of Swedish novels published in French translation since the turn of the millennium is largely explained by the so called "boom" of Scandinavian crime fiction. In 2013, Swedish was the fifth most important source language for translated novels published in France. He concludes by affirming that the circulational approach to the concept of world literature, may strengthen the centripetal forces of world literary space.

In her contribution, **Chatarina Edfeldt** aims at mapping out some starting points for how gender can operate as a mediating category in the circulation of literature, by examining the migration of African lusophone literatures into the contemporary Portuguese book market. Discussing Mani's concept of bibliomigration and Owen's identification of exclusion of women's experiences in Mozambican national literary discourse, Edfeldt stresses that accessibility to literary agency can be restricted by gender identity, which further affects the ability for the literary experience of women to circulate, or even to be written. Additionally, the lusophone literary system contains two centres (Portugal and Brazil), which means that Brazilian authors do not need to be recognised in Portugal and vice-versa for their wider consecration and circulation, while African authors are still dependent on being recognised in one of these two centres to enable their dissemination into a world market through translation. The essay rounds up with a discussion underlining how a gender-oriented reading of the Mozambican author Paulina Chiziane can provide an understanding of how *strategic exoticism* can be in place as a strategy both by the market forces, as well as a writer's strategy in the commodification process.

Erik Falk, finally, discusses some of the challenges facing the scholar approaching African literature from the sociological world literary studies perspective of Pascale Casanova. It draws throughout on postcolonial theory – and occasionally on book chain studies – to highlight central aspects of her theorisation that need questioning from an East African perspective or elaboration to be applicable. With the oppositions in theory between Casanova and Prendergast and using Kalliney's studies of Caribbean-British author relations, Falk discusses three general points in which the East African literary field differs from other fields. The first point is the impact of the dual economy, favouring the publication of educational literature in place of fiction. The second is the impact of the status of English as a national language, which means that the passage to literary fame look very different from European authors, who are established first in the national literary field and subsequently on the world stage through translation and/or foreign publication, processes which depend on recognition by literary institutions. The third point is that the cultural feedback loops need particular attention and empirical elaboration with respect to East African anglophone writing. The chapter ends with a discussion of the marketing of Ugandan author Doreen Baingana's short story collection, *Tropical Fish*, a concrete illustration of the points made.

To conclude the introduction I would like to underline that the focus of the chapters in this section has been on the exploration of the complex cosmopolitan and vernacular dynamics in literary translation and mediation. The methodological aspects of the presented research have also been foregrounded, since most of the participating scholars are in the initiating phase of their projects. This *Ansatzpunkt* might on the one hand have left the paramount economic aspect of transnational circulation of literature in the shade, on the other hand not so traditional but equally challenging aspects has been debated and brought out into the light.

25. Translation Bibliomigrancy: The Case of Contemporary Caribbean Literature in Scandinavia

Yvonne Lindqvist
Translation Studies, Stockholm University

This paper presents the theoretical framework for the project *The Meeting of Literary Peripheries by means of Translation – Prerequisites for Caribbean Literature in Scandinavia*. The framework is derived from the so-called "social turn" of translation studies where the general aim according to Wolf is:[1]

> … to contribute to the conceptualisation of a general translation sociology and … to deliver a comprehensive methodological framework, substantiated by empirical studies, which would allow us to analyse the social implications of the translation process in its various contexts.[2]

This general translation sociology is based on the cultural sociology of Pierre Bourdieu as further developed by for instance

---

[1] Michaela Wolf, "Translating and Interpreting as a Social Practice – Introspection into a New Field", in *Übersetzen–Translating–Traduire: Towards a "Social Turn"?* ed. Michaela Wolf (London: Transaction Publishers, 2006), 9–23.
[2] Wolf, "Translating and Interpreting as a Social Practice", 9.

How to cite this book chapter:
Lindqvist, Yvonne. "Translation Bibliomigrancy: The Case of Contemporary Caribbean Literature in Scandinavia". In *World Literatures: Exploring the Cosmopolitan-Vernacular Exchange*, edited by Stefan Helgesson, Annika Mörte Alling, Yvonne Lindqvist, and Helena Wulff, 295–309. Stockholm: Stockholm University Press, 2018. DOI: https://doi.org/10.16993/bat.y. License: CC-BY.

Pascale Casanova, John Heilbron and Gisèle Sapiro.[3] It is commonly conceived of as hosting three main research areas: 1) the sociology of translators 2) the sociology of translating 3) the sociology of translations. The first area deals with translator status, prestige and working conditions. The second studies the act of translating – the translation process, practices and norms. The third area studies translations as products on an international market.[4] The current research project belongs mainly within the third area of research within the sociology of translations. It examines the uneven and hierarchical "flows" of literature in the "world republic of letters" materialised in translation. Considered from a sociological perspective, translations are a function of the social relations between language groups and their transformations over time.[5]

Cultural exchanges such as translation have their own dynamics largely depending on the global market structures. Hence, the project constructs the market as a relatively autonomous global field with economic, political and symbolic dimensions. More specifically, the project examines the prerequisites for the meeting by means of translation of two local literary peripheries on the global translation field. It explores the necessary

---

[3] Pascale Casanova, *La république mondiale des lettres* (Paris: Éditions du Seuil, 1999); Pascale Casanova, "Consécration et accumulation de capital littéraire. La traduction comme échange inégal", *Actes de la recherche en sciences sociales,* 144 (2002); Johan Heilbron, "Towards a Sociology of Translation. Book Translations as a Cultural World System", *European Journal of Social Theory* 2 (1999): 429–44; Johan Heilbron, "Responding to Globalization: The Development of Book Translations in France and the Netherlands", in *Beyond Descriptive Translation Studies. Investigations in Homage to Gideon Toury* ed. Anthony Pym, Miriam Shlesinger & Daniel Simeoni.(Amsterdam/Philadelphia: Benjamins Translation Library, 2008), 187–99; Gisèle Sapiro, ed. *Translatio: Le marché de la traduction en France à l'heure de la mondialisation* (Paris: CNRS, Collection Culture et Société, 2008). Gisele Sapiro, "Globalization and Cultural Diversity in the Book Market: The Case of Literary Translations in the US and in France", *Poetics* 38 (2010), 419–39.

[4] Andrew Chesterman, "The Name and Nature of Translator Studies", *Hermes* 42 (2009), 16.

[5] Heilbron, "Towards a Sociology of Translation", 431.

consecration mechanisms for translation taking place from one local periphery to another, Caribbean to Scandinavian literature. Consecration is a term from the cultural sociology of Pierre Bourdieu, which in short means recognition and legitimation by the agents of the field under study.[6] To be consecrated by autonomous agents on the literary field signifies the crossing of a literary border – a metamorphosis of ordinary (literary) material into "gold", into absolute literary value. And translation is from a global point of view a form of consecration. It constitutes the principal means for access to the literary world for writers outside the centre.[7]

The aim of the project is to examine the bibliomigrancy dynamics on the global translation field. Bibliomigrancy is an umbrella term that describes the migration of literary works in the form of books from one part of the world to the other.[8] The term comprises two strands:

- Physical migration of books, i.e. book production and trade, translations, library acquisitions and circulation.
- Virtual migration, i.e. adaptations and appropriation of narratives; in more recent times the technical term for digitalisation of books.

Bibliomigrancy promotes and facilitates the processes of a "worlding"[9] of literature – the most basic condition for connections between central and peripheral positions on the global translation field. Translation gives a wider audience to this "world-making" by helping literary texts to escape the confines of the national

---

[6] Pierre Bourdieu, *Konstens regler. Det litterära fältets uppkomst och struktur* (Stockholm: Symposion, 2000), 326–27.
[7] Pascale Casanova, *The World Republic of Letters*, trans. M B. DeBevoise (Cambridge: Harvard University Press, 2004), 126.
[8] Venkat Mani, "Bibliomigrancy: Book Series and the Making of World Literature", in *The Routledge Companion to World Literature*, ed. Teo D'haen, David Damrosch and Djelal Kadir (London and New York: Routledge 2014), 289.
[9] Pheng Cheah, "What is a World? On World Literature as World-Making Activity", *Dædalus* 3 (2008): 34–25.

borders from which they have emerged to enter other contexts.[10] The bibliomigrancy concept encapsulates both the material and ideational dimensions of literary cosmopolitanism.

One methodological step in the study of translation bibliomigrancy dynamics is to test the double consecration hypothesis[11] stating that this kind of literature needs to be consecrated primarily within the centre(s) of the former colonial power, and secondly – due to the strong impact of the Anglo-American culture and literature in Scandinavia – within the British and American literary cultures. Caribbean literature written in French, Spanish and English has to be "filtered", so to speak, through the central British and American cultures in order to reach Scandinavian readers in translation. The relations are schematically represented in figure 5 showing the bibliomigrancy dynamics of Caribbean and Scandinavian literatures.

Nevertheless, each Caribbean language group will probably manifest a specific dynamic depending on how centralised the contemporary literary culture in question is. Casanova has shown that the French literary culture is strongly mono-centric with Paris as the sole consecration centre.[12] The English contemporary literary culture on the other hand is hypothesised in this study as duo-centric counting New York and London as the most important consecration centres. The Spanish contemporary literary culture eventually, is hypothesised as pluri-centric in the sense that literary consecration takes place in several centres alike, notably in Madrid, Barcelona, Mexico City and Buenos Aires for example. However, the British and American "filters" for reaching Scandinavia will be a common denominator for the involved

---

[10] Kathryn Batchelor, "Translation: Spreading the Wings of Literature", in *Intimate Enemies. Translation in Francophone Contexts*, ed. Kathryn Batchelor & Claire Bisdorf (Liverpool: Liverpool University Press, 2013), 100.

[11] Yvonne Lindqvist, "Det globala översättningsfältet och den svenska översättningsmarknaden. Förutsättningar för litterära periferiers möte", in *Läsarnas marknad, marknadens läsare. En forskningsantologi utarbetad för litteraturutredningen*, ed. Ulla Carlsson and Jenni Johannisson (NORDICOM. Göteborgs universitet, 2012), 10.

[12] Casanova, *Consécration et accumulation*, 7–20.

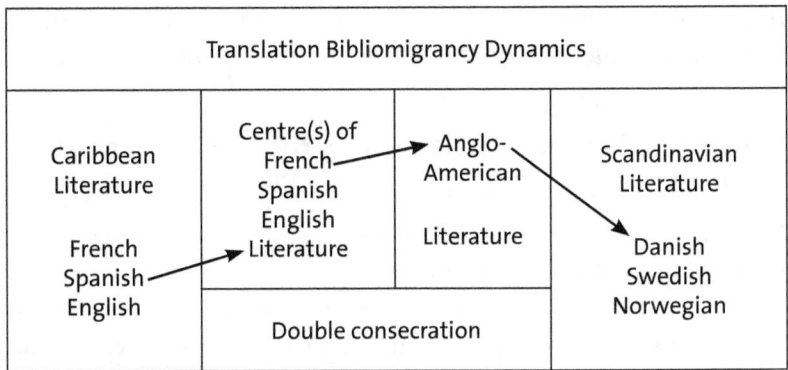

Figure 5. Schematic representation of the double consecration hypothesis concerning bibliomigrancy dynamics of Caribbean and Scandinavian literatures.[13]

literary cultures in order to be translated into the Scandinavian languages. These complex dynamics probably also vary over time and according to genre. The project covers cosmopolitan and vernacular translation dynamics, i.e. literary migration on the global translation field from mainly dominated positions to the dominating in the first case, and from dominating to dominated in the latter, during the period 1990–2010.

Consequently, the hypothesis of the study claims that for this kind of literary translation to take place *double consecration* within the dominating cultures for each language group on the global translation field is necessary, i.e. writers from peripheral cultures selected for translation into Swedish, Danish and Norwegian have to be consecrated within the centre(s) of their previous (colonial) culture on the global translation field and *then* within the centres of the British and American cultures. The hypothesis is a specification of a more general hypothesis put forward by Heilbron, Casanova and Moretti: Literature translated from one periphery to another is a consequence of what is translated from the peripheral language in question to the central languages and cultures and

---

[13] An earlier version of the schematic representation of French Caribbean literature as an example has been published in Lindqvist 2012.

that, as Moretti puts it, "movement from one periphery to another (without passing through the centre) is almost unheard of".[14]

Centre and Periphery Relations on the Global Translation Field

In order to map out the bibliomigrancy dynamics on the global translation field power relations between language groups have to be taken into consideration. As Mona Baker[15] has pointed out, translation is rarely the peaceful linear transfer of literary and semantic devices described in textbooks in translation. On the contrary, the global translation field has its own rules of functioning based on positions gained from constant struggles of accumulated symbolic power.

One of the most cited databases for statistically surveys of the most dominating – hence most central – source languages on the global translation field is Index Translationum of UNESCO. The percentages in Table 1 are compiled from the findings of Heilbron and Sapiro and then compared to the numbers from 2015 in Index Translationum of UNESCO.[16] Table 1 shows that the ranking of centrality in the global translation field has not changed essentially during the last 30 years in the central positions – except for the decline of Russian in the 1990s – English, French, and German remain as the hyper-central and central languages, respectively. Some minor alterations concern the semi-central languages. Spanish and Italian have changed place in terms of importance comparing the 1990s and 2015 and Danish has lost ground from the seventh position of importance in 1980s to the

---

[14] Heilbron, "Towards a Sociology", 437; Casanova, *Consécration et accumulation*, 8; Franco Moretti, "More Conjectures", *New Left Review* 20 (2003): 76.

[15] Mona Baker, "Editor's Introduction", in *Critical Readings in Translation Studies.* ed. Mona Baker (London and New York: Routledge, 2010), 285.

[16] Heilbron, "Towards a Sociology", 433–35; Sapiro, "Translatio", 68–72, 423. For a discussion of the reliability of this database, see for instance Heilbron, "Globalization"; Sapiro, *Translatio*; Johan Svedjedal (ed.), *Svensk litteratur som världslitteratur: en antologi* (Uppsala: Uppsala University, 2012).

Table 1. The ten most central source languages on the global translation filed during the period 1980–2015. Percentage of the source language of the total amount of published books on the global translation market.[17]

1980–1989 (Heilbron 1999)		1990–1999 (Sapiro 2008)		Index Translationum 2015[18]	
Language	Percentage	Language	Percentage	Language	Percentage
English	40	English	59	English	63
French	12	French	10	French	10
German	11	German	10	German	9
Russian	10	Spanish	3	Russian	5
Italian	3	Italian	3	Italian	3.5
Spanish	3	Swedish	2	Spanish	3
Danish	2	Japanese	2	Swedish	2
Swedish	2	Latin	2	Japanese	1.5
Polish	1	Russian	1.5	Danish	1
Czech	1	Danish	1	Latin	1

tenth in 1990 – surpassed by Japanese and Latin – and to the ninth position in the year 2015. The climb of Latin on the scale in the 1990s can probably be ascribed to a worldwide increase of translation of the literary classics and other medieval text genres for educational use.[19]

---

[17] I am aware of the fact that Table 1 is rather unorthodox. The data in the overview shown should only be interpreted as indications of tendencies in the global translation field, since exact numbers are virtually impossible to produce. An earlier version of this table has been published in Lindqvist 2015.

[18] http://www.unesco.org/xtrans/bsstatexp.aspx?crit1L=3&nTyp=min&topN=50&lg=0 accessed 25 November 2016.

[19] Emily Wilson, "Translating the Classics". Society for Classical Studies 2014, http://apaclassics.org/blogs/emilywilson/translating-classics#sthash.rUe8ppA1.dpuf accessed 16 October 2016.

The tendency in the global translation field is towards greater diversification of the amount of source languages mainly due to the decline of the Russian language from 11 per cent in the 1980s to 1.5 per cent in the 1990s, shifting from a central position to a semi-central position and then gaining ground again in 2015 with 5 per cent of the translation market. Swedish has, on the other hand, advanced in the scale of importance from eighth place in the 1980s to sixth place in the 1990s as source language in the global translation field. Due to the Russian climb in 2015, Swedish is, however, pushed down to seventh place in that year.

Table 2 shows that domination dynamics in the global translation field are reproduced on a smaller scale within the Swedish literary space. The most dominant source languages occupy a given position even within Swedish literature, but the regional languages – Norwegian and Danish – also play a crucial role, thereby signalling the existence of a regional translation subfield, where Stockholm plays the role of centre in the regional periphery.[20] This constitutes an explanation of the fact that two of the Scandinavian languages occupy a semi-peripheral position on the global translation field.

The average of translations among books published in the European countries[21] amounts to 15 per cent.[22] Nonetheless, the Swedish literary space is proven the most closed in Scandinavia – a decisive indication of centrality in the peripheral subfield.[23] Hence the Scandinavian literary field fits the third category of four kinds of dominated languages from a global translational

---

[20] Yvonne Lindqvist, "The Scandinavian Literary Translation Field from a Global Point of View – A Peripheral (Sub)field?" in *Institutions of World Literature – Writing, Translation, Markets* eds. Stefan Helgesson and Pieter Vermulen (New York & London: Routledge, 2015), 185–87.

[21] Pascale Casanova, *The World Republic of Letters* (Cambridge: Harvard University Press, 2004), 168.

[22] It has long been disputed where one should draw the line between open and closed systems based on publication statistics (cf. Bassnett 1998, Pym 1999). A pragmatic solution is to consider an average of 20 per cent or more as open systems.

[23] Lindqvist, "The Scandinavian Literary Translation Field", 184–86.

Table 2. In polysystemic terminology, the Swedish literary system can be qualified as an open literary system, where more than 20 per cent of the total amount of published literature during the first decade of the twenty-first century consisted of translations.[24] The five most dominating source languages within the totality of published books in the Swedish literary field during 2000–10 (The Swedish National Bibliography).

Year/Language	2001	2002	2003	2004	2005	2006	2007	2008	2009	2010	Total
English	1978	1821	1859	2095	2339	2141	2169	2490	1897	1889	20678
Norwegian	127	122	152	190	162	130	149	179	130	157	1498
Danish	93	111	90	140	130	133	151	161	141	136	1286
German	88	116	86	116	104	109	118	175	130	113	1155
French	76	100	104	127	138	125	96	151	124	115	1156

---

[24] Itamar Even-Zohar, "Polysystem Studies", *Poetics Today* 11 (Tel Aviv: Duke University Press, 1990), 47–53. See the Swedish National Bibliography 2000–2010. The percentage has fallen considerably during the last ten years mainly due to the strong consolidation of the Swedish book market and to the substantial increase of non-fiction publications. During the 1980s the percentage reached over 40 per cent of the total of published books in Sweden (Lindqvist 2002, 36).

point of view discussed by Casanova.[25] She distinguishes between oral languages with young writing systems and Creole languages (for example Yoruba and Haitian Creole), languages with newly gained national status (Catalan), languages of established cultures with relatively small populations (Swedish, Danish and Norwegian) and languages spoken by large populations possessing a rich literary tradition but nevertheless positioned in the very periphery of the global translation field (Hindi and Chinese). In the world republic of letters the accumulation of literary capital is decisive for the position on the global translation field. From the statistics and categorisations presented above it is possible to discern two overall orientations for literary translations on the global translation field: cosmopolitanising and vernacularising translation.[26] The orientations reveal the basic bibliomigrancy dynamics of translated literature on the global translation field and are presented in Figure 6.

The central positions of dominating literatures and languages are constructed by their historically high access to literary capital and relative autonomy vis-à-vis other national literatures and languages. Cornerstones of literary capital are on the one hand the age of the literary culture and its highly specialised literary institutions, on the other literary criticism, literary values and literary renown.[27] High access to literary capital means that the culture in question possesses a very well-developed literary institution and a literary repertoire, which does not need to count on translations to assert itself in competing with repertoires of other literary cultures. When a text is translated into such a culture it is considered especially valuable by the dominated cultures, which does not possess an equally developed literary repertoire. Translation in this case then becomes a proof of the high literary quality of the text. In the terminology of

---

[25] Casanova, *Consécration et accumulation*, 8.
[26] I have schematically organised the main arguments in Casanova (2004) to create the model and adapted it to my study by adding the double consecration dynamics at the centre of my interest. The original terms in Casanova (2002:10) are Traduction accumulation and Traduction consécration.
[27] Casanova, "The World Republic", 14–15.

Cosmopolitanising translation	Vernacularising translation
A. Dominated → Dominating (Swedish, Danish, Norwegian → English)	C. Dominating → Dominated (English →Swedish, Danish, Norwegian)
B. Dominating → Dominating (French → Spanish)	D. Dominated→ Dominated* (Caribbean French, Spanish, English → Swedish, Danish, Norwegian)
* D. Dominated →Dominating→Dominating →Dominated (Double consecration)	

Figure 6. The basic bibliomigrancy dynamics on the global translation field – cosmopolitanising and vernacularising translation – with examples of relations from the involved languages of the presented project.

Bourdieu,[28] this process constitutes a means for consecration of the text by the literary agents of the leading institutions of the target culture – a case of cosmopolitanising translation. A typical example of a cosmopolitansing translation is shown in figure 6, case A, when Scandinavian, i.e. Swedish, Danish and Norwegian, crime fiction novels translated into English are launched into the Anglo-American market. The novels then gain in literary prestige, accumulating literary capital by the consecration, and consequently become more interesting for other dominating literary cultures, for instance the French culture. A famous example from Swedish crime fiction is the Millennium Trilogy by Stieg Larsson, in 2009 sold in 10 million copies.[29] Other examples of Scandinavian peripheral writers in cosmopolitanising translation are the Norwegian Torkil Damhaug's *Oslo Crime Files Quartet* and the Danish writer Jussi Adler-Olsen winner of the Glas Key Prize in 2010 for best Scandinavian crime fiction novel.

Case B in figure 6 shows another dynamic of cosmopolitanising translation – translation taking place between two dominating cultures, for instance between the French and Spanish literary

---

[28] Bourdieu, "*Konstens regler*", 326–27.
[29] Erica Treijs, "Litteraturens ansikte", *Svenska Dagbladet*, 11 September 2009.

cultures. It is highly probable that the French Goncourt Prize-winner will be translated into Spanish and reversely that the Nadal Prize-winner will be translated into French. Consequently, the Goncourt Prize-winner of 2010, Michel Houellebecq with the novel *La carte et le territoire*, for instance, was translated into Spanish in 2012 under the title *La mapa y el territorio*. And Clara Sánchez, The Nadal Prize winner of 2010 with the novel *Lo que esconde tu nombre*, which was translated into French under the title *Ce que cache ton nom* in 2012.

The position of the dominated literatures and languages on the global translation field is, on the other hand, due to their lack of literary capital and relative autonomy. The translation relations occurring in these cultures are vernacularising translations, i.e. translations stemming from the dominant positions and languages. A prototypical example of vernacularising translation is from English to Swedish, case C in figure 6. As we have seen in table 2, this translation relation is by large the most common relationship in Sweden. In fact, 71 per cent of all published translations in Sweden during the period 2000–2010 had English as source language.[30] The dynamics of English source language translations are very similar in Norway and Denmark[31] (a veritable wave in the Moretti sense[32]).

Case D in figure 6 – the vernacularising translation in focus in the project – is elucidated in case D* and illustrates the double consecration hypothesis. That is, in order for two literary peripheries on the global translation field – the Caribbean and the Scandinavian – to meet by means of translation, the migrating source texts have to be primarily consecrated within two central literary cultures, revealing cosmopolitanising dynamics in vernacularising translation as well. This is probably the prerequisite for Scandinavian publisher's decision to publish French, Spanish and English Caribbean writers in translation. Proceeding from this theoretical framework the project will examine the multidirectional dynamics of cosmopolitanising and vernacularising translation on the global translation field.

---

[30] Swedish National Bibliography, 2000–2010.
[31] Lindqvist, "The Scandinavian", 180–83.
[32] Franco Moretti, "Conjectures on World Literature", *New Left Review* 1 (2000): 67.

Bibliography

Baker, Mona. "Editor's Introduction. Chapter 16". In *Critical Readings in Translation Studies*, edited by Mona Baker, 285–86. London and New York: Routledge, 2010.

Batchelor, Kathryn. "Translation: Spreading The Wings of Literature. Veronique Tadjo in Interview with Kathryn Batchelor". In *Intimate Enemies: Translation in Francophone Contexts*, edited by Kathryn Batchelor and Claire Bisdorf, 98–108. Liverpool: Liverpool University Press, 2013.

Cheah, Pheng. "What is a World? On World Literature as World-Making Activity". *Dædalus* 3 (2008): 26–38.

Bourdieu, Pierre. *The Field of Cultural Production: Essays on Art and Literature*. Cambridge: Polity Press, 1993.

———. *Kultur och kritik*. Göteborg: Daidalos. 1997.

———. *Konstens regler: Det litterära fältets uppkomst och struktur*. Translated by Johan Stierna. Stockholm: Symposion, 2000.

Casanova, Pascale. *La République mondiale des lettres*. Paris: Éditions du Seuil, 1999.

———. "Consécration et accumulation de capital littéraire. La traduction come échange inégal". *Actes de la recherche en sciences sociales* 144 (2002): 7–20.

Casanova, Pascale. *The World Republic of Letters*. Translated by M. B. DeBevoise. Cambridge: Harvard University Press, 2004.

Casanova, Pascale. "Literature as a World". *New Left Review* 31 (2005): 71–90.

Chesterman, Andrew. "The Name and Nature of Translator Studies". *Hermes* 42. 2009. 13–22.

Even-Zohar, Itamar. "Polysystem Studies". *Poetics Today* 11, no. 1 (1990).

Heilbron, Johan. "Towards a Sociology of Translation: Book Translations as a Cultural World System". *European Journal of Social Theory* 2, no. 4 (1999): 429–44.

———. "Responding to Globalization. The Development of Book Translations in France and the Netherlands". In *Beyond Descriptive Translation Studies. Investigations in Homage to Gideon Toury*, edited by Anthony Pym, Miriam Shlesinger and Daniel Simeoni, 187–99. Amsterdam/Philadelphia: Benjamins, 2008.

Lindqvist, Yvonne. *Översättning som social praktik. Toni Morrison och Harlequinserien. Passion på svenska*. Diss. Stockholm Studies in Scandinavian Philology. N.S. 26. Stockholm: Almqvist & Wiksell International. 2002.

———. "Det globala översättningsfältet och den svenska översättningsmarknaden. Förutsättningar för litterära periferiers möte". In *Läsarnas marknad, marknadens läsare. En forskningsantologi utarbetad för litteraturutredningen*, edited by Ulla Carlsson and Jenni Johannisson, 197–209. NORDICOM. Göteborg: Göteborgs universitet, 2012.

———. "The Scandinavian Literary Translation Field from a Global Point of View – A Peripheral (Sub)field?" In *Institutions of World Literature: Writing, Translation, Markets*, edited by Stefan Helgesson and Pieter Vermulen, 174–87. New York: Routledge, 2015.

Mani, Venkat. Bibliomigrancy: "Book Series and the Making of World Literature". In *The Routledge Companion to World Literature*, edited by Teo D'haen, David Damrosch, Djelal Kadir, 283–96. New York: Routledge, 2014.

Moretti, Franco. "Conjectures on World Literature". *New Left Review* 1 (2000): 54–68.

———. "More conjectures". *New Left Review* 20 (2003): 73–81.

Treijs, Erica. "Litteraturens ansikte". *Svenska Dagbladet* 11 September 2009.

Sapiro, Gisèle *Translatio: Le marché de la traduction en France à l'heure de la mondialisation*. Paris: CNRS, 2008.

———. "Globalization and Cultural Diversity in the Book Market: The Case of Literary Translations in the US and in France". *Poetics* 38 (2010): 419–39.

Svedjedal, Johan, ed. *Svensk litteratur som världslitteratur: en antologi*. Uppsala: Uppsala University, 2012.

Wilson, Emily. "Translating the Classics". Society for Classical Studies 2014. http://apaclassics.org/blogs/emily_wilson/translating-classics#sthash.rUe8ppA1.dpuf. Accessed 16 October 2016.

Wolf, Michaela. "Translating and Interpreting as a Social Practice – Introspection into a New Field". In *Übersetzen–Translating–Traduire: Towards a "Social Turn"?*, edited by Michaela Wolf, 9–23. London: Transaction Publishers, 2006.

26. Profiles of Italy: Localising Practices of Swedish Publishing Houses

Cecilia Schwartz
Italian, Stockholm University

Is it possible to pinpoint the status of a foreign literature in a receiving culture? In this chapter, I will briefly suggest a methodological path that can be followed in order to find out more about attitudes towards translated literature, by focusing on the selection of titles and the packaging of books. Why is selection and packaging crucial to the understanding of transnational literary relations?

According to Lawrence Venuti, the translation process is a "localizing practice" that involves a whole series of actions that are "mediated by values, beliefs, and representations in the receiving situation. Far from reproducing the source text, a translation rather transforms it by inscribing an interpretation that reflects what is intelligible and interesting to receptors".[1] Even though Venuti mainly pays attention to the discursive strategies performed in the translated texts, he also argues that the process of inscription "operates at every stage in the production, circulation, and reception of the translation".[2]

---

[1] Lawrence Venuti, *Translation Changes Everything: Theory and Practice* (London, New York: Routledge, 2013), 193.
[2] Lawrence Venuti, *The Scandals of Translation: Towards an Ethics of Difference* (London, New York: Routledge, 1998), 67.

How to cite this book chapter:
Schwartz, Cecilia. "Profiles of Italy: Localising Practices of Swedish Publishing Houses". In *World Literatures: Exploring the Cosmopolitan-Vernacular Exchange*, edited by Stefan Helgesson, Annika Mörte Alling, Yvonne Lindqvist, and Helena Wulff, 310–323. Stockholm: Stockholm University Press, 2018. DOI: https://doi.org/10.16993/bat.z. License: CC-BY.

The suggested analysis takes into consideration the localising practices in the part of the production that does not include the translated texts, but rather some of the actions performed by the publishing houses: the selection and packaging of Italian texts for a Swedish readership. Furthermore, while this perspective is mainly relevant to the understanding of contemporary Italian literature's status in Sweden, it will also shed light on the relations between semi-peripheral literatures[3] that tend to be overlooked in the studies of world literature.[4] According to recent statistics, Italian is today the sixth or seventh most translated language into Swedish.[5] Yet, Italian literature seems rather unheard of except for some worldwide bestselling writers such as Umberto Eco, Roberto Saviano and Elena Ferrante. So what is the overall status of Italian literature in Sweden today? To answer this question, the researcher has to start out with an analysis of Swedish publishing houses specialised in Italian literature.

Publishing houses are crucial gatekeepers when literature travels from one culture to another. In the years 2009–11, no fewer than four publishing houses with special focus on Italian literature were founded in Stockholm.[6] This peculiar situation – four

---

[3] Gisèle Sapiro, "The sociology of translation. A new research domain", in *A Companion to Translation Studies*, ed. Sandra Bermann et al. (Chichester: Wiley Blackwell, 2014), 85. According to Sapiro, until 1989, Italian and Swedish, together with Spanish, Danish, Polish, Russian and Czech, belonged to the happy few in the literary semi-periphery, which means that these languages had a share that varied from one to three per cent of the languages in the world system of translations. After the fall of the Berlin wall, Polish and Czech lost their semi-peripheral position, while Italian, Spanish and Swedish literature remained stable.

[4] Cf. Theo D'haen, *The Routledge Concise History of World Literature* (New York: Routledge, 2012), 153.

[5] Due to these statistics provided by the National Library of Sweden, Italian was preceded by English, Norwegian, French, German and Danish in 2016 and by the same languages plus Finnish in 2017. Kungliga biblioteket. *Nationalbibliografin i siffror 2016* (Stockholm: Nationalbibliografin, Kungliga biblioteket, 2017), 14–15; Kungliga biblioteket. *Nationalbibliografin i siffror 2017* (Stockholm: Nationalbibliografin, Kungliga biblioteket, 2018), 11.

[6] Cartaditalias bokserie (2009–2012) was established in the wake of a bilingual cultural magazine, *Cartaditalia*, both initiatives by the Italian

publishing houses founded in a two-year-period – raises questions closely related to the status of Italian literature in Sweden:

- Which texts, authors and genres were published by these four newcomers?
- How were these texts and authors presented to the Swedish readership?
- How can an analysis of the selection and packaging contribute to the understanding of the status of Italian literature in contemporary Sweden and of semi-peripheral relations in world literature?

In the following, I will briefly outline a useful methodological path for analysing these four newcomers in the publishing field. First of all, a bibliographical research must be carried out in order to get a panoramic view of the Italian literature published in Sweden in the studied period.[7] In this specific case, since the publishing houses were all founded in the years 2009–11, I suggest starting from at least year 2005 and list *all* Italian titles translated into

---

Cultural Institute in Stockholm. The house published novels, poetry, essays and short stories of Italy's most prestigious authors (Italo Calvino, Pier Paolo Pasolini, Elsa Morante etc). In 2010 another publishing house arose, Astor (2010–2014), which mainly focused on contemporary literature from the Italian and Spanish language area. Astor published novels, short stories and essays by writers from the younger generation (born in the 1970s), who had never been translated into Swedish before. Still in 2010, another firm with an Italian profile was established in Stockholm, Laurella & Wallin (2010–2014). Their idea was to publish texts written in the borderland between fiction and travel literature. All in all, Laurella & Wallin published eight titles, of which the first five focused on one Italian city each (Palermo, Rome, Florence, Venice and Naples). The only publishing house that has survived until the present day is Contempo, which was founded in 2011 by a father and his daughter. As the name chosen for the house indicates, it concentrates on contemporary Italian novels, all very successful in their homeland. Currently they have published 15 titles.

[7] On the importance of making lists and bibliographies, see Anthony Pym, *Method in Translation History*, (Manchester: St Jerome Publishing, 1998), 38–54.

Swedish up until 2015.⁸ This temporal perspective offers a frame for the analysis by mapping the importation of Italian literature into Sweden before and during the rise of these specific publishing houses. It also offers an objective context to which the following steps of the analysis can be related. To complete the picture, a quantitative analysis of optional variables – such as genre, publisher, author's and translator's gender etc. – is needed. Then of course the publications of the four publishers must be compared to the general picture.

However, if we want to consider the publishing houses' selection of titles as a localising practice, it has to be considered from a qualitative perspective, not least of all because the selection is "always an exclusion of other foreign texts and literatures".⁹ One factor that is crucial to an analysis focusing on publishing houses is the distinction between big and small publishing houses in the translation field. When it comes to foreign literature, big publishers tend to contribute to standardisation since they prefer traditional novels written in English, while smaller firms rather contribute to innovation by introducing new authors and translating from languages other than English.¹⁰ The *discovery* of new (or ignored) authors, which might lead to true innovation in the literary field, is actually perceived as one of the most important functions of small publishing houses.¹¹ In order to survive in the competition with larger publishers, small firms often concentrate on a *niche*. One such *niche* strategy consists in choosing literature from a specific language area, which "explains the role they play in discovering writers in peripheral or semi-peripheral languages".¹² But what are the consequences of this niche strategy in terms of localising practices? Are the selections made concerning

---

⁸ The easiest way would be to make a search on the Nationalbibliografin (Swedish National Bibliography).
⁹ Venuti, *Scandals*, 67.
¹⁰ Gisèle Sapiro, *Translatio: Le marché de la traduction en France è l'heure de la mondialisation* (Paris: CNRS Éditions, 2008).
¹¹ Sapiro, *Translatio*, 190.
¹² Gisèle Sapiro, "Translation and the field of publishing. A commentary on Pierre Bourdieu's 'A conservative revolution in publishing'", *Translation studies* 1, no. 2 (2008): 157.

the source or target culture? Or do the publishers instead rely on the transnational circulation of the chosen literature? And what localising practices are visible in the presentations and packaging of the chosen language area?

In order to answer these questions, the selection of titles can be approached by using different analytical tools. A proficient way is to examine which other languages the selected works have already been translated to. This approach not only contributes to a better understanding of the circulation patterns of semi-peripheral literature, it also tests the legitimacy in Sapiro's statement that "the chance for a work published in a peripheral language to be translated in another peripheral language depends greatly on its being first translated into a central language".[13] Similarly, Franco Moretti argues "that movement from one periphery to another (without passing through the centre) is almost unheard of".[14] Is this assumption confirmed in our case as well? If not, the analysis must go beyond the macro-dimension and focus on other aspects, such as the agents involved in the importation.

The selection of texts could also be perceived as a way of "challenging domestic canons for foreign literatures and domestic stereotypes for foreign cultures",[15] and on the contrary, the selection could confirm such domestic canons and stereotypes. For instance, if Swedes associate Italy with *mafia*, then one might expect that publishers specialised in Italian literature will be inclined to relate to this cliché in one way or another. Do they reinforce the cliché or do they try to challenge it by offering alternative perspectives of Italy?[16]

In terms of inclusion it is even more intriguing to compare the titles selected by the foreign publishers with the same titles' status in the national field, since canons of the source literature

---

[13] Sapiro, *Sociology*, 86.
[14] Franco Moretti, "More Conjectures", *New Left Review*, 20 (2003): 75.
[15] Venuti, *Scandals*, 81.
[16] Cf. Hanne Jansen, "*Bel Paese* or *Spaghetti noir*? The image of Italy in contemporary Italian fiction translated into Danish", in *Interconnecting translation studies and imagology*, ed. by Luc van Doorslaer, Peter Flynn and Joep Leerssen, (Amsterdam: John Benjamins, 2015), 163–79.

often differ from the target literature.[17] Especially in the cases in which the publishing houses make their decisions in close relation to the source culture, it is appropriate to analyse the selected author's position in the source field. A useful tool for conducting this analysis is offered by Sapiro, who distinguishes between four ideal-typic writers: the notables, the aesthetes, the popular and the avant-garde writers.[18]

If the selection is made in a closer relation to the receiving culture or with an international perspective, another appropriate model is suggested by Danielle Risterucci-Roudnicky (2008),[19] who argues that it is possible to locate every translation in the field by combining two opposing axes: the canonisation-discovery dimension and the distancing-naturalisation dimension, where the latter relies on the ways in which a translation is included in the new system: is the foreignness of a literary work highlighted (distancing) or hidden (naturalisation)?[20] According to Risterucci-Roudnicky, the place that a translation occupies alongside these axes determines its symbolic position in the editorial landscape: a naturalised canonised title would have a higher symbolic capital than an unknown author's work where the distance from the receiving culture is underscored.[21] Is this the case

---

[17] Cf. Mads Rosendahl Thomsen, *Mapping World Literature. International Canonization and Transnational Literatures* (London: Continuum, 2008).

[18] Gisèle Sapiro, "Le champ littéraire français. Structure, dynamique et formes de politisation", in *Art et société. Recherches récentes et regards croisés, Brésil/France*, ed. Alain Quemin et al. (Marseille: Open Edition Press, 2016), accessed 23 January 2017, doi: 10.4000/books.oep.475. Even though Sapiro's distinction regards the French literary field, I argue that it could be applied on many other national fields. In the case of Italian literature, it is particularly appropriate since the boundaries between the French and the Italian literary fields are very strong.

[19] Danielle Risterucci-Roudnicky, *Introduction à l'analyse des œuvres traduites* (Paris: Armand Colin, 2008).

[20] See also Lawrence Venuti's discussion on foreignising and domesticating translations in *The Translator's Invisibility: A History of Translation* (London, New York: Routledge, 2008).

[21] Risterucci-Roudnicky, *Introduction*, 18.

in a semi-peripheral culture as well? Or could the underscored foreignness – for instance in the packaging – be a way to gain symbolic capital?

Another method is put forward by Sapiro. Drawing on Bourdieu, she has elaborated a model for analysing translated literature that can be applied to the selection in order to find out about the criteria used more or less deliberately by the publishers when choosing titles for translation.[22] Suggesting how works translated into French can be classified, the method combines a vertical depoliticised-politicised axis with a horizontal axis that goes from the particular (left) to the universal (right). By crossing these two axes, four different categories, in which the selected titles can be inserted and roughly classified, are distinguished:

> **Depoliticised particularism:** This dimension is particularly strong when it comes to the selection of foreign literature, as it focuses on the ethnographic dimension of culture and often balances on the edge of exoticism.
> **Depoliticised universalism:** literary texts marked by individualism, subjectivism and formalism. By expressing a subjectivity that can be shared over time and space these works inscribe themselves into the "universal" literature – the classics. In this category, Sapiro inserts the catalogues of a prestigious publisher such as Gallimard as well as many smaller highbrow publishers.
> **Politicised universalism:** Even though this category includes works that are conceived as universal, it differs from the former as it features the historical and moral dimension of literature. Although these works are often believed to grasp the universal from the particular, as for instance in memoirs and ethical world fiction, they dissociate from exoticism and identity politics by encouraging hybrid identities.
> **Politicised particularism:** When the socio-political dimension is combined with the particular identity dimension, we find a category of works defined as identity political. These are narratives in which the author's identity is crucial and where the cultural particularity, as well as the political or social dimension, is privileged.

---

[22] Sapiro, *Translatio*, 204–9.

When applying this model, the researcher must be aware of the fact that it is a description of translations into French during the years 1984–2002. Obviously, not only the dimensions are likely to differ from one literature to another (and from one time to another), but there will always be works that do not fit into such schematic representations.[23] This brings us to the next step in the analysis, which takes into account more concrete signs of localising practices visible in the surroundings of the literary text, the *paratext*.

In his seminal work *Seuils*,[24] Gérard Genette outlines a theory of the paratext, which includes all the elements that accompany the literary text: covers, titles, the author's name, notes, prefaces, interviews with the author etc. According to Genette, the concept of paratext should be conceived as an umbrella term that is bifurcated into two main areas: the *peritext* and the *epitext*. The elements of the peritext are more closely related to the text *per se* – prefaces, titles, titles of the chapters, footnotes, covers, blurbs – while the epitext addresses all the messages outside the actual volume, such as interviews with the author, private conversations, letters, diaries etc. Genette mainly focused on literary works in their original language, and the theory has only recently been adapted to the area of translated literature, where much remains to be done.[25]

---

[23] However, in the case of the four "Italian" publishing houses it seems that the selection could be inserted in all categories described above, except one, the politicised particularism. This suggests that publishing houses with an Italian focus deliberately exclude postcolonial narratives from their catalogues.

[24] Gérard Genette, *Seuils* (Paris: Seuil, 1987). Translated by Jane E. Lewin as *Paratexts. Thresholds of interpretation* (Cambridge: Cambridge University Press, 1997).

[25] Until now only a few volumes that combine the paratextual perspective with the translational to any lengthier extent have been published: Richard Watts, *Packaging Postcoloniality: The Manufacture of Literary Identity in the Francophone World*, (2005), Danielle Risterucci-Roudnicky, *Introduction à l'analyse des œuvres traduites*, (Paris: Armand Colin, 2008); Anna Gil-Bardají et al. (eds.), *Translation peripheries: Paratextual Elements in Translation* (Bern: Peter Lang, 2012); Chiara Elefante, *Traduzione e paratesto*, (Bologna: Bononia University Press,

I would argue that when it comes to translated works, an analysis of the paratext is even more relevant than it might be for source texts. Why is that? Generally, it has to do with the mediating role performed by paratextual items in the transmission of literary texts between cultures. Paratexts represent *hybrid spaces* where source and target cultures meet.[26] Since the current research task concerns the status of Italian literature in present Sweden, an analysis of the localising practices performed by the publishers is required: to what extent do the publishers remain faithful to the source edition, and to what extent do they adapt the surroundings of the text to the receiving culture? Focusing on the publisher's paratext reveals motives for publishing a certain text as well as suggestions on how to read and use the volume: the paratext invites the reader to share the publisher's own interpretation of the text,[27] and at the same time it designs and defines the publishing houses' target readers.

Even though the most intriguing part of the paratext, at least for the purpose of the research task presented here, concerns the *publisher's peritext* (and especially covers, titles, prefaces and notes), a proficient starting point would be to examine the *publisher's epitext*, i.e. presentation texts on the website, interviews and articles in the press in order to trace the publishers' profile and self-perceived function in the Swedish field.[28] This first step of

---

2012), Valerie Pellatt (ed.), *Text, Extratext, Metatext and Paratext in Translation* (Cambridge: Cambridge Scholars Publishing, 2013). For studies on translation and paratexts with a particular attention given to the Swedish literary field, see Jerry Määttä, *Raketsommar. Science fiction i Sverige 1950–1968* (Lund: Ellerströms) and Cecilia Alvstad "The Strategic moves of Paratexts: World Literature through Swedish Eyes", *Translation Studies*, 5 (1) (2012): 78–94.

[26] Cf. Risterucci-Roudnicky, *Introduction*, 30.

[27] Alberto Cadioli, "Il patto editoriale nelle edizioni moderne e contemporanee", in *I dintorni del testo. Approcci alle periferie del libro*, ed. Marco Santoro et al. (Rome: Edizioni dell'Ateneo, 2005), 664. According to Alberto Cadioli, the very edition of a literary text reflects the publisher's intention to establish a pact with the reader, "il patto editoriale" ("the publisher's pact").

[28] If the analysis considers contemporary publishers, the researcher can contact them in order to carry out interviews. An example of such a

the analysis would clearly indicate the publisher's view on Italian literature. Following Sapiro, other aspects that should be taken into consideration in the publisher's epitext are statements regarding innovation and tradition, language areas and niche strategies. This part of the analysis will contribute interesting facts about the publishers' own analysis of the sector and their choice to focus on Italian writers in that particular moment.

However, the publishers' localising efforts are mainly visible in the peritext. The elements of the cover and its appendages have been thoroughly listed by Genette.[29] Among these, the localising practices are most explicit in the translation of the title (see below), in the choice of pictures, photos or other iconographic illustrations, and in the texts on the back cover as well as on the inside front and back covers, where presentations of the author and the intrigue share the space with blurbs and other promotional statements. All these items, which reflect the publishers' attempts to address a certain readership and to express an interpretation of the text, are likely to become revealing representations of the source culture.

The title, which Adorno once addressed as "the microcosm of the work",[30] has been studied from various perspectives and disciplines. Linguists, for instance, have underscored the function of the determinative article in book titles, while others might have concentrated on the nominal style or the numbers of words used for the title. From a paratextual point of view, the title, being a compromise between the author, the translator and the publisher, is a hybrid space that lends itself to comparison between the source edition and target editions in different languages. What happens, for instance, when Valeria Parrella's novel *Lo spazio bianco* ("The white space") is translated into German (*Zeit des Wartens*, "Time

---

case study is Andreas Hedberg's article "Small Actors, Important Task: Independent Publishers and their Importance for the Transmission of French and Romance Language Fiction to Sweden Since the Turn of the Millennium". *Moderna Språk*, 110, no. 2 (2016): 21–30.
[29] Genette, *Paratexts*, 23–26.
[30] Theodor W. Adorno, *Notes on Literature* (New York, Oxford: Columbia University Press, 1992), 4.

of waiting"), French (*Le temps suspendu,* "The suspended time") and Swedish (*Väntrum,* "Waiting room")? Well, it is significant that while the French and German titles emphasise the temporal aspect, the Swedish title remains more faithful to the spatial dimension in the Italian original, but on the other hand the Swedish title concretises the somewhat elusive Italian title, which is better preserved in the French and German variants. This is just one illustration of how localising practices become visible in the paratext, and we could go on by analysing the presence and functions of footnotes and pre- and postfaces, not to mention the publisher's choice of the preface writer.[31] Genette defines several functions of these peritextual elements, which he basically divides into the *themes of the why* and the *themes of the how.*[32] When translated works eventually contain a translator's preface, Ellen McRae has shown that in a corpus of contemporary fiction translated into English, the main functions of the translator's fore- or afterword were to call for the reader's attention to the translator's role, as well as to promote a mutual understanding between cultures.[33]

Concluding remarks

The research task proposed in this chapter draws on the conviction that current ideas of Italian literature and its overall status in present Sweden are manifested in the publishing houses' localising practices, which are expressed in the selection of titles as well as in paratexts. However, depending on the aim of the research task, the presented methods and models might be used together or separately, on similar material.

---

[31] For instance, Ulf Norberg argues that in Sweden, "the writers of prefaces usually have a large literary capital (literary critics, literary scholars or authors)". *Translation peripheries,* ed. Anna Gil-Bardají (Bern: Peter Lang, 2012), 105.

[32] Genette, *Paratexts,* 198–223.

[33] Ellen McRae, "The role of translators' prefaces to contemporary literary translations into English: An empirical study", in *Translation Peripheries: Paratextual elements in translation,* ed. Anna Gil-Bardají et al. (Bern: Peter Lang, 2012), 81.

The methods presented in this brief chapter are only samples of the resources that are available for a researcher today. It is important to keep in mind, though, that most of the existing models originate from the Anglo-American and French-speaking areas, which might not be adequate for describing the situation in semi-peripheral or peripheral language areas. As researchers we must therefore presume that the overall picture might differ from one literature to another and from one time to another. From this we can draw the intriguing and stimulating conclusion that methods that are better suited for describing (semi-)peripheral relations need to be elaborated and developed if we want to obtain a deeper understanding of neglected areas of world literature.

Bibliography

Adorno, Theodor W. *Noten zur Literatur*. Frankfurt am Main: Suhrkamp Verlag, 1974. Translated by Shierry Weber Nicholsen as *Notes on Literature*. New York, Oxford: Columbia University Press, 1992.

Alvstad, Cecilia. "The Strategic moves of Paratexts: World Literature through Swedish Eyes". *Translation Studies* 5, no. 1, (2012): 78–94.

Cadioli, Alberto. "Il patto editoriale nelle edizioni moderne e contemporanee". In *I dintorni del testo. Approcci alle periferie del libro*, vol. II, edited by Marco Santoro and Maria Gioia Tavoni, 663–672. Rome: Edizioni dell'Ateneo, 2005.

D'haen, Theo. *The Routledge Concise History of World Literature*. London, New York: Routledge, 2012.

Elefante, Chiara. *Traduzione e paratesto*. Bologna: Bononia University Press, 2012.

Genette, Gérard. 1987. *Seuils*. Paris: Editions du Seuil. Translated by Jane E Lewin as *Paratexts: Thresholds of Interpretation*. Cambridge: Cambridge University Press, 1997.

Gil-Bardají, Anna, Pilar Orero, and Sara Rovira-Esteva, eds. *Translation Peripheries: Paratextual Elements in Translation*. Bern: Peter Lang, 2012.

Hedberg, Andreas. "Small Actors, Important Task: Independent Publishers and their Importance for the Transmission of French and Romance Language Fiction to Sweden Since the Turn of the Millennium". *Moderna Språk*, 110, no. 2 (2016): 21–30.

Jansen, Hanne. "Bel Paese or Spaghetti noir? The Image of Italy in Contemporary Italian Fiction Translated into Danish". In *Interconnecting Translation Studies and Imagology*, edited by Luc van Doorslaer, Peter Flynn and Joep Leerssen, 163–79. Amsterdam: John Benjamins Publishing, 2015.

Kungliga biblioteket. *Nationalbibliografin i siffror 2016*. Stockholm: Nationalbibliografin, Kungliga biblioteket, 2017.

Kungliga biblioteket. *Nationalbibliografin i siffror 2017*. Stockholm: Nationalbibliografin, Kungliga biblioteket, 2018.

McRae, Ellen. "The Role of Translators' Prefaces to Contemporary Literary Translations into English: An Empirical Study". In *Translation Peripheries: Paratextual Elements in Translation*, edited by Anna Gil-Bardají, Pilar Orero and Sara Rovira-Esteva, 63–82. Bern: Peter Lang, 2012.

Moretti, Franco. "More conjectures". *New Left Review* 20 (2003): 73–81.

Määttä, Jerry. *Raketsommar. Science fiction i Sverige 1950–1968*. Lund: Ellerströms, 2006.

Norberg, Ulf. "Literary translators' comments on their translations in prefaces and afterwords: the case of contemporary Sweden". In *Translation Peripheries: Paratextual Elements in Translation*, edited by Anna Gil-Bardají, Pilar Orero and Sara Rovira-Esteva, 101–16. Bern: Peter Lang, 2012.

Pellatt, Valerie, ed. *Text, Extratext, Metatext and Paratext in Translation*. Cambridge: Cambridge Scholars Publishing, 2013.

Pym, Anthony. *Method in Translation History*. Manchester: St Jerome Publishing, 1998.

Risterucci-Roudnicky, Danielle. *Introduction à l'analyse des œuvres traduites*. Paris: Armand Colin, 2008.

Rosendahl Thomsen, Mads. *Mapping World Literature: International Canonization and Transnational Literatures*. London: Continuum, 2008.

Sapiro, Gisèle, ed. *Translatio: Le marché de la traduction en France à l'heure de la mondialisation*. Paris: CNRS Éditions, 2008.

———. "Translation and the Field of Publishing. A Commentary on Pierre Bourdieu's 'A Conservative Revolution in Publishing'". *Translation studies* 1, no. 2 (2008): 154–66.

———. "The Sociology of Translation. A New Research Domain". In *A Companion to Translation Studies*, edited by Sandra Bermann and Catherine Porter, 82–94. Chichester: Wiley Blackwell, 2014.

———. "Le champ littéraire français. Structure, dynamique et formes de politisation". In *Art et société. Recherches récentes et regards croisés, Brésil/France*, edited by Alain Quemin and Glaucia Villas Bôas. Marseille: Open Edition Press, 2016.

Venuti, Lawrence. *The Translator's Invisibility: A History of Translation*. 2nd ed. London, New York: Routledge, 2008.

———. *The Scandals of Translation: Towards an Ethics of Difference*. New York: Routledge, 1998.

———. *Translation Changes Everything: Theory and Practice*. New York: Routledge, 2013.

Watts, Richard. *Packaging Post/coloniality: The Manufacture of Literary Identity in the Francophone World*. Lanham: Lexington Books, 2005.

27. Literary Migration as Transformation
Paul Tenngart
Comparative Literature, Lund University

Examining how literature circulates across geographical, cultural and linguistic borders is a central task for contemporary literary studies. As other chapters in this section also demonstrate, nuanced insights into the patterns and conditions of what B. Venkat Mani calls "bibliomigrancy"[1] – literary circulation by way of books – enhance our understanding of intercultural traffic and intercultural relations in general. Such studies may focus on the material conditions for circulation – the economic reality of producing and distributing books, the establishment and maintenance of libraries or potential readers' various degrees of access to books – but in order to reach literature's significance on a more general and substantial level of intercultural communication another point of view is just as important: that of transformation. A work of literature, David Damrosch reminds us, "*manifests* differently abroad than it does at home", and the ways in which literature transforms when it travels tell us a great deal about intercultural manifestations as such.[2]

My case in point will be British and American translations of Swedish working-class fiction from the 1930s. This literary

---

[1] B. Venkat Mani, "Bibliomigrancy: Book series and the making of world literature", in Theo D'haen, David Damrosch and Djelal Kadir (eds.), *The Routledge Companion to World Literature* (London and New York: Routledge, 2011).

[2] David Damrosch, *What Is World Literature?* (Princeton: Princeton University Press, 2003), 6.

How to cite this book chapter:
Tenngart, Paul. "Literary Migration as Transformation". In *World Literatures: Exploring the Cosmopolitan-Vernacular Exchange*, edited by Stefan Helgesson, Annika Mörte Alling, Yvonne Lindqvist, and Helena Wulff, 324–339. Stockholm: Stockholm University Press, 2018. DOI: https://doi.org/10.16993/bat.aa. License: CC-BY.

current has a central position in Swedish twentieth-century literature, with a distinct connection to the particularly Swedish version of the welfare state – a compromise between socialism and capitalism. The English translations of these novels amount to 13 publications: four of these are British, five are American, and four of them are published in the USA and the UK simultaneously. In two cases, the same translation is published in the US and the UK separately by different publishers. Five of the translated texts are from the 1930s, one is from the 1940s, one is from the 1970s, five are from the 1980s, and two are published in the 1990s.[3] This material is, then, quite diverse: it involves two different literary markets, several historical periods, and six translators. A common

---

[3] The 13 publications are: Harry Martinson, *Cape Farewell* (London: Cresset Press, 1934), transl. Naomi Campbell (*Kap Farväl!*, Stockholm: Bonniers, 1933); Harry Martinson, *Cape Farewell* (New York: Putnam, 1934), transl. Naomi Cambell (*Kap Farväl!*, Stockholm: Bonniers, 1933); Harry Martinson, *Flowering Nettle* (London: Cresset Press, 1936), transl. Naomi Campbell (*Nässlorna blomma*, Stockholm: Bonniers, 1935); Vilhelm Moberg, *Memory of Youth* (New York: Simon & Schuster, 1937), transl. Edwin Björkman (*Sänkt sedebetyg*, Stockholm: Bonniers, 1935); Vilhelm Moberg, *The Earth is Ours* (New York: Simon & Schuster, 1940), transl. Edwin Björkman (*Sänkt sedebetyg*, Stockholm: Bonniers, 1935; *Sömnlös*, Stockholm: Bonniers, 1937; *Giv oss jorden!*, Stockholm: Bonniers, 1939); Eyvind Johnson, *1914* (London: Adam Books, 1970), transl. Mary Sandbach (*Nu var det 1914*, Stockholm: Bonniers, 1934); Jan Fridegård, *I, Lars Hård* (Lincoln and London: University of Nebraska Press, 1983), transl. Robert E. Bjork (*Jag Lars Hård*, Stockholm: Schildt, 1935); Jan Fridegård, *Jacob's Ladder & Mercy* (Lincoln and London: University of Nebraska Press, 1985), transl. Robert E. Bjork (*Tack för himlastegen*, Stockholm: Schildt, 1936; *Barmhärtighet*, Stockholm: Schildt, 1936); Moa Martinson, *Women and Appletrees* (New York: Feminist Press, 1985), transl. Margaret S. Lacy (*Kvinnor och äppelträd*, Stockholm: Bonniers 1933); Moa Martinson, *Women and Apple Trees* (London: Women's Press, 1987), transl. Margaret S. Lacy (*Kvinnor och äppelträd*, Stockholm: Bonniers, 1933); Moa Martinson, *My Mother Gets Married* (New York: Feminist Press, 1988), transl. Margaret S. Lacy (*Mor gifter sig*, Stockholm: Bonniers, 1936); Ivar Lo-Johansson, *Breaking Free* (Lincoln and London: University of Nebraska Press, 1990), transl. Rochelle Wright (*Godnatt, jord*, Stockholm: Bonniers, 1933); Ivar Lo-Johansson, *Only a Mother* (Lincoln and London: University of Nebraska Press, 1991), transl. Robert E. Bjork (*Bara en mor*, Stockholm: Bonniers, 1939).

ground for the 13 publications, however, is the fact that they all execute a circulation from a peripheral literary language to a central one.[4]

When this domestically central Swedish literature, then, migrates to the very different political and cultural contexts of twentieth century UK and USA, its significance changes. Swedish working-class fiction is something else abroad. But *how* is it different? Well, that question needs multiple answers. The Swedish versions of these novels are not only reshaped into another language, but also repackaged and recontextualised. As a result of a first examination of these publications, this chapter will point out nine different kinds of transformations and a diverse set of theoretical frameworks required to analyse the changes. Faced with another material, some of these transformations may prove irrelevant, and other changes not evident in my material may instead emerge as crucial. I do think, however, that a similar set of aspects may be applied to all kinds of migrated literary material.

Situation, Format and Language

First of all, when a literary work enters a new market, it is doing so in a particular situation. The text is translated by a particular translator, edited by an editor, and published, distributed and marketed by a particular publisher. To analyse these situational conditions – and perhaps compare them to how the original text was situated in the source culture – requires theories and methods from book history and translation sociology.[5] In my material, four

---

[4] The notion of central and peripheral literary languages is primarily drawn from Johan Heilbron's analysis of translation patterns, "Towards a Sociology of Translation: Book Translations as a Cultural World-System", *European Journal of Social Theory* 2 (1999): 429–44. Heilbron argues that English is a "hyper-central" language and Swedish is a "semi-peripheral" language, but his statistics are based on a particular period, the 1970s and the 1980s, whereas my material covers many decades. Therefore, Heilbron's more detailed relations between literary languages cannot be applied.

[5] For introductions to book history and translation sociology, see Leslie Howsam, "The Study of Book History", in *The Cambridge Companion*

different types of publishers are evident: small publishing houses with a narrow back list of literary fiction from abroad, large companies with a distinct commercial agenda, politically driven publishers with an ideological agenda and university presses with educational ambitions. These four types of publishers use different kinds of distribution and reach different kinds of readers. The translators can be divided into three groups: those whose principal profession is translation, those who translate texts alongside a principal occupation as writers or journalists, and academics who translate literature as a parallel activity to research and teaching.

More concrete and evident situations are created by the peritexts accompanying the translated texts in the books, including covers framing the narratives in quite a new way compared to the different Swedish editions.[6] Observations like these require a book historical approach, but also narratological ideas about the role of peritexts as well as intermedial theories on the impact of covers. None of the books in my material, for example, use the same cover or cover artist as the Swedish versions. In some cases, the different versions make contrasting impressions and create contrary expectations of the novel at hand.

The most apparent situational transformation in my material occurs when Moa Martinson's novels *Kvinnor och äppelträd* and *Mor gifter sig* are published in the 1980s as *Women and Appletrees* and *My Mother Gets Married* by the New York–based Feminist Press. The publisher's political agenda is highlighted by the translator Margaret S. Lacy's afterword, in which Martinson is portrayed as a feminist rather than a proletarian writer. Martinson's narratives are removed from one political situation in the Swedish 1930s to quite another political situation in 1980s America. The new situation makes her texts function in another way, which is further stressed by the cover paintings: American

---

to the History of the Book, ed. Leslie Howsam (Cambridge: Cambridge University Press, 2015) and Andrew Chesterman, "The Name and Nature of Translator Studies", *Hermes* 42 (2009): 13–25.

[6] Peritext is Gérard Genette's term for the kind of paratext that is part of the volume as such: introductions, afterwords, endnotes, covers etc. Gérard Genette, *Seuils* (Paris: Seuil, 1987).

artist Mary Cassatt's *Baby Reaching for an Apple* from 1893 on *Women and Appletrees* and German artist Paula Modersohn-Becker's *Mädchenbildnis* from 1905 on *My Mother Gets Married*. Cassatt's picture of a woman and a baby underneath an apple tree and Modersohn-Becker's portrait of a girl looking straight back at her observer signal womanhood and girlhood rather than poverty and class struggle.

In addition to these situational changes, editorial decisions also repackage the narratives into new text and book formats. In the migration process, several of the Swedish novels from the 1930s have undergone substantial changes as to the arrangement of chapters, shortenings, and volumes. For example, *1914* is a translation of the first book of Eyvind Johnson's autobiographical tetralogy *Nu var det 1914*, *Här har du ditt liv!*, *Se dig inte om!* and *Slutspel i ungdomen*. In the UK, the first part of this series is published as a single, isolated novel, giving it a sense of finality and closure it does not have in a Swedish context. Similarly, Vilhelm Moberg's trilogy *Sänkt sedebetyg*, *Sömnlös*, and *Giv oss jorden!* is published in two different ways. In 1937, the first part of the trilogy appears in the US as a separate novel, *Memory of Youth*, and in 1940 the whole series is published in a single volume, *The Earth is Ours*. These two publishing strategies have contrasting effects: in the first case a part is isolated from the rest of the narrative, in the second case three distinctly published parts are presented as a unity.

A more important change of format in my material, however, is abbreviation. All translated texts are not abridged, but some of them are considerably shorter than their Swedish counterparts. This is especially the case in the early translations: the practice of abbreviation tends to disappear in the last decades of the twentieth century. Exclusions appear on different levels: whole chapters, sections of chapters, paragraphs, sentences, and parts of sentences. Another kind of format change, just as important as shortenings, is the inclusion of footnotes and endnotes. This kind of peritext, interweaving the literary text with asterisks or numbers, is rare in the early publications but richly used in the translations from the 1980s and 1990s. Abbreviations and added notes are apparent examples of how literature changes shape when it migrates. In her book on African editions of John Bunyan's *The Pilgrim's Progress*, Isabel Hofmeyr notes that migrated literary works are "excised, summarized, abridged, and bowdlerized by the new intellectual formations into which they migrate".[7] This holds true for Swedish realist narratives in the UK and the USA as well as for African versions of British Christian classics.

The most evident change in any translated material is of course the very shift from one language to another. It is crucial, however, to bear in mind that the translators' detailed work is only one kind of transformation among many in the migration process. In relation to my material, Emily Apter's notion of "untranslatability" has proven constructive to discuss the translators' struggles with certain words and concepts, especially those naming domestic and everyday phenomena,[8] and Lawrence Venuti's take on the old terms "domestication" and "foreignisation" offers a good starting point to describe different translators' solutions to these problems.[9] Judging from these translated texts there is, for example, one Swedish phenomenon proving more difficult to translate than any other: the habit of drinking liquor. The verb "supa" (drinking heavily, as opposed to just drinking, "dricka"), is simply translated as "drinking", and the word "brännvin" is dealt with in a variety of ways: "brandy",[10] "potato-spirit",[11] "booze",[12] "aquavit"[13] and, finally, kept as a foreign word in italics, "*brännvin*".[14] Whereas "drinking" is a neutralisation of "supa", the words "brandy" and "booze" domesticate the kind of drink referred to,

---

[7] Isabel Hofmeyr, *The Portable Bunyan: A Transnational History of* The Pilgrim's Progress (Princeton: Princeton University Press, 2004), 2f.
[8] Emily Apter, *Against World Literature: on the Politics of Untranslatability* (London: Verso, 2013).
[9] Lawrence Venuti, *The Translator's Invisibility: A History of Translation* (New York: Routledge, 1995).
[10] Harry Martinson, *Flowering Nettle*, 7; Fridegård, *I, Lars Hård*, 19; Moa Martinson, *Women and Apple Trees*, 25.
[11] Johnson, *1914*, 28.
[12] Lo-Johansson, *Breaking Free*, 29.
[13] Lo-Johansson, *Only a Mother*, 229.
[14] Moberg, *Memory*, 21.

while "potato-spirit", "aquavit" and "*brännvin*" foreignise the Swedish liquor.

Distance and Integration

Distributed on other literary markets, these texts are read in new cultural contexts framing and conditioning the understanding of the narratives. Interpreting literature, hermeneutics tells us, is very much about bridging gaps between the characters', the author's, and the reader's different historical positions.[15] In translations, there is an added *cultural* gap, creating a cultural distance between author and reader. This recontextualisation has fundamental representational effects. Distributed and read in another context, far from its place of origin, a literary text often comes to represent more general phenomena than it represents in a context closer to home. The tendency in my material is that the translations are less distinctly connected to particular instances – a specific author, literary current, historical period and social stratum – and instead represent Swedish or Scandinavian literature, culture, society or ways of life. The hardships and injustices depicted come forth as generally Swedish, and the stylistic, thematic and narrative characteristics of these particular novels become characteristics of Swedish literature.

This kind of transformation due to cultural distance, however, not only reduces but also enlarges the novels' significance. Hermeneutic distance does not necessarily make us see less, but may enable us to acknowledge other kinds of significance, unnoticeable at a close range. Moa Martinson's novels are lifted from their firm position in Swedish literary history as proletarian narratives to a cosmopolitan context of women writers from different parts of the world. She contributes with a Swedish perspective on a vastly significant global issue. The same kind of transformation is evident in all the other novels: Moberg's, Fridegård's, Lo-Johansson's and Harry Martinson's narratives become

---

[15] Hans-Georg Gadamer, *Gesammelte Werke: Band 1: Hermeneutik I: Wahrheit und Methode: Grundzuge Einer Philosophischen Hermeneutik* (Mohr Siebeck: Tübingen, 2010).

internationally significant accounts of injustice, frustration, exposure and vulnerability rather than depictions of particular instances in Swedish history.

Furthermore, translations often bring an additional historical gap to the process of interpretation: that between the author and the translator. Moa Martinson's *My Mother Gets Married*, for example, is written in the early 1930s with a 30-year distance from when it is set. With Margaret S. Lacy's translation and afterword, these two historical positions are clothed with words and perspectives from the 1980s, including, for example, a late twentieth-century discourse of gender and feminism. The American translation also includes a foreword by the author written for a new edition of the novel in 1956. Interpreting the novel involves, then, a navigation through five layers of different historical positions: the reader's own position, the translator's 1980s, the foreword's 1950s, the 1930s of Martinson's writing, and the setting's first decade of the twentieth century. These historical gaps interfere with the cultural distance between reader and author, and vice versa: the cultural gap between translator/reader and writer/characters complicates the process of abridging the historical distance, threatening to blur the impressions of historical distinctness.

The ways in which cultural phenomena in the texts are understood differently by target culture readers compared to source culture readers is a hermeneutic question with a distinct anthropological significance. In Gabriele Schwab's words, translated literary texts function as "imaginary ethnographies",[16] interpreted with the help of other sets of references than the original text. For a Swedish reader, for example, these novels have a distinct position in twentieth-century literary history and are understood as a special kind of literature, *arbetarlitteratur*, written from a particular social and historical point of view. For British and American readers, however, these narratives first and foremost come forth

---

[16] Gabriele Schwab, *Imaginary Ethnographies: Literature, Culture, & Subjectivity* (New York: Columbia University Press, 2012).

as Swedish, and the depiction of customs and conditions is given a cultural rather than a social and historical significance.

At the same time, the translations also become integral parts of the target culture. With the help of polysystem theory, the Swedish novels can be related to different existing literary cultures, for example the tradition of social realism in the UK and the USA.[17] There are many ways in which a translated text can be connected to a particular domestic sphere in the target culture. In my material, cover texts, afterwords and footnotes include quite a few comparisons to British and American literary and social events and phenomena. Other integrating connections are made in reviews and introductions. Furthermore, readers themselves have most certainly been prone to understand these narratives from their own cultural points of view via domestic counterparts. Here, it is important to bear in mind that the USA differs distinctly from the UK in that it has a Scandinavian-American minority culture for which these novels have a special audience. This is illustrated by the fact that three out of four American translators have Scandinavian roots: Edwin Björkman (Moberg), Robert E. Bjork (Fridegård and Lo-Johansson) and Margaret S. Lacy (Moa Martinson). The different ways in which these novels become integral parts of British and American majority or minority cultures of course affect the way in which the cultural phenomena depicted are perceived and understood.

Formal, Generic and Thematic Changes

Since there is never a one-to-one relation between different languages, literary translations often include changes in the use of literary devices. This kind of formal transformation is also found in British and Americans versions of Swedish working-class fiction. Due to substantial differences between Swedish and English, the translators have occasionally been forced to make significant changes in the novels' narrative techniques. This happens,

---

[17] See Itamar Even-Zohar, "Polysystem Studies", *Poetics Today* 11, no. 1, (1990).

for example, when dramatic shifts of tense are skipped or a dialect-based free indirect speech has proven too difficult to keep. The tendency is that the translators make the narrative techniques less complex and more smoothly accessible, but these changes not only neutralise the narrative and the stylistic peculiarities of the Swedish authors, but also, and more significantly, create new kinds of narratives from the stories at hand. In Eyvind Johnson's *1914*, for example, the translator Mary Sandbach has added inverted commas to separate the characters' thoughts from the words of the anonymous narrator. Thereby, Johnson's fuzzy boundaries between narrator and characters are made distinct, and the narrative becomes more of an outside gaze into a foreign world than an account from within. A substantial analysis of this kind of observation requires a narratological framework.[18]

A couple of texts in my material undergo slight generic changes when translated. For example, a peritext can stress the autobiographical element of a novel so much that the text appears to be more of a direct testimony of a foreign life than an aesthetic account of a general experience. The use of explaining footnotes and endnotes enhances this impression, rendering the novels a distinct anthropological value and reshaping them from fiction to ethnographic sources. This kind of transformation occurs much more in the later than in the early translations, with a distinct shift around 1980. The most evident reason for this change is the fact that the later translations are predominantly published by university presses, with a focus on educational distributions and readerships. Generic changes are best studied through the lens of

---

[18] The modern fundamentals of this framework are found in Gérard Genette's *Figures I–III* from 1967–1970 (*Figures I*, Paris: Seuil, 2007; *Figures II*, Paris: Seuil, 2007; *Figures III*, Paris: Seuil, 1999), of which *Narrative Discourse: An Essay in Method* (Ithaca: Cornell University Press, 1983) is a selection, and in Dorrit Cohn, *Transparent Minds: Narrative Modes for Presenting Consciousness in Fiction* (Princeton: Princeton University Press, 1978). A more recent approach to the relation between narrator and character is found in Alan Palmer, *Fictional Minds* (Lincoln: University of Nebraska Press, 2004).

genre studies and its development within and outside the discipline of literary studies.[19]

The cultural gap also has the tendency to affect the very themes of the novels. The new cultural context frames the understanding of the text in a way that makes it appear to be about something slightly different. To analyse this kind of thematic transformation, we need a hermeneutic perspective based on the texts' recontextualisations. Being isolated on the autumnal potato fields in northern Sweden, for example, the young protagonist of Johnson's *1914* is ignorant of the war going on in many parts of Europe. For a Swedish reader, this ignorance enhances the theme of alienation. The protagonist is stuck. He is trapped in the outskirts of the world, too remote from everyone and everything else to be able to change his situation. In Britain, where young working-class men were forced unto the continent to be killed en masse at the front, this non-participation in the world events may very well be seen as a lucky stroke of God's grace. The protagonist is spared, and when the war ends he will get on with his life. In Moa Martinson's *Women and Appletrees* and *My Mother Gets Married*, the cultural and historical gaps work together in transforming the narratives from being working-class novels written from a female point of view to being feminist or proto-feminist narratives from a working-class perspective. This substantial shift is first and foremost enforced by the translator's afterword and the publishing situation, and it has a fundamental impact on the understanding of the narratives, putting some of the novels' motifs in focus at the expense of others.

World Perspectives

Finally, in recent literary scholarship, world literary theory has revitalised the concept of world-making in order to discuss what kind of relation to the world literary texts from different traditions encompass and evoke.[20] Culturally recontextualised texts

---

[19] For an overview, see John Frow, "'Reproducibles, Rubrics, and Everything You Need': Genre Theory Today", *PMLA* 122, no. 5 (2007).

[20] Pheng Cheah, "What is a World? On World Literature as World-making Activity", *Dædalus* 137, no. 3 (2008): 26–38.

are especially relevant cases to study from this perspective, since they are able to offer significantly different alternative outlooks upon the world we all share. At the end of Moberg's *The Earth Is Ours*, for example, the protagonist Knut Toring experiences a strong feeling of a two-fold belonging: he belongs in the small Swedish village of Lidalycke and "on this earth".[21] This existential insight is prompted by the conflict between Adolf Hitler and Neville Chamberlain at the negotiation in Munich in 1938 and the threat of a new European war. The novel's concept of "this earth" is thus primarily European. From a Swedish perspective, Knut's insight reflects a similar position for the reader: every Swedish city, town or village is dangerously close to the escalating conflict down south. But whereas a Swedish reading perspective is placed within Knut's world, an American perspective exists outside its borders. In one sense, then, the American reader is an outsider looking into European affairs from a distance, but by reading about the world through the eyes of the protagonist he or she is simultaneously invited to share Knut's perspective. Unlike the contemporary Swedish reader, the translation reader is thus offered a negotiation of perspectives.[22]

An analysis of a text's world can be done in a number of ways. A method that has proven very fruitful in my material is a simple mapping of geographical and cultural references in order to grasp the scope of the novels' and their characters' worlds.[23] In this respect, the narratives show huge differences. Eyvind Johnson's *1914*, for example, contains mostly local and very few international references, whereas Harry Martinson's *Flowering Nettle* is crammed with associations to and thoughts of places and phenomena from all over the world. Physically, the protagonists in these novels are equally bound to a limited place, but in their

---

[21] Moberg, *The Earth*, 621.
[22] For a discussion of the dynamics between the regional, the national and the cosmopolitan in all these novels, see Paul Tenngart, "Local Labour, Cosmopolitan Toil: Geo-Cultural Dynamics in Swedish Working-Class Fiction", *Journal of World Literature*, no. 6, 2016.
[23] For preliminary results of this mapping, see Paul Tenngart, "The Bamboos of Blekinge: The Writing of Cultures in Swedish Proletarian Fiction", *Journal of Literature and Art Studies* 5, no. 7, 2015.

minds their worlds are very different in geographical and cultural scope. Johnson's and Martinson's narratives thus represent two very different ways of experiencing the world, reminding us that outlooks upon the world are not merely conditioned by broadly drawn national, cultural and social belongings. Taken together, Swedish working-class narratives from the 1930s will give the reader a very diversified account of the world, despite the fact that they are all Swedish and written from a common historical and social perspective. Read separately and at a cultural distance, however, any of these novels may be understood as encompassing a general Swedish 1930s working-class perspective on the world.

Conclusion

The kinds of transformation due to literary migration observed here are very different from one another. They are caused by different conditions, they have different effects, and they require different theoretical frameworks in order to be substantially analysed. Examining them one by one from separate theoretical perspectives is clearly possible, but it will not enable us to reach a general impression of how a text or a set of texts manifests in new languages and contexts. All these kinds of transformation are active at the same time, impacting each other – sometimes confirming each other, sometimes enhancing each other, and at other times ruling each other out or giving contradictory impressions. In other words, their interrelations are very complex, and we need to address them all together.

One fundamental distinction is important to make. Five of these transformations exist on a more basic level than the others. Changes in situation, format, language, hermeneutic distance and cultural context are all necessary recodings that constitute the migration process. The other four – formal, generic and thematic changes, and changes in world perspectives – are rather secondary effects prompted by the inevitable recodings. In addressing all the transformations together, this distinction will help us see their interconnections and structure our further examinations.

Bibliography

Apter, Emily. *Against World Literature: On the Politics of Untranslatability*. London: Verso, 2013.

Cheah, Pheng. "What is a World? On World Literature as Worldmaking Activity". *Dædalus* 137, no. 3 (2008): 26–38.

Chesterman, Andrew. "The Name and Nature of Translator Studies". *Hermes*, 42 (2009): 13–25.

Cohn, Dorrit. *Transparent Minds: Narrative Modes for Presenting Consciousness in Fiction*. Princeton: Princeton University Press, 1978.

Damrosch, David. *What Is World Literature?* Princeton: Princeton University Press, 2003.

Even-Zohar, Itamar. *Polysystem Studies. Poetics Today* 11, no. 1 (1990).

Fridegård, Jan. *Jag Lars Hård*. Stockholm: Schildt, 1935.

———. *Tack för himlastegen*. Stockholm: Schildt, 1936.

———. *Barmhärtighet*. Stockholm: Schildt, 1936.

———. *I, Lars Hård*. Translated by Robert E. Bjork. Lincoln: University of Nebraska Press, 1983.

———. *Jacob's Ladder & Mercy*. Translated by Robert E. Bjork. Lincoln: University of Nebraska Press, 1985.

Frow, John. "'Reproducibles, Rubrics, and Everything You Need': Genre Theory Today". *PMLA* 122, no. 5 (2007).

Hans-Georg Gadamer. *Gesammelte Werke: Band 1: Hermeneutik I: Wahrheit und Methode: Grundzuge Einer Philosophischen Hermeneutik*. Mohr Siebeck: Tübingen, 2010.

Genette, Gérard. *Narrative Discourse: An Essay in Method*. Ithaca: Cornell University Press, 1983.

———. *Seuils*. Paris: Seuil, 1987.

———. *Figures III*. Paris: Seuil, 1999.

———. *Figures I*. Paris: Seuil, 2007.

———. *Figures II*. Paris: Seuil, 2007.

Heilbron, Johan. "Towards a Sociology of Translation: Book Translations as a Cultural World-System". *European Journal of Social Theory*, 2 (1999): 429–44.

Hofmeyr, Isabel. *The Portable Bunyan: A Transnational History of The Pilgrim's Progress*. Princeton: Princeton University Press, 2004.

Howsam, Leslie. "The study of book history". In *The Cambridge Companion to the History of the Book*, edited by Leslie Howsam, 1–13. Cambridge: Cambridge University Press, 2015.

Johnson, Eyvind. *Nu var det 1914*. Stockholm: Bonniers, 1934.

———. *1914*. Translated by Mary Sandbach. London: Adam Books, 1970.

Lo-Johansson, Ivar. *Godnatt, jord*. Stockholm: Bonniers, 1933.

———. *Bara en mor*. Stockholm: Bonniers, 1939.

———. *Breaking Free*. Translated by Rochelle Wright. Lincoln and London: University of Nebraska Press, 1990.

———. *Only a Mother*. Translated by Robert E. Bjork. Lincoln: University of Nebraska Press, 1991.

Mani, B. Venkat. "Bibliomigrancy: Book Series and the Making of World Literature". In *The Routledge Companion to World Literature*, edited by Theo D'haen, David Damrosch and Djelal Kadir, 283–96. New York: Routledge, 2011.

Martinson, Harry. *Kap Farväl!*. Stockholm: Bonniers, 1933.

———. *Cape Farewell*. Translated by Naomi Walford. London: Cresset Press, 1934.

———. *Cape Farewell*. Translated by Naomi Walford. New York: Putnam, 1934.

———. *Nässlorna blomma*. Stockholm: Bonniers, 1935.

———. *Flowering Nettle*. Translated by Naomi Walford. London: Cresset Press, 1936.

Martinson, Moa. *Kvinnor och äppelträd*. Stockholm: Bonniers 1933.

———. *Mor gifter sig*. Stockholm: Bonniers 1936.

———. *Women and Appletrees*. Translated by Margaret S. Lacy. New York: Feminist Press, 1985.

———. *Women and Apple Trees*. Translated by Margaret S. Lacy. London: Women's Press, 1987.

———. *My Mother Gets Married*. Translated by Margaret S. Lacy. New York: Feminist Press, 1988.

Moberg, Vilhelm. *Sänkt sedebetyg*. Stockholm: Bonniers, 1935.

———. *Sömnlös*. Stockholm: Bonniers, 1937.

———. *Giv oss jorden!* Stockholm: Bonniers, 1939.

———. *Memory of Youth*. Translated by Edwin Björkman. New York: Simon & Schuster, 1937.

———. *The Earth is Ours*. Translated by Edwin Björkman. New York: Simon & Schuster, 1940.

Palmer, Alan. *Fictional Minds*. Lincoln: University of Nebraska Press, 2004.

Schwab, Gabriele. *Imaginary Ethnographies: Literature, Culture, & Subjectivity*. New York: Columbia University Press, 2012.

Tenngart, Paul. "The Bamboos of Blekinge: the Writing of Cultures in Swedish Proletarian Fiction". *Journal of Literature and Art Studies* 5, no. 7 (2015): 495–504.

———. "Local Labour, Cosmopolitan Toil: Geo-Cultural Dynamics in Swedish Working-Class Fiction". *Journal of World Literature* 1, no. 4 (2016): 484–502.

Venuti, Lawrence. *The Translator's Invisibility: A History of Translation*. New York: Routledge, 1995.

28. A Cosmopolitan North in Nordic Noir: Turning Swedish Crime Fiction into World Literature

Louise Nilsson

English, Stockholm University

World literature does not carry itself across borders solely by the force of its words or at the behest of book reviewers vouching for the quality of the narratives. When translated literature travels outside its domestic context and becomes, following David Damrosch's definition, *a work of world literature*, its journey and perception is governed by a multifaceted (re)presentation that goes beyond common-sense perceptions of the book as an inert, unchangeable object.[1] Literature is visually embedded in print and digital media, film adaptations or marketing strategies as alluring jacket designs. Through these modes of representation that produce as well reproduce meaning about cultures and societies, a domestic literature in translation becomes a visually *glocal* literature, depicting universal themes in a local setting. When studying how literature is perceived in a foreign context, the power of representation should never be underestimated. In the circulation of world literature, media plays a seminal part that exemplifies how the perception of a book is a negotiating between its *content* and *context*.[2]

---

[1] David Damrosch, *What Is World Literature?* (Princeton: Princeton University Press, 2003), 5–6.

[2] Louise Nilsson et al., "Introduction", in *Crime Fiction as World Literature*, ed. Louise Nilsson et al. (New York: Bloomsbury, 2017),

---

How to cite this book chapter:
Nilsson, Louise. "A Cosmopolitan North in Nordic Noir: Turning Swedish Crime Fiction into World Literature". In *World Literatures: Exploring the Cosmopolitan-Vernacular Exchange*, edited by Stefan Helgesson, Annika Mörte Alling, Yvonne Lindqvist, and Helena Wulff, 340–354. Stockholm: Stockholm University Press, 2018. DOI: https://doi.org/10.16993/bat.ab. License: CC-BY.

A highly important aspect here, for the circulation of literature on the transnational book market, is how the book cover plays a key role in the representation of literature. When a domestic literature is integrated – and often assimilated – into other national and cultural contexts, the appearances of the books become especially crucial, either in reinforcing the branding of a known author or series, or else in setting the tone for a new entry into the market. The book cover is a highly relevant source for a deeper understanding of the circulation and perception of world literature, as it visually encloses the narrative.

This essay serves – by departing from the book cover as a source – as a *minor* sample example on how to *methodologically* approach the circulation of literature outside its own national context. The focus will be on the circulation of crime fiction outside its domestic context, focusing on works grouped together in the subgenre Nordic Noir, and it centres on Swedish crime fiction as a minor case study.

The aim is to examine, by departing from *one* cover, how translated literature becomes visually framed – as a foreign literature – on a transnational book market and how this domestic literature intersects with the cosmopolitan mediascape. The essay raises the question: how is a novel's narrative visually framed outside its domestic context on a transnational book market?

The investigation will discuss how the perception of Nordic Noir as exotic and well-marketed with wintry covers rests upon a culturally forged and globally disseminated idea of the north, found worldwide in various cultural expressions such as myths, folklore, fairy tales, literature and contemporary cinema and trails centuries back in cultural history. This idea embraces narratives of fear, as well as elements of the supernatural and fantastic, political dimensions or specific topographies. The main argument is that the perception of Swedish crime fiction as a local literature – often

---

1ff. Louise Nilsson, "Uncovering a Cover: Marketing Swedish Crime Fiction in a Transnational Context", *Journal of Transnational American Studies*, 7, no. 1 (2016): 1–16. My understanding of representation follows: Stuart Hall (ed.), *Representation: Cultural Representations and Signifying Practices* (London: Sage: The Open University, 1997), 1–3.

perceived as exotic – rests upon the shoulders of cultural history, popular culture as well as fine arts and in sum, a cosmopolitan cluster of shared ideas and values. The circulation of literature across borders is a multilayered and multifaceted process; the narrative itself is in fact only a part of the process that presents the novel to new potential readers. Therefore, the representation of literature in different media (film, magazines, marketing, blogs) contributes not only to our perception of literature's fictional narratives, but also to its surrounding cultural contexts and geographical location. The perception of world literature, I argue, is a negotiation between content and context, and the circulation of images, such as book covers, connects to other dimensions of culture and historically embedded ideas, often cosmopolitan in their orientation.

The choice of study object – the crime fiction genre – is motivated in several different ways. Crime fiction is a globally shared genre, intimately connected to the local place: the depicted milieus provide the *settings* for the plots and often play a thematic role in the novels.[3] Crime fiction is one of the most widespread of all literary genres, read worldwide and known for portraying and formulating a social critique of its own native context. It is deeply rooted in a *local* place, yet at the same time dealing with universal questions about life and death, crime and punishment, conflicting values and morals. The genre blends together reality and fiction, depicting its own society through fictional plots and characters. The genre's intimate connection to other media, such as film adaptations, occupies a unique niche and offers as empirical departure an opportunity to closely investigate the dynamics between fictional narratives and perception of culturally embodied geographical places.[4]

---

[3] Paul Geherin, *The Dragon Tattoo and Its Long Tail: The New Wave of European Crime Fiction in America* (Jefferson, North Carolina: McFarland & Company, 2012), 5–8. For further reading see Leonard Lutwack, *The Role of Place* (Syracuse: Syracuse University Press: 1984); Barbara Pezotti, *The Importance of Place in Contemporary Italian Crime Fiction: A Bloody Journey* (Madison: Fairleigh Dickinson University Press, 2012).

[4] Nilsson et al., *Crime Fiction*; Hans Bertens et al. (eds.), *Contemporary American Crime Fiction* (New York: Palgrave Macmillan, 2001).

The contemporary and internationally successful subgenre Nordic Noir is deliberately chosen as an empirical example as it is known narratively for its uniqueness or exoticism and aesthetically for its wintry book covers, due to its geographical northbound location in Europe.[5] Within academic research the focus has been on "the success story" in the aftermath of bestselling writers such as Henning Mankell and Stieg Larsson. The claim is that the success story is interwoven with a changed publishing industry that has merged into multimedia conglomerates and marketing strategies, drawing aesthetically upon the snowy landscapes of the Nordic countries.[6]

This encapsulation belies the complexity of marketing foreign literatures and simplifies how domestic crime fiction enters the transnational book market and merges into a cosmopolitan mediascape knit together by universal questions and shared ideas. Another aspect too substantial to disregard is the concept Nordicity, a research field developed by Canadian researchers in the 1960s, and that problematise the perception of high latitude regions – real and imagined – and how these connect to culturally forged ideas about the north in relation to natural conditions as well as culture and human psychology and identity.[7] The following

---

[5] I'm here using the word "aesthetically" in regard to the visual framing of crime fiction, for example, marketing. The term applies also, however, as a concept within literature studies, arching the aesthetic dimension of *language*.

[6] Nilsson, *Uncovering*, 2016.

[7] For research about Nordicity, see especially Daniel Chartier, "Towards a Grammar of the Idea of North: Nordicity, Winterity", *Nordlit* 22 (2007): 35–47; Sherrill E. Grace, *Canada and the Idea of North* (Montreal: McGill-Queen's University Press, 2001). Further reading, see: Margaret Atwood, *Strange Things: The Malevolent North in Canadian Literature* (Oxford:Clarendon Press, 1995); B. J. Epstein (ed.), *True North: Literary Translation in the Nordic Countries* (Newcastle upon Tyne: Cambridge Scholars Publishing, 2014); Carolyn Strange et al. (eds.), *True Crime, True North: The Golden Age of Canadian Pulp Magazines* (Vancouver: Raincoast Books, 2004); Sumarliði Ísleifsson et al. (eds.), *Iceland and Images of the North* (Quebec; Presses de l'Université du Québec; Reykjavík: The Reykjavík Academy, 2011); Sverrir Jakobsson et al. (eds.), *Images of the North: Histories – Identities – Ideas* (Amsterdam; New York; Rodopi, 2009); Dolly Jørgensen et al. (eds.), *Northscapes: History,*

analysis will therefore by taking on the surface of a narrative – the cover – contextualise it and, in relation to the novel's content, show how the local place intersects with the cosmopolitan space and shared beliefs and ideas from cultural history.

Theoretical and Methodological Considerations

A common approach to studying covers is quantitative and finds its inspiration in the work of Gérard Genette, statistically surveying paratexts (blurbs on the back cover, titles, additional text appearances on the cover).[8] My own approach is qualitative and employs discourse analysis as a theoretical and methodological point of departure. Theoretically inspired by discourse analysis understand crime fiction as a discursive field – a network consisting of elements and nodal points that connect and build on each other. The nodal points forming this discursive field can include subgenres, authors, domestic literature or iconic works, which I will show further ahead play key roles in forging of marketing tropes. In my use of *iconic* I mean an "image that refers to something outside of its individual components, something (or someone) that has great symbolic meaning for many people".[9]

Technology, and the Making of Northern Environments (Vancouver: University of British Columbia Press, 2013).

[8] Gérard Genette, *Paratexts: Thresholds of Interpretation* (Cambridge: Cambridge University Press, 1997). See also Karl Berglund, *Mordförpackningar. Omslag, titlar och kringmaterial till svenska pocketdeckare 1998–2011* (Uppsala: Avd. för litteratursociologi; Uppsala universitet: 2016); Nicole Matthews et al. (eds.), *Judging a Book by Its Cover: Fans, Publishers, Designers, and the Marketing of Fiction* (Aldershot: Ashgate, 2007). For an introductory study to literature and its commercial context a seminal study is: Claire Squires, *Marketing Literature: The Making of Contemporary Writing in Britain* (Basingstoke: Palgrave Macmillan: 2009).

[9] For further reading about iconic and in relation to visual displays in culture, see: Marita Sturken and Lisa Cartwright, *Practices of Looking: An Introduction to Visual Culture*, Oxford: Oxford University Press, 2001, quote from s. 36. For reading about iconic in relation to a northern setting, see: Robert G. David, *The Arctic in the British Imagination, 1818–1914*, Manchester: Manchester University Press, 2000.

The discursive field is not static but flexible, yielding an openness where new nodal points can emerge. As an established genre, crime fiction holds a power position on the book market, intersecting with a number of other discourses, belonging to, for example, entertainment culture where female crime fiction heroines challenges gender stereotypes, or social critique, focusing on malfunctions and flaws in the societal system as law, police enforcement or power misuse in politics. My approach follows Ernesto Laclau's and Chantal Mouffe's development of discourse as a system of social relations consisting of both linguistic and non-linguistic phenomena, including forms of behavior or visual representations.[10]

The following analysis connects specifically to the nonlinguistic dimension. Within this discursive field, elements appear continuously, striving to establish identities and subject positions. Elements then compete to strengthen their position and become nodal points, which are constructed through linguistic as well as nonlinguistic practices. Consider a foreign literature or unknown writer, both elements within this discursive field. Through articulatory practices including the many elements that go into the construction of a compelling paratext, these can merge successfully into the field, connecting to other nodal points, then establishing independent identities to become fixed nodal points connected to others. As discourses are open, identities continuously change and evolve. Meaning, therefore, is only partially fixed within the field.[11]

As Laclau and Mouffe discuss, a subject position can possess a number of social relations, all providing different identities. Thus, a domestic literature may represent the local or national, and can circulate within the transnational field as a cosmopolitan literature. A crime fiction novel may spur entertainment-oriented movie or television adaptations, yet at the same time spotlight a

---

[10] For further reading about discourse, see: David R. Howarth, *Discourse* (Buckinghamshire: Open University Press, 2000) 101; Ernesto Laclau et al., *Hegemony and Socialist Strategy: Towards a Radical Democratic Politics* (London: Verso, 1985).

[11] Howarth, *Discourse*, 101–7.

specific social problem (thereby connecting to another discourse). Swedish crime fiction has gone from being a foreign element to a well-established nodal point in many markets – a nodal point connecting to the node for the cluster of Nordic Noir – by successfully articulating its own identity and by connecting to other nodal points of the discursive field, via genre, nationality, author-branding, bestseller status or place-representation, and its specific geography that intersect with the cosmopolitan idea of the *north*.

In the following case study the analysis focuses on the Swedish crime fiction writer Arne Dahl and departs empirically from his novel *En midsommarnattsdröm* (2003) and its German translation, *Ungeschoren* since its jacket design displays a typically snowy Nordic Noir cover.

A Contradictory Cover

The author Arne Dahl's *En midsommarnattsdröm – A Midsummer Night's Dream* – is the sixth novel in the series of ten about the Stockholm-based crime-fighting squad called *A-gruppen* (A-unit, the *Intercrime Group* in English translation) and was adapted to the screen in 2015. Dahl's Intercrime Group series has been translated internationally and its Swedish TV-adaptation has been exported to Argentina, Chile, Finland, Germany, Japan and the UK among other countries. The plot in *A Midsummer Night's Dream* begins with the discovery – over a short time – of four dead bodies in Stockholm: a corpse in Riddarfjärden, a polish nurse killed with an axe, a Swedish television-manager involved in a popular reality TV-show and a murder, which appears to be an honor killing. The murder victims become connected by tattoo; each body has a small tattoo on the back of their knee and that together spell *PUCK*.[12]

The novel's title (its *paratext*) presents a multilayered meaning. Besides paraphrasing Shakespeare's well-known play *A Midsummer Night's Dream*, it refers to the Swedish holiday

---

[12] For information about translations and film adaptations of Arne Dahl's novels, see: http:// www.arnedahl.net (accessed February 2017).

midsommar (*midsummer*) in June. In regard to geography and climate, the midsummer holiday spawns the year's brightest night in Sweden, known as the night the sun never goes down. Traditionally it is celebrated by dancing outdoors around a flower-decorated maypole that resembles a cross (taking place during daytime, oriented towards families with children), eating traditional food (potatoes, herring, bread), singing traditional drinking songs and toasting in Swedish hard liquor served as shots.

In addition, the novel's plot takes place during the week before midsummer celebrations. The week before midsummer is when Sweden is gearing into vacation mode for a smooth and slow shut down before disappearing away to midsummer celebrations. The letters spelling PUCK is another reference to Shakespeare's play, and with a slightly different spelling it forms the old-fashioned Swedish word *Puke*, which refers to the devil or a devilish creature. Shakespeare figures, of course, as a source of inspiration for this novel.

The chosen title, *En midsommarnattsdröm*, intersects with an intertextual universe of literature as well as with culturally embedded customs and Swedish habits. The book covers for the releases in the Nordic countries also share the same image: the eerie silhouette of a flower-decorated midsummer pole against a dramatic dark and orange-coloured evening sky. In translation the novels have received a variety of covers, which also applies for new domestic editions: silhouettes at the end of roads, a corpse in water, a pocket knife or eerie faces, which all are images that follow the marketing tropes for the crime fiction genre at whole.[13]

However, there's a remarkable deviation to be found regarding Piper Verlag's German translation, re-titling the novel *Ungeschoren*. The front cover makes no sense in regard to the novel's plot. It depicts a snow-covered pine tree with two black ravens, leading the mind into a winter mystery, despite the original title – and fellow cover design – that indicates that the plot actually takes place in *June*. In addition, a wintry climate or wilderness

---

[13] Louise Nilsson, "Covering Crime Fiction: Merging the Local into Cosmopolitan Mediascapes", in *Crime Fiction as World Literature*, ed. Louise Nilsson et al.

has nothing to do with the novel's plot, which connects the murders to the Polish mafia, and the geographical setting for the plot is the capital Stockholm.[14] The German cover may be used as one example of many for the exoticism of Nordic Noir. This contradicting cover exemplifies the need for a qualitative analysis, which reveals the complexity of literature's visual representation when circulated on the book market.

Snow, ravens and forest are all *iconic* symbols and imageries that hold special symbolic positions in the discursive field of the crime fiction genre, stemming from a variety of key films and literature. As such these expressions can be understood as nodal points and when applied on book covers to capture attention, they become marketing tropes. Swedish crime fiction can be understood – from this sample case and my discussion in the beginning about discourse analysis – how it is an *element* in the discursive field connected to established nodal points in striving for becoming its own nodal point with a specific identity: Swedish crime fiction, which in turn connects to the node of Nordic Noir.

In regard to the use of marketing trope, the aesthetic framing of Dahl's *Ungeschoren* through its book cover, the novel becomes located on the book market as a crime fiction novel. Its title in turn – *Ungeschoren* – is a German expression that means "getting away with something". It locates the foreign novel as a story on the book market belonging to the crime fiction genre. This is only one minor example, though, of a wider pattern that defines the visual framing for the circulation of crime fiction as whole.

Birds, especially crows and ravens, are iconic and widely used within both the horror and crime fiction genre. Placed on book or DVD covers these not only represent the product but trigger associations and represent a myriad of cultural, mythological, religious and folkloristic references, including film and literature. By employing certain images, a foreign literature may be integrated into a transnational book market. Displaying a couple of black ravens stirs up association encompassing a wide array of symbols,

---

[14] Arne Dahl, *Ungeschoren* (Munich: Piper Taschenbuch, 2009).

images or iconic scenes in literature and film from the discursive field of crime fiction.

Edgar Allan Poe, often dubbed the father of crime fiction, should be understood as an iconic nodal point in the field amongst his seminal world-known poem *The Raven*. Birds occur often in Alfred Hitchcock movies, most notably *The Birds* (based in turn on a literary work, Daphne du Maurier's story) and when adapting Robert Bloch's *Psycho* for film, Hitchcock lets the killer Norman Bates nurture an intimate and highly personal relationship to birds, both as a concept and in the physical form of a stuffed bird – an echo back to Poe's raven. Given Hitchcock's iconic status, he is another nodal point that other elements connect to when positioning themselves in the discursive field and that marketing seeks to connect to.[15]

It is not surprising that birds frequently appear on the covers of Swedish crime novels. Håkan Nesser's *Am Abend Des Mordes*, featuring a red house in the forest flanked by a black bird, and his *Mensch ohne Hund* and *Die Einsamen* have sepia windows through which birds can be seen. The American edition of Liza Marklund's *Lifetime* carries the silhouette of a bird with its wings spread against murky yellowish tones and the Dutch edition of Kristina Ohlsson's *Engelbewaarders* shows a black, blood-dipped feather against white snow. As established symbols, ravens become – connected to other established, and often iconic, nodal points – attractive strategies in the articulatory practice for new literature, an element to apply and integrate in its appearance in the discursive field.[16]

As I've previously argued, snow-powdered Nordic Noir covers, outside their domestic contexts, do not furnish an exotic and

---

[15] Ravens are also depicted on all three mass-market paperback covers of American crime writer Michael Connelly's trilogy (2006–2010) about a killer named *The Poet*, in which Poe's works are an important clue for solving the case. On the inaugural novel, a bird circles over a red-coloured Los Angeles, embedded in black. Nilsson, *Crime Fiction*, 120ff.

[16] Håkan Nesser, *Die Einsamen* (München: Btb Verlag, 2011); Håkan Nesser, *Am Abend Des Mordes* (München: Btb Verlag, 2012); Kristina Ohlsson, *Engelbewaarders* (Amsterdam: The House of Books, 2012); Liza Marklund, *Lifetime* (New York: Atria/ Emily Bestler Books: 2013).

unique framing. Instead these covers intersect with a cosmopolitan mediascape of shared imaginaries that embrace glocal literature and holds an aesthetic rooted in the history of literature and film, as well as in cultural history.[17]

Wintry sceneries displayed on covers for Nordic Noir connects to a greater set of universally spread ideas about the *north* as a mysterious place. A part of Nordic Noir's foreign allure rests therefore upon this culturally forged idea of *the north* – on Dahl's *Ungeschoren* cover merged with the iconic ravens – and that can be found in various cultural expressions such as myths, folklore, fairy tales, literature and contemporary cinema and trails centuries back in cultural history. In *The Idea of the North* the renaissance historian Peter Davidson discusses how perception of a north connects to various geographical locations. He points out that everyone carries a notion of the north. For example, in China, the Great Wall marks the beginning of the north, in Japan it is the Hokkaidō Island, for a Swede, the north entails Lappland or, farther still, Iceland or the North Pole. Imaginations and artistic portrayals of the north have a long tradition in art and literature as well, intimately entwined with ghost stories and the fantastic: the Snow Queen or Ice Witch, as in Hans Christian Andersen's tale *Snow Queen* about a heroine who journeys to save her friend, kidnapped by the Snow Queen.[18]

Snowy covers are very common within the crime fiction genre. To mention a few: the different editions of Stephen King's *Misery* that circulate with snow-covered typewriters, houses and landscapes, or the winterscape on Mark Henshaw's *The Snow Kimono,* or the icy blue-coloured *Winter at the Door* by Sarah Graves. Other examples are the vampire battle taking place on a snow-covered field in the Twilight movie series and Quentin Tarantino's bedazzling Japanese winter garden for the sword-fight in *Kill Bill,* where the heroine Beatrix Kiddo fights her enemy

---

[17] Nilsson, "Uncovering"; Nilsson, "Covering".
[18] Peter Davidson, *The Idea of North* (London: Reaktion Books, 2005), 9, 109f.

O-ren Ishii.[19] When employed as a strategic marketing tool, the northern imagery gives Swedish literature a dramatic setting and labels domestic crime fiction through its home geography. This aesthetic belongs though to a multilayered and multifaceted mediascape where visual expressions intertwine with the circulation of literature, allowing not only foreign literature to enter the transnational book market for world literatures but also contributing to forging new narratives, as well as imaginaries of foreign places.

Bibliography

Arne Dahl homepage. Accessed February 2017. http:// www.arnedahl. net/ ?rID=1056&page=internationellt.

Atwood, Margaret. *Strange Things: The Malevolent North in Canadian Literature*. Oxford: Clarendon Press, 1995.

Bertens, Hans, and Theo D'haen, eds. *Contemporary American Crime Fiction*. New York: Palgrave Macmillan, 2001.

Berglund, Karl. *Mordförpackningar. Omslag, titlar och kringmaterial till svenska*

Pocketdeckare 1998–2011. Uppsala: Avd. för litteratursociologi; Uppsala universitet, 2016.

Connelly, Michael. *The Narrows*. New York: Grand Central Publishing, 2006.

———. *The Poet*. New York: Grand Central Publishing, 2009.

———. *The Scarecrow*. New York: Grand Central Publishing, 2010.

Dahl, Arne. *En midsommarnattsdröm*. Stockholm: Bonnier förlag, 2003.

---

[19] Mark Henshaw, *The Snow Kimono* (Melbourne: The Text Publishing Company, 2014); Sarah Graves, *Winter at the Door* (New York: Bantam, 2015), Stephen King's book covers. http://www.coverbrowser.com/covers/stephen-king-books (Accessed May 2017).

———. *Ungeschoren*. Munich: Piper Verlag; Piper Taschenbuch, 2009.

Damrosch, David. *What is World Literature?* Princeton: Princeton University Press: 2003.

Chartier, Daniel. "Towards a Grammar of the Idea of North: Nordicity, Winterity". *Nordlit* 22 (2007): 35–47.

Davidson, Peter. *The Idea of the North*. London: Reaktion Books, 2005.

Epstein, B. J., ed. *True North: Literary Translation in the Nordic Countries*. Newcastle upon Tyne: Cambridge Scholars Publishing, 2014.

Geherin, David. *The Dragon Tattoo and Its Long Tail. The New Wave of European Crime Fiction in America*. Jefferson, North Carolina: McFarland & Company, 2012.

Genette, Gérard. *Paratexts: Thresholds of Interpretation*. Cambridge: Cambridge University Press, 1997.

Grace, Sherrill E. *Canada and the Idea of North*. Montreal & Kingston: McGill-Queen's University Press, 2001.

Graves, Sarah. *Winter at the Door*. New York: Bantam, 2015.

Hall, Stuart (ed.). *Representation: Cultural Representations and Signifying Practices*. London: Sage in association with The Open University, 1997.

Henshaw, Mark. *The Snow Kimono*. Melbourne: The Text Publishing Company, 2014.

Howarth, David R. *Discourse*. Buckinghamshire and Philadelphia: Open University Press, 2000.

Ísleifsson, Sumarliði and Daniel Chartier. *Iceland and Images of the North*. Québec: Presses de l'Université du Québec; Reykjavík: The Reykjavík Academy, 2011.

Jakobsson, Sverrir, ed. *Images of the North: Histories – Identities – Ideas*. Amsterdam; New York; Rodopi, 2009.

Jørgensen, Dolly and Sörlin, Sverker, eds. *Northscapes: History, Technology, and the Making of Northern Environments.* Vancouver: UBC Press, 2013.

Laclau, Ernesto and Chantal Mouffe. *Hegemony and Socialist Strategy: Towards a Radical Democratic Politics.* London; New York: Verso, 1985.

Lutwack, Leonard. *The Role of Place in Literature.* Syracuse: Syracuse University Press, 1984.

Marklund, Liza. *Lifetime.* New York: Atria/ Emily Bestler Books, 2013.

Matthews, Nicole and Nickianne Moody. *Judging a Book by Its Cover. Fans, Publishers, Designers, and the Marketing of Fiction,* Aldershot: Ashgate, 2007.

Nesser, Håkan. *Mensch ohne Hund.* München: Btb Verlag, 2007.

———. *Die Einsamen.* München: Btb Verlag, 2011.

———. *Am Abend Des Mordes.* München: Btb Verlag, 2012.

Nilsson, Louise, "Covering Crime Fiction: Merging the Local into the Cosmopolitan Mediascape". In *Crime Fiction as World Literature,* edited by Louise Nilsson, David Damrosch and Theo D'haen. New York: Bloomsbury, 2017.

———. "Uncovering a Cover: Marketing Swedish Crime Fiction in a Transnational Context". *Journal of Transnational American Studies* 7:1 (2016), 1–16.

Ohlsson, Kristina, *Engelbewaarders.* Amsterdam: The House of Books, 2012.

Pezzotti, Barbara. *The Importance of Place in Contemporary Italian Crime Fiction: A Bloody Journey.* Madison: Fairleigh Dickinson University Press, 2012.

David G. Robert. *The Arctic in the British Imagination, 1818–1914,* Manchester: Manchester University Press, 2000.

StephenKing'sbookcovers.AccessedMay2017.http://www.coverbrowser.com/covers/stephen-king-books

Sturken Marita, Cartwright Lisa, *Practices of Looking: An Introduction to Visual Culture*, Oxford: Oxford University Press, 2001.

Squires, Claire. *Marketing Literature: The Making of Contemporary Writing in Britain*. Basingstoke: Palgrave Macmillan, 2009.

Strange, Carolyn and Tina Loo. *True Crime, True North: The Golden Age of Canadian Pulp Magazines*. Vancouver: Raincoast Books, 2004.

29. Swedes in French: Cultural Transfer from Periphery to Literary Metropolis

Andreas Hedberg
Literature, Uppsala University

There is a long tradition of cultural exchange between Sweden and France.[1] Typically, this exchange has been dominated by cultural phenomena moving northward, from Paris to Stockholm. However, in the context of understanding the relationship between the vernacular and the cosmopolitan, between the dominated and the dominating, one should not neglect the cultural products that have traveled the opposite route. Translations into French have played an important role for the continued mediation of Swedish fiction to the literary world. For instance, France was among the first major foreign markets for Stieg Larsson's now world-famous crime novels.[2] But there are several older examples. A French translation of the Swedish Nobel prize laureate Selma Lagerlöf's debut novel *Gösta Berlings saga* (1891) was published as early as 1904 and marked the beginning of a half-century-long heyday for

---

[1] Cf. e.g. *Une amitié millénaire: Les relations entre la France et la Suède à travers les ages*, L'historie dans l'actualité, edited by Marianne and Jean-François Battail (Paris: Beauchesne, 1993).

[2] Sylvain Briens and Martin Kylhammar, *Poétocratie. Les écrivains à l'avant-garde du modèle suédois* (Paris: Ithaque, 2016), 357.

How to cite this book chapter:
Hedberg, Andreas. " Swedes in French: Cultural Transfer from Periphery to Literary Metropolis". In *World Literatures: Exploring the Cosmopolitan-Vernacular Exchange*, edited by Stefan Helgesson, Annika Mörte Alling, Yvonne Lindqvist, and Helena Wulff, 355–368. Stockholm: Stockholm University Press, 2018. DOI: https://doi.org/10.16993/bat.ac. License: CC-BY.

Lagerlöf in France.³ The French were also quick to discover two other Swedish Nobel prize laureates, Eyvind Johnson (published in French as early as 1927)⁴ and Harry Martinson (eight works translated since 1938, not counting single poems published in anthologies or magazines). Furthermore, the Swedish existentialist writer Stig Dagerman was published by the prestigious Éditions Gallimard in the 1950s, and has been praised by French Nobel prize laureates Jean-Marie Le Clézio and Patrick Modiano.⁵

The research project "From Periphery to Center. Swedish Literature on the French Book Market 1945–2013" addresses the question of how a peripheral (or semi-peripheral) literature is established on a central literary field, with a special focus on the role of literary mediators in this venture. Drawing on bibliographical data⁶ and using qualitative methods including interviews, the study investigates how translators, publishers and mediators shape the transmission process. The objective of the study is to analyse the logics at work in the meeting of two literary systems and to make a general contribution to the understanding of literary circulation as such. In this introductory essay, the project's theoretical framework will be established through a discussion of

---

³ Guy de Faramond, *Svea & Marianne: Les relations franco-suédoises, une fascination réciproque* (Paris: M. de Maule, 2007), 24. Cf. Karin Andersson, "Selma Lagerlöf en France", in *La Nord à la lumière du Sud: Mélanges offerts à Jean-François Battail*, Deshima: Revue d'histoire globale des pays du Nord, 3, ed. Sylvain Briens and Martin Kylhammar (Strasbourg: Départements d'études néerlandaises et scandinaves, Université de Strasbourg, 2013, 161–175.

⁴ May-Britt Lehman, "*Lettre recommandée, Stad i ljus*: heurs et malheurs de la publication d'un roman d'Eyvind Johnson" and Birgit Munkhammar, "Eyvind Johnsons franska debut", both in *La Nord à la lumière du Sud: Mélanges offerts à Jean-François Battail*, Deshima: Revue d'histoire globale des pays du Nord, 3, ed. Sylvain Briens and Martin Kylhammar (Strasbourg: Départements d'études néerlandaises et scandinaves, Université de Strasbourg), 2013, 177–204/205–19.

⁵ Cf. Karin Dahl, *La Mythification d'un écrivain étranger. La réception de l'œuvre de Stig Dagerman en France et en Italie* (Göteborg: Avdelningen för franska och italienska, Göteborgs universitet, 2008).

⁶ The main source for bibliographical data will be Dennis Ballu's *Lettres nordiques. Une bibliographie 1720–2013* (Stockholm: Kungl. biblioteket, 2016).

the concept of world literature and the introduction of a a number of factors contributing to the circulation of literary works outside their original context. Some preliminary conclusions, based on earlier bibliographical research, will also be drawn.[7]

A Circulational Approach to the Concept of World Literature

My understanding of the concept of "world literature" is a circulational one.[8] The study of world literature, I contend, is the study of all literature crossing borders, circulating outside its original context, no matter what kind of literature, in no matter what source language. This understanding has been popularised since the turn of the millennium by such scholars as Pascale Casanova (*The World Republic of Letters* [1999/2004]) and Franco Moretti (e.g. "Conjectures on World Literature" [2000]).

For Moretti, world literature is not a canon or a set of works – it is not even an object, "it's a *problem*, and a problem that asks for a new critical method".[9] If one accepts his view, world literature should be a new way to study literature as a border-crossing phenomenon and on a much larger scale than before. Moretti is chiefly interested in genres and the spread and development of genres throughout the world. Reading at a distance, he identifies configurations common to the literary development in several different cultures. He uses these pieces of evidence "to reflect on the

---

[7] An earlier version of this essay has been published in Swedish. Cf. Andreas Hedberg, "Ett unikt kulturflöde. Den svenska litteraturens väg till Frankrike", in *Médiations interculturelles entre la France et la Suède: Trajectoires et circulations de 1945 à nos jours*, edited by Sylvain Briens and Mickaëlle Cedergren (Stockholm: Stockholm University Press, 2015), p. 111–17.

[8] Cf. Stefan Helgesson, "Going Global: An Afterword", in *Literary History: Towards a Global Perspective*, Vol. 4: *Literary Interactions in the Modern World* 2, ed. Stefan Helgesson (Berlin: W. de Gruyter, 303–21.

[9] Franco Moretti, "Conjectures on World Literature and More Conjectures" (2000/2003), in *World Literature: A Reader*, ed.Theo D'haen, César Dominguez and Mads Rosendahl Thomsen (London; New York: Routledge, 2013), 161–62.

relation between market and [literary] forms" in order to uncover what he terms "*laws of literary evolution*".[10]

Moretti's approach to world literature is true to Johann Wolfgang von Goethe's original statement on world literature, given in the poet's conversations with his personal secretary Johan Peter Eckermann: that national literature "means little now", that "the age of *Weltliteratur* has begun" and that "everyone should further its course".[11] For Moretti too, national literatures mean little, because he considers them abstractly, as examples to be studied from a great distance. Goethe's stance has been called "idealistic" and "too optimistic",[12] but if we follow Moretti, the age of world literature might very well be upon us, at least in the field of literary scholarship. When studying peripheral literatures and their relation to the world republic of letters using Moretti's methods, one might be able to formulate general points that can be applicable to other cases of how a minor language literature is mediated to the world.[13] This, however, is difficult to achieve without an operational understanding of the relationship between nation states and literature as an international phenomenon.

According to Casanova, there is, in the development of world literary space, a constant tendency towards autonomy, towards "literary emancipation in the face of political (and national) claims to authority".[14] But at the same time, literature suffers from an "original dependence" on the nation. Its medium, language, is "invariably appropriated by national authorities as a symbol

---

[10] Moretti, "Conjectures on World Literature and More Conjectures", 163.

[11] Johann Wolfgang von Goethe, "On World Literature" (1827), in *World Literature: A Reader*, ed. Theo D'haen, César Dominguez and Mads Rosendahl Thomsen (London; New York: Routledge, 2013), 11.

[12] Mads Rosendahl Thomsen, *Mapping World Literature: International Canonization and Transnational Literatures* (London; New York: Continuum International Publishing Group, 2008), 11.

[13] Nevertheless, one should not forget that, as Casanova puts it, "not all those who are literarily dominated find themselves in the same situation" and that "each one is dependent in a specific way" (Pascale Casanova, *The World Republic of Letters*, trans. M. B. Debevoise [Cambridge MA; London: Harvard University Press, 2004], 83).

[14] Casanova, *World Republic of Letters*, 39.

of identity", and literary resources are "inevitably concentrated [...] within the boundaries of the nation itself".[15] Consequently, Casanova, while insisting that the international literary space is relatively independent of the everyday world, that its boundaries does not completely coincide with those of the political or economic world, also criticises the naïve conception of literature as "pure", denationalised and dehistoricised.[16]

Literature, Economy and Sweden

Casanova's stance is an important theoretical starting point for the project at hand. To understand the logic at work in the transnational flows of literature, one needs to consider, among other things, the economic importance of the countries in which these languages are spoken. If we – for example – establish every language's share of the total Gross Domestic Product of the world, Swedish (whose relation to French is the main focus of this project) ends up high on the list. Sweden's economic power makes Swedish more than ten times more important than it should be, considering that Swedes only make up 0.14 per cent of the world's population.[17] Swedish publishers have the economic means to

---

[15] Casanova, *World Republic of Letters*, 34.
[16] Casanova, *World Republic of Letters*, 23. For a somewhat critical discussion of Casanova's view on the relation between literature and nation, see Alexander Beecroft, "World Literature without a Hyphen. Towards a Typology of Literary Systems", in *New Left Review*, November–December 2008, eg. 97–98. Beecroft's criticism echoes Christopher Prendergast's in his review of Casanova's book (Christopher Prendergast, "Negotiating World Literature", in *New Left Review*, March–April 2001, 100–21). Prendergast is severe in his critique of what he calls Casanova's "national-competitive model", claiming that it dangerously simplifies her account of literary history (109). He also points to weaknesses in Casanova's "ethnocentric" and print-centred definition of "literature" (118–19).
[17] Johan Svedjedal, "Svensk skönlitteratur i världen: Litteratursociologiska problem och perspektiv", in *Svensk litteratur som världslitteratur: En antologi*, Skrifter utgivna av Avdelningen för litteratursociologi vid Litteraturvetenskapliga institutionen i Uppsala, 65, edited by Johan Svedjedal (Uppsala: Avdelningen för litteratursociologi, Uppsala universitet, 2012), 28.

advertise their products abroad. Also, the Swedish state has the means to create and uphold institutions such as the Swedish Institute, advertising Sweden and Swedish culture abroad and financing the teaching of Swedish around the world. The Swedish Arts Council, also financed by the Swedish state, makes important economic contributions to the translation of Swedish fiction.[18]

These facts are not to be forgotten when studying the cultural relationships between Sweden and France. Statistics from The Swedish Arts Council show that French publishers and translators are very active when it comes to applying for translation grants (17 applications in 2012, making France number five on the list of countries with the most applications). Furthermore, according to statistics from the Swedish Institute, France is the fifth country in the world when it comes to the number of university students studying Swedish (approximately 800 students in 2015). Teaching is partly financed by the Swedish Institute, which spends more money per student in France than in any other country, except for Russia and Poland. These, of course, are factors that contribute to patterns in the mediation of Swedish literature to the French book market.

Paris: The Capital of the Literary World

As Casanova has suggested, world literature should be studied as a separate literary field, with mechanisms of consecration similar to those at play in the national literary fields. This means that we have to consider not only economic factors, but also factors unique for the literary or cultural fields, such as the reversed economy, as understood by Casanova's teacher Pierre Bourdieu, and strong ideas about literary centres and peripheries. Such an idea is Casanova's of Paris as "the capital of the literary world", which means that a writer who wants to be part of world literature must

---

[18] For a comprehensive history of state support for Swedish literature abroad, cf. Agnes Broomé, *Swedish Literature on the British Market 1998–2013: A Systemic Approach* (London: Department of Scandinavian Studies, UCL, 2015), 213–32.

be consecrated in the literary milieu of the French capital.[19] This hypothesis has been called into question[20] – especially following the rise of other literary centres, such as London and New York – but no matter if Casanova is right or wrong, the idea, or perception, of Paris as a centre, is sufficiently strong and widespread to influence the literary world in tangible ways. As Casanova herself puts it: a literary centre exists "both in the imaginations of those who inhabit it [and, one might add, those who inhabit the entire world republic of letters] and in the reality of the measurable effects it produces".[21] The recitation of the glories of Paris, "by virtue of being repeated as something obvious, gradually comes to acquire a reality of its own".[22]

For example, writers from minor languages, such as Sweden's August Strindberg, have gone to great pains in order to have their work translated into French.[23] (Strindberg's contemporary, the Danish literary scholar Georg Brandes contended – much like Casanova – that "[w]hen an author is acknowledged in France, he is known across the entire earth".)[24] Efforts like Strindberg's, and of other writers from what literary sociologist Robert Escarpit has

---

[19] Casanova, *World Republic of Letters*, 24, 127.
[20] Alexander Beecroft, for example, suggests that Casanova's model has "the perhaps unintended effect of re-inscribing a hegemonic cultural centre", even though her "avowed desire is to globalize literary studies" (Beecroft, "World Literature without a Hyphen. Towards a Typology of Literary Systems", 88). Beecroft also points to the limited scope of Casanova's (and Moretti's) theories: "If we wish our model of the world to extend deeply into the past, then [these theories], useful as they are in their own context, will not suffice" (91). Furthermore, he claims that Casanova's model is too focused on the national literatures, which makes it "inadequate", since "a number of languages and their literatures transcend national borders and because the de-centring of the nation state brought about by contemporary global capitalism alters literary circulation" (98).
[21] Casanova, *World Republic of Letters*, 24.
[22] Casanova, *World Republic of Letters*, 26.
[23] Concerning Strindberg's attempt to "conquer Paris", cf. Casanova, *World Republic of Letters*, 137–138.
[24] Georg Brandes, "World Literature" (1899), in *World Literature: A Reader*, edited by Theo D'haen, César Dominguez and Mads Rosendahl Thomsen (London; New York: Routledge, 2013), 25.

called "le circuit lettré",[25] have meant that canonised literature makes up a larger share of the fiction translated from Swedish to French than of fiction translated from Swedish to many other languages.

Looking closer at the translation of Swedish fiction into French, it is possible to collect statistical data that tests Casanova's suppositions about France's unique position in the literary world. For example, one might consider the translations of children's books. Statistically, children's books make up an impressive share of all fiction translated from Swedish: about 60 per cent. But the proportion varies between the different target languages. Among the translations to English, the share of children's books is close to the average, with 57 per cent. For translations to Japanese, it is as high as 84 per cent. But – coming back to Casanova – for translations to French, it is only 39 per cent.[26] The popular Swedish children's book author Astrid Lindgren, whose dominance is overwhelming in almost every target language, is in French surpassed by both the Nobel prize laureate Selma Lagerlöf and August Strindberg.[27] Similarly, still active writers who can be considered part of Sweden's literary canon – "le circuit lettré"– are comparatively widespread in France. These facts can be partly explained with reference to France's reputation as a major literary power. Canonised writers have made active efforts to have their work translated into French, in the belief that if they take Paris first, they can then move on to take the world.

---

[25] Robert Escarpit, *Sociologie de la littérature*, Que sais-je?, 777, 8 ed. (Paris: Presse Universitaire de France, 1992 [1958]).
[26] Andreas Hedberg, "Språk, genrer, författare. Sökningar i Kungl. bibliotekets bibliografi *Suecana Extranea*", in *Svensk litteratur som världslitteratur: En antologi*, Skrifter utgivna av Avdelningen för litteratursociologi vid Litteraturvetenskapliga institutionen i Uppsala, 65, ed. Johan Svedjedal, (Uppsala: Avdelningen för litteratursociologi, Uppsala universitet, 2012), 121–22.
[27] Ballu, *Lettres nordiques 1720–2013*, 913.

The Changing Itineraries of World Literary Space

Translations to certain languages – like French – seem to be particularly important for continued distribution and translation of literary works written in minor languages. These *transit languages* play integral parts in the global network of literature. Much like people, books tend to follow established routes from one country to another; a translation into one language often means a translation into another. In the case of fiction translated from Swedish, German – by far the most important of the Germanic languages – has played an essential role as a transit language.[28]

However, the itineraries of literature are changing rapidly. Today, books can find new routes, and their journey into the world is much quicker. Of course, many factors contribute to this remarkable development, of which several have been discussed by the Danish literary sociologist Hans Hertel, who speaks of *concentration* (a direct consequence of the conglomerisation of the media market; whereby the large-scale economics of the modern book industry force publishers to merge into larger units in order to survive ever harsher competition) and *polarisation* (a growing gap on the book market, between big and small publishers, between big and small book shops and chain stores and between bestsellers and failed titles) as two dominant trends of the modern book market.[29] Large-scale economics and media conglomerates contribute to a fast-paced bestseller culture, dominated by enormous book fairs and a system of literary agents, where Swedish publishing houses have made pioneering

---

[28] Lars Lönnroth, "Den svenska litteraturen på världsmarknaden", in *Den svenska litteraturen, 7: Bokmarknad, bibliografier, samlingsregister* (Stockholm: Bonnier, 1990), 38.

[29] Hans Hertel, "Boken i mediesymbiosens tid", in *Litteratursociologi: Texter om litteratur och samhälle*, edited by Lars Furuland and Johan Svedjedal, 2 ed. (Lund: Studentlitteratur, 2012), 225. For a critical discussion of Hertel's points, cf. Andreas Hedberg, "Small Actors, Important Task: Independent Publishers and their Importance for the Transmission of French and Romance Language Fiction to Sweden Since the Turn of the Millennium", in *Moderna Språk* 110, no. 2 (2016): 21–30.

contributions.³⁰ This development of the modern book market has meant considerable changes in the mediation of Swedish fiction to the international market, not only when it comes to pace and itineraries, but also when it comes to selection.

As a consequence of the phenomena studied by Hertel, Swedish fiction now has a different face or image in the eyes of the world. In the 1960s, while Astrid Lindgren unquestionably was the most translated of all Swedish writers, there was still quite a large share of canonised authors on the "top list". But today, the situation is completely different. Canonised literature has disappeared, replaced by crime fiction, which, together with the always popular children's books, make up Sweden's contribution to world literature.³¹ Effects of this development are clearly visible also on the French book market. The significant rise of the number of Swedish novels published in French translation since the turn of the millennium (18 novels in 2000, 73 in 2013)³² can be largely explained with reference to the so called "boom" of Scandinavian crime fiction. In 2013, Swedish was the fifth most important source language for translated novels published in France (after English, German, Spanish and Italian).³³ These patterns will be further examined in the project at hand.

In keeping with the theoretical framework and research principles outlined in this introductory essay – such as the focus on e.g. translation grants, Scandinavian studies and the role of literary mediators – the research project "From Periphery to Center" will discuss translations of Swedish fiction published on the French book market since the second world war. Translation flows will be followed through time, developments traced and highs and lows identified and explained. Also, the importance of specific genres will be studied, e.g. children's books, poetry and crime fiction.

---

30 Karl Berglund, "A Turn to the Rights. The Advent and Impact of Swedish Literary Agents", in *Hype. Bestsellers and Literary Culture*, edited by Jon Helgason, Sara Kärrholm and Ann Steiner (Lund: Nordic Academic Press, 2014), 67–87.
31 Svedjedal, "Svensk skönlitteratur i världen: Litteratursociologiska problem och perspektiv", 49–51.
32 Ballu, *Lettres nordiques 1720–2013*, 916–17.
33 Ballu, *Lettres nordiques 1720–2013*, 912–13.

Finally, a study of a small number of translated works will aim at a description of how Swedish fiction is mediated to the French readers, using, for example, Lawrence Venuti's distinction between foreignisation and domestication.[34] Already, one might point to some interesting characteristics of Sweden and France as literary spheres; Swedish literature, fuelled by for example a strong economy and strong institutions, seems more semi-peripheral than peripheral while France – as a result of a traditional and still important belief in Paris as a literary center – comes across as an important transit market and generator of literary value.

A study of this kind – in which literature is regarded as a travelling phenomenon – seems true to Goethe's idealistic stance on literature. In the wake of nationalist movements in today's Europe, this seems an important undertaking. Interestingly, Goethe, in his conversations with Eckermann, leaves room for hesitation. He calls upon us to "further [the] course" of world literature, as if this is something that needs to be done. This combination of optimism and concern is mirrored in Casanova's *The World Republic of Letters*, where the formation of a world literary space is described as a constant struggle between "the centripetal forces that strengthen the autonomous and unifying pole" of literature and "the centrifugal forces associated with the national poles of each national space".[35] Closed borders, Casanova suggests, never meant anything good for literature; instead, they bring literary development to a staggering halt. National literatures bring stylistic conservatism; international culture, on the other hand, brings literary innovation.[36] The study of literature as an international phenomenon, especially when guided by a circulational approach to the concept of world literature, may very well strengthen the centripetal forces of world literary space.

---

[34] Lawrence Venuti, *The Translator's Invisibility. A History of Translation* (London; New York: Routledge, 1995), 20.
[35] Casanova, *World Republic of Letters*, 109.
[36] Casanova, *World Republic of Letters*, 112.

Bibliography

Andersson, Karin. "Selma Lagerlöf en France". In *La Nord à la lumière du Sud. Mélanges offerts à Jean-François Battail*, Deshima. Revue d'histoire globale des pays du Nord, 3, edited by Sylvain Briens and Martin Kylhammar, 161–75. Strasbourg: Départements d'études néerlandaises et scandinaves, Université de Strasbourg, 2013.

Ballu, Dennis. *Lettres nordiques. Une bibliographie 1720–2013*. Stockholm: Kungl. biblioteket, 2016.

Battail, Marianne and Jean-François Battail, eds. *Une Amitié millénaire: Les relations entre la France et la Suède à travers les ages*, L'historie dans l'actualité, Paris: Beauchesne, 1993.

Beecroft, Alexander. "World Literature without a Hyphen: Towards a Typology of Literary Systems". In *New Left Review* (November–December 2008), 87–100.

Berglund, Karl. "A Turn to the Rights. The Advent and Impact of Swedish Literary Agents". In *Hype: Bestsellers and Literary Culture*, edited by Jon Helgason, Sara Kärrholm and Ann Steiner, 67–87. Lund: Nordic Academic Press, 2014.

Brandes, Georg. "World Literature" (1899). In *World Literature: A Reader*, edited by Theo D'haen, César Dominguez and Mads Rosendahl Thomsen, 23–27. London; New York: Routledge, 2013.

Briens, Sylvain and Martin Kylhammar. *Poétocratie. Les écrivains à l'avant-garde du modèle suédois*. Paris: Ithaque, 2016.

Broomé, Agnes. *Swedish Literature on the British Market 1998–2013: A Systemic Approach*. London: Department of Scandinavian Studies, UCL, 2015.

Casanova, Pascal. *The World Republic of Letters*. Translated by M. B. Debevoise. Cambridge MA: Harvard University Press, 2004 [1999].

Dahl, Karin. *La Mythification d'un écrivain étranger. La réception de l'œuvre de Stig Dagerman en France et en Italie*. Göteborg: Avdelningen för franska och italienska, Göteborgs universitet, 2008.

Escarpit, Robert. *Sociologie de la littérature*, Que sais-je? 777, 8 ed. Paris: Presse Universitaire de France, 1992 [1958].

Faramond, Guy de. *Svea & Marianne. Les relations franco-suédoises, une fascination réciproque*. Paris: M. de Maule, 2007.

Goethe, Johann Wolfang (von). "On World Literature" (1827). In *World Literature: A Reader*, edited by Theo D'haen, César Dominguez and Mads Rosendahl Thomsen, 9–15. New York: Routledge, 2013.

Hedberg, Andreas. "Språk, genrer, författare. Sökningar i Kungl. bibliotekets bibliografi *Suecana Extranea*". In *Svensk litteratur som världslitteratur: En antologi*, Skrifter utgivna av Avdelningen för litteratursociologi vid Litteraturvetenskapliga institutionen i Uppsala, 65, edited by Johan Svedjedal, 117–34. Uppsala: Avdelningen för litteratursociologi, Uppsala universitet, 2012.

———. "Ett unikt kulturflöde. Den svenska litteraturens väg till Frankrike". In *Médiations interculturelles entre la France et la Suède: Trajectoires et circulations de 1945 à nos jours*, edited by Sylvain Briens and Mickaëlle Cedergren, 111–17. Stockholm: Stockholm University Press, 2015.

———. "Small Actors, Important Task: Independent Publishers and their Importance for the Transmission of French and Romance Language Fiction to Sweden Since the Turn of the Millennium". *Moderna Språk* 110, no. 2 (2016): 21–30.

Helgesson, Stefan. "Going Global: An Afterword". In *Literary History: Towards a Global Perspective*, Vol. 4: *Literary Interactions in the Modern World 2*, edited by Stefan Helgesson, 303–21. Berlin: W. de Gruyter, 2006.

Hertel, Hans. "Boken i mediesymbiosens tid". In *Litteratursociologi: Texter om litteratur och samhälle*, edited by Lars Furuland and Johan Svedjedal, 2 ed., 221–42. Lund: Studentlitteratur, 2012.

Lehman, May-Britt. "*Lettre recommandée, Stad i ljus*: heurs et malheurs de la publication d'un roman d'Eyvind Johnson". In *La Nord à la lumière du Sud. Mélanges offerts à Jean-François Battail*, Deshima. Revue d'histoire globale des pays du Nord, 3, edited by

Sylvain Briens and Martin Kylhammar, 177–204. Strasbourg: Départements d'études néerlandaises et scandinaves, Université de Strasbourg, 2013.

Lönnroth, Lars. "Den svenska litteraturen på världsmarknaden". In *Den svenska litteraturen*, 7: *Bokmarknad, bibliografier, samlingsregister*, 38–43. Stockholm: Bonnier, 1990.

Moretti, Franco. "Conjectures on World Literature and More Conjectures" (2000/2003). In *World Literature: A Reader*, edited by Theo D'haen, César Dominguez and Mads Rosendahl Thomsen, 160–75. London; New York: Routledge, 2013.

Munkhammar, Birgit. "Eyvind Johnsons franska debut". In *La Nord à la lumière du Sud. Mélanges offerts à Jean-François Battail*, Deshima. Revue d'histoire globale des pays du Nord, 3, edited by Sylvain Briens and Martin Kylhammar, 205–19. Strasbourg: Départements d'études néerlandaises et scandinaves, Université de Strasbourg, 2013.

Prendergast, Christopher. "Negotiating World Literature". *New Left Review* (March–April 2001), 100–21.

Svedjedal, Johan."Svensk skönlitteratur i världen: Litteratursociologiska problem och perspektiv". In *Svensk litteratur som världslitteratur: En antologi*, Skrifter utgivna av Avdelningen för litteratursociologi vid Litteraturvetenskapliga institutionen i Uppsala, 65, edited by Johan Svedjedal, 9–82. Uppsala: Avdelningen för litteratursociologi, Uppsala universitet, 2012.

Thomsen, Mads Rosendahl. *Mapping World Literature: International Canonization and Transnational Literatures*. London: Continuum, 2008.

Venuti, Lawrence. *The Translator's Invisibility: A History of Translation*, London; New York: Routledge, 1995.

30. Gender and the Circulation of African Lusophone Literature into the Portuguese Literary System

Chatarina Edfeldt

Portuguese, Dalarna University

When literary works travel from one geographical and linguistic literary circuit into another they, just like migrants, need to cross border controls in the form of literary and cultural gatekeepers and/or mediators (e.g. literary critique and consecration, publishing houses, translators, agents, book fairs etc.), which all affect their chance to make the journey. In addition to market conditions, literary circulation also encompasses various literary, cultural and socio-political processes, both regarding the source culture and the target culture, such as an author's access to subjective and literary agency in a society, geopolitical conditions, choice of source language and literary genre. Furthermore, the writer's nationality, gender and ethnicity are features that will condition their commodity value and influence the probability of their literature reaching a wider circulation.

The aim of this chapter is to map out the importance of gender as a mediating category in the circulation of literature, by the example of the migration of Mozambican literature (written in Portuguese) into the contemporary Portuguese book market. As such, it will outline some possible theoretical, methodological and gender political starting points for examining how the

---

How to cite this book chapter:
Edfeldt, Chatarina. "Gender and the Circulation of African Lusophone Literature into the Portuguese Literary System". In *World Literatures: Exploring the Cosmopolitan-Vernacular Exchange*, edited by Stefan Helgesson, Annika Mörte Alling, Yvonne Lindqvist, and Helena Wulff, 369–382. Stockholm: Stockholm University Press, 2018. DOI: https://doi.org/10.16993/bat.ad. License: CC-BY.

contemporary Portuguese literary community conceptualise and incorporate Mozambican literature into an imagined literary lusophone system.[1] More specifically, I will address how gender and ethnicity differences can function as mediating categories in the circulation processes of this literature.

The mapping that follows departs from the assumptions that, on one hand, a worldly directionality (desire)[2] is detectable in both the field of contemporary Portuguese literary criticism, as well as in the book market to inclusively conceptualise (by its parts) Luso-Brazilian-African literatures into a wider world literature in Portuguese. As such, it could be argued that the Portuguese literary community is expected to open up to inclusively incorporate also the vernacular specificities (for example, national languages, orality and rural culture) of African lusophone literature into its literary system. On the other hand, the intertwined gender and geopolitical power relations still imbedded in the lusophone literary system are of course problematic, considering that the contemporary idea of a lusophone community (*lusofonia*) is rooted in a common colonial historical past.

The theoretical and methodological framework for this mapping is informed by a combination of recent studies interested

---

[1] Constituted by a contemporary body of literary works by internationally well-established authors Mia Couto and Paulina Chiziane from Mozambique, published in Portugal in 1990–2016. The date range is determined by the publication period of these authors, in Mozambique as well as in the Portuguese book market.

[2] This reflexion on a "worldly directionality and desire" is inspired by, and adopted from, Mariano Siskind's concept "deseo del mundo" [desire for the world], which he derived from the writings of (Brazilian) Latin American authors of the nineteenth century. Siskind detected in this literature a universal tendency and directionality – "cosmopolitan desires" – which he argues is a common epistemological structure for literatures situated in, and written from, global peripheries. Although Siskind's concept is constructed upon literary text production, it is perfectly transportable for explaining a similar directionality towards the world held in the Portuguese scholarly field of world literature and the book market. See Mariano Siskind, *Cosmopolitan Desires: Global Modernity and World Literature in Latin America* (Evanston, Illinois: Northwestern University Press, 2014), 3.

in world literature and how literature travels between different literary systems (e.g. Damrosch, Mani, Buescu, addressed below), as well as by lusophone gender and postcolonial studies (e.g. Almeida, Owen, Martins, addressed below).

This latter perspective is important to this essay's parallel theoretical objective to contest the gender-blind readings that most of these paradigmatic studies in world literature thus far has fostered.

The absence of an implemented gender analysis in the area of world literature studies (so far) and its consequences could be analysed through various approaches.[3] This is a broad issue that has to be addressed in another article, though it could be concluded that the disinterest seems to have been mutual; literary gender scholars have also shown little interest (so far) in engaging with the concept of world literature. This is probably due to a scepticism towards the accumulated outcome of these studies. A fear that they would (again) be creating, and only be concerned with, a super canon (of mostly male writers from national canons) on a global scale, remitting historically marginalised literature (for example, of women authors) to the margins. The last decades' revitalisation of the research area of world literature studies has developed along different strands, and my interest here is not so much to criticise and point out problems following the lack of a gender perspective but rather to map out some points of relevance and usefulness that an integrated gender and ethnicity perspective can provide to these studies. Especially interesting, in this sense, is the recent study of Venkat B. Mani, *Recoding World Literature,* which, although not fostering an explicit gender perspective, nevertheless integrates a power perspective that opens up a theoretical framework for it. Mani conceptualises world literature as *bibliomigrancy:* "the physical and virtual migration of literature as books from one part of the world to another", works of literature that travel beyond their linguistic and cultural origins

---

[3] See, for example, Debra A. Castillo, "Gender and Sexuality in World Literature", in *The Routledge Companion to World Literature,* ed. Theo D'haen et al. (London: Routledge, 2012), 393–403. See also the essay by Katarina Leppänen in this volume.

and are recoded with new meanings in the target culture.[4] Mani's perspective allows for acknowledging literature's important role of representing collective memory and ways of imagining and understanding the world, alongside the importance of the dimension of political and institutional power at the core of the literary circulation process:

> world literature as a literary catalog of the world is far from a neutral, alphabetically organized bibliography of masterpieces translated into world languages. Translations of literary works into other languages and their circulation and reception beyond cultural and national origins do not happen in a historical, sociocultural, or political vacuum.[5]

In addition to this, all literature is created, read, studied, interpreted, translated and marketed in communities and societies which are always historically and culturally situated, they are also, to a higher or lesser degree, organised and structured according to different social (hierarchical) categories. Therefore, a gender and ethnicity perspective on the processes of literature's circulation, translation and reception is relevant when investigating socio-political and geopolitical conditions of who gets translated and why. Depending on the general condition and social status of women in different societies and literary establishments, there could be many a *glass ceiling* to break through on the path to worldwide circulation of their literature. In Mozambique, Portuguese was established as the official language after independence in 1975, creating a literacy and democracy problem when a high rate of the population, especially women, could not read or write in Portuguese. In her study on Mozambican women writers, Hilary Owen points to several political and material paths responsible for the exclusion of women's experiences in the national literary discourse and, as a consequence, in the formation of the new Mozambican national identity:

---

[4] Venkat Mani, *Recoding World Literature: Libraries, Print Culture, and Germany's Pact with Books* (New York: Fordham University Press, 2017), 10–11.

[5] Mani, *Recoding World Literature*, 12.

Women's lack of access both to the Portuguese language as the means through which culture nationhood came to be imagined, and to written language as the means of its dissemination, were relevant factors in delimiting women's self-identification through nationhood as a narrated process.⁶

In addition to this marginalisation through the lack of access to the Portuguese language, there is the symbolic exclusion through various symbolic rhetorical figurations of African women in national and male literary discourses, representing a sexualised exotic and/or nostalgic image of Mother Africa. According to Owen, this "feminine fetish image [was] equally available to colonial and anticolonial nationalism" in Mozambique which further hampered women's access to literary and political agency and subjectivity.⁷ These are some examples of how one's accessibility to literary agency can be restricted by a gender identity, which further affects the ability for the literary experience of women to circulate, or even to be written in the first place.

Towards an Inclusive World Literature in Portuguese

Recent Portuguese and lusophone literary studies, aspiring to revitalise the research area of literary history and criticism, expresses a worldly directionality of situating literature written in Portuguese into a wider world literary system. Mainly this is being done by broadening the scope of literary studies by moving away from conceptualising literature and authors within an exclusively national framework, instead, suggesting that all national literatures written in Portuguese should be studied in a comparative manner in a global network of cultural exchange that could be conceptualised as "worlding literatures in Portuguese".⁸ Likewise, a newly published collection of essays on rethinking literary history writing suggests: "[i]nstead of privileging the writing of the

---

⁶ Hilary Owen, *Mother Africa, Father Marx: Women's Writing of Mozambique, 1948–2002* (Lewisburg: Bucknell University Press, 2007), 21.
⁷ Owen, *Mother Africa, Father Marx*, 21–25.
⁸ Helena Buescu, "Wordling Literatures in Portuguese", *1616: Anuario de Literatura Comparada*, 3 (2013): 19–31.

national literary history of Portugal, or Brazil, or of Mozambique, or of Angola, and so forth and so on, we should privilege the study of the interrelations and crossings that constitute the lusophone predicament".[9] However, in spite of the discernible aspiration, on a global scale, of being more inclusive, using sophisticated theoretical tools to advocate for the diversity and plurality of literatures in Portuguese, a gender consciousness is not yet part of the theoretical framework in any of these studies.

A shift to inclusively categorise Portuguese, Brazilian and Luso-African literatures into its own linguistic "world literature in Portuguese", could give these (by its parts) peripheral literatures a stronger platform and visibility, both in cultural as well as economical terms, in a global landscape. On the other hand, the idea of defining cultural expressions from Portugal, Brazil, Angola, Mozambique, Cape Verde, São Tomé and Príncipe, Guinea Bissau and East Timor into a lusophone community is not new. In this sense, the idea of founding a cultural community on its historical roots of linguistic and cultural (colonial) affinities go way back and has historically and situationally expressed itself in many different forms and served different political interests.[10] The current idea of a lusophone community (*lusofonia*), based on common

---

[9] João Cezar de Castro Rocha, introduction to "*Literary Histories in Portuguese*", *Portuguese Literary and Cultural Studies* 26 (2014): 2.

[10] It is not possible here to address the various ideas (cultural theories) that resemble the current meaning of *lusofonia*. Some, though, are of great importance for this kind of study, and this points at gender issues as crucial for its constitution, such as the ideas of Gilberto Freyre's *lusotropicalism*, being a theory of a specific (national) identity for people colonised by Portugal. These ideas continue to influence and take various forms in the identity formation of Portuguese-speaking postcolonial societies. At its core is the idea of the Portuguese colonisers' racial mixing with the colonised as a token for their more "humane" approach to the colonised. An idea of miscegenation that in the reality played itself out in an (violent) unequal (racist) sexual relation between the white male coloniser and the black colonised woman. See, e.g. Miguel Vale de Almeida, *An Earth-Colored Sea: "Race" Culture, and the Politics of Identity in the Postcolonial Portuguese-speaking World*. (Oxford: Berghahn Books, 2004).

historical, linguistic and cultural foundations is promoted by cultural and political institutions in Portuguese-speaking countries.[11]

However, several gender and postcolonial studies have drawn the attention to the importance of decolonising (racially and sexually) the notion of *lusofonia*, on the basis that it still maintains reminiscences of its hierarchical (colonial) power structure.[12] Furthermore, many of the writers from Mozambique and Angola have contested the label of being a "lusophone writer" or writing "lusophone literature", among them, Paulina Chiziane and Mia Couto. The latter approaches and problematises the question of *lusofonia* through the idea of embracing cultural inclusion and linguistic diversity: "For the lusophone project to be relevant in Mozambique, it must support the defence of other Mozambican cultures". ("Para que o projeto da lusofonia funcione em Moçambique, ele deve apoiar a defesa de outras culturas moçambicanas").[13] It is then important from an ethical perspective to problematise *lusofonia*, in gender and geopolitical terms, and recognise that it often is implemented with cultural indifference in the hegemonic Portuguese literary community.[14]

As David Damrosch has pointed out, when literary works cross borders it "involves shifting relations both of literary history and cultural power. Works rarely cross borders on the basis of full equality".[15] This is even more intricate when considering the circulation of works within a limited (although widespread globally)

---

[11] See CPLP, Comunidade dos Países da língua Portuguesa homepage: https://www.cplp.org/.

[12] See, e.g. Almeida, *An Earth-Colored Sea;* Ana Margarida Martins, *Magic Stones and Flying Snakes: Gender and the Postcolonial Exotic in the Work of Paulina Chiziane and Lídia Jorge* (Oxford: Peter Lang, 2012), 6; Alfredo Margarido, *A Lusofonia e os Lusófonos: Novos Mitos Portugueses* (Lisboa: Edições Universitárias Lusófonas, 2000).

[13] Mia Couto, "Luso-Afonias – A Lusofonia entre Viagens e Crimes", in *E se Obama Fosse Africano: Interinvenções* (Alfragide: Editorial Caminho, 2009), 194.

[14] What complicates the use of "lusophone" even further is that it is also used as an adjective, in a neutral manner, to designate all African literatures written in Portuguese for practical reasons, not having to name all the countries in referring to them.

[15] Damrosch, *What Is World Literature*, 24.

linguistic community founded on a common colonial historical past. The centre/periphery within the lusophone system, in economic and cultural terms, is as prevalent as in any other linguistic system rooted in the colonial enterprise. However, as Jean-Marc Moura concludes when comparing the francophone literary system with the lusophone literary system, the latter appears to be "poly-centric". That is, while the francophone system is organised through one centre (France) the lusophone contains two centres (Portugal and Brazil). Still, according to Moura, this also means that Brazilian authors do not need to be recognised in Portugal and vice-versa for their wider consecration and circulation. African authors, however, are still dependent on being recognised in one of these two centres to enable their dissemination into a world market through translation.[16]

For various historical, political and socio-economic reasons, the main market for African literatures written in Portuguese have until recently exclusively been the Portuguese book market, although lately the Brazilian book market also shows a rapidly increasing interest in this literature. There is then a relation of dependency between the dissemination of this African literature and the lusophone literary system, much like the one Moura concludes in relation to the francophone situation that the "institutional system facilitates the circulation of writers and works within the French-speaking world".[17] Portugal's cultural institutions, like Camões give financial support for publishing translations of Portuguese as well as African literature written in Portuguese into other languages. The "lusophone literary system", that is, the current institutional character of the Portuguese-speaking literary community, can then be said to still incorporate a cultural inequality. It remains to be seen if a methodological shift towards

---

[16] Jean-Marc Moura, "French-Language Writing and the Francophone Literary System", *Contemporary French and Francophone Studies* 14, no. 1 (2010): 31.

[17] Moura, Francophone Literary System, 31. See also, Ellen Sapega, "Que mundo? Apontamentos sobre a recepção e a circulação da literatura e cultura caboveridianas", in *Literaturas Insulares: Leituras e Escritas de Cabo Verde e São Tomé e Príncipe*, ed. Margarida C. Ribeiro et al. (Porto: Afrontamento, 2011), 107.

to conceptualise and read this literature in the framework of a "world literature written in Portuguese" have a potential for harbouring a more inclusive and egalitarian approach.

Short Notes on Gender and Commodification Processes

The format of this text does not allow for a gender-critical approach to the variety of disciplinary theoretical frameworks engaged in explaining how literature circulates across borders. However, as noted, a gender- and ethnicity-critical perspective has not been prevalent in the most influential studies in, for example, those of literary sociology conducted by Gisèle Sapiro and Gérard Genette.[18] In the analysis that follows, the aim is to provide some examples of how gender and ethnicity function as mediating categories in the commodification processes of Mozambican literature.

Shifting the attention to the Portuguese literary book market and its marketing strategies, the same worldly directionality as observed before to conceptualise literatures written in Portuguese into a common entity can be detected. Entering a book store in Lisbon in 2017 shows an increased tendency of reorganising the categorisation of literatures written in the Portuguese language. From being organised by nationality, Portuguese, Brazilian, Luso-African literature, these literatures can now be found indiscriminately by author, in alphabetic order under "Literatura Lusófona".[19] The largest publishing house in Portugal of African literature in Portuguese, Caminho, is also undergoing a change in relation to its packaging of this literature. Until very recently, it was organised in a special book series, which by name signalled

---

[18] Gisèle Sapiro, "The Sociology of Translation", in *A Companion to Translation Studies*, ed. Sandra Bermann et al. (Blackwell: John Wiley & Sons Ltd, 2014), 82–94. Gérard Genette, *Seuils* (Paris: Seuil, 1987).

[19] This is a general observation, conducted in 2017, that still contains some varieties. For example, the high prestige Livraria Bertrand and Livraria Buchholz still maintain the distinction between national (Portuguese) and foreign literature written in Portuguese (as lusophone), whereas more recently established book stores, like FNAC Portugal and Pó dos Livros and others organise all literature written in Portuguese as lusophone literature.

its geo-marginal status: "Outras margens" (Other margins), and a uniform blue book cover containing an African design or artwork. Today the African authors published by Caminho could be considered more integrated in the Portuguese literary system by no longer being published in a separate series. Nevertheless, the new and recent designs on the book covers of Mia Couto's and Paulina Chiziane's novels still contain images transmitting a strong ethnic and gendered identity of "africanness".

This recent development in the packaging of literature on the Portuguese book market consists of giving each author a specially designed theme on their covers, which makes it easy for the reader to quickly identify a book and connect it with a specific author. This development towards an "individualised" book cover is not exclusive to African authors, rather it is ruled by the general increased predicament of brand thinking in the publishing industry. Authors have to work on, or at least be marketed (by the publisher) as, an exclusive brand, enhanced through representation in social media, at literary book fairs etc. This "branding", in turn, seems to be conducted by an excavation (although superficial) of the singularity and specificity of an authorship. In Couto's and Chiziane's cases, this is achieved by emphasising vernacular elements, such as the geographical and local affiliation of the authors, as well as their gender identity.

The new editions of Mia Couto's novels are designed in a strong colour (different for each book) with a graphic figure (in black) of a person, fauna or item that unmistakably connotes to a masculine sphere of the rural vernacular (exotic) Africa. Equally, the new editions of Paulina Chiziane's books display variations of a graphic pattern of a traditional African cloth, transmitting a traditional African women's sphere. The new designs on these book covers then highlight the vernacular and gendered features of their literature at the expense of their possible universal and cosmopolitan qualities, but at the same time, present a more a universal stereotyped image of Africa than a specific "Mozambiqueness". In this sense, there is still a resemblance with the stereotyped covers, criticised by scholars, of the Heinemann's African Writers Series (launched in 1962), which are described by Venkat B. Mani as containing "a particular 'packaging' of a continent [...] invocations of 'ethnicized' art reminiscent of Gauguin's Tahiti-period against a bright orange background!"[20]

A gender and ethnicity analysis is also important to understand the complexity of other strands of the commodification processes in how this literature crosses borders, and I will end this mapping by providing some examples related to the authorship of Paulina Chiziane.

Chiziane's literary work has been acknowledged internationally for its political and ethical commitment in discussing several topics of recent Mozambican history (colonial war, post-independence and civil war), intrinsically connected to the issues of national identity and racial and gender relations. All her writing departs from an explicit women-centred focus, which, by its gendered perspective, has provided a powerful rethinking of the transformation processes of the political systems in Mozambique.[21] A gender-informed analysis is therefore called for when investigating how her literature is recoded when migrating into new literary circuits.

In Portugal, Chiziane's work is heavily marketed as an authentic (exotified) African literature written by a woman. In an important study on Chiziane's authorship, Ana Margarida Martins addresses the commodification process and reception of Chiziane's work in Portugal and shows the importance of a gender perspective to grasp Chiziane's agency in this process. Although Martins's study draws heavily on Huggan's theories of the "postcolonial exotic" and the "global market reader", she nevertheless criticises his lack of gender approach and suggests that it takes away the women writers' "agency over the commodification of their work" and "neglects the writers' strategic ways of turning their often multiple marginal (in the West) and central (in their own countries)

---

[20] B. Venkat Mani, "Bibliomigrancy: Book series and the Making of World Literature", in *The Routledge Companion to World Literature*, ed. Theo D'haen et al. (London: Routledge, 2012), 292. Mani's chapter contains a thorough critique of the series.

[21] See Martins, *Magic Stones and Flying Snakes*; and Owen, *Mother Africa, Father Marx*.

identities to their own advantage in situated contexts".[22] Martins's gender-oriented reading of Chiziane's authorship calls for an understanding of how *strategic exoticism* (which emphasises gender and African identity) can be in place as a strategy both by the market forces, as well as a writer's strategy in the commodification process. An example of this double process can be seen in a quotation by Chiziane, included in the author's presentation on all her book covers (regardless of edition): "They say that I am a novelist and that I was the first Mozambican woman to write a novel, but I say: I am a storyteller and not a novelist. … I am inspired by the tales from the bonfire" ("Dizem que sou romancista e que fui a primeira mulher moçambicana a escrever um romance, mas eu afirmo: sou contadora de estórias e não romancista. … Inspiro-me nos contos à volta da fogueira").[23]

The aim of this chapter was to map out some reading paths that consider the importance of gender as a mediating category in the circulation of literature from one literary (national) circuit into another. By addressing different parts of this journey, with special attention to literacy and the accessibility to subjective and literary agency, both in writing and in the commodification processes, I have wanted to show examples of how a gender analysis can contribute to a deeper understanding of literature's migration process.

Bibliography

Almeida, Miguel Vale de. *An Earth-Colored Sea: "Race" Culture, and the Politics of Identity in the Postcolonial Portuguese-speaking World*. Oxford: Berghahn Books, 2004.

Arenas, Fernando. *Lusophone Africa: Beyond Independence*. Minneapolis: University of Minnesota Press, 2011.

Buescu, Helena. "Wordling Literatures in Portuguese". *1616: Anuario de Literatura Comparada* 3 (2013): 19–31

---

[22] Martins, *Magic Stones and Flying Snakes*, 29.
[23] On all book covers, for example, Paulina Chiziane, *O Sétimo Juramento*. (Lisboa: Caminho, 2000).

———. *Experiência do Incomum e Boa Vizinhança: Literatura Comparada e Literatura-Mundo*. Porto: Porto Editora, 2013.

Castillo, Debra A. "Gender and Sexuality in World Literature". In *The Routledge Companion to World Literature*, edited by Theo D'haen, David Damrosch and Djelal Kadir, 393–403. New York: Routledge, 2011.

Chiziane, Paulina. *O Sétimo Juramento*. Lisboa: Caminho, 2000.

Couto, Mia. *E se Obama Fosse Africano: Interinvenções*. Alfragide: Editorial Caminho, 2009.

Damrosch, David. *What is World Literature?* Princeton: Princeton University Press, 2003.

Genette, Gérard. *Seuils*. Paris: Seuil, 1987.

Helgesson, Stefan. "Litteraturvetenskapen och det kosmopolitiska begäret". *Tidskrift för Litteraturvetenskap* 1 (2013): 81–92

———. *Transnationalism in Southern African Literature: Modernists, Realists, and the Inequality of Print Culture*. London: Routledge, 2009.

Mani, B. Venkat. "Bibliomigrancy: Book Series and the Making of World Literature". In *The Routledge Companion to World Literature*, edited by Theo D'haen, David Damrosch and Djelal Kadir, 283–296. London: Routledge, 2012.

———. *Recoding World Literature: Libraries, Print Culture, and Germany's Pact with Books*. New York: Fordham University Press, 2017.

Margarido, Alfredo. *A Lusofonia e os Lusófonos: Novos Mitos Portugueses*. Lisboa: Edições Universitárias Lusófonas, 2000.

Martins, Ana Margarida. *Magic Stones and Flying Snakes: Gender and the Postcolonial Exotic in the Work of Paulina Chiziane and Lídia Jorge*. Oxford: Peter Lang, 2012.

Moura, Jean-Marc. "French-Language Writing and the Francophone Literary System". *Contemporary French and Francophone Studies* 14, no. 1 (2010): 29–38

Owen, Hilary. *Mother Africa, Father Marx: Women's Writing of Mozambique, 1948–2002*. Lewisburg: Bucknell University Press, 2007.

Rocha, João Cezar de Castro. "Introduction to '*Literary Histories in Portuguese*'". *Portuguese Literary and Cultural Studies* 26 (2014): 1–14.

Rothwell, Phillip. *A Canon of Empty Fathers: Paternity in Portuguese Narrative*. Lewisburg: Bucknell University Press, 2007.

Sapega, Ellen. "Que mundo? Apontamentos sobre a recepção e a circulação da literatura e cultura caboveridianas". In *Literaturas Insulares: Leituras e Escritas de Cabo Verde e São Tomé e Príncipe*, edited by Margarida C. Ribeiro and Silvio R. Jorge, 99–110. Porto: Afrontamento, 2011.

Sapiro, Gisèle. "The Sociology of Translation". In *A Companion to Translation Studies*, edited by. Sandra Bermann and Catherine Porter, 82–94. Oxford: Blackwell, 2014.

Siskind, Mariano. *Cosmopolitan Desires: Global Modernity and World Literature in Latin America*. Evanston, Illinois: Northwestern University Press, 2014.

31. World Literary Studies and East African Anglophone Literature

Erik Falk
English, Nordic Africa Institute

In an article from 2008, Peter Kalliney uses the fate of East African author Moyez Vassanji's novel *The Gunny Sack* to address a question he sees as long overdue in postcolonial literary scholarship: the relation between what he calls globalisation theory and postcolonial theory. A central point in his argument concerns the circulation of literature. Vassanji's complex and narratively intricate story of migration and dispossession, Kalliney argues, becomes attractive to scholars of postcolonial literature because it combines an aesthetic value – complexity – with what is ostensibly a political value – the novel's theme of subordination and marginalisation. These values exist, Kalliney suggests, in tension. The fact that the novel is read and discussed at all in northern academic circles is proof of its circulation, indeed its literary success, in metropolitan centres where the relevant institutions grant it recognition. On the other hand, success is anathema to the novel's political value, which depends instead on it being as marginalised as the individuals and communities it represents. To Kalliney, the failure in much postcolonial study to recognise the relation between literary theme and/or narrative form and the fate of the book object undermines its relevance, and in the article, he turns to globalisation theory to flesh out a literary studies approach which combines attention to the literary text with analysis of the

---

How to cite this book chapter:
Falk, Erik. "World Literary Studies and East African Anglophone Literature". In *World Literatures: Exploring the Cosmopolitan-Vernacular Exchange*, edited by Stefan Helgesson, Annika Mörte Alling, Yvonne Lindqvist, and Helena Wulff, 383–395. Stockholm: Stockholm University Press, 2018. DOI: https://doi.org/10.16993/bat.ae. License: CC-BY.

mechanisms that enable, or prevent, the circulation of, and access to, literature.[1]

Kalliney's critical intervention is an instance of what Sarah Brouillette has subsequently called a "material turn" within postcolonial literary studies – a turn Brouillette herself helped realising – that addresses precisely the status, the circulation, and the material conditions of postcolonial literature.[2] Despite this recent direction, it is arguably world literature studies which, over the last decades, has most successfully established itself as a research and teaching discipline that brings globalisation theory into literary study through analyses of the development and history, the circulation, the transformation and the recognition of literature on a global scale.[3]

Because of its theoretical ambitions, its comparative global scope, and its European origins as a conceptual framework, world literary studies continuously risk being too abstract to be useful, or, which amounts to the same thing, ignoring historical and cultural particularities and contexts which shape literary cultures. Historical and cultural nuance, of course, are central values to postcolonial studies (if not always given due attention[4]). In a manner akin to Kalliney's approach above, this chapter discusses some of the challenges that face the scholar who approaches African literature from the sociological world literary studies perspective of Pascale Casanova. It draws throughout on postcolonial theory – and occasionally on book chain and book history studies – to

---

[1] Peter Kalliney, "East African Literature and the Politics of Global Reading", *Research in African Literatures* 39, no. 1 (2008): 4–5.

[2] Sarah Brouillette, "Postcolonial Print Cultures", *Journal of Commonwealth Literature* 48, no. 1 (2013): 3.

[3] David Damrosch, Franco Moretti, and Pascale Casanova are household names but the field is too wide to summarise here. One point of entry is the introduction to *Institutions of World Literature: Writing, Translation, Markets*, ed. Stefan Helgesson and Pieter Vermeulen (New York: rouledge, 2015), 1–20.

[4] Neil Lazarus, in *The Postcolonial Unconscious* (Cambridge: Cambridge University Press, 2011), 1–19, argues precisely that postcolonial literary studies has detached itself from specific political and historical specificities and shrunk the canon of texts to a minimum.

highlight central aspects of her theorisation that need questioning from an East African perspective or elaboration to be applicable. The chapter ends with a brief discussion of the marketing of Ugandan author Doreen Baingana's short story collection, *Tropical Fish*, which is intended to give concrete example of the points made.

In Casanova's highly influential model of the international space of literature – "the world republic of letters" – nations are locked into competition and struggle for literary superiority. The space that results from the relations between nations is structured in centre and periphery where certain languages, locations, and therefore literatures, dominate others. The internationally dominant centre (or centres, such as regional ones), establishes what counts as literary value at each historical point in time and becomes the model of literature which the dominated literary nations receive, emulate, revolutionise, or rebel against. Such revolutionising occurred, in Casanova's account, in the turn to popular national-language literature in nineteenth-century Europe, where German intellectuals and writers, drawing on the philosophical ideas developed by Herder and others, began arguing the value of a distinct national literature. It happened again in the postcolonial era in which newly independent countries "moved to assert linguistic and literary claims of the their own".[5]

The struggle between nations mirrors the struggles that take place in the national arenas. Every author, Casanova writes, "is situated once according to the position he or she occupies in a national space, and then once again according to the place that this occupies within the world space".[6] Authors enter the literary field through publication and compete for literary capital by being recognised by critics, prize juries and other institutions.

In this international literary space, exchange between the national literary fields happens through translation, through importation of ideas, and through the movement of writers, all of which may serve different ends. Translations may be a means for

---

[5] Pascale Casanova, *The World Republic of Letters*, trans. M. B. DeBevoise (Cambridge: Harvard University Press, 2007), 78–80.
[6] Casanova, *The World Republic of Letters*, 81.

a nation to confirm a position of dominance, such as the "belles infidèles" translations of the French 17th century, or they may be attempts to "catch up" with dominant nations from a position of subordination by accumulating literary capital.[7] As a rule, however, dominant languages and nations are less open to influences from the other nations through translation, as measured, for instance, by the proportion of translations of foreign works to the publication total in a country.[8] For the individual writer, translation and/or publication abroad are additional ways of furthering the literary career, just as the adoption of a more central language, such as English, or the relocation to a literary metropolis, like Paris, are potential roads to literary fame.

Although the idea is not developed extensively, it is clear that in Casanova's world literature model, translators and travelling or migrant writers are important. Whatever their own motives, they perform the vital role of enriching literary fields by introducing new literary ideas and by sending home new impulses from the new host culture. The traffic may run from the older and more venerable national field to the younger, from the younger to the older (less common), or combine the two. Thus, in Casanova's description, Paul Valéry's French translation of *Ulysses* helped establishing James Joyce as an important modern writer capable of revitalising an old and prestigious literary culture. As a consequence, he became a central author in Irish literary culture as well. In similar fashion, Gertrude Stein's residence in Paris not only advanced her literary career but also contributed importantly to American literary culture, which at the time was comparatively undeveloped.[9] Nathan Suhr-Sytsma provides a Nigerian example of this process by analysing how writers connected to Ibadan University in the 1950s fashioned new idioms for an emerging

---

[7] Casanova, *La Langue Mondiale* (Paris: Seuil, 2015), 77–95.
[8] Heilbron, "Translation as a Cultural World System", *Perspectives: Studies in Translatology* 8, no. 1 (2000): 12–15. See the contributions by Tenngart, Lindqvist, Hedberg, Schwartz, and Edfeldt in the current section for discussions of various cases of translations between central and peripheral languages, or from one periphery to another.
[9] Casanova, "Literature as a World", *New Left Review* 31 (2005): 86–87

Nigerian literary culture by transforming British metropolitan modernism in ways that also made them attractive to publishers in London.[10]

The central advantage of a model of world literary space like Casanova's lies in its comparative international perspective. Its occasionally sweeping arguments have, however, attracted criticism. One of the critics is Christopher Prendergast who turns against what he sees as Casanova's exaggerated dependence on the notions of *nation* and *struggle*. This single focus, he claims, preclude other, potentially more valuable, units and dimensions of analysis, such as region, class and gender, and other possible relations, like negotiation or collaboration. The result is loss of theoretical precision and historical nuance. Prendergast illustrates his point through historical example: French authors in the 17th century used Shakespeare not simply as model to emulate, but as a means to combat the dominant aesthetic of Racine – that is they enlisted the English playwright in a domestic aesthetic struggle rather than for competition with another nation.[11]

Peter Kalliney's study of the literary group around the BBC *Caribbean Voices* radio programme is a *de facto* elaboration of Prendergast's second point of criticism. What Kalliney demonstrates is that Caribbean and British authors simultaneously helped and competed with one another, and that the new impulses feeding into British literary culture in the 1950s from the West Indies in and outside of Britain became means in a literary struggle against the aesthetic of the dominating realism.[12]

Prendergast's response to Casanova, and Kalliney's analysis of Caribbean-British author relations both point to aspects of East African literary culture that must be addressed for a world literature studies comparative model to be relevant: the role of the national literary field, the role of language, and the nature of the

---

[10] Suhr-Sytsma, "Ibadan Modernism: Poetry and the Literary Present in Mid-Century Nigeria", *The Journal of Commonwealth Literature* 48, no. 1 (2013): 44–45
[11] Prendergast, "Negotiating World Literature", *New Left Review* 8 (2001): 109–11.
[12] Kalliney, *The Commonwealth of Letters*, 118–19.

feedback or transfer between literary fields. All three of them are conceptual and empirical at once.

First, in contrast to the European or American literary fields which Casanova discusses, East African literary fields are not divided into a pole of small-scale literary fiction – in which book production strives towards value defined as literary quality – and a pole of large-scale popular fiction – where book production is governed primarily by an economic logic in which value equals sales.[13] Rather, from the colonial period into the present, literary markets have been dominated by the publishing of educational books.[14] Foreign aid organisations and intergovernmental organisations with publication interests or literary support strategies have also impacted heavily on book production and book trade.[15] As a result, markets have been less autonomous, hybrid arenas in which literature for education has constituted the only profitable market – but a market in which money can be made through the publication of quality literature. During the late colonial and early post-colonial period foreign publishers found this "dual economy", as Caroline Davis calls it, very lucrative. The publishing of Wole Soyinka by Oxford University Press, one of Davis' examples, illustrates this clearly. The publisher exploited the characteristic to market Soyinka as a serious African writer in Britain, a labelling that added to the cultural prestige of the publisher. In Nigeria, he became a commercially successful author due to his inclusion in school reading lists and curricula.[16] The situation has not changed significantly, and

---

[13] Gisèle Sapiro, "The Sociology of Translation: A New Research Domain", in *A Companion to Translation Studies*, ed. Sandra Bermann and Catherine Porter (Chichester, UK: Wiley 2014), 88.
[14] Bgoya, "Publishing in Africa from Independence to the Present Day", *Research in African Literatures* 44, no. 2 (2013): 22.
[15] Sarah Brouillette, "UNESCO and the Book in the Developing World", *Representations* 127 (2014): 27.
[16] Caroline Davis, "Publishing Wole Soyinka: Oxford University Press and the Creation of 'Africa's Own William Shakespeare'", *Journal of Postcolonial Writing* 48, no. 4 (2012): 346.

international publishers remain the central actors in the East African literary landscape.[17]

Secondly, English remains one of the national languages in East Africa and is the medium of instruction in school above the lower forms. The situation, according to some critics, significantly hampers the establishment of broad reading publics that can support a commercially viable trade in sophisticated books in *any* language used in the region.[18] It also means, however, that individual authors may choose to write in a language which, if not their first, is deeply familiar and at the same time a central language globally (an option that may appear as much an opportunity as a necessity in the absence of established routes to a literary career at home). The consequence is that the passage to literary fame may look very different from European or American authors who are usually established first in the national literary field and subsequently on the world stage through translation and/or foreign publication, processes which depend on recognition by additional literary institutions.

Thirdly, the cultural feedback loops need examination and empirical elaboration with respect to East African anglophone writing. Postcolonial literary studies have from its inception been concerned with questions of canon and literary influence. More recently, it has turned its attention to audiences. Sarah Brouillette has demonstrated that readers of anglophone postcolonial fiction that are found in former colonising nations are generally made up of immigrants from the same countries as the authors whose fiction they read, or readers – in university courses, for instance – with relatively deep knowledge of the places they read about. At the same time, postcolonial authors are frequently published and marketed as spokespersons of sorts for a country, or a culture. Authors, acutely aware of these strategies strain against them,

---

[17] Bgoya notes that the "traditional" publishing model in which commercially successful books may support the publishing of narrower titles is counteracted by the presence of international publishers whose operations effectively prevent smaller national or local ventures. "Publishing in Africa", 22. See, however, Doreen Strauhs' discussion of the role of literary non-governmental organisations, for a complementary view. Strauhs, "African Literary NGOs", e.g. 11–41.

[18] Bgoya, "Publishing in Africa", 22.

with the result that their texts are often marked by a certain anxiety around representativeness.[19]

Against the background of the general points made about the characteristics of literary fields in East Africa, and the challenges they pose to a world literature perspective, I want now to turn to Doreen Baingana and her collection of short stories, *Tropical Fish*, to illustrate how some of the issues introduced play out in one particular case.

Baingana's short story collection, which is her literary debut, recounts the life of three sisters of the same wealthy Ugandan family (at one point they own a Mercedes-Benz) in Entebbe. Romances and sexual discoveries are central to the story and are narrated as part of explorations of identity that move between the liberatory and the destructive. The tentative and adventurous lives the sisters try out are also connected to deep feelings of disorientation and self-doubt, and in one instance events take a sinister turn. Christine, the central character, in one short story compares herself to the tropical fish her then-boyfriend, a white Englishman, exports to Britain. In a following short story, she struggles and fails to be at home in Los Angeles where she settles with her new American boyfriend in a destructive relationship, before she returns to Uganda. Her sister Rosa, equally explorative, ends up dying from AIDS, while Patti, her second sibling, becomes a new-born Christian. The stories' historical and political background is the period after Idi Amin's rule in Uganda.

Even a short description like this brings home the central themes of cultural identity and belonging that the stories develop. The summary also makes clear that the text's demographic setting – a middle class and "modern" Ugandan family with the ability to travel – makes it very different from Vassanji's novel. The anxiety that Brouillette charts in her analyses, however, is readily observable in Baingana's text. In a preface to the stories, Baingana writes that her text should not be read as "stories of African womanhood" but be regarded as "examples, fantasies".[20]

---

[19] Sarah Brouillette, *Postcolonial Writers in the Global Literary Marketplace* (Houndmills, Basingstoke: Palgrave Macmillan, 2007), 26–44.

[20] Doreen Baingana, "Preface to the Harlem Moon Edition", *Tropical Fish: Tales from Entebbe* (New York: Harlem Moon, 2005), n.p.

A brief look at the publication history and the packaging of Baingana's literary work will shed further light on the place Baingana and her short stories occupy in the "world republic of letters". In a very concrete manner, her text speaks to the American literary market. She has chosen to write in English, and several of the stories from the collection have been published in literary magazines in the USA. Some of them are smaller, like *Glimmer Train*, based in Portland, and others have high reputation, like *Callalloo*, placed at A&T University in Texas. The collection was published by the US publisher Harlem Moon in 2005 – now an imprint of Penguin Random House, one of the world's largest publishers with a tradition of publishing quality literature as well as popular fiction.[21]

The book's cover reinforces the impression that its intended audience is primarily American. Book covers play important roles in the marketing of literature.[22] The paperback cover features an image of a female face, a colour photograph centred on a black woman's mouth in which a yellow flower is placed. The cover is striped horizontally in bright colours, and printed on top of them are excerpts from reviews, praise from author colleagues, and mentions of literary prizes. On the front page is a quotation from a review by *Vanity Fair* magazine which links Baingana's writing to Jhumpa Lahiri and Monica Ali, Indian-American and Bangladeshi-British authors respectively, by stating that these writers have in common an interest in "the modern, messy, intimate politics of home life" rather than "the history and politics of the homeland". Taken together,

---

[21] Penguin Random House, accessed 20 May 2017, www.penguinrandomhouse.com.
[22] Gérard Genette, *Thresholds of Interpretation*, trans. Jane E. Lewin (Cambridge, Mass: Cambridge University Press, 1997). Genette divides the *paratext* – that is, texts outside the literary text proper, into *peritext* – the texts and images immediately surrounding the literary text, such as covers and forewords, and the *epitext* – more distant texts like interviews. Different publishers may aim for different readerships on separate markets, by varying the cover of books, just as new editions may signal a new audience. For an example, see Andrew van der Vlies' discussion of the different covers of Zakes Mda's *Heart of Redness* in *South African Textual Cultures: White, Black, Read All Over* (Manchester: Manchester University Press, 2007).

these elements of the *peritext* – the cover, the blurb, the excerpts – illustrate how the publisher creates an intended audience for the text. The image creates an arresting contrast between colours, but more importantly, draws attention to aestheticisation, to beauty, sensualism and sex that are central elements in the stories. It also uses sensualism (and sex) as a device to capture the attention of the potential book buyer. The excerpt from *Vanity Fair*, placed centrally on the front page, performs several significant tasks at once. In his reading of the cover of *The Gunny Sack*, Kalliney comments on a quotation which states that the novel is "Africa's *Midnight Children*". The comparison serves as marker of recognition, highlights a (post-)modernist and literary aesthetic shared by the two authors, and simultaneously emphasises the novel's difference and continental belonging – *Africa's Midnight's Children*.[23] The *Vanity Fair* quotation is similarly multi-layered. It bestows popular (rather than elite) recognition upon Baingana's text; it places it in the company of other, and more established, authors who span the popular-quality divide and are well read in the USA and Britain; and it furnishes a global-but-particular communal identity for the text and the author in addition to the local belonging signalled by the subtitle's geographical marker "Entebbe".

Baingana's text testifies to the anxiety around representativity Brouillette discusses, and the marketing of her book, as signalled by the *peritexts*, seemingly displays the publisher's efforts to direct it to an American audience. Baingana, however, is far from an estranged migrant writer. On the contrary, she is a literary activist of sorts who divides her time between the USA and Uganda. She is associated with Uganda women writers' organisation, FEMRITE and has been on the juries of several African literary prizes. She has written a column for a Ugandan women's magazine, taught creative writing in Kenya, and contributed to the South African literary magazine *Chimurenga*.[24]

---

[23] Kalliney, "East African Literature and the Politics of Global Reading", 13–16

[24] FEMRITE. Femrite.org. Pilgrimages collaboration between Chimurenga and Kwani? Magazines, accessed 20 May 2017, https://www.pilgrimages.org.za/pilgrimages/doreen-baingana/.

Her option to write in English does not exclude her from the national literary market, nor does it necessarily make her fiction more exclusive than it would have been in other languages. It does not follow from this, however, that her short story collection is readily available in Ugandan bookshops, though research would have to establish that. Lastly, Baingana, in very concrete ways acts as a point of contact and feedback between the literary fields she belongs to and contributes to the literary culture of Uganda.

This chapter has identified some of the challenges that research into East African literature need to address when approaching it from a world literature perspective. More precisely, it has argued that central concepts used by scholars like Pascale Casanova need calibration before they are applicable in East African contexts. The brief discussion of the marketing and writing activities of Ugandan author Doreen Baingana has illustrated, further, the need for discussion of feedback loops and cultural transfers to be empirically based.

Bibliography

Baingana, Doreen. *Tropical Fish: Tales from Entebbe*. New York: Harlem Moon, 2005.

Bgoya, Walter and Mary Jay. "Publishing in Africa from Independence to the Present Day". *Research in African Literatures* 44, no. 2 (2013):17–34.

Bourdieu, Pierre. *The Field of Cultural Production: Essays on Art and Literature*. Edited by Randal Johnson. New York: Columbia University Press, 1984.

Brouillette, Sarah and David Finkelstein. "Postcolonial Print Cultures". *Journal of Commonwealth Literature* 48, no.1 (2013): 3–7.

———. *Postcolonial Writers in the Global Literary Marketplace*. Houndmills, Basingstoke: Palgrave Macmillan, 2007.

———. "UNESCO and the Book in the Developing World". *Representations* 127 (2014): 33–54.

Casanova, Pascale. "Literature as a World". *New Left Review* 31 (2005): 71–90.

———. *La Langue Mondiale*. Paris: Seuil, 2015.

———. *The World Republic of Letters*. Translated by M. B. DeBevoise. Cambridge: Harvard University Press, 2007.

Davis, Caroline. "Publishing Wole Soyinka: Oxford University Press and the Creation of 'Africa's Own William Shakespeare'". *Journal of Postcolonial Writing* 48, no. 4 (2012): 344–58.

———. *Creating Postcolonial Literature: African Writers and British Publishers*. Houndmills, Basingstoke: Palgrave Macmillan, 2013.

Genette, Gérard. *Paratexts: Thresholds of Interpretation*. Translated by Jane E. Lewin. Cambridge: Cambridge University Press, 1997.

Heilbron, Johan. "Translation as a Cultural World System". *Perspectives: Studies in Translatology* 8, no. 1 (2000): 9–26.

Helgesson, Stefan and Pieter Vermeulen, eds. *Institutions of World Literature: Writing, Translation, Markets*. New York: Routledge, 2015.

Kalliney, Peter. "East African Literature and the Politics of Global Reading". *Research in African Literatures* 39, no. 1 (2008): 1–23.

———. *The Commonwealth of Letters: British Literary Culture and the Emergence of Postcolonial Aesthetics*. Oxford: Oxford University Press, 2013.

Lazarus, Neil. *The Postcolonial Unconscious*. Cambridge: Cambridge University Press, 2011.

Prendergast, Christopher. "Negotiating World Literature". *New Left Review* 8 (2001): 100–21.

Sapiro, Gisèle. "Translation and the Field of Publishing. A Commentary on Pierre Bourdieu's 'A Conservative Revolution in Publishing'". *Translation studies* 1, no. 2 (2008): 152–166.

———. "The Sociology of Translation: A New Research Domain". In *A Companion to Translation Studies*. Edited by Sandra Bermann and Catherine Porter. Chichester: Wiley, 2014.

Strauhs, Doreen. *African Literary NGOs: Power, Politics, and Participation.* Basingstoke: Palgrave Macmillan, 2013.

Suhr-Sytsma, Nathan. "Ibadan Modernism: Poetry and the Literary Present in Mid-Century Nigeria". *The Journal of Commonwealth Literature* 48, no. 1 (2013): 41–59.

Van der Vlies, Andrew. *South African Textual Cultures: White, Black, Read All Over.* Manchester: Manchester University Press, 2007.

Notes on contributors

Annika Mörte Alling is Associate Professor of French literature at Lund University. Most of her publications have dealt with the nineteenth-century French novel, from various angles: the translation and reception of French literature in Sweden in the nineteenth century, the "Bovarysm" of Jules de Gaultier in novels by Stendhal and Flaubert, the problem of endings and closures in Balzac, mimetic desire in Stendhal (doctoral thesis, 2003). Currently, she has two main areas of research: firstly, the dynamics between the vernacular and the cosmopolitan in the nineteenth-century French novel; secondly, the role of emotion in literature teaching. ORCID: https://orcid.org/0000-0001-8163-8468

Helena Bodin is Professor of Literature at the Department of Culture and Aesthetics, Stockholm University, and Senior Lecturer at The Newman Institute in Uppsala, Sweden. Her research concerns the functions of literature at boundaries, such as between languages, nations, arts and media. She has particularly studied modern literature's engagement with the Byzantine Orthodox Christian tradition, from the various perspectives of intermedial studies, cultural semiotics, and translation studies, including aspects of multilingualism. ORCID: https://orcid.org/0000-0003-1711-5798

Christian Claesson is Associate Professor of Spanish at Lund University. He received his PhD in Hispanic Literatures from Harvard University in 2009, focusing on Latin American 20th and 21st century literature. Since 2012, he has worked extensively on subjectivity and social criticism in the different narratives of the ongoing Spanish crisis. He has published several articles on contemporary Spanish literature, and participates in several research groups working on this area. He is the editor of the anthology *Crisis y subjetividad en la España contemporánea*, forthcoming in early 2018. ORCID: https://orcid.org/0000-0002-7764-0001

Chatarina Edfeldt is a Senior Lecturer in Portuguese and a member of the Literature, Identity and Transculturality research group (ISTUD) at Dalarna University. She is a member of the research groups of CEMRI, at University of Aberta, and of "Intersexualities" at ILCML, University of Porto, Portugal. She has published books and articles on the topics of gender issues, literary historiography and Portuguese-speaking women writers. Her most recent book is a co-edited volume, *Transcultural Identity Constructions in a Changing World* (Peter Lang 2016).

Bo G. Ekelund is Associate Professor at the English Department, Stockholm University. His research has dealt with US fiction after 1940, both at the level of individual authors and sociological studies of the access to authorship. Recent projects have focused on citation studies, the field of translation in Sweden, and spatiality in Anglophone Caribbean fiction. ORCID: https://orcid.org/0000-0001-9831-3053

Erik Falk has a PhD from Karlstad University, Sweden. His field of research is anglophone literature from Africa and the Caribbean and his project within the research programme compares markets for contemporary East African Anglophone literature with a focus on its publication, packaging and reception in Uganda, Tanzania, Kenya, USA and Britain. Erik works as an external relations officer at Södertörn University. His research project is placed at the Nordic Africa Institute, Uppsala University. ORCID: https://orcid.org/0000-0002-1903-576X

Ashleigh Harris is Associate Professor of English at Uppsala University. Her current monograph focuses on the contemporary African novel and she is the primary investigator in a research project entitled "African Street Literatures and the Future of Literary Form". ORCID: https://orcid.org/0000-0002-6207-3067

Andreas Hedberg is Doctor of Philosophy in Literature, acting lecturer at the Department of Literature, Uppsala University. His research interests include sociology of literature, world literature, processes of canonisation, ecocriticism and literature as critique of modernisation. Since 2011, he is part of the research group Swedish Literature in the World (SIV) at the Section for the Sociology of Literature, Uppsala University.

Stefan Helgesson is Professor of English at Stockholm University and the principal investigator of the cosmpolitan-vernacular research programme. His research interests include southern African literature in English and Portuguese, Brazilian literature, postcolonial theory, translation theory and theories of world literature. He is the author of *Writing in Crisis: Ethics and History in Gordimer, Ndebele and Coetzee* (2004) and *Transnationalism in Southern African Literature* (2009), and is co-editor (with Pieter Vermeulen) of *Institutions of World Literature: Writing, Translation, Markets* (2015). He has published widely in journals such as *PMLA*, *History and Theory*, *Research in African Literatures*, *Interventions* and *Translation Studies*. ORCID: https://orcid.org/0000-0002-2222-1037

Christina Kullberg, Associate Professor of French literatures at Uppsala University, is specialised in contemporary Caribbean, and in Early Modern French travel literature. She has published extensively on Caribbean literature, including *The Poetics of Ethnography in Martinican Narratives* (University of Virginia Press, 2013). Currently, she is completing a book manuscript on Dominican missionary to the Antilles J-B Du Tertre (1610–1687), and has started a project that interrogates the inclusion of other languages and voices in French seventeenth century travel writing to Africa and the Caribbean, entitled "Tropical Engagements" and funded by The Swedish Foundation for Humanities and Social Sciences.

Katarina Leppänen is Professor in Intellectual History and coordinator of the Master's Program in Critical Studies at Gothenburg University, Sweden. Her doctoral thesis was on the feminist Elin Wägner and the European feminist movement in the interwar era, especially focusing on issues of alternative social orders and ecological feminist ideas. Leppänen's research covers women's independent nationality, education for internationalism and trafficking in women in the interwar era. Her ongoing project deals with the importance of transnational, international and regional exchanges of political ideas, in the Nordic and Baltic countries, in the early 20th century. ORCID: https://orcid.org/0000-0001-5241-3120

Anna Ljunggren is Professor of Russian at Stockholm University. Her main area of research has been 19th and 20th century poetry (Boris Pasternak, Elena Guro, Innokentii Annenskii, Fedor Tiutchev). She has also conducted a project dedicated to contemporary Russian prose at the turn of the millennium. She is originally from St Petersburg, where she got her MA in Romance languages. She taught for a number of years in the U. S.

Yvonne Lindqvist is Associate Professor, Senior Lecturer in Translation Studies, and Deputy Director of the Institute for Interpreting and Translation Studies at the Department of Swedish Language and Multilingualism, Stockholm University. Her current research within the Sociology of Translation and World Literature studies multidirectional cosmopolitanising and vernacularising translation dynamics and translation as a social practice. ORCID: https://orcid.org/0000-0002-5413-3891

Adnan Mahmutović is a Bosnian-Swedish writer and Lecturer at Stockholm University. His works include *Future in Comics* (McFarland Press, 2017), *Ways of Being Free* (Rodopi, 2010), *Thinner than a Hair* (Cinnamon Press, 2010), *How to Fare Well and Stay Fair* (Salt Publishing, 2012). He leads an MA in Transnational Creative Writing at Stockholm University. ORCID: https://orcid.org/0000-0002-0367-249X

Louise Nilsson holds a PhD in History of Science and ideas and is a researcher at English Department, Stockholm University where she is currently working on the project, "Mediating the North in a Transnational Context: Vernacular and Cosmopolitan Places in Nordic Noir," within the research program *Cosmopolitan and Vernacular Dynamics in World Literatures*. She's the co-editor of Crime Fiction as World Literature with David Damrosch and Theo D'haen and a member of the Australian- based research network *Detective Fiction* *on the Move* (Newcastle University) and one of the contributors to the network's collection *Criminal Moves* (forthcoming). Further information: http://worldlit.se ORCID: https://orcid.org/0000-0001-9079-3929

Anette Nyqvist is Associate Professor of Social Anthropology, at Stockholm University. Within the research program *Cosmopolitan and Vernacular Dynamics in World Literatures*, she is re-visiting her previous occupation as a journalist and author as she, from an anthropological perspective, investigates the role of travel literature as a literary genre that "mediates the world". Nyqvist's other research interests are focused at the nexus of statecraft and market-making. Her contributions within political and economic anthropology are noted in volumes such as the monographs *Reform and Responsibility in the Remaking of the Swedish National Pension System. Opening the Orange Envelope* (Palgrave Macmillan, 2016) and *Ombudskapitalisterna. Institutionella ägares röst och roll* (Liber, 2015).

Irina Rasmussen is Assistant Professor at the Department of English, Stockholm University, specialising in British, American, and Russian modernisms. She has published articles and reviews in *James Joyce Broadsheet*, *James Joyce Quarterly*, and *Modernism/modernity* and co-edited an essay collection *Ethics and Poetics* (Cambridge Scholars Publishing, 2015). ORCID: https://orcid.org/0000-0003-1356-9047

Lena Rydholm is Professor of Chinese at the Department of Linguistics and Philology at Uppsala University. Rydholm's research interests are ancient and modern Chinese literature, mainly classical poetry and fiction, and literary theories, theories of genre and style. Her publications include e.g. Cullhed and Rydholm (eds.). *True Lies Worldwide: Fictionality in Global Contexts* (2014), "Theories of Genre and Style in China in the Late 20th Century," *Orientalia Suecana LIX* (2010), "The Theory of Ancient Chinese Genres," in Lindberg-Wada (ed.). *Literary History: Towards a Global Perspective* (2006), "Lao She's Fiction and *Camel Xiangzi*" (*The Routledge Handbook of Modern Chinese Literature*, forthcoming).

Cecilia Schwartz is Associate Professor in Italian at Stockholm University. Her research interests concern cultural transfer and literary mediators, the idea of the North in contemporary Italian novels and travel writing as well as the idea of Italianness in Scandinavia. The current research project "Made in Italy. A diachronic study of literary circulation and translation in the semi-periphery" focuses on the translation flow from Italy to Sweden and seeks to provide a better understanding of the semi-peripheral dynamics in world literature. Schwartz is also a translator and she contributes to various Swedish newspapers. ORCID: https://orcid.org/0000-0002-5751-8834

Irmy Schweiger (PhD Heidelberg) is Professor of Chinese Literature and Culture at the Department of Asian, Middle Eastern and Turkish Studies, Stockholm University. Her research interests are situated in the realm of modern and contemporary sinophone literature, including historical trauma and cultural memory, literature as counter narrative to official discourse, cultures in contact. Together with Frank Kraushaar (Riga) she is the editor of the EUROSINICA book series.

Per Ståhlberg is a media anthropologist and Senior Lecturer in media- and communication studies at Södertörn University, Sweden. His research interests include mass media and popular culture in India and eastern Europe. Among his publications is *Writing Society Through Media: Ethnography of a Hindi Daily* (Rawat, 2013). ORCID: https://orcid.org/0000-0001-5150-7731

Paul Tenngart, Associate Professor of Comparative Literature at Lund University, has published several books on Swedish and French poetry, including a monograph on the politics of Charles Baudelaire's *Les Fleurs du Mal* and the biographical study *Livsvittnet Majken Johansson*. He has also published articles on climate change fiction and on English translations of Swedish working-class novels.

Paula Uimonen is Associate Professor of Social Anthropology, Stockholm University. She specialises in digital anthropology,

anthropology of art, visual culture, media and globalisation. Her current project *African women writers* has a web site at http://womenwriters.one/. Her recent publications focus on mobile photography in Tanzania, mobile infrastructure in Africa, and mourning rituals for Mandela. Her research on digital media and intercultural interaction at a national art institute in Tanzania was published in the monograph *Digital Drama: Teaching and Learning Art and Media in Tanzania* (2012), with a website at http://innovativeethnographies.net/digitaldrama. She has produced documentary films, such as *Efuru@50* (2017). ORCID: https://orcid.org/0000-0002-4228-3403

Mattias Viktorin received his BA (2001) and PhD degrees (2008) in Social Anthropology from Stockholm University, where he currently works as a researcher and Senior Lecturer. Previously he has been a Fulbright visiting scholar at the University of California, Berkeley (2006–2007), a post-doc fellow at the Stockholm Centre for Organisational Studies (2009–2011) and the secretary of the Swedish Society for Anthropology and Geography (2009–2011). He is the author of *Exercising Peace: Conflict Preventionism, Neoliberalism, and the New Military* (2008) and the co-editor of *Antropologi och tid* (2013; Anthropology and Time).

David Watson is an Associate Professor specialising in American Literature at the Department of English, Uppsala University. He has published on modernist poetry, nineteenth-century and contemporary American literature, and transnational and translation studies. His current research focuses on translation networks and inter-imperial formations in 19th century American literature, as well as depictions of migration and security in the contemporary American novel.

Helena Wulff is Professor of Social Anthropology, Stockholm University. Her research is in the anthropology of communication and aesthetics, based on a wide range of studies of the social worlds of literary production, dance and visual culture, currently on migrant writing in Sweden as world literature. Among her publications are the monographs *Ballet across Borders:*

Career and Culture in the World of Dancers (1998), *Dancing at the Crossroads: Memory and Mobility in Ireland* (2007) and *Rhythms of Writing: An Anthropology of Irish Literature* (2017), and the edited volume *The Anthropologist as Writer: Genres and Contexts in the Twenty-First Century* (2016). ORCID: https://orcid.org/0000-0002-8200-7980

Index

A

A History of Modern Chinese Fiction, 1917–1957 55
A Madman's Diary 73, 79–85
Abdülhamid II
Abidjan 108
Achebe, Chinua 135, 181
Adichie, Chimamanda Ngozi 135
Adiga, Aravind 169, 275, 276, 278, 279, 280, 281, 282
Adler-Olsen, Jussi 306
Adorno, Theodor 319
aesthetic world 166, 176, 249, 253, 254, 256, 257, 258
Afghanistan 119
Africa 24, 105, 108, 110, 130, 135, 144, 152, 153, 378
African literature 370, 376, 377
Agee, James 167, 188, 190, 191, 196
Ahmed, Rehana 142
Aidoo, Ama Ata 181
Akropong 155
Alabama 190
A-lai 42
Albania 95
Ali, Monica 391
Allred, Jeff 192
Almeida, Miguel Vale de 371

America: see USA
American literature 59–68; American literary field 64, 65, 68
American Muslim writing 105, 140–48
Americas 24
Amin, Idi 390
Andersen, Hans Christian 350
anglophone 4, 17, 53, 106, 293, 389
Angola 374, 375
Anguilla 157, 158
Ansatzpunkt 7, 294
Antheil, George 188, 189
anthropocene 1
anthropology 133, 217, 230, 232, 239, 250; literary 120
Antigua 158
antillanité 150
Appadurai, Arjun 143, 216
Apter, Emily 3, 4, 96, 195, 203, 291, 329
Arabic 2, 6, 108, 144, 146, 147, 249
Arac, Jonathan 68
Aráfi 266
archipelagic (thinking) 150
Arendt, Hannah 166, 175–76
Arfa, Riza 249

Argentina 346
Ari, India 134
art 45, 131, 132, 176, 188, 193, 194, 195, 196, 203, 204, 213, 222, 238, 250, 270, 350, 379
Ashcroft, Bill 152, 153, 155
Asia 144, 283
Atatürk 251
Auerbach, Erich 7
Augé, Marc 216
Australia 144, 181, 220, 257

B

Bachchan, Amitabh 280
baihua (vernacular language) 45, 74, 83
Baillie, E. C. C. 246
Baingana, Doreen 293, 385, 390, 391, 392, 393
Baker, Mona 300
Bakhtin, Mikhail 54, 218
Baltic countries 95
Balzac, Honoré de 167, 199, 200, 201, 203, 205, 206, 208
Ban Gu 74
Barbados 108, 154
Barcelona 298
Basque 32, 37
Basque Country 33, 35
Battuta, Ibn 262
Baudelaire, Charles 158
Baugh, Edward 157
Beaujour, Elizabeth Klosty 221
Beecroft, Alexander 5, 6, 8, 9, 19, 20, 21, 27, 105, 140, 143, 144, 147, 173

Benjamin, Walter 194
Bhabha, Homi K. 103
Bhagat, Chetan 169, 275, 276, 278, 279, 280, 281, 282, 283
bibliomigrancy 290, 297, 298, 299, 300, 304, 305, 324, 371
Bishop, Peter 264
Bjork, Robert E. 332
Björkman, Edwin 332
Bloch, Ernst 153, 193
Bloch, Robert 349
Boist, Victoire 21
book history 2, 291, 326, 384
Book of Job 234, 235
Booth, Marilyn 250
born translated 278, 281
Boston 156
Bougainville, Louis Antoine de 263
Bourdieu, Pierre 295, 297, 305, 316, 360
bovarysme 204, 206
Boyle, Danny 281
Braddock, Jeremy 192
Brandes, Georg 361
Brändström, Elsa 231, 233
Brathwaite, Edward Kamau 151–59
Brazil 2, 293, 374, 376
Brazilian literature 374, 377
Britain: see UK
Brixton 155
Brodsky, Joseph 167, 214, 215, 217, 219, 222, 223

Brouillette, Sarah 384, 389, 390, 392
Brown, Dan 284
Brown, John 60
Brown, William W. 60
Brubaker, Rogers 125
Buck, Pearl S. 42
Buenos Aires 298
Buescu, Helena 371
Bunyan, John 329
Byron, Lord 203, 204

C

canon (canonicity, canonisation) 4, 15, 50, 85, 90, 91, 92, 93, 96, 98, 155, 172, 182, 192, 193, 199, 230, 314, 357, 362, 364, 371, 389
Cape Town 107, 108, 180
Cape Verde 374
Caribbean 2, 105, 106, 150–60
Caribbean literature 297, 298
Casanova, Pascale 3, 19, 20, 21, 22, 27, 173, 293, 296, 298, 299, 357, 358, 359, 360, 361, 362, 365, 384, 385, 386, 387, 393
Cassatt, Mary 328
Castilian 16, 31, 32, 33, 34, 36
Castilian literature 38
Castillo, Debra A. 91, 94, 97
Castronovo, Russ 64
Catalan 32, 33, 37, 304
Catalonia 31, 33

Chakrabarty, Dipesh 46
Chamberlain, Neville 335
character system 249, 253, 258
Cheah, Pheng 4, 136, 137, 165, 174, 175, 176, 230
Chekhov, Anton 168, 181, 229, 233, 235, 236, 238
Chen Duxiu 71, 73, 75, 77, 78, 79, 80
Chenier, André 203
Chile 346
Chimurenga Magazine 107, 108, 392
China 2, 5, 16, 42, 43, 45, 48, 49, 51, 70, 72, 73, 75, 79, 81, 82, 83, 200, 350
Chinese 6, 17, 42, 48, 52, 53, 54, 304
Chinese literature 16, 17, 42, 43, 45, 46, 50, 51, 52, 54, 55, 71, 72, 77
Chinese poetry 5
Chineseness 43, 51–55
Chiziane, Paulina 293, 375, 378, 379, 380
Christianity 65, 66
chronotope 169, 218
Clarke, James Freeman 67
classical language 45, 47, 76
Coelho, Paulo 284
Coetzee, J. M. 172, 178
Cold War 51, 182
colonialism 54, 141, 186
colonisation 44
commodification 46, 293, 377, 379, 380

common-place 27
comparative literature 96, 125
Confucianism 52, 74, 75, 81, 83, 84
connectedness 168, 249, 253, 254, 258
consecration 290, 293, 297, 298, 305, 360, 369, 376: see also double consecration
Constantinople 2, 168, 246, 247, 249, 251, 252, 253, 257
Cornis-Pope, Marcel 95
cosmopolitan 1, 2, 5, 6, 8, 9, 15, 16, 19, 27, 32, 35, 52, 60, 61, 62, 63, 68, 97, 98, 105, 106, 130, 131, 132, 133, 134, 141, 142, 143, 144, 146, 147, 151, 152, 154, 157, 158, 159, 160, 165, 166, 168, 169, 172, 181, 182, 185, 186, 187, 193, 200, 206, 213, 224, 233, 251, 262, 278, 281, 289, 294, 299, 330, 342, 344, 355, 378; Russian 211, 212; Constantinople 246
cosmopolitan literature 140, 345; literary ecology 146
cosmopolitan mediascape 291, 341, 343, 350
cosmopolitan practices 186, 187
cosmopolitanisation 151
cosmopolitanising translation 289, 291, 304, 305, 306, 307
cosmopolitanism 8, 130, 135, 185, 186, 187, 188, 195, 196, 212, 225, 298
cosmopolitics 167, 186, 193; literary 192
cosmopoltitan language 21, 27, 147

countryside 201, 204, 205
Couto, Mia 375, 378
Covarrubias, Sebastián de 33
creole 304
créolité 150
crime fiction 291, 292, 341, 342, 344, 346, 348, 351, 364
Cuba 181, 189
cultural brokers 257
Cultural Revolution 84
Cunard, Nancy 166, 188, 196
Czech Republic 95

D

Dagens Nyheter 122, 266
Dagerman, Stig 356
Dahl, Arne 291, 346
Damhaug, Torkil 306
Damrosch, David 3, 4, 92, 95, 173, 324, 340, 371, 375
Danish 289, 290, 299, 300, 302, 305
Dar es Salaam 108, 131
Davidson, Peter 291, 350
Davis, Caroline 388
De Wette, Wilhelm Martin Leberecht 66, 67
Debaene, Vincent 238
Delgado, Luisa Elena 37
de-nationalise 43, 52, 54
Denmark 306
de-sinicise 43, 52, 54
development discourse
diaspora literature 125
Dickens, Charles 79

Dictionaries 20, 21, 23, 24, 25
Dictionnaire critique de la langue française (1787–88) 26
Dictionnaire de l'Académie française (1694) 25
Dictionnaire de la langue française (1872–77) 21
Dictionnaire universel de la langue française (1823) 21
Diderot and d'Alembert 23
Dikobe, Modikwe 181
dispossessive collectivism 195
distant reading 15, 200, 277
domestication 9, 329, 365
Doroshevich, Vlas 239
Dostoevsky, Fyodor 167, 211, 229, 230, 233, 234, 235, 240
double consecration 290, 299, 307
Douglass, Frederick 60
Drum 180
Du Bellay, Joachim 20, 27
dual economy 293, 388
duo-centric 298
Dutch 150, 251
Duyckinck, Evert 61
Duyckinck, George 61

E

East Africa 390
East African literature (writing) 289, 389, 393
East Timor 374
Eckermann, Johann Peter 358, 365
Eco, Umberto 311

Ede, Amatoritsero 115
Edjabe, Ntone 107
Edrissy, Sulaiman 250
Eichhorn, Johann 66
El Guindi, Fadwa
Emerson, Ralph Waldo 59, 67
Emerson, William 67
emotions 200, 207
Encyclopédie ou Dictionnaire raisonné des sciences, des arts et des métiers 23, 24
English 7, 9, 42, 74, 93, 105, 113, 132, 133, 135, 136, 143, 144, 146, 147, 150, 169, 180, 181, 182, 220, 221, 230, 233, 257, 275, 276, 279, 280, 281, 284, 289, 290, 293, 298, 300, 305, 306, 313, 320, 325, 332, 346, 362, 364, 386, 389, 391, 393
Entebbe 390, 392
epitext 317, 318, 319
Escarpit, Robert 361
ethnicity 369, 370, 371, 372, 377
ethnography 192, 195, 239; fictionalised 236, 237
Europe 2, 3, 4, 8, 33, 50, 61, 70, 75, 161, 212, 214, 217, 221, 233, 257, 258, 334, 343, 385; provincialising 46
European explorers 262, 263
European literature 62
Evans, Walker 167, 188, 190, 191, 196
Everett, Edward 67

exile 121, 126, 167, 168, 211, 212, 214, 215, 223, ; Siberian 229–40
exotic 23, 379; exoticism, exoticising 262, 263, 269, 272, 293
explorers 262, 263
expressionism 193

F

Farrokhzad, Athena 122
Farsi: see Persian
Fassin, Didier 236
Felińska, Ewa 230, 233
feminism 94 , 97, 331
feminist literary studies 17, 18
FEMRITE 392
Féraud, Jean-François 26
Ferrante, Elena 311
Fichte, Johann Gottlieb 67
Fieldwork 130, 239
Finland 168, 238, 249, 346
Finnish 251
Flaubert, Gustave 167, 199, 200, 205
foreignisation 9, 329, 365
Foucault, Michel 213
France 48, 292, 355, 360, 362, 364, 365, 376
francophone 17, 53, 376
French 9, 16, 20, 23, 24, 25, 42, 150, 158, 215, 217, 219, 224, 251, 257, 289, 290, 292, 298, 300, 306, 316, 320, 362, 363, 386
French Academy (*Academie française*) 26, 215

Fridegård, Jan 330
Fukienese 48
Fuller, Margaret 59, 67
Furetière, Antoine 25

G

Galician 32, 37
Ganguly, Debjani 165
Gao Xingjian 42, 55
Gaultier, Jules de 204, 206
gender 17, 18, 89, 92, 93, 94, 97, 331, 369, 371, 372, 374, 375, 377, 379, 380
Genette, Gérard 317, 319, 320, 344, 377
Genoa 156
genre 59, 60, 61, 94, 104, 110, 127, 131, 132, 146, 165, 168, 169, 187, 188, 192, 218, 220, 229, 256, 262, 281, 292, 299, 313, 334, 342, 345, 346, 347, 348, 350, 369
German 67, 108, 224, 251, 300, 319, 320, 346, 347, 363, 364
Germany 48, 346
Ghana 155
Gleize, Joëlle 207
global translation field 296, 299, 300, 304, 307
globalisation 1, 45, 47, 130, 133, 141, 142, 185, 187, 213, 383, 384
glocal 340
Godefroy, Frédéric 21
Goethe, Johann Wolfgang von 91, 203, 358, 365
Gogol, Nikolai 81, 181

Goodman, Nelson 174, 261, 264
Gordimer, Nadine 178
Gramática sobre la lengua castellana (1492) 33
Grand dictionnaire universel du XIXe siècle (1866–77) 21
Granta 115, 116
Graves, Sarah 350
Gray, Richard 142
Grenada 158
Grisham, John 284
Grünewald, Isaac 247, 254
Guadeloupe 158
Guillén, Claudio 3
Guinea Bissau 374
Gumby, L. S. Alexander 167, 188, 189, 196
Gupta, Suman 276, 284

H
Ha Jin 42, 55
Hakka 48
Hamdi Bey, Osman 247
Hamid, Mohsin 105, 142, 143, 145
Hannerz, Ulf 133
harem 168, 246, 247, 248, 250, 252, 254, 255, 256, 257, 258
Harlem 155, 190
Harlem Renaissance 189
Hasselblatt, Ivar 231, 233
Hastrup, Kirsten 131
Hauptmann, Gerhart 79
Hausbacher, Eva 219
Havanna 155

Hayot, Eric 1, 166, 173, 176, 249, 252, 253, 258
Heath, Jennifer
Hedge, Frederic Henry 67
Hegel, Friedrich 67
Heidegger, Martin 249
Heilbron, Johan 296, 299
Hemingway, Ernest 181
Henshaw, Mark 350
Henson, Josiah 60
Herder effect 27
Herder, Johann Gottfried 385
Hertel, Hans 292, 363, 364
Herzen, Alexander 211
heteroglossia 53
Higonnet, Margaret 97
Hindi 304
hispanophone 53
Historia y crítica de la literatura española (1980–) 36
Hitchcock, Alfred 349
Hitchcock, Peter 3
Hitler, Adolf 335
Hofmeyr, Isabel 329
Holland 181
Hong Kong 42, 47, 50, 53
Honwana, Luís Bernardo 181
Hosseini, Khaled 142, 145
Houellebecq, Michel 306
Hsia, C. T. 50, 55
Hu Shi 71, 73, 75, 77, 79, 80
Huggan, Graham 4, 379
Hughes, Langston 189, 190
Hugo, Victor 79

I

Iakubovich, Pëtr 229, 233, 234, 235, 237, 239
Iceland 350
iconic 348, 349
Illusions perdues 200, 203
imaginaries 108, 165, 166, 168, 284, 292, 350, 351
imperialism 186
India 2, 169, 170, 181, 275, 276, 278, 280, 281, 282, 283, 284
Indian literature 276, 284
Indonesia 47
intellectual history 96
intermedial 327
international literary space 359, 385
Iran 104, 119, 120, 121, 122, 123, 124
Iraq 119
Ireland 121
Islam 105, 141, 144, 146; cosmopolitan heritage of 141
Ismond, Patricia 151, 152, 153, 157
Italian 300, 311, 320, 364
Italian literature 290, 311, 312, 314
Italy 314

J

Japan 48, 70, 79, 80, 200, 346
Japanese 2, 301, 362
jazz 188, 189
Jerichau-Baumann, Elisabeth 246
Jockers, Matthew 92
Johannesburg 108
Johansson, Eva 126
Johnson, Eyvind 328, 333, 334, 335, 336
Joyce, James 92, 181, 386
Julien, Eileen 108
Jusdanis, Gregory 46

K

Kahf, Mohja 105, 142, 145
Kahora, Billy 104, 110, 111, 112, 113, 115
Kalliney, Peter 293, 383, 384, 387, 392
Kampala 108, 135
Kandinsky, Vasily 239
Kant, Immanuel 67
Katanga 108
Katlehong 180
Kennan, George 233
Kenya 109
Kimberley 180
King, Stephen 350
Kinshasa 108
Kirkwood, Mike 178
Kisambaa 132
Kiswahili 113, 132, 133, 136
Knapp, Samuel Lorenzo 64
Knickerbockers 61, 63, 64
Knight, Michael Muhammed 105, 142, 143, 145, 146
Korolenko, Vladimir 229, 237
Kropotkin, Peter 233
Kyrklund, Willy 124

L

Laclau, Ernesto 345
Lacy, Margaret S. 327, 331, 332
Lagerlöf, Selma 355, 356, 362
Lagos 108
Lahiri, Jhumpa 391
Lalami, Leila 142
Lamar, Kendrick 172
Lamartine, Alphonse de 203
Langer, Joakim 268, 270, 271
langue vulgaire 25
Lansdell, Henry 233
Lappland 350
Larousse, Pierre 21
Larrimore, Mark 234
Larsson, Stieg 306, 343, 355
Late Qing fiction 72
Latin 6, 20, 22, 23, 25, 300; alphabet 182
Le Clézio, Jean-Marie 356
Le Rouge et le Noir 200, 201
Lectures on American Literature, with Remarks on Some Passages on American History (1829) 64
Lee, Leo Ou-fan 52
Leningrad 213, 216
Levine, Caroline 196, 208
Lewis, John Frederick 247
Liang Qichao 72, 73, 75, 76, 78, 80
Lindberg-Dovlette, Elsa 168, 247–59
Lindberg-Wada, Gunilla 173
Lindgren, Astrid 169, 268, 269, 271, 271, 362, 364

lingua franca 49
Lisbon 156
literary agency 293, 369, 373, 380
literary ecologies 6, 7, 140, 142
literary field 293, 388
literary history 2, 7, 10, 15, 17, 20, 28, 36, 45, 50, 60, 64, 68, 90, 92, 94, 95, 96, 143, 165, 330, 331, 373, 374, 375
Littré, Émile 21, 26
localising practice 311, 313, 314, 317, 318, 319, 320
location 103–106, 119, 126, 130, 138, 154, 168
Lo-Johansson, Ivar 330
London 171, 233, 298, 361
Loti, Pierre 246
Lotman, Yuri 213
Lu Xun 17, 71, 73, 79–85
Luanda 108
Lukács, Georg 193, 194
Lundahl, Mikela 90, 91
Luso-African literature 374, 377
lusofonia 370, 374, 375
lusophone 53, 292, 376
lusophone literary studies 373
lusophone literature 370

M

MacGillivray, Alex 141
MacKenzie, John M. 250
Madame Bovary 200, 204, 206
Madrid 298
Maghreb 108
Mainer, José Carlos 34

Makine, Andreï 167, 168, 215, 216, 217, 219, 220, 224
Malabo 108
Malangan art 270
Malaysia 42, 47
male gaze 252
Malinowski, Bronislaw 239
Mamin-Sibiryak 237
Mandarin 48, 49
Mani, B. Venkat 292, 324, 371, 372, 378
Mankell, Henning 343
Mao Zedong 44
maps 108. 109, 11, 112, 155, 180, 205
marketing 141, 166, 293, 340, 342, 343, 344, 347, 348, 349, 351, 377, 385, 391, 392, 393
Marklund, Liza 349
Martinique 189
Martins, Ana Margarida 371, 379, 380
Martinson, Harry 330, 335, 336, 356
Martinson, Moa 327, 330, 331, 332, 334
Matshoba, Mtutuzeli 178
Mau forest 109, 110, 111, 112, 113, 117
Maughan-Brown, David 177
Mauriac, François 205
Maurier, Daphne du 349
May Fourth Movement 45, 48, 49, 71, 78
May Fourth period 44
Mbembe, Achille 109, 110, 111, 116

McConckey, James 231
McConnell, Justine 219
McRae, Ellen 320
Mecca 181
media 264, 267
media convergence 280
medialisation 264
Mediterranean 156
Melanesia 270
Melville, Herman 61
Menéndez Pelayo, Marcelino 35, 38
Menéndez Pidal, Ramón 35, 36
methodological eurocentrism 4
methodological nationalism 4, 237
Mexico City 298
Middle Passage 153
migrant literature 125
Milton, John 62
Moberg, Vilhelm 328, 330, 332, 335
modernisation 44, 70, 187
modernism 44, 166, 185, 186, 192, 193, 195, 238, 387; documentary 167, 185–97, 238; British 387; localist 190; Russian 214
modernity 42, 44, 45, 47, 51, 66, 167, 185, 186, 194, 196, 275, 280
Modersohn-Becker, Paula 328
Modhi, Narendra 283
Modiano, Patrick 356
Mombasa 108
Monegal, Antonio 37

Mongolia 53
mono-centric 298
monolingual paradigm 33
Moretti, Franco 2, 173, 174, 277, 299, 300, 314, 357, 358
Mörner, Birger 266
Moscow 213
Mouffe, Chantal 345
Moura, Jean-Marc 376
Moyez Vassanji, Moyez
Mozambican literature 369, 370
Mozambique 372, 373, 374, 375, 379
Mphahlele, Es'kia 178, 181
Mshengu 181
Mufti, Aamir 3, 4, 279
multilingualism (multilingual approach) 8, 15, 33, 225

N

Nabokov, Vladimir 167, 215, 217, 219, 220, 221, 222, 223
Naficy, Hamid 127
Nairobi 108, 155
Nansen, Fridtjof 233
national allegories 55
national language 48, 293, 385
nationalism 20, 34, 48, 50, 55, 185, 186, 187, 195, 196
Ndebele, Njabulo 178
Nebrija, Antonio de 33
négritude 150
Nerman, Einar 247
Nesser, Håkan
Neubauer, John 95

New Culture Movement 43, 44, 47, 52, 71, 77, 81
New Novel 76
New York 155, 171, 190, 298, 361
New Youth 77, 78, 79
Nguni (languages) 180
Nicot, Jean 25
Nigeria 388
Nivat, Georges 221
Nixon, Rob 104, 110
Nobel prize for literature 42, 355, 356, 362
Nomani, Asra 148
Non-Governmental Organisations (NGOs)
Nordic Noir 291, 341, 343, 346, 348, 349, 350
Nordic region (Nordic-Baltic) 97, 343, 347
Nordicity 343
Nordström, Ester Blenda 231
north (the north) 341, 346
North America 2
North Pole 350
Norway 168, 238, 306
Norwegian 233, 289, 290, 299, 302, 304, 305
novel 93, 119, 120, 121, 122, 124, 125, 126, 146, 147, 148, 181, 201, 205, 206, 207, 208, 216, 219, 222, 247, 278, 279, 281, 282, 283, 306, 319, 327, 328, 331, 333, 342, 345, 346, 347, 348, 355, 380, 383, 390, 392; nineteenth-century French 200, 208

O

O'Toole Fintan 121
occidentalism 214
Oceania 261, 263, 265, 272
Ohlsson, Kristina 349
orientalism (orientalist) 250
orientation 103–106, 119, 126, 130, 138, 154
Orsini, Francesca 169, 276, 281, 284
Osmonde, Gabriel 215, 219
Ottoman society 257
Owen, Hilary 292, 371, 372, 373

P

Pacific Ocean 261, 263, 267, 271
Packer, Barbara 66
Pamuk, Orhan 92
Pantagruel ou le Quart livre 20
Papua New Guinea 265, 266, 271
paradise 263
paradise on Earth 261, 263, 265
paratext 318, 320, 346
Paris 22, 108, 155, 167, 171, 200, 201, 202, 203, 204, 205, 206, 211, 219, 298, 355, 360, 361, 362, 365, 386
Parker, Theodore 17, 59, 60, 61, 64–68
Parrella, Valeria 319
Pasha, Kamran 142
Pasternak, Boris 222

Peabody, Ephraim 60
performativity (performative) 131
peritext 317, 318, 319, 328, 333, 392
Persian (Farsi) 2, 9, 144, 249
Petri, Kristian 231
Pettersson, Anders 173
Pettersson, Carl-Emil 169, 261, 262, 265, 266, 267, 268
Ping Chen 74
Pippi Långstrump (Pippi Longstocking) 268, 269
Plaatje, Solomon T. 181
planetary thinking 1
Poe, Edgar Allan 349
Poland 360
Polish 230, 233
Pollard, Charles 159
Pollock, Sheldon 8, 9, 19, 151
polysystem theory 332
popular culture 281, 291, 342
Portugal 293, 374, 376, 377
Portuguese 369, 370, 372, 373, 374, 376, 377
Portuguese literary studies 373
Portuguese literature 36, 374, 377
postcolonial literature (fiction) 383, 384, 389
postcolonial studies (postcolonial criticism) 85, 91, 171, 375, 384
postcolonial theory 383, 384
post-loyalist 54, 55
postmodernism 46

postmonolingual approach 39
Pound, Ezra 158
Prendergast, Christopher 293, 387
print culture 20
putonghua (common language) 49

R

Rabelais, François 16, 20, 22, 23, 27
racialisation 123, 126
Racine, Jean 387
racism (racist) 48, 119, 169, 269, 270
Rashmi, Sadana 284
Ravan Press 177
regionalism 186
Regius, Hélena 270, 271
remediation 169, 264
Renaixença 34
representation 18, 90, 93, 94, 110, 11, 202, 235, 262, 340, 341, 342, 346, 348, 378
Reshetnikov, Fyodor 237
Resina, Joan Ramón 36
Rexurdimento 34
Rico, Francisco 36
Rilke, Rainer Maria 222
Rimbaud, Arthur 158
Risterucci-Roudnicky, Danielle 290, 315
Rive, Richard 178
Robbins, Bruce 195
Roberts, Mary 251, 252, 253, 258
Roberts, Shabaan 132

Rohi, Pooneh 104, 120, 122–27
romanticism 8
Rothberg, Michael 142
Rousseau, Jean-Jacques 202, 204
Rushdie, Salman 92, 279
Russia 2, 168, 211, 212, 216, 217, 223, 229, 230, 231–40, 360
Russian 215, 219, 221, 223, 224, 233, 300, 302
Russo-Japanese war 80
Rustenburg 180

S

Said, Edward W. 250, 262
Sakhalin Island 235, 238, 239
Saltykov, Mikhail 237
Sánchez, Clara 306
Sand, George 205
Sandbach, Mary 333
Sanskrit 6
Santana, Mario 36, 37, 39
São Tomé and Principe 374
Sapiro, Giséle 290, 296, 314, 315, 316, 319, 377
Saviano, Roberto 311
Scandinavia 2, 290, 298, 304
Scandinavian literature 330
Schiller, Friedrich 203
Schwab, Gabriele 331
Scott, Walter 62, 203, 204
scrapbook 166, 187, 188, 189, 190,
Sebokeng 180

Sedakova, Olga 214
Selepe, Magoleng wa 180, 181
semi-peripheral literature 314, 356
semi-pheripheral position 302, 311, 312,
Seng'enge Zuhura 105, 129–38
Shakespeare, William 61, 92, 172, 346, 347, 387
Sharpeville 180
Shih, Shu-mei 53, 54
Shishkin, Mikhail 167, 168, 215, 217, 219, 223
short story 73, 79, 81, 103, 109, 124, 127, 182, 224, 252, 255, 293, 385, 390, 393
Shternberg, Lev 239
Siberia 168, 229–39
Simpson, Jessie
Singapore 42, 47
Singdo-Misse 265, 266
sinocentricism 43, 50
Sino-Japanese war 70
sinophone 53–55
sinophone literature 53–54
slave narrative 17, 59, 60, 63, 64, 67, 68
slavery 64
Slemani 108
slow violence 104, 110
sociological functionalism 237
sociology of translation 291, 295, 296, 326
Solzhenitsyn, Aleksandr 214
Sotho 180
South Africa 177, 180

South America 2
South Seas 169, 269
Soweto 177, 180
Soyinka, Wole 388
Spain 16, 31, 32, 35, 37, 39
Spanish 31, 32, 34, 37, 150, 290, 298, 300, 306, 364
Spanish literature 32, 38, 39
Spivak, Gayatri Chakravorty 3, 4, 89, 95, 175
St Lucia 154, 156
Staffrider 166, 172, 173, 177–82
Stalin, Joseph 222
Stein, Gertrude 386
Stendhal 167, 199, 200, 201, 206
Stockholm 120, 265, 271, 346
storytelling 111, 264
Strauss, David Friedrich 67
Strindberg, August 361
suffrage 251
Suhr-Sytsma, Nathan 386
Swahili : see Kiswahili
Sweden 9, 104, 119, 121, 123, 124, 125, 168, 200, 238, 249, 251, 267, 269, 290, 311, 312, 355, 359, 360, 362, 364, 365
Swedish 233, 247, 248, 290, 292, 299, 302, 305, 306, 311, 313, 320, 327, 359, 360, 362, 363, 364
Swedish Arts Council 360
Swedish Institute 360
Swedish literature (fiction) 292, 302, 325, 326, 330, 332, 341, 351, 356, 360, 364, 365

Swedishness 125
Switzerland 223
Sydney 267
Syria 119

T

Tabar Islands 265, 266, 267, 270, 271
Tahiti 263
Taiwan 42, 47, 50, 51, 52, 53
Tanzania 105, 130, 133, 135
Tarantino, Quentin 350
Telemaque, Harold 158
Teochew 48
Tesoro de la lengua castellana o española 33
The Chronic 107, 108
The New Novel (*Xin xiaoshuo*, 1902) 76
The Position and Duties of the American Scholar (1849) 59
Themba, Can 181
Thieme, John 157
Thiong'o, Ngugi wa 135
Thomsen, Mads Rosendahl 4, 91, 224
Thoreau, Henry David 59
Tibet 53
Ticknor, George 67
tidalectics 150
Tlali, Miriam 178
Tolstoy, Leo 168, 229
Toronto 156
transcendentalism 60, 67
transcultural literature (writing, prose) 218, 220, 224, 225
transculturalism 168, 217
transit languages 363
translation 2, 9, 10, 15, 50, 61, 68, 96, 97, 98, 171, 289, 290, 291, 292, 293, 294, 295–307, 310, 313, 315, 316, 317, 319, 324, 325, 326, 328, 330, 331, 332, 333, 340, 347, 355, 362, 363, 364, 376, 386
translation studies 96, 289
translingual autobiography 218, 220, 222, 223
translingualism 52
transmedial 264
transnational tangle 130, 133, 134, 138
transnationalism (transnational approach) 15, 52, 55, 68
travel literature (writing) 24, 262, 263, 264
traveller (travellers) 111, 169, 219, 262, 263
travelling stories 169, 261
travelogue 246, 251, 252, 257, 258, 263
Tripoli 108
Trouillot, Michel Rolph 93
Tu Wei-ming 51–52
Turkey 2, 251
Turkish 247, 248

U

Uganda 135, 390
UK (Britain) 48, 65, 168, 238, 325, 326, 328, 329, 332, 334, 346, 387, 388, 390
Ukraine 95

Ummah 141, 144, 146
UNESCO 300
untranslatability 96, 291, 329
Urdu 144
USA (America) 48, 62, 63, 70, 145, 146, 190, 200, 215, 221, 233, 238, 325, 326, 327, 329, 332
Uspensky, Boris 213
Uspensky, Gleb 237
USSR (Soviet Union) 167, 212, 213, 214

V

Valdés, Mario 174
Valéry, Paul 386
van Kesteren, Geert 109, 114, 115
Vassanji, Moyez 383, 390
Vaughan, Michael 177
Vava, Husluma 42
Vecko-Journalen
veil (veiling) 247, 251, 253, 256, 258
Venuti, Lawrence 290, 310, 329, 365
vernaculaire 16, 24
vernacular 2, 5, 6, 8, 9, 15, 16, 17, 19, 20–28, 32, 33, 47, 48, 49, 59, 60, 61, 63, 64, 68, 71, 72, 73, 74, 75, 76, 77, 78, 82, 83, 94, 87, 98, 106, 116, 127, 131, 133, 134, 140, 143, 146, 147, 151, 154, 155, 157, 159, 160, 165, 166, 172, 180, 181, 182, 187, 190, 195, 200, 212, 216, 230, 278, 280, 281, 283, 289, 355, 370, 378; culture 34, 59, 60, 62, 281; language 16, 20, 24, 32, 33, 45, 73, 74, 83, 251, 276; literature 6, 140; photography 190
vernacular literary culture (tradition) 8, 9, 132, 151
vernacular literary value 9
vernacular revolution 21, 27, 28
vernacularisation 16, 19, 28, 43, 48, 116, 151
vernacularising translation 289, 304, 306, 307
vernacularism 8; strategic 180
Vietnam 181
vulgar (language) 25, 26, 76

W

Walcott, Derek 151–59
Walkowitz, Rebecca 217, 278
Wang Gungwu 52
Wang, David 60, 77
Wang, David Der-wei 53, 54
Warwick Research Collective (WReC) 5
Watts, Andrew 206
Wen Jiabao 278
Weng Xiaoming 47
wenyan (literary language) 45, 74, 75, 82, 83
West Indies 387
western Europe 167, 217, 221, 258
westernisation 44, 212
White, Patrick 181
Wilde, Oscar 79
Wolf, Michaela 295

working-class fiction 291, 326, 332, 334, 336
world republic of letters 171, 296, 358, 385, 391
worldedness 1, 258
worlding 1, 249
worldliness 2, 92, 96
world-literature 5
world-making 7, 10, 130, 131, 136, 137, 165, 166, 168, 172, 173, 174, 176, 177, 182, 191, 196, 232, 247, 252, 261, 262, 263, 264, 272, 278, 297, 334
world-system theory 1, 5, 7
Wright, Richard 181

X

Xhosa 180, 181
Xinjiang 53

Y

Yildiz, Yasemin 33
Yoruba 304
Young America 61, 63, 64
Yurchak, Alexei 213

Z

Zhang Longxi 91
Zilliacus-Tikkanen, Henrika
Zola, Émile 79, 201, 206
Zulu 180

www.ingramcontent.com/pod-product-compliance
Lightning Source LLC
Chambersburg PA
CBHW061925220426
43662CB00012B/1806